Urban Fears and Global Terrors

Urban Fears and Global Terrors explores the disruption around the 7/7 London bombings in 2005, taking people back to the events of that day and the sense of loss, fear and mourning that followed. By framing a new landscape of urban fear, Victor Jeleniewski Seidler shows how new technologies helped to shape responses to a global terror that had been anticipated but was dreadful in its reality. By listening to the narratives people shaped for themselves, Seidler shows the need for new forms of social theory that can come to terms with the contemporary realities of urban fear, complex identities and belongings. This book:

- explores the relationship of Islam to the West and ways this has been forgotten within traditional forms of social theory;
- engages with a crisis of masculinities and the particular histories of migration and diaspora from the sub-continent;
- follows the discussions around citizenship, identity and difference, and the possibilities of belonging that were being fought out through different visions of multiculture and integration that followed.

This book will prove an incredibly useful resource for students and researchers of Political Sociology and Citizenship, Gender Studies, Race and Ethnic Studies, Diaspora Studies, Terrorism and Political Violence, Social and Cultural Theory, Ethics and Philosophy.

Victor Jeleniewski Seidler is Professor of Social Theory in the Department of Sociology, Goldsmiths, University of London. He has written widely in areas of social and cultural theory and philosophy. He has a particular interest in gender, in relation to men and masculinities.

International library of sociology
Founded by Karl Mannheim
Edited by John Urry
Lancaster University

Recent publications in this series include:

Urban Fears and Global Terrors

Citizenship, multicultures and belongings after 7/7

Victor Jeleniewski Seidler

Routledge
Taylor & Francis Group

LONDON AND NEW YORK

First published 2007
by Routledge
2 Park Square, Milton Park, Abingdon, Oxon OX14 4RN

Simultaneously published in the USA and Canada
by Routledge
270 Madison Ave, New York, NY 10016

Routledge is an imprint of the Taylor & Francis Group, an informa business

© 2007 Victor Jeleniewski Seidler

Typeset in Sabon by Wearset Ltd, Boldon, Tyne and Wear
Printed and bound in Great Britain by TJI Digital, Padstow, Cornwall

British Library Cataloguing in Publication Data
A catalogue record for this book is available from the British Library

Library of Congress Cataloging in Publication Data
Seidler, Victor J., 1945–
Urban fears and global terrors after 7/7 : citizenship, multicultures
and belongings / Victor J. Seidler.
p. cm.
'Simultaneously published in the USA and Canada.'
1. London Terrorist bombings, London, England, 2005. 2.
Muslims–Cultural assimilation–Great Britain. 3. Terrorism–Religious
aspects–Islam. 4. Political violence. 5. Marginality, Social. 6. Social
sciences–Philosophy. 7. Fear–Social aspects. 8. Masculinity. 9. Mass
media–Influence. I. Title.
HV6433.G713L653 2007
303.6'250941–dc22   2007005571

ISBN10: 0-415-43614-1 (hbk)
ISBN10: 0-203-94053-9 (ebk)

ISBN13: 978-0-415-43614-4 (hbk)
ISBN13: 978-0-203-94053-2 (ebk)

In memory of all those who have been killed in the 'War on Terror' since 9/11

I walk among the fragments and limbs of men. This is what is terrible for my eyes, that I find man in ruins and scattered as over a battlefield or a butcher-field.

(Nietzsche, *Thus Spoke Zarathustra)*

The relationship between Earth, *Terra*, territory and terror has changed and it is necessary to know that this is because of knowledge, that is, because of technoscience. It is technoscience that blurs the distinction between war and terrorism.

(Jacques Derrida, *Philosophy in a Time of Terror: 101*)

The 'War on Terror' has been a disaster and the metaphor was rotten from the start. Language shapes ideas and policy and this abuse of language has led to a state of permanent lawlessness and exceptionalism – the festering sore of Guantánamo Bay, the extraodinary science of extraordinary rendition.

(Shami Chakradarti, Director of Liberty)

I'm writing about human beings, not heroes . . . writing is to travel towards discovering others; it's a day to listen to and love them.

(Elias Khourv, Review, *Saturday Guardian* 28th July 2007: 12)

The cause of integration has become so fetishised since the July bombings that it has been elevated to the level of an intrinsic moral value – not a means to an end but an end in itself.

(Gary Younge, *Guardian* 19th September 2007: 23)

Contents

Preface and acknowledgements

I want to share a journey that was initially carried out in 'real time' of making sense of the traumatic and disruptive events of 7 July in London as they unfolded both locally but also globally. As we lived through days of shock and misrecognition it was often difficult to find the words for events that had so suddenly and radically unsettled traditional ways of thinking and feeling. Often it was just a matter of keeping up with the news and drawing upon skills of attention and judgement to keep a sense of balance in a rapidly changing situation. Often this involved listening to different views, often as they were being formulated in the heat of the moment as they were seeking to articulate their own sense of shock and relief. Many lives were to be broken and many hopes were to be destroyed particularly for those who were directly involved and who had families and friends who were killed or injured.

Reflecting on the shock that followed the London bombings on 7 July 2005, and the fears that were felt by so many people as global terror hit home that it could 'so easily have been me', this work explores these new landscapes of fear and the ways they oblige us to rethink the terms of social theory. Transformed by globalised media and the Internet, what would have been a local event becomes a global event unfolding in real time around a networked planet. Living in the West post-9/11 has involved living with an expectation that cities could become targets and that innocent people from any background could be caught up in these traumatic events. By tracing connections between new urban landscapes of fear that people have had to adjust to as they move across urban spaces and the global terrors that can also be used by those in power to restrict civil liberties, we need to reflect upon *new* dangers to democratic civil society and politics. We also have to question the terms of traditional social theory that have been shaped through the implicit terms of a secular Enlightenment rationalism which makes it difficult to illuminate shifting religious allegiances and changing relationships between the West and Islam.

If we are to be able to revise social theory to allow for spaces of dialogue between different religious and secular traditions, we need to challenge the terms of an Enlightenment modernity through which, as

Levinas explored, 'the other' aspired to become like 'the same'. We have to allow for the dignity of difference in ways that also appreciate *how* questions of gender and sexualities have become contested sources of human dignity and self-worth. As Wittgenstein helps to frame, 'Hegel seems to me to be always wanting to say that things which look different are really the same. Whereas my interest is in showing that things which look the same are really different.' If this explains why Wittgenstein felt his later philosophy could not really be appreciated within an Enlightenment modernity, it is an insight we need to develop further to appreciate narratives of difference that can also engage with embodied memories, traumatic histories and emotional lives.[1]

The July 7 bombings in London provided a deadly reminder to European governments of the chilling reality they confront with new forms of international terrorism. As the events of July 7 quickly morphed in the mass media into 7/7 they became part of a global narrative of international terror that suggested that we had come to live in a radically different world that had been indelibly marked with 9/11. There was a world before 9/11 and a radically different world after 9/11. Life, at least in the West had become precarious in new ways. Though people who travelled across the city to work had long expected that London would be a target of global terror ever since 9/11 and the participation of the Blair government in the wars in Afghanistan and later Iraq, the bombings still came as a shocking surprise. People had got so accustomed to the expectation of the worst that, when it happened, there was a moment of relief. The worst had finally happened, even though it had surprised people and now it might be the turn of others. Most Muslims deplore the violence that has been committed in Islam's name but, at the same time, they understand the anger and frustration of a younger generation having to witness the deaths of civilians in Afghanistan and Iraq and aware of the West's refusal to intervene justly in the Israel–Palestine conflict. They see the double standards of Western foreign policy and feel angry at what seems to them to be a war against Islam.

If we are to understand such traumatic events as the London bombings of 7/7, we need to shape forms of narrative social theory that can listen to the different voices of those who were involved. I wanted to bring different voices into relationship with each other not in the defence of a pre-given position but out of an awareness that it was through *listening to others* that we might create a different vision of multicultural politics that recognised the transnational lives of so many in a newly globalised world. It was not enough to conceive of multiculturalism in a single country or to think that the events of 7/7 somehow meant that multiculturalism had failed in Britain and had to be replaced by a new vision of integration within a more generous vision of 'Britishness'. By returning to these traumatic days we can also hear how people at moments of loss also find depths within themselves to speak out to articulate future hopes for living together with differences. Through a vision of critical multiculturalism we can honour the routine and everyday forms of multiculture that have become very much part of urban lives. Somehow London held together when there were so many fears that it might fall apart. Through grief and a recognition of shared pain and an awareness of the precariousness and vulnerability of lives, a critical multiculturalism was being imagined that went beyond traditional liberal conceptions of citizenship.

As we are aware of how we were positioned by the event, so we can be sensitive to the destructive impacts upon those more directly involved, either through being caught up in the London underground system that was directly impacted, or else through the personal losses of relatives and friends who went to work in the morning never to return home to their families. Like a stone thrown into a lake, the ripples move out from the centre where the explosions took place. But what is clear is that everyone in London carries memories from that day, and that the events of 7/7 will be inscribed in the history and memory of London as a global city. The landscapes of fear changed, and even if people were eventually to return to similar routines, at some level they carried a sense of uncertainty that transformed their experience of urban life.

If London could be bombed once, it could be bombed again. If what had seemed unimaginable a few years back had actually happened, it meant that a boundary had been crossed. In some way it mattered who you were on that day, in the sense that if you were from an Islamic background or 'looked Muslim' in some way you became under suspicion. This might mean that if you come from a Muslim background you might write differently about the events of that day and you might be sensitive to voices that could otherwise be ignored. But what was defining for these events was that anyone who lived or worked in London could have been a target on that day. In this sense, the bombing was indiscriminate and many people with Muslim backgrounds were caught up in the terrors of that day. It was the sense that 'it could so easily have been me or anyone I know' that marked the events of the day. There was something indiscriminate in the bombings that was also perversely democratic. Possibly this made a difference to the ways different communities came together in the wake of the events of 7/7.

There are different kinds of stories that need to be told. But there are also challenges to traditional forms of social theory that would seek to capture these events in their own way. Traditionally, there has been a disdain for journalism within the human sciences as if they necessarily got too caught up in the event itself and so lacked the distance and objectivity that is necessary for rational understanding. But there has been a shift in journalism that allows for a different kind of relationship with social theory since, in the face of traumatic events – for instance, the death of Princess Diana – the traditional categories through which they might have been tempted to grasp a royal event seemed to collapse as microphones were handed over to the gathering crowds to record their own experience of witnessing. These voices helped to shape a more engaged and direct response and so helped to produce a different understanding of what happened in London on those crucial days after Diana's body was returned from Paris. If this was a narrative that rationalists sought to reclaim as a moment of 'irrational' grief, it remains part of a counter-discourse that still needs to be told when the striking diversity of people came into the streets to affirm their responsibility for a public sharing of mourning for a princess so many felt the establishment had betrayed.[2]

Nietzsche recognised that it *took time* for people to come to terms with traumatic events that disrupt the flow of everyday life and shape a kind of pause in which people have to gather their thoughts and feelings. The body has experienced a shock that it can take time for the mind to be able to reflect upon. Nietzsche warns us against thinking too fast with the mind working as an 'unstoppable machine' (1974: 33). Nietzsche writes of the importance of achieving a certain distance in order to gain perspective, it is through allowing the pause to become the creative well-spring from which 'everything else follows' (1968: 486). Opposing this inner directional force will exhaust the body's nervous energy (1997: 204–205), whereas a person becomes stronger by deciding (*entscheiden*) slowly and holding fast to the decision taken in the pause (1968: 485–486).[3]

Nietzsche writes of the importance of immersion in the 'lives experience' of life (the Erlebnis) through the body as a way to achieve wisdom, rather than just observing life with the detachment of the conscious mind. He recognises that we need to allow the moments of disruption to discover through their own creative pauses the narratives that will help to open up the traumatic events bodies have registered for themselves. What characterises Nietzsche's 'searcher after knowledge' is a liminal condition where embodied intuition and conscious formation co-exist. He recognises that it takes time and a creative pause for the mind to recognise what the body has already experienced as it has lived through a traumatic event. Of course, events can be traumatic in different ways, and often there is an uneasy tension between personal memories and the ways these can be mediated through public memories of these events.

If, for Nietzsche, existence means undergoing a gradual process of revelation of unfolding, of 'laying itself out', there is a recognition of social life as a process that is working itself out on different levels of experience: personal, institutional and structural. This calls for a listening to a diversity of different voices that help to create a moving exposition, something that constantly lends itself to shifting interpretations ('this is how it is becoming'). Multiplicity comes from *Falte*, meaning a fold, and indicates 'many folds'. This spiral is Nietzsche's evolutionary image, where 'onward development' (*Fortentwickling*) combines with the 'necessity of turning' (*Nothwendigkeit*). In contrast, progress is linked to a purely linear development – a 'false idea' in Nietzsche's view though, as Gramsci recognised, a view that implicitly has informed traditions of classical social theory.

As we learn how to listen to different stories, so we begin to recognise how traumatic events can impact differently, both in individual lives and within the larger community or country. As we begin to appreciate how the meaning of events is to be grasped within the terms of specific cultural and national memories, so we learn to recognise the diversity of cultures and the different ways that conflicting groups might interpret these events. As social researchers, it is not our task to seek reconciliation between these different narratives or to assume we have inherited a disciplinary expertise that grants us authority to be able to decide between them. Rather, we need to *listen* to these different narratives in ways that empower people within a democratic community to enter into dialogue across differences. If the need for creative dialogues across cultural differences has become vital in the wake of the rifts that have opened up between the West and Islam, it also calls upon us to rethink taken-for-granted disciplinary assumptions, particularly in relation to traditions of secular rationalism that often stand in the way of dialogue. It can also make it harder for us to listen and learn appropriately from individual stories.

In Europe, unlike the United States, Australia and Canada, the foundational myths of nation-states do not recognise a story of formation through immigration. What individual European states recognise is the existence of minority cultures within national borders. Different responses in Europe have largely been framed in terms of how to assimilate these diverse immigrations into discrete hegemonic national projects. Consequently, questions around multiculturalism and the 'problems' of immigrants have largely been posed as relatively recent, post-Second World War phenomenon. My family came as refugees from Nazi controlled Europe just before the outbreak of that war and found refuge in London. I was partly shaped through aspirations towards belonging framed through a culture of assimilation. Growing up within the Jewish communities of North West London we very much wanted to 'integrate' so that we could become 'like everyone else'. But the life that I knew in 1950s London was still being framed very much as multiculturalism in one country. But the requirements of citizen rights in a globalised world of mass migration and transnational movements of labour across the local boundaries of the nation call for different visions of a *critical multiculturalism* that recognises that integration is multifaceted and multi-located. We need to recognise histories of transnational affiliation that have long existed as we re-vision possibilities of complex belongings. But this also means listening and learning from different stories that can acknowledged complex interrelations between 'race' and religion.

Myriam, 48, was born in Tunisia and moved to France when she was eight and became a French citizen. The last time she saw her son Peter was in May 2004. He was leaving the public-housing project where they lived just north of Paris. Peter's father, who died when the boy was just 14, was a Roman Catholic from the French Antilles in the Caribbean. But Peter took a different path and, in 2003, when he was 23, he converted to Islam, after years of worshipping little more than video games and French rap stars. He told his mother he was leaving for Syria to study Arabic and the Koran. He kept in contact by email, sending her photos and news of his studies in Damascus. Then, in July, he told her he was heading for a 'spiritual retreat' and would be out of touch for a while. She heard nothing until December 2005, when she received a brief phone call from a French government official who told her that Peter had been captured by US soldiers in the Iraqi city of Fallujah. Today he is one of five French citizens held at Abu Ghraib prison outside Baghdad.

His mother is still trying to understanding what has happened and how young Muslims like her son had come to give up their lives in the West to pursue their version of jihad. 'They saw aggressive, violent images on the Internet, and asked questions about why Muslims were suffering abroad while European countries were doing nothing,' she says. 'It's like they set off a bomb in their heads' (*Time*, 31 October 2005: 32). She is now asking the same questions, and we need to be able to listen and learn from what she has to say if we are to enter into a creative dialogue. At the same time we need to recognise that there is not a single answer but a *multiplicity of pathways* that we need to be able explore if we want to understand these movements not as regressions, but as very much part of a contemporary, postmodern, globalised world. These radical Islamist movements have become part of the contemporary world and, if they are to be defeated, then we also need to question the wisdom of a 'war on terror' that suggests a military solution is possible without grasping the complex historical, cultural and psychological sources that can help to explain what draws these young men into jihadist movements. But it also means engaging with the injustices they discern and being ready to recognise connections between their senses of injustice and the destructive actions they sometimes take.

Most Muslims in Europe, of course, are not radicals, but British Muslims were shocked to discover that it was second-generation Muslims who were responsible for the London bombings. What had been framed as an external enemy that could be defeated through a US-led 'war on terror' suddenly had to be rethought. This provoked a discussion that challenged prevailing notions of identity, citizenship and belonging, not only in Britain but across Europe. People began to question ideas of nationality and citizenship across different European countries and the different ways in which migrant communities had been integrated.

What was being too quickly interpreted, without a proper pause, as a weakness in British models of multiculturalism that had somehow prevented governments from taking action to secure the freedom and human rights of the population, had to be rethought when the uprisings took place in late October in the working-class neighbourhoods surrounding French cities. When the *banlieues* erupted and youths fought running battles with the police, this exposed the underlying ills that remained unattended within the French republican tradition that talked of integrating others as French citizens with equal legal and political rights. While it was unclear what part religion was playing, many of these young men identified themselves as Muslim and had been exposed to images of what was happening in Afghanistan and Iraq. Although discrimination is illegal, many felt rejected and ignored by the Republic whose elite institutions remained exclusively white.

With disturbing frequency, young Muslims across Europe are finding spiritual and political homes within radical, anti-Western strains of Islam. Rather than feeling a sense of identification with the democratic states they have been born into, they can feel ignored, disdained and rejected. But this is not a matter of employment alone. Often it is educated young people who have, at some level, seemed more integrated who have turned away and felt an added burden of guilt and responsibility for the actions that Western governments have taken in a war against Islam, as they would perhaps describe the conflicts in Afghanistan and Iraq. While their fathers kept their heads down, working at the woollen mills in northern towns, sons of Pakistani immigrants who had arrived in the early 1960s, like Khaddam, had to cope with racism at school. 'I was the only Asian in the whole school,' he says. 'Day in and day out I got beaten up and some teachers just stood there' (*Time*, 21 November 2005: 32). Soon, though, there were very few whites left in the Manningham district, where his family lived. As he grew older, young men complained of police insensitivity and brutality.

The eruption came when a minor clash between white and Asian gangs exploded into three days of violence in July 2001 in Burley, Bradford and Oldham. Young Asian men turned their rage on the police and ravaged the symbols of 'white culture' like a BMW showroom and a club for white working-class men. Many of the older generation were shocked that their sons were involved. But young men with Bradford accents were no longer operating by their fathers' rules. They might show the necessary respect demanded by fathers at home, but they lived their own lives, often locked away in their rooms on the Internet. They felt a distance from their parents, who have little understanding of what they are into or little grasp that their children have grown up in very different worlds. They have created a culture and identities of their own. The government-sponsored report by Ted Cantle into the disturbances between Asian and white youths found people living 'parallel lives' and made proposals for tackling segregation and promoting 'community cohesion' to deal with the fracturing of communities along ethnic and faith lines.[4]

According to Ted Cantle:

> Multiculturalism was a defence against racism, The focus in this country has been on controlling people's behaviour, stopping them discriminating and trying to ensure fair play. We are now in an era of multiculturalism on a totally different scale from the 1950s and 60s. Virtually every modern multicultural city has not just dozens, but possibly hundreds of different communities now interacting. And we don't understand how they interact, or what stops them. So we have to develop new models.
>
> (*Guardian*, 21 September 2005: 5)

Cantle can help us to identify some of the weaknesses of traditional multi-culturalism and ways it has been allowed to develop to keep communities apart from each other. He is convinced that 'Unless there is political and economic integration, I believe it is not possible to have mutual trust and reciprocity.'

Cantle is keen not to be labelled an assimilationist – unlike, perhaps, Trevor Phillips, head of the Commission for Racial Equality (CRE), who seems prepared to imagine a move from multiculturalism towards a notion of integration closer to a traditional notion of assimilation in response to his perception that Britain is 'sleepwalking' into segregation on the scale identified in New Orleans after Hurricane Katrina. As he argues:

> I want to preserve cultural identities, which means you need a critical mass of different people in an area to support separate shops, temples, mosques. The problem is when that becomes total exclusion. It is so easy then for each community to then develop an ignorance of each other that is exploited by the BNP [British National Party].
>
> (Ibid.)

An unpublished government study has reportedly analysed for the first time unemployment and economic activity by religions and found that Britain's 1.6 million Muslims are more than three times more likely to be unemployed than the general population.

As Cantle acknowledges, 'There is no doubt that poverty and class play a big role. You can't have a cohesive society when one group is so disadvantaged and marginalized that it doesn't have a stake in that society.' But, he adds, 'Just lifting them out of poverty is not necessarily going to dispel the distrust and myths they have of each other.' As he sees it, 'We've got to agree what the areas of difference that we're prepared not just to tolerate but to celebrate, and what are the areas where we are not going to accept difference' (ibid.). This is linked to Cantle's recognition that we need to address notions of citizenship in Britain in new ways:

> Citizenship is something we shy away from. It's not seen as terribly British to have citizenship days. But it does seem to have some value.

'We all belong to Canada' is their [i.e. the Canadians'] big slogan. When you move there, you receive a big pack stating, 'This is what you can expect from us and this is what we expect from you.' That is valuable.

(Ibid.)

Although he readily concedes that British foreign policy played its part in the London bombings in July, he says, 'You have to feel some commitment to a sense of society and a sense of belonging. It's about where people's loyalties lie' (ibid.).

But issues of loyalty and uncertain belonging, traditionally framed within the terms of the nation state, need to be revised within a newly globalised world that has seen major shifts of population so many people live in multicultural societies and feel *complex loyalties* that reach across different spaces. This raises issues that go beyond the terms of Cantle's analysis that still envisage multiculturalism within a single country and force us to rethink the terms we have inherited within social and political theory to think about issues of identity and belonging. These are questions that I have lived with, since my own family were refugees, but from Nazi-controlled Europe. I grew up within terms of a culture that sought to 'integrate' through a process of assimilation that involved a readiness to be 'like everyone else', so being prepared to pay the price of belonging. But within an assimilationist culture, this often meant a shaming of differences that were often hidden and concealed, as I explored in *Shadows of the Shoah: Jewish Identity and Belonging.*[5]

Of course the situation with other migrations is quite different, particularly within a globalised world in which so many more people live with transnational identifications, but there are also significant resonances, particularly around issues of identity, difference(s) and belonging. There are also issues of religious practices and ways these can be experienced differently within secular societies in the West, and the challenges this creates for traditions of social theory that have been largely framed within terms of a secular rationalism. An awareness of marginality and a sense of the fears and rejections that often accompany difference and a desire to belong allowed me to write from a particular position that could learn from a Muslim–Jewish dialogue, without minimising the sources of conflict, not least over Israel/Palestine. But as we recognise that we are living in a world whose terror has a reach that goes beyond that we knew with the IRA, there are also new dangers to civil liberties within a democractic society that has come to rely so heavily upon surveillance.

We also need to fully engage with the ways landscapes of fear can so easily be manipulated by those in authority to further their own purposes. There is a way that fear is undermining at both an individual and collective level and it was not for nothing that the German filmmaker Fassbinder calls his film picturing the travails of immigrant life 'fear eats the soul'.

Through a discourse on human rights that have helped challenge entrenched inequalities and discriminations in relation to class, 'race', ethnicities, gender, sexualities and able-bodiedness, we have helped shape a more tolerant and democratic civil society. We need to listen to the voices of young people who are drawn into radical Islamist politics while recognising that there is important not to misrecognise a turn towards religion with a commitment to Jihadist politics. Through exploring the masculinities of the young men who were involved in the London bombings I hope to identify significant strains that do not simply identify them with an anti-politics of death and martyrdom but which also illuminates pressures in their everyday lives in Yorkshire that could lead them in this direction. As 7 July has been transposed to 7/7 and the London bombings linked to 9/11 and the attacks on the World Trade Centre we can be tempted away from thinking about relations between the local and the global and the ways these relations are mediated through global communications on the Internet. We need to recognise different colonial histories and different upbringings if we are to grasp the diverse sources of anger and frustration.

As Judith Butler wrote in *Precarious Life*, her reflections after 9/11:

> That we can be injured, that others can be injured, that we are subject to death at the whim of another, are all reasons for both fear and grief. What is less certain, however, is whether the experience of vulnerability and loss have to lead straightaway to military violence and retribution. There are other passages. If we are interested in arresting cycles of violence to produce less violent outcomes, it is no doubt important to ask what, politically, might be made of grief besides a cry for war.
>
> (2004: xii)[6]

If Muslim communities are not to feel marginalized and threatened by state policies so exacerbating the appeals towards terror, we need to discover other passages. We need to find other ways of including, recognising and affirming. If this means listening to different voices and learning from the experience of different communities, it has to go beyond an important affirmation of the dignity of differences towards a vision of shared life together that is willing to rethink traditional liberal distinctions between private and public life. We have to imagine a critical multiculturalism that goes beyond the terms of a secular rationalism while honouring the importance of secular state institutions. This involves engaging with histories of empire that still resonate in the present and being prepared to radically rethink the terms of contemporary 'Britishness'.

Acknowledgements

Many people have supported me with this project, sometimes through sharing their own experiences and reflections in the wake of 7/7 and the different kind of questions, both theoretical and personal, this has raised for them. I have learnt from these discussions, particularly from Ilyas Mohammed who shared his experience of growing up in Keighley, not far from Beeston, the Leeds suburbs where Mohammed Sidique Khan and the other young men responsible for the London bombings lived, as a second-generation young man who has come to identify with Islam. He was around the Department of Sociology at Goldsmiths, University of London, that summer where he is doing research for a PhD on Islamic militant groups. Dialogues with him helped me to understand something about where these young men were coming from.

He understood how Khan, in a video released months after the bombings, could denounce Europe's 'democratically elected governments' for carrying out 'atrocities' against Muslims. 'We are at war and I am a soldier,' Khan warns. 'Now you too will taste the reality of this situation.' Feeling that few seemed to care about what was happening to civilians in Iraq, Chechnya, Afghanistan and Palestine, there were feelings of guilt and responsibility. These young men felt that if only people could experience what Muslims were already suffering on a daily basis, they might they do something about it. They wanted to bring the war home. Like other young radical jihadists in different European countries, they wanted to bring the reality of suffering to the countries in which they were raised.

Many people in the Department of Sociology, as well as in the Centre for Urban and Community Research, have been concerned with issues around urban cultures, particularly in relation to issues of 'race', ethnicities and multiculturalisms. Through discussions with scholars, both present and past, such as Les Back, Chetan Bhatt, Fran Tonkiss, Paul Gilroy, Michael Keith, Nikolas Rose, Ben Gidley, Allison Rooke, Caroline Ramanzanoglu, Celia Lury, Marsha Rosengarten, Bev Skeggs, Nirmal Puwar, Brian Alleyne and Brett St-Louis, I have learned how to think about urban space, fear and difference(s). There has also been a lively debate around issues of citizenship, identity and belonging, particularly within the unit on Global Justice that includes, amongst others, Vikki Bell, Kirsten Campbell, David Hirsh and Kate Nash. I have been very fortunate to be able to work in such a stimulating environment that has also fostered discussions across disciplinary boundaries.

Within the Philosophy and Human Values group, I have been particularly supported by Howard Caygill and Josh Cohen who have helped produce intellectual spaces that allowed us to think about some of the philosophical assumptions that so often silently shape discussions around identity and belonging with Joanna Ryan. The embodied psychic and life politics research group in the sociology department centre (CISP) that we formed together provided an invaluable exploratory space to present some of this work. I also appreciate discussion at the staff and postgraduate seminar in sociology at Bristol University in November 2006 that helped me shape ideas around a critical multiculturalism. Particular thanks are due to Les Back, Ben Gidley and Steven Jones who gave helpful responses at critical moments and Lily Ickowitz Seidler for bibliographic help. Outside Goldsmiths I have been encouraged and supported in recent years by Zygmunt Bauman and Larry Blum and by Richard Sennett, Craig Calhoun and the NYLON culture project research group. Although they work in different fields, their influences have helped to shape the responses I have been able to make to 7/7. John Urey has believed in this project and with my editor Gerhard Boomgaarden have encouraged me to bring it to completion. Hannah Dolan and Carl Gillingham at Wearset have helped to craft its production.

Closer to home, my partner Anna Ickowitz and our children Daniel and Lily watched the development of this work and shared some of their insights into what was happening in those fearful and anxious days. For a time at least, it seemed imperative to risk thinking differently so that one could respond to changing situations, but also to interrupt some of the state responses that still endanger democratic and human rights that have so long been fought for. Many voices have been raised against the dangers that anti-terror legislation could pose in further marginalising communities that we need to be able to listen to.

It is only if we are prepared to share our own vulnerability that we can listen to the diverse voices of young Muslims in Britain and across Europe. Only if people experience themselves as being heard and feel that, rather than assuming a project of multiculturalism has failed, it is to be revised and strengthened so that it can no longer also sometimes work as a cover for indifference, can we imagine a just and democratic multicultural society. This means rethinking the terms of citizenship and belonging within a critical multiculturalism, not as a return to an assimilationist ethic of integration, but to visions of human rights and dignities that ensure loyalty to democratic politics and culture that can both respect and celebrate the dignities of diverse difference(s). Within a fragile and endangered planet it will only be through a renewed commitment to global justice and respect for complex belongings that a viable future can be hoped for.

Victor Jeleniewski Seidler
August 2007

1 Introduction
Traumatic events, precarious lives and social theory

Traumatic events

Traumatic events like the London bombings of 7/7 can change people's lives in ways they could never have anticipated. People can feel disturbed and shaken up, even if they were not directly involved but have spent time feeling anxious about relatives or friends who had not immediately replied to phone calls. People can have been affected in different ways, often quite surprising to themselves. Suddenly everyday routines and taken-for-granted assumptions about their lives had been shaken and they can feel that, as they are obliged to live within new landscapes of fear, they are bereft of a language that can help them to make sense of how the world seems to have changed so utterly while, in other ways, they are still surrounded by their familiar relationships and routines of work. The terrorist attacks of 11 September 2001 in New York, 11 March 2004 in Madrid and 7 July 2005 in London showed how Western capitals were no longer to be considered invulnerable but had become targets of attacks that governments could no longer hope to protect their citizens from. As there was a new landscape of urban fear, so there were global risks and terrors that could make themselves felt with devastating consequences.

Traditional forms of social theory had often assumed a form of expertise that sought to explain to people the changing forms of national life. Largely framed within the terms of the nation state, social theory already needed to rework critical assumptions if it was to come to terms with the precarious lives so many people were obliged to live within a newly globalised world, where there were enormous shifts of capital, people and media communication across national boundaries. With changes in work within the new capitalism, people could no longer assume a job for life, or with staged progressions towards seniority within organisations. Neo-liberalism had brought a transformation in organisational cultures that created its own forms of insecurity, as people were encouraged to develop entrepreneurial relationships to a self that had to be constantly regulated and re-skilled if it was to keep up with the demands of a changing global market. This was also reflected in a crisis of confidence in political institutions.[1]

Part of the appeal of postmodern theories for a younger generation was that they seemed to allow for the precariousness that characterised young-people's lives, where they were obliged, across distinctions of class, gender, 'race' and ethnicities, to live uncertain lives.[2] Traditionally it had been the promise of different kinds of work shaping the visions of the future for different social classes that organised the temporalities assumed by classical social theory. Max Weber had offered an understanding of the relationship between a Protestant ethic that still seemed to reverberate in anxieties about performance within competitive cultures of work and the spirit of capitalism that, for many, who were fortunate enough to still have jobs, seemed to have intensified with a long-hours culture.[3] A largely unforeseen consequence of feminisms was the pressure on young women to also identify with these intensified work cultures within new capitalism. They felt capable of competing on equal terms with men, and so felt that feminism was a discourse that might have made sense for the generation before them, but no longer illuminated the world of gender equality that they had inherited.

But Max Weber also helped to shape an interpretative tradition with social theory that allowed for individuals to define the meanings of their own experience. He helped to create spaces of reflection in which people could feel they had control over their lives through being able to shape meanings they gave to their own experience. But this was a control that had been threatened in the new capitalism where young people often felt a need to redefine the boundaries between their work lives within the public sphere and their private lives where they could hopefully allow themselves to be vulnerable. Post-structuralist theories had proved illuminating in the 1980s and 1990s because they could recognise the uncertainties, fragmentations and fluidities of identities that seemed to be articulated differently through prevailing discourses in different spheres of life. It also allowed for a certain distancing and self-protection that an earlier feminism had threatened through its notion that the 'personal is political'.[4]

If some felt that this insight endangered the recognition of the value of impersonal institutions and public life, it could have worked as a reminder that lives cannot be so firmly compartmentalised and that, as C. Wright Mills had already recognised, people's personal sufferings and distress often need to be understood through a sociological imagination that helps to situate their experience within larger structures of social and political power.[5] Feminism rediscovered and defined this insight for genders and sexualities at the same time as showing the need to also be able to think across the boundaries of reason and emotion, minds and bodies, nature and culture that had become settled dualities within rationalist forms of social theory that often assumed a dominant white European masculinity.[6]

Within the new landscapes of fear established in the wake of 9/11 and the globalised realities of mass media and networked relations, it can be difficult to know where risk and danger lies. Often it is the disruptive impact of unexpected traumatic events that tend to throw people and unsettle their understandings. It takes time to come to terms with how people have been affected and also to begin to shape narratives that can help people to grasp changes not only in their embodied psyches but also in their life politics. This is a task that calls for more open forms of social theory that *open up* a conversation between people who are equally searching for forms of self-understanding rather than speaking from a position of authority and power in which they deliver the assured truths of their expertise.

As Richard Sennett has also suggested, this calls for different ways of thinking and writing that are more open and democratic.[7] Rather than speaking with the authority of expertise, too often framed within a technical discourse that works to exclude, it searches for more accessible ways of writing and communicating within a public sociology that is committed to listening to those who are often silenced. If this is to recognise how we might be ill-served by certain traditions of positivist social theory that too-easily work to close down conversations and refuse to engage with the complexities of social life, it means shaping forms of social theory that also allow for social actions and practices of reflection that can help to shape alternative institutions that are empowering and democratic.[8]

If social theory is too important to be left to experts, this was an insight we should have already learned from Socrates about ethics and philosophy. It is in refusing a sharp positivist distinction between philosophy and social theory and in recovering insights from traditions of critical theory that we can begin to shape a more democratic and empowering form of sociological imagination that is both creative and engaged with transforming social relationships. This means separating from those in power who are engaged with controlling and managing populations for their own political ends. Whatever promise was felt in the New Labour project in Britain, and whatever benefits it has been able to deliver, it has failed to regenerate a democratic politics and, in its insistence on following the United States into the war in Iraq, it showed it had lost contact with its own citizens who demonstrated in their millions for a different outcome.

An ICM poll reported in the *Guardian* (3 November 2006) showed that 71 per cent of British voters now say the invasion was unjustified, a view shared by 89 per cent of Mexicans and 73 per cent of Canadians. As a result, US President George W. Bush is 'ranked with some of his bitterest enemies as a cause of global anxiety'. The pole also 'exposes high levels of distrust'. In Britain, 69 per cent of those questioned say they believe US policy has made the world less safe since 2001, with only 7 per cent thinking action in Iraq and Afghanistan has increased global security.

'The finding is mirrored in America's immediate northern and southern neighbours, Canada and Mexico, with 62% of Canadians and 57% of Mexicans saying the world has become more dangerous because of US policy' (ICM interviewed a random sample of 1,010 adults by telephone from October 27–30. Interviews were conducted across the country and the results have been weighed to the profile of all adults. Polling was by phone in Canada (sample 1,007) and Mexico (1,010)) (*Guardian*, 3 November 2006: 1).

In the week that followed soon after the fourth anniversary of 9/11, the details of civilian deaths were reported for the first time, from media reports about the terrible casualties of suicide bombings in Iraq that have devastated so many lives, in a war where, for so long, Iraqi civilian casualties were not properly accounted for. We are reminded in a particularly intense way of the vulnerability and precariousness of human life, particularly in war zones, but also of the difficulties of accepting the *equal value* of human life when, for so long, civilian deaths went unreported in the Western media. This helps to fuel the anger that many young Muslims feel about the double standards in the West's relationships to the Islamic world in the aftermath of 9/11 and Bush's 'war on terror' that has helped to make the world more dangerous.

Rather than make the world safe from terror, the war in Iraq has proved itself to have been a terrible misjudgement that has made Britain and other countries involved in the coalition direct targets for a global terror campaign by al-Qaida. As Tim Collins, commander in the Royal Irish Regiment during the invasion of Iraq, told a meeting at Chatham House (the Royal Institute of International Affairs, 22 September 2005): 'We are relying entirely, it seems to me, on military muscle to impose freedom and democracy.' He said the British commanders had 'no idea' about the complexities of Iraq at the time of the invasion. They seemed unprepared on many different levels.

Sometimes it is only through listening to the pain of army families who have lost their husbands and fathers that we can appreciate the sacrifices that some families are making, with and the conflict in Iraq being 'brought home' to many. But the constant images, that become almost routine, of terrible losses of life that seem to match the loss of life in the London bombings on a daily basis, remind us of the value of 'other' lives and the devastation that is brought to them. Though the global media makes us aware of wars that would have traditionally been hidden from view, the images and stories that emerge are often tightly controlled. We read about the losses of life and the casualties in Baghdad and other Iraq cities, but it can be difficult for those in the West who feel disconnected from the people there to fully appreciate both the sufferings and also the anger these sufferings generate within Islamic communities in the West. Diverse Muslim communities feel identified with the terribly losses and casualties and fear that, despite the public denials, the 'war on terror' has somehow become a 'war on Islam'.

In identifying with the pain and suffering of shattered lives in the zones of conflict in Iraq, Afghanistan, Israel/Palestine, Chechnya, Muslims can feel that it is intolerable that life seems to go on 'as normal' in the West.

To recognise that it is often a kind of desperation that encourages terror is not to condone it. Rather, we have a moral responsibility to listen and learn, and so recognise *connections* that otherwise would not be made. We need to develop forms of social theory that are open to listening to a diversity of different voices that can somehow be brought into dialogue with each other.

Caught up within cycles of violence and revenge, and wanting to hold people individually responsible for their terrorist actions against civilians, it can seem initially incomprehensible that the tragic carnage on the London Underground and on the No. 38 bus need to be connected with issues of global injustice, religious fundamentalisms, and a politics of uprootedness and uncertain belongings. But within a globalised world, traumatic events in individual lives can often only be grasped through also appreciating and making visible connections between the individual and the global, the psyche and the social, as these are mediated through the complex diasporic histories of peoples and nation states.

Lives torn apart

The video released on 1 September 2005 by Mohammed Sidique Khan shows him claiming responsibility for the London bombings of 7/7. He explains his reinvention from the young man who grew up in Beeston, outside Leeds and the transcultural influences that had shaped his present. We heard his familiar sounding voice that indicated how he belonged to the place of his birth. His accent showed his past and indicated traces of belonging at the very moment that he disavowed and did his best to erase them. When he talked about 'my people' he was expressing his identification with Islam and the sufferings of Muslims around the world. It is not that he lacked opportunities to acquire a British identity but that he partly felt shamed by it because of its actions in Afghanistan and Iraq. It was not an identity he could erase even if he did his best to disavow his cultural and emotional attachments to Britain. In fact it was his very Britishness, marked by his voice, that seemed to have added an intensity to his drive towards action. It was as if he had to do something extreme to *wipe out* the traces of his own identifications. The impossibility of the task is what shapes this act of self-reinvention, as if you can strip yourself of your everyday culture and remake yourself through an act of will. The attempt to remake yourself through an individual act of will also has sources within Western culture, possibly most evident in revolutionaries that have felt impelled to prove their commitment through actions that disavowal their middle class backgrounds.

I want to set reflections on the video against the memories of a survivor who is struggling to come to terms with how the events shattered her life, showing how 'events' impact differently upon different lives. I also show the need for social theories to learn how to listen to what people have to say about being affected by traumatic events and so help to shape narratives that can open up to different levels of experience. I have learned this often this means that researchers have to be willing to ask themselves questions and so do the required *inner work* for themselves if they want to be able to connect to people they are listening too. Often this means searching for a similar experience of loss in your own life and a willingness to do the inner work that allows for a more equal relationship to be established. In this way the interview becomes more equal and people are careful to only ask questions they have been willing to ask themselves. This produces a different kind of atmosphere in which the interview takes place so creating different responses and often more meaningful encounters. Listening to how people frame their own narratives shows how different lines through events are shaped and the ways events shape future lives in radically different ways.

One image replays in Martine Wright's head. Dressed in jeans and her new Adidas trainers, she is running towards the open doors of a tube train, jumping on and sitting in the first seat available. It was a split-second decision, the instinctive action of a Londoner rushing to get to work. It was 8.49 am on Thursday, 7 July. Some 30 seconds later, her life had changed forever. She should never have been on a Circle line train, but with the Northern line down that morning, she was forced to take an alternative route to get from her flat in Stroud Green, North London, to her office at Tower Hill, in the city where she works as an international marketing manager.

> I remember it was just a normal Thursday. I got to this platform and saw this tube arriving and thought, 'Ah, it's a Circle line train, excellent, quick, jump on.'
>
> The doors shut and I sat in the first seat in front of me. Thirty seconds later ... what I can only describe as a white noise, I don't remember a boom, just a white noise. I couldn't see anything but blinding white, and it wobbled like a cartoon effect and I was being rocked from side to side.
>
> It was a tube then all of a sudden it wasn't a tube, its just devastation, black, black devastation and I'm thinking, 'Where has the carriage gone, I mean where has it gone?'
>
> Then just screams, screams, what the hell's happened, help me, help me, just raw screaming in this dark and dust and devastation.
>
> (*Guardian*, 24 September 2005: 1)

Martine Wright was one of the most seriously injured survivors of the July 7 suicide bombings – the last person to be pulled out of the carnage of the Aldgate tube station. She lost both legs above the knee and suffered a fractured skull when Shehzad Tanweer exploded his backpack bomb 3 feet from where she was sitting. Three people around her were killed outright. As she tells Sandra Laville her story, for the *Guardian*, she sit in a wheelchair in the garden of the Douglas Bader rehabilitation unit in South

London and remembers every detail of that day, using her hands to describe the moment of the blast – 'Dooff' – and hesitating only over the words 'bomb' and 'explosion': 'I can't say these words,' she says, 'I have to call it an accident' (*Guardian*, 24 September 2005: 1). Language has also been *fractured* for her and it is as if certain words can no longer be spoken – as if these words have become traumatised and carry too much pain to be uttered.

Three months on, the severity of her injuries is still a daily shock – but she has no feelings about the bombers:

> Maybe I will be angry one day, but at the moment I don't waste my energy. I just think the world has gone mad. I wake up in the morning. I feel OK. Then I go and have a wash in the wheelchair and just look down at my legs and think, but I'm Martine Wright, this doesn't happen to me.
>
> Sometimes I say, why me, why me? But you can't think that. I keep trying to tell myself I am lucky, I am here and other people died. But I don't feel lucky. Maybe one day, if I keep telling myself, it will finally sink in.
>
> (*Guardian*, 24 September 2005: 3)

Responsibilities

The video of the Beeston suicide bomber Mohammed Sidique Khan was only released by the Arabic news channel al Jazera two months after the attacks on London, on 1 September, only days before the anniversary of 9/11. The video was followed by one of Ayman al-Zawahiri, the second-in-command of al-Qaida, suggesting the network was more involved in the attacks than Western intelligence had previously thought. Khan spoke in English in a calm, native Yorkshire accent, aiming specifically at British Muslims and using words like 'spin' that have a special resonance in Britain under New Labour.

In the video, he praised Osama bin Laden and the Iraqi insurgency leader Abu Musab al-Zarqawi as 'heroes'. He appeared wearing an olive-green jacket, clutching a pen and glancing at notes. Speaking in his Yorkshire accent, he said:

> Our words have no impact upon you, therefore I am going to talk to you in a language that you understand. Our words are dead until we give them life with our blood.
>
> I am sure by now the media has painted a suitable picture of me. This predictable machine will naturally try to put a spin on things to suit the government and scare the masses into conforming to their power and wealth-obsessed agenda.
>
> I and thousands like me have forsaken everything for what we

believe. Our drive and motivation does not come from tangible com-
modities that this world has to offer.

The rhetoric he used was not new but it was calibrated to touch on the
sore points about Western policy felt by Muslims bitterly opposed to violence, as well as to speak directly to British people in general, saying:

> This is how our ethical stances are dictated. Your democratically
> elected governments continually perpetuate atrocities against my
> people all over the world and your support of them makes you directly
> responsible, just as I am directly responsible for protecting and aveng-
> ing my Muslim brothers and sisters.
>   Until we feel security you will be our target. Until you stop the
> bombing, gassing, imprisonment and torture of my people we will not
> stop this fight. We are at war and I am a soldier. Now you too will
> taste the reality of this situation.
>
> (*Guardian*, 2 February 2005: 11)

Khan's video was released exactly four weeks after a previous video fea-
turing Al-Zawahiri praising the bombings and exactly eight weeks after
the July 7 bombings. The video also featured a graphic of a simulated
explosion on an Underground train in which a carriage erupts in flames.
The accompanying caption read: 'He guided the knights of Tawheed to
explore the volcano of Islamic anger in the heart of the capital of the cross,
London.' A-Zawahiri, unlike Khan, is pictured next to a grenade launcher,
suggesting possibly that Khan's segment of the film was filmed in the UK,
used his speech in Arabic to blame Blair for the attacks. He said:

> I talk to you today about the blessed London battle which came as a
> slap to the face of the tyrannical, Crusader British arrogance. It's a sip
> from the glass that the Muslims have been drinking from.
>   This blessed battle has transferred – like its glorious predecessors in
> New York, Washington and Madrid – the battle to the enemies.
>   Blair has brought catastrophes to his people in the middle of the
> capital, and will bring more, God willing, because he is still fooling his
> people and insisting and stubbornly treating them like ignorant fools
> when he keeps repeating that what happened in London has nothing to
> do with the crimes he has committed in Palestine, Afghanistan and Iraq.
>
> (*Daily Mail*, 2 September 2005: 2)

He mocked British Muslims who condemned the attacks: 'We tell them
treatment in kind is just,' he said.
    Blair's immediate strategy, according to the *Guardian*'s Westminster
correspondent, David Hencke, appeared to be that any response from
Downing Street 'would give further oxygen to the terrorists, so no

comment would be issued'. It was left to Jack Straw, the Foreign Secretary, who was attending talks on Turkish membership of the EU in Newport, to simply say: 'there is no excuse, no justification for terrorism of any kind, and it happens those who, entirely wrongly, claim to speak in the name of Islam are mainly killing their fellow Muslims.'

Hencke reported that, earlier the same day, Kenneth Clarke had launched a fierce attack on the government's involvement in the Iraq War. One of the few Tory MPs who voted against the war, he said Mr Blair must be the only person left who saw no connection between his 'disastrous' decision to go to war in Iraq and the recent bombings in London. He told the Foreign Press Association at Westminster:

> The war did not create the danger of Islamic terrorism in this country . .. [but] the decision by the UK government to become the leading ally of President Bush in the Iraq debacle has made Britain one of the foremost targets for Islamic extremists.
>
> (*Guardian*, 2 September 2005: 11)

As an editorial in the *Guardian* acknowledged:

> When even the bomber himself says he was motivated by actions abroad, it is perverse for the government to continue to deny this.... If it wants its message to be listened to by British Muslims, it must first establish credibility and it is very hard to do that while denying the blindingly obvious. Iraq cannot be a justification for the London bombings – but Mr Blair should stop pretending it is not a factor.
>
> (*Guardian*, 3 September 2005: 19)

There is a difference between denying that the war in Iraq provides a cause or justification for the bombings and acknowledging the influence of the war in creating particular pressures for young Islamic men who feel identified with the sufferings of other Muslims. At the very least we need to acknowledge the *influence* of these transnational identifications for they have become a significant feature of a globalised world. In a speech focusing primarily on civil liberties and community relations, Clarke warned, before the Khan video emerged:

> New laws after every terrorist atrocity can feed a sense of panic. They can also encourage the terrorists because, if our response is an ever-more repressive set of laws, they will know that those laws are most likely to impact on communities from which they derive sympathy.

He added: 'You do not beat the enemies of freedom by taking freedoms away.' This was a critical reminder which was to prove significant in the arguments around restrictions of civil liberties. The government had also to be careful not to reproduce a widespread culture of fear to justify limitations on civil liberties if they were not further to isolate and threaten Islamic communities in Britain.

Richard Norton-Taylor reported (*Guardian*, 3 September 2005: 10) that M15 still felt, at that time, that there was nothing in Khan's video of his last testimony to show that al-Qaida was more closely linked to the attacks than previously assumed. "It leaves us in the same position," a senior source said. They still believed that plotters were 'homegrown' and said there is no evidence of any 'mastermind' behind the attacks. They described the broadcast as 'the al-Qaida leadership, post-event, trying to stake some kind of claim' to the July 7 attacks, stating that Khan did not actually say that he was inspired by 'today's heroes' or that he had acted under their orders. Norton-Taylor might be right about this but, as we know, influences work in complex ways and as it became clear that they had visited Pakistan and made connections there, it became more difficult to trace the exact nature of al-Qaida influence.

Norton-Taylor also reports that, at the time, though late to be questioned, officials are convinced there was no link between the July 7 and the failed July 21 attacks, which they regard as a 'copycat' plan. They base their view chiefly on the unplanned bombing of the bus in London's Tavistock Square by Hasib Hussain, one of the July 7 suicide bombers. But what worries intelligence officials, according to Norton-Taylor, is al-Qaida's ability to use the media to mount a huge propaganda exercise directed at a British audience and the Arab world, albeit weeks after the event. But

> what most worries M15, M16 and the police, is what, or who, persuades an intelligent, British educated, 30-year-old to blow himself up and persuade others to do the same, killing scores of innocent members of the public in the process.
>
> (Ibid.)

Denial

In the two months since Khan left his wife and young baby in their flat at Dewsbury, some of his friends who had played football with him or knew him as youth workers have been living in denial. One young man who gave his name as Saj, who had been on day trips quad biking with the 30-year-old youth worker, said:

> A lot of people loved him round here. I have known him all my life, he was a friend to everyone.[...] He never talked of terrorism to me. I just don't accept that he or the others did this. I am suspicious of what the police say, there is no proof and look how they shot that Brazilian guy who was innocent.
>
> (Ibid.)

But, provided with what seemed to be evidence, the video statement of Khan apparently admitting to his role in the bombings, his protégés were left confused. Saj was one of the few young men to admit it was evidence of a kind: 'That is proof I suppose. It just shows you doesn't it?' (ibid.).

But others were harder to convince. Refusing to give their names for fear of being investigated by M15, one said, 'It's a fake. Look at the way his lips were moving; they looked odd, the whole thing is a fake.' Many older men also believe that Khan, a dedicated teaching assistant at Hillside Primary School, is the victim of conspiracy. 'It's crap,' said Mohammed Afsal, a father of five and member of the Hardy Street mosque.

> I know people can change in a second, but I can't say he is one of them. He taught my son, he was a very good teacher. He was never hardline – no one could say he was an extremist – he was peaceful and dedicated to his children. They all loved him.
>
> (Ibid.)

At Friday prayers each week, families are urged to look out for their young sons. The unspoken fear seems to be that others may follow in Kahn's footsteps. Afzal Choudhry, a youth worker who spent six months working with Khan in Beeston, hopes they will not. He said the video may have a positive impact in the long term, forcing young people to accept he was involved: 'It makes it more clear that he perpetrated these acts, it was definitely him, it was his voice and his face, that cannot be denied' (ibid). He also believes that it was only in the last five years that Khan became particularly religious. Others fear that the video could make things harder. Dr Hassan from the Leeds Forum of Mosques also had to accept what the police had been saying, that Khan was one of the suicide bombers. His fear now is 'This video will make some see him as a martyr, definitely. ... We are very concerned. We are trying to reach out to his circle of friends to find out what influence he still holds on them and to try and eradicate it' (ibid.).

Polly Toynbee recognised that, while we were witnessing hundreds of people being massacred in Iraq in one bloodbath after another, thus magnifying the horrors that were experienced in London many times over within a single week, it was difficult to know the impact upon Muslim communities in Britain and globally. She wrote:

> But if Iraq is all but absent, the war on terror is hot politics. Charles Clarke's new proposals emanate from the increasingly unreal planet of No 10, which still insists on no connection between the Iraq war and July 7. No one else believes it; most ministers have trouble speaking the words. But double-think and double-speak are leading us into a disastrous clash of civilisations.
>
> (*Guardian*, 20 September 2005: 29)

She continued:

> Even if the intention is good – ridding the world of Saddam or trying
> to stop bombers murdering tube travellers – any action that makes the
> threat worse is a mistake. Labour is keen on what works; Iraq has
> made the world more dangerous and these anti-terror laws risk the
> same.... Clarke's move to jail for up to five years anyone who
> 'glorifies, exalts or celebrates' terrorist attacks is as daft as it is
> dangerous.
>
> (Ibid.)

While Toynbee recognises 'Islamist killers took terror to a new level on
9/11', she cites the UK's experience with the IRA: 'Most attempts to quell
terror made things worse by disproportionate action taken in anger.'

> Never forget the IRA murdered publoads of ordinary people and came
> within a splinter of slaughtering the prime minister and cabinet.
> Ordinary Muslims may detect an elemental horror of dark-skinned
> bombers that strikes a deeper fear that Irish Catholics. Why else yet
> more draconian action? ... It seems as if we fear these new terrorists
> as more alarmingly alien, less one of us, though Catholic and Islamist
> bombs have the same effect.... Or is it just that politicians need to be
> seen taking 'new' action, despite perfectly good existing laws?
>
> (Ibid.)

Similar fears are expressed by Salim Lone, a former spokesman for the
UN mission in Iraq, who recognises that 'Since the London terror attacks
in July, Tony Blair has dramatically elevated the question of "incitement"
by aggressively defining it as one of the root causes of extremism'. It was a
campaign that began right after July 7 'with an astonishing attempt to
silence those exploring any link between British policies in the Middle East
and the growth of domestic militancy'. As Lone acknowledges, 'Few
dispute the need to outlaw incitement to terrorism' but there are worries
that 'it may threaten free speech, the bedrock of democracy and the rule of
law. Terms such as "potential" or "indirect" incitement could include any
advocacy of armed resistance ... is force now to be the preserve of the
powerful?' (*Guardian*, 22 September 2005: 33).
Along with the threats to freedom of speech, Lone thinks:

> it is alarming that Blair seems to be focussing only on Muslim actions
> ... The many Western scholars and writers who incite their countries
> to undertake wars of aggression are not to be affected by anti-
> incitement legislation. Such incitement is more deadly due to the
> awesome destructive power of the states that are being urged, invari-
> ably, to attack a much weaker country.... Bush and Blair have repeat-

edly pointed to their cultures' compassionate values, and condemned the barbarity of Muslim militants. Such talk offends many mainstream Muslims, not only militants.

(Ibid.)

Lone further points out:

nothing that the US and the UK are doing is winning over moderate Muslim opinion. The two leaders' refusal to countenance a speedy end to the occupation of Iraq and Afghanistan and the threats aimed at Iran and Syria are achieving the opposite – and so making it harder for Muslims to turn against the extremists.

(Ibid.)

Multicultures/integrations

Gary Younge has written: 'The cause of integration has become so fetishised since the July bombings that it has been elevated to the level of an intrinsic moral value – not a means to an end but an end in itself.' Though he appreciates the warnings of Trevor Phillips, the head of the Commission for Racial Equality, that Britain is a country that is 'sleep-walking' into a 'New Orleans-style' quagmire of 'fully fledged ghettos', he also realises that 'unless integration is coupled with the equally vigorous pursuit of equality and anti-racism, it does not go very far'. He reminds us that 'Rwanda had plenty of inter-ethnic marriages before the genocide' and that 'Jews were more integrated into German society than any other European nation before the Holocaust'.

He readily acknowledges 'Common-sense suggests that the more contact you have with different races, religions and ethnicities, the less potential there is for stereotyping and dehumanising those different from yourself', but insists that 'even that small achievement depends on the quality and power dynamics of the contact'. In other words, Younge explains, 'the value of integration is contingent on whom you are asking to integrate, what you are asking them to integrate into and on what basis you are asking them to do so'. He thinks the framing of the current debate post-7/7 is flawed on all three counts (*Guardian*, 19 September 2005: 23).

What we have to question, as Younge does, is the way integration is so often treated as a one-way street:

not a subtle process of cultural negotiation but full-scale assimilation of a religious group that is regarded by many liberals and conservatives as backward and reactionary. It is hardly surprising that many Muslims would not want to sign up to that.

(Ibid.)

Younge insists Britain has a great many qualities where race is concerned,

> but the image so eagerly touted after the bombings, of an oasis of tolerant diversity that has been exploited by Islamic fundamentalists who hail from a community determined to voluntarily segregate, simply does not square with the facts. If fair play is a core British value, racism is no less so.
>
> (Ibid.)

Also, the most likely victims of race attacks are Pakistanis and Bangladeshis – the dominant ethnic groups among Muslims – and this was before the bombs sparked a significant rise in Islamophobia.[9] Given the high levels of unemployment, according to Younge:

> if they need to be integrated into anything as a matter of urgency, it is to the workforce and the education system. A decent job with a decent income is still the best path out of the crudest forms of racism and fundamentalism.
>
> (Ibid.)

As Younge recognises, 'Equality of opportunity is the driving force behind integration, not the other way round, but their relationship is subtle and symbiotic, not crude and causal' (ibid.).

But, at the same time, Younge knows that the four young men who were responsible for the London bombings led neither deprived nor segregated lives. This means that the questions they raise are complex and related to complex dynamics that include issues of gender, sexuality and belonging as well as class and exclusion. But if this means questioning some of the terms of British multiculturalism, it also means engaging with the very different experiences and histories within different communities in different parts of the country. There are complex histories and geographies of migration and (dis)placement that need to be explored. Rather than assuming that a certain model of multiculturalism has failed so that we have to move towards an alternative vision of integration, we need to grasp the complex histories of post-war assimilations and migrations as well as the complex relationships between diverse communities.

This also means engaging critically with religious and faith traditions, rather than assuming the existence of homogeneous communities with their own traditions, cultures and values that need to be respected. We need to recognise tensions, histories and conflicts within communities and the ways they are constantly transforming and mutating with diverse generational experiences and through the interactions with other communities. We have to recognise how issues of gender and sexuality are also being contested and how silences and resentments can be created across the boundaries of generation. This means exploring the complex masculinities that have emerged, and the tensions that exist between the 'secular' and the 'religious' that can no longer be grasped within the terms of an Enlightenment rationalism that had traditionally disdained religious belief as a sign of 'backwardness'.

We need to explore the particular appeal of religious traditions to young men who might have grown up in secular worlds and been educated within local schools. Sometimes it can help them to affirm threatened masculinities and give them a sense of place and belonging. But it can also remove them from intimate contact with those they are closest to, and shape tensions in their relationships with women where they might be tempted to assume a masculine superiority they might otherwise have questioned. It can *reinforce* traditional masculinities and notions of respect and honour that can work to legitimate the subordination of women. It can encourage young men to put pressure on the young women they know to behave and dress more modestly than they might have chosen for themselves. This can also encourage women to speak out for themselves and so create dialogues across genders as young women and men learn to negotiate their complex identities with each other. As they learned to respect the particular decisions they have made for themselves, so it can be significant for women to feel they are making decisions for themselves – say, around wearing the hajib. Again there are often movements in different directions and people can respect the very different decisions young women and men might be making within the same families as they are seeking to define their own spiritualities and religious practices.[10]

Masculinities/intimacies

In her reflections upon what made her husband Jermain Lindsay become a suicide bomber, responsible for the bomb on the Piccadilly line train near King's Cross that killed 26 people, Samantha Lewthwaite said:

> The killing of innocent British civilians was something I could never comprehend because he was always a peaceful man who loved people.
>
> He was so angry when he saw Muslim civilians being killed on the streets in Iraq, Bosnia, Palestine and Israel – and always said it was the innocent who suffered.
>
> Then he is responsible for doing the same thing – but to his fellow British citizens.
>
> (*Sun*, 23 September 2005: 4)

She had married Lindsay in October 2002. She had become a Muslim at 18. At the time she met Lindsay, she was studying religion and politics at the School of Oriental and African Studies in London. A friend had given her his email address because he too had recently converted to Islam. She said, 'I wanted to marry a British Muslim and so did he. We didn't want an arranged marriage so I suppose in a way we kind of arranged our own.' Her first face-to-face contact with Lindsay – who later changed his name to Jermal – was on a Stop the War march in London's Hyde Park. She said, 'He wanted to qualify as a human rights lawyer and I was a member of an Amnesty International group at school. We wanted to make a difference to the world by peaceful means.' She added: 'The Jamal I met and married was a man of peace' (ibid.: 6). Her father Andy, a former British soldier, did not approve of the marriage and stayed away. As she said, 'He found it hard enough when I converted to Islam without marrying a Muslim I had hardly met.'

They went to live in Huddersfield and, she insisted, 'When he was living up North he was a peace-loving person. He was so naïve he couldn't believe anyone could hurt anyone. He was just lovely.' Lindsay was Jamaican-born but came to live in the UK with his mother when he was six-months old. He grew up in Huddersfield. As Samantha described it:

> He was very bright and had learnt Arabic and knew the Koran inside out. He left school early, which was a surprise as he had nine GCSEs – most of them at A grade. But he wanted to travel to an Islamic country like Saudi Arabia and learn more.
>
> (*Sun*, 24 September 2005: 4)

She recalled:

> When we got together we were fantastic and we prayed five times a day together. When I became pregnant life just got better and better. But all that changed when we moved South. I firmly believe if we had stayed up North he would be the same Jamal.
>
> (Ibid.)

As Samantha tried to make sense of what changed, she said,

> But he got involved in mosques in London and Luton and became a changed person. Women and men are separated in mosques when they pray so I never knew who he was meeting. ... In October through to November 2004 he met a group who changed his life. He became a man I didn't recognise. I have no doubt that his mind was twisted in there.
>
> (Ibid.)

Looking back, Samantha, who had taken the name 'Asmantera', noticed changes in his behaviour. At one time he spent ten days and nights in the Regent's Park Mosque. His life seems to have changed and he was distancing himself, possibly having assumed a different sense of Islamic masculinity and relationships with women. As she recalled,

When he came back he was different. He was snappy and verbally aggressive. It was a turning point – a different Jamal I saw from now on. It was nothing instant, but gradual over the months as his attitude to me changed. It was as if he was driving me away.

(Ibid.)

She added, 'Jamal still prayed five times a day but didn't want me to pray with him. I had no idea of what was happening in his life' (ibid.).

She shows how difficult it can be to discern changes, even in those we are closest to, and how you also need to trust your intuition in these matters.

According to the *Sun* interview, he also took to disappearing into a locked room where he would spend much of his time on the Internet. The Sun report goes on to say that he wept as he read a story about a Muslim girl being raped and tortured while being held in prison in Iraq. As Asmantera told Jamie Pyatt:

The police told me it is a recognised pattern that a person who has been recruited to do something like this begins to detach himself from his life. It makes it easier for them to go out and commit an atrocity.

(Ibid.)

She believed Jamal said an abstract 'goodbye' to her and her son, Abdullah, now 17 months, by taking them on fun park outings he had never previously suggested.

She had little doubt that he communicated to like-minded people during his long Web sessions. She added: 'He just said he wanted space and began to seclude himself from me.' After one trip away, he returned home with a dramatically changed image. She recalled:

He was dressed in trendy designer Western clothes and had ditched all his Arab-style gowns. He shaved off the beard he had grown since he was 14 and had never even trimmed. This shocked me as the beard is Sunnah – an example to the Prophet Muhammad. The change was directly against everything Jamal ever believed in.

(Ibid.: 4)

As she recalled more recent times, she said:

With hindsight he was clearly preparing himself for the suicide bombing. I didn't think much of it at the time because his behaviour was so odd. I didn't think for a moment he was involved. Why should I? I'd send him to sort his head out. I didn't think the very next morning he would be blowing up a train.

He had taken to disappearing for days and I told him to go to a mosque and talk to his brothers and come back to me again when he was the Jamal I married.

She recalled watching the reports of the London bombings:

> I saw the images on TV and got very upset. My dad phoned and told me I had better take off my Islamic clothing in case there was a backlash. I ignored him. ... 'I was crying when I saw people looking for family members, Obviously I didn't know then I was linked to what I was seeing.'

Reflecting back, she said:

> He loved his son more than anything and loved me. Yet these people manage to twist him so much that he could turn his back on those who meant so much.
> It shows why all good Muslims have to fight against evil.
>
> (*Sun*, 23 September 2005: 5)

Ethics

Zadie Smith is one of those writers who recognises that writing a novel, as well as reading a novel, is an ethical practice, a practice place for morals where we watch, in safety, people choosing what they must do and what they lose when they choose wrongly. It is the closest possible thing to the real thing. Zadie Smith is also convinced that 'Good writing requires – demands – good being.' This is something she seems to have learnt from E.M. Forster who she celebrates in the 2003 Orange Word Lecture, saying:

> He allowed the English comic novel the possibility of a spiritual and bodily life, not simply to exist as an exquisitely worked game of social ethics, but as a messy human concoction. He expanded the comic novel's ethical space (while unbalancing its moral certainties) simply by letting more of life 'in'.
>
> (*Guardian Review*, 3 September 2005: 16)

For Smith, this open multiplicity is an article of faith – 'we find ourselves caring about people who are various, muddled, uncertain and not quite like us (and this is good)' (ibid.). Of course there are limits, but we need to explore their nature, rather than to assume them in advance. This is something that social theories also need to learn from, as they explore different ways to let more life in.

But this is to refuse the idea that to seek to understand how British-born and educated young men could turn to terror is to impart some legitimacy to terrorist acts. Norman Geras has condemned those who seek to understand their motivations as 'fellow travellers' but I think this is mistaken, for unless we can understand how these young men have been drawn into these fundamentalist positions and prepared themselves to act as suicide bombers, we will *not* be able to engage with other young men who feel similarly drawn. We have to reject the arguments of those like Tom Friedman, a columnist for the *New York Times*, who would curtail critical intellectual engagement. Quoting James Rubin, the former US state department spokesman, Friedman wrote:

> the excuse makers ... who come out after every major terrorist incident ... to explain why imperialism, Zionism, colonialism or Iraq explain why terrorists acted. [The excuse-makers] are just one notch less despicable than the terrorists.
>
> (Quoted by Salim Lone, in the *Guardian*, 22 September 2005: 33)

This becomes a way of foreclosing the discussions we need to have about how people are to learn to live together with their differences respected in precarious and often dangerous times. This involves establishing bonds of trust between individuals and communities that can help dissolve economies of fear. This is not simply a matter of bringing different voices into relationship with each other as if we can decide upon these different views on the basis of an impartial and dispassionate reason. Rather we have to listen beyond an attempt to discern similarities and differences that can help shape a common ground towards an *ethics of judgement* that allows us to recognise what matters in individual and collective lives. This involves a willingness to think beyond certain dualities, say between tradition and modernity and the secular and the religious that have traditionally shaped forms of social theory. This means thinking beyond the terms of liberal tolerance that have tended to assume that religions can be integrated into a multicultural project through being largely left to themselves.

Within an Enlightenment vision of modernity religion is largely regarded as a matter of individual belief and even though we refer to a 'return to religion' in 'post-secular societies' religion is still separated from politics and religions are rarely provoked to give moral accounts of themselves, say in relation to issues of gender and sexualities. Questions of faith are framed in terms of self-identification and belonging and as matters of belief and unbelief. There are issues that pertain to representation and community leadership but relatively little engagement with *how* religious traditions interpret their sacred texts and traditions of reading. But politics remains essentially secular and little regard is given to religions as ethical traditions with their own values and traditions that can be engaged with critically. Rather reference is made to the 'shared values' of the 'great faiths' in ways that prefer to forget their bloody and difficult histories.

The advocates of integration and nation-building on the one hand and defenders of a cosmopolitan multicultural polity tend to accept the opposition between national and religious categories. Ulrich Beck, for example, accepts that in a globally interconnected and economically governed age, you have to look beyond national boundaries while accepting that the ability to oppose a religious faith depends upon putting faith in the moral authority of the state.[11] Although Paul Gilroy is less inclined to disregard the idea and usefulness of the nation, he recognises the false dreams that accompany 'postcolonial melancholia' when Britain refuses to face its imperial histories of violence and colonial rule.[12] But, like Beck, he tends to see politics as a means by which religions can be rescued from being positioned as the sources of categories about which conflict arises. In their different ways they seem committed to an Enlightenment vision that radically separates reason from faith.

It becomes tempting to assume that democracy can only be part of Islam through 'Europeanisation' or secularisation and that Islam can only be rescued from its radical extremes if it accepts secular political norms. But this denies Islam recognition of its own ethical resources and capacities to *renew itself* through its own traditions. But if we are to take the theology and politics of religious traditions seriously we have to go beyond thinking of them exclusively as sources of identity and viewing them as markers for conflicts that run much deeper and have exclusively material sources. When Beck seeks to separate Islamic terrorism from Islamic faith, he does this through radically separating religion from politics and insisting that terrorism is profoundly modern and so political so that it is *political* Islam rather than political *Islam*.[13]

If we forget the need to question the moral foundations of law so keeping alive the challenges the ethics can make to politics we can so easily be confined within the legitimations offered by legislators. This is partly why An-Na'im refuses to accept that it is not a matter of giving assent to the moral authority of the state's laws or the moral authority of one's religious laws, but of recognising that these laws function best when they are seen as coextensive. The task of politics is to ensure that the normative claims of religion do not ossify into hollow and unchallengeable rites and rituals. According to An-Na'im the point of laicite is not to silence religions but to open them to dissent and change.

But this means recognising the normative claims made by religions so that they are not denied a voice. In An-Naim's words "politics and religion do not operate in distinct realms; the one continually informs and is informed by the other."[14] The question of religion's place in politics is in many ways inseparable from morality's place in politics. Within postmodern cultures in which we can only speak of religions within the frameworks of integration or multiculturalism we often fail to appreciate the difficulties we have in speaking meaningfully about moralities and how they are to be politically voiced. As Zygmunt Bauman recalls the words of the novelist Max Frisch which seem resonant to the moment, "At the end of our progress, we stand where Adam and Eve once stood: all we are faced with now is the moral question."[15]

Coming to terms with complex ethical issues is made more difficult, as Amoz Oz recognised in his speech when he was awarded the Goethe prize in Frankfurt on 28 August 2005, by the silences within traditional social theories about issues of good and evil. As Oz argued:

> To them, all human motives and actions derive from circumstances, which are often beyond personal control. 'Demons,' said Freud, 'do not exist any more than gods do, being only the products of the psychic activity of man.' We are controlled by our social background. For about a 100 years now, they have been telling us that we are motivated exclusively by economic self-interest, that we are mere products of our ethnic cultures, that we are no more than marionettes of our own subconscious.
>
> (*Guardian Review*, 3 September 2005: 4)

Though I think he over-generalises, he makes an important insight when he says: 'For the first time since the book of Job, the devil found himself out of a job. He could no longer play his ancient game with human minds. Satan was dismissed. This was the modern age.'

According to Oz: 'Satan is no longer in the details. Individual men and women cannot be "bad", in the ancient sense of the book of Job ...' Against this, he affirmed:

> Personally I believe that every human being, in his or her own hearts, is capable of telling good from bad. Even when they pretend not to. We have all eaten from that tree of Eden whose full name is the tree of knowledge of good from evil ... it may sometimes be hard to define good; but evil has its unmistakable odour: every child knows what pain is. Therefore, each time we deliberately inflict pain on another, we know what we are doing. We are doing evil.
>
> (Ibid.)

Oz insisted that

> Satan might have been sacked, but he did not remain unemployed. The 20th C was the worst arena of cold-blooded evil in human history. The social sciences failed to predict, encounter or even grasp this modern, highly technologised evil. Very often this 20th C evil disguised itself as world reforming, as idealism, as re-educating the masses or 'opening their eyes'. Totalitarianism was presented as secular redemption for some, at the expense of millions of lives.
>
> (*Guardian Review*, 3 September 2005: 4)

As we learn to think critically in the twenty-first century – including in relation to religious forms of redemption – we need to be able to revision social theories in ways that allow us to explore issues of 'good' and 'evil' in ways that refuse President Bush's dualistic notion that 'we are good, they are evil'. We have to be able to imagine 'the other' in ways that also appreciate how human pain can also breed evil and the complex identifications that people can learn to feel for the sufferings of others.[16]

We have to explore the complex processes of identity and belonging that so often shape the tensions and anxieties carried by young men whose families have experienced migration and displacement. We also need to investigate the appeals of religious fundamentalisms that can work to encourage young men to sacrifice their lives as suicide bombers.

These are difficult questions that we will need to return to once we have revisited the traumatic events of the London bombings. Recalling those times will help us to acknowledge how other sufferings, perpetrated away from the gaze of the Western media, equally impact on the lives of others. For Oz, Goethe who wrote his *West-Eastern Divan*:

> was neither an orientalist nor a multiculturalist. It was not the extreme and imagined exoticism of the east that tempted him, but the strong and fresh substance that eastern cultures, eastern poetry and art may give to universal human truths and feelings.... He takes humans, all humans, seriously. East or west, good men weep.
>
> (Ibid.: 5)[17]

2　Urban fears and terrors of 7/7

Events

It took time to realise that a major event was unfolding in London on 7 July 2005, and that life in London would never quite be the same again. It was hard to realise that it might turn out to be one of those events that disrupts linear visions of time and memory you would recall in ways that can define the experience of a generation. If you can remember where you were when the news that President Kennedy was shot in Dallas, it can help to locate yourself in generational time and help shape cultures. If you can recall the moment when you heard the nuclear plant at Chernobyl had exploded, spreading nuclear dust over Europe, or when Princess Diana was killed in Paris, or when you first realised there had been an attack on the Twin Towers in New York, these very different events can help to locate you in time and space.

With the development of global media, what might have been local events that you only hear about much later have become global events that you can witness unfolding. Often it is events that stop us in our tracks and disrupts time that bring an awareness that we need to think differently if we are to understand how the world that we had known had somehow changed in decisive ways. It might be that it is the presence of the global media and the speed of delivery of images that makes people complicit in events in new ways and helps to define a postmodern age.[1]

Often it can take time for the impact of these events to be absorbed, and for us to recognise the need to develop new forms of social and political theory if we are to illuminate the realities we have witnessed. The significance of some events, for instance, the 'liberation' of Belsen, Dachau and other concentration camps, and the dropping of nuclear bombs on Hiroshima and Nagasaki, were immediate. People quickly realised that they were living in a new world with different fears, terrors and possibilities. There were different kinds of awareness that people were now living in a world 'after Auschwitz' or 'after Hiroshima', and that it might take considerable time for people to adjust their ways of thinking and living to these new realities. Sometimes these were events that they did not witness directly, though they saw television newsreels later. But, with 9/11 and the attack on the Twin Towers, there was a globalisation of the mass media that allowed people to feel involved in the unfolding of events in different ways. They became witnesses in a way relatively few could have been in previous times. This allowed for a transformation of experience that implicated people in new ways as they realised that relationships between radical Islam and the West had entered a new and terrifying phase. If this was an event they watched happening in New York, it meant that people felt unsafe in London, Paris, Berlin and Madrid, and anywhere else that could be identified as part of 'the West'. It was unclear where the next attack would take place and what countries had to do to, if anything, to make themselves safe from attack.[2]

From the moment of the attack on the Twin Towers, there were new global landscapes of fear and it was obvious that life had suddenly become unsafe in new ways in London. There were immediate fears that there might also be an attack on Canary Wharf and there were evacuations carried out in tall buildings in the City of London. If an attack did not happen then, it could always happen later. There was fear and uncertainty as people realised that the London Underground could be a target. There were warnings that told people they had to be on constant alert and watchful. People became suspicious because they did not know where the threat was coming from and what they could do to make themselves safe. There were new boundaries to be drawn between private and public spaces, as public spaces seemed to carry more dangers, and people were initially scared of using public transport or working in high buildings that could be attacked by aircraft. There was an awareness that the attack would come from a different direction, but what seemed to make life so precarious is that it was difficult to know how you might make yourself safe.

Everyday life had become threatening and social theories needed to think in new ways about how 'events' had disrupted and transformed social life. Possibly, events were revealing threats that already existed, though they had gone largely unrecognised, but sometimes they were showing that we lived in a different kind of world in which quite different social forces were at work. With the imminent threat of global warming, it also showed that boundaries between nature and culture had to be imagined differently because they were making human life *precarious* in different, but equally significant, ways.[3]

Often it is through relating personal narratives to the larger events as they are unfolding that we recognise that there is a difference between the speed with which information is moving and the psychic time and space that it takes people to undo the shock and begin to integrate some of their own experiences. In this way, individual lives can be related to global events as people learn to narrate their own experiences. It is also a way of people learning to value their own narratives as they learn how to listen to others who may have been more directly involved. Through a social theory of events that values narrative methods, we can explore *how* it took time for people to realise that a major terrorist events was unfolding on 7 July 2005.

Time takes its own shape as the 'event' develops, and people in different urban spaces find themselves in different spacial relationships as well as different temporalities. Everyone in London carries their own stories of what happened that day. Later, people will reflect back in different terms as they become aware of the time it takes to undo some of their shocked responses. It is the different ways in which events help to shape individual and collective lives and futures that needs to be carefully explored. Sometimes people are shaken momentarily, only to return to familiar and habitual ways of thinking and behaving. For others, it can lead to long-term changes in behaviour as they become *aware* of their lives as precarious in new ways.[4]

Narratives

Often it can help to recall our own experience of events and the particular intensities of affect. I had been working at home in North West London on a paper for a conference since 8.00 am so that I was a little late when I arrived at the side entrance of Brent Station. It was closed and I was a little surprised as this was a working day. When I walked around to the front of the station, there were people walking away and an older man stopped to tell me that there was no power on the Northern line and they were advising everyone to take buses. It was on the number 210 bus to Finsbury Park that I talked to an Asian woman who said that two trains had collided at Moorgate and that it was going to be difficult to get into Central London. She worked in a bank and they had insisted that she find her way in. She knew that the tube system had gone down and she had also heard that there had been a terrorist incident. It seemed pointless to make it to Finsbury Park so I got off at Golders Green, where I discovered that there was no way of getting through Central London – and that there had indeed been a terrorist incident of some kind.

I was determined to get to Goldsmiths in New Cross, South East London, where I work, because I had to examine a PhD candidate at 2.00 pm, and I knew that the candidate was coming from Geneva and the external examiner was coming in on a train from Edinburgh. It was difficult for me to accept that I had no control of the situation, and that the best thing was to return home. But the disturbance in my routine was difficult to handle. I had my day worked out and I had been planning it for days. I felt thrown as I took the bus back home and immediately turned on the television. They were talking about explosions that had gone off at different places, but they were not saying what we already knew, that this was a major terrorist attack on London and that these different explosions were related to each other. They were talking about six separate bombings and they named the tube stations and showed images of King's Cross as well as an image of the bus that had had its roof blown off in Tavistock Square. Gradually you realised that you were watching short clips and that on the divided screens you were being shown the same images over and over again. I changed the channel over to the BBC, but found a pretty similar scene. I just kept watching, hoping to understand what was going on.

I pass through King's Cross on my way to London Bridge whenever I go to work, and I was shaken to realise that, if I had gone a little earlier and not delayed my journey today, I could have somehow been involved. At that stage it was quite unclear what you would have been involved in, but as the time moved on, it was scary to realise that people were caught in a tube station below ground. There were a few reports from people who had made narrow escapes, and who spoke with fear in their voices and a sense of relief, but it was pretty clear that there had been tight controls on what was being shown and that more could be learned from listening to the radio, even though you might see less. As I learned later, only ITV had been carrying related breaking news, while the BBC was still editorially hung up on the idea of power surges even as late as 11.30am, after Sir Ian Blair of the Metropolitan Police had spoken, and shortly before Tony Blair made his first announcement talking about a terrorist attack on London with the loss of life. Very soon after, we were listening to narratives of people caught up in the bombings and exposed to the fears and terrors circulating, as well as the myths being produced in the face of limited news reporting. People were 'being affected', knowing 'it could so easily have been me or someone I know'.

Images/horrors

As Kathryn Flett recognised: 'We may finally be having our 9/11, but it soon becomes clear that this will not be accompanied by such extra-ordinarily powerful and emotive images.' She recalled:

> Oddly the atmosphere – at least as it is televised – is so calm we could be watching a disaster simulation rather than the real thing, Though the mind boggles at the thought of what sort of hellishness may be unfolding in the underground tunnels, none of what we are watching is entirely unprecedented – is, indeed, in effect, a replay of the fallout from the King's Cross fire or the Moorgate crash. We've been here before, sort of, and, to be honest, many of us have been expecting to be here again for a while.
>
> (*Observer*, 10 July 2005: 19)

By early evening, when the situation had become clearer and the boundaries of the terrorist attack established, there were signs of how new technologies had transformed everyone who had been present into a reporter. Telephone technologies have allowed for a democratisation of newsgathering. There is grainy footage from inside tube trains and tunnels and from the streets outside in the immediate aftermath. Flett is right that 'The stilted, pixelated quality of the images and lack of sound in no way diminish the impact of the reportage' (ibid.: 19). It had been at 8.51 am when the London transport system was coping with the peak of the morning rush hour that the coordinated terror attack that the capital had feared became a reality. The first bomb ripped through the second carriage of a Circle line train 100 yards inside the tunnel between Liverpool Street and Aldgate station. Although this was being reported in the early coverage as two incidents, it was produced by a single bomb that had been left by a door. The blast sent a flash of flame outside of the train as the carriages reared up, flinging the 700 or so passengers onto the floor and filling the darkened carriages with smoke, grit and debris.

'The first thing I knew I saw silver travelling through the air, which was glass, and a yellow flash,' said Michael Henning, 39, a City worker from Kensington. 'Then I was getting twisted and thrown down on the ground. The blast just twisted and turned me. I was in the next carriage but within 10ft of where the bomb went off, I feel extremely lucky' (*Guardian*, 8 July 2005: 4). For a moment after the explosion, there was a stunned silence inside the train, but as the realisation of what had happened began to sink in, the survivors started to fear the wreckage was about to be consumed in flames. 'It was very dark all around us,' Mr Henning said.

> People panicked and were screaming and a few of us were telling them to calm down. The girls were the calmest and had things under control quickly. We tried to open the doors, we were trying to pull them. The London underground drivers were trying to get them open from the outside but they weren't moving. There was a lot of dust and smoke. There was no communication, no Tannoy, no feedback.'
>
> (Ibid.)

Like many passengers in his carriage, Mr Henning had been injured by flying debris. He had glass in one eye and dozens of cuts and scratches on his face. As some passengers used their mobile phones to let people know they were alive, some of the walking wounded – a phrase I had not really heard before, but which became strangely familiar through the day – were moving into less-damaged carriages through the connecting doors to get away from the smoke. 'There was blood dripping off them, they were all white,' said Loyita Worley, 49, who had also been travelling in the third carriage. It was only when they finally made it out on the tracks and were being led to safety that the survivors realised the scale of the carnage. Mustafa Kurtuldo, a 24-year-old graphic designer from Hackney, said, 'As they led us down the track past the carriages where the explosion was, we could see the roof was torn off it, and there were bodies on the track' (ibid.).

Mr Henning said:

> There was part of the side wall missing. Some of the seats were missing, People were still in their seats and they were screaming

with pain and were covered in blood down one side of their body. There was other people that were trapped and they were just left there.

(Ibid.)

Scott Wenbourne, another survivor, said:

> I saw three bodies on the track. I couldn't look it was so horrific. I think one was moving but I'm not too sure.
> There were also, I think, some bodies in the carriages, some were moving but I couldn't really look. No one was attending to them.
>
> (Ibid.)

Derik Price, 55, from Essex, said he was surprised how calm the survivors were as they were led along the tracks past the wreckage. 'Some people were upset but there wasn't panic, considering you could only see a few feet in front of your face' (ibid. 4).

One regular commuter on the packed Piccadilly line tube train said they instinctively knew a bomb had gone off when the train drew slowly to a halt after a blinding flash and a loud bang. The blast hit the train at 8.56 am about three minutes south of King's Cross station. Survivors were led out of both ends of the tunnel – to the station the train had just left and Russell Square, the next on the line. One woman caught in the incident at Russell Square said:

> Some people were able to carry other people who were much more badly injured than them. There were a lot of people with terrible burns. People were starting to get very dehydrated and very unwell. When the emergency services got there they had to carry people in blankets who had lost limbs.
>
> (Ibid.)

Jo Herbert, in an email to the *Guardian Unlimited* website, wrote:

> I was stuck in a smoke-filled, blackened tube that reeked of burning for over 30 minutes. So many people were hysterical. I truly thought I was going to die and was just hoping it would be from smoke inhalation and not fire. I felt genuine fear but kept calm (and quite proud of myself for that).
> 'Eventually people smashed through the windows and we were lifted out, all walked up the tunnel to the station. There was chaos outside and I started to walk down Euston Road (my face and clothes were black) towards work and all of a sudden there was another huge bang and people started running up the road in the opposite direction to where I was walking and screaming and crying.
> I now realise that it must have been the bus exploding.

Another survivor, Fiona Trueman, 26, who works in marketing for Sky News, said outside the Royal London Hospital, Whitechapel:

'It was just horrendous; it was like a disaster movie. You can't imagine being somewhere like that – you just want to get out. I kept closing my eyes and thinking of outside. It was frightening because all the lights had gone out and we didn't hear anything from the driver, so we wondered how he was.'

(*Guardian*, 8 July 2005: 4)

Tom Curry, 28, who works for an Internet provider, was also on the Piccadilly line train. He said:

We were coming out of King's Cross and there was a really big bang, a big, bright flash of light and loads of black smoke started to pour into the carriage.

Immediately, loads of black smoke was everywhere. I think it was soot from the inside of the tunnels. It was acrid and really hard to breathe.

(Ibid.)

The Circle Line tube train was just pulling out of Edgware Road station towards Paddington when it was also rocked by a huge blast, at 9.17am. Sara, 23, who was on her way to work at Wapping, said: 'Our carriage filled with thick smoke and we were plunged into darkness. The next thing we heard was this unholy scream and this guy crying "Help me, help me, someone please help me." It was pretty chilling.' She said she later heard that the man had lost both his legs. Travis Banko, a 24-year-old Australian insurance worker, had just boarded the train and said the explosion had hit just ten seconds after it pulled out of the station: 'It wasn't very full but then there was a massive explosion.' He had been in the first carriage, in front of the one in which the explosion took place. 'It blew out the side of the train. It was dark. Everyone was screaming. When the smoke cleared the second carriage was ripped apart like it had been done with a can opener.' As Mr Banko recalled, people were 'screaming and crying' but, after an initial period of panic, people realised they were OK and started to help those who were injured (ibid.).

Somehow the decision each passenger had taken about what carriage to go into had meant all the difference between life and death. What might have seemed an inconsequential decision had turned out to be one of the most crucial in their lives. This is a scary realisation, but it was to take time to register. It shows how lives have become precarious in new ways. As Ulrick Beck recognised, global risks were being intentionally created in the wake of 9/11 so that we need to rethink the terms of a globalised risk society.[5]

Many of the survivors were too traumatised to speak. One of the most seriously injured, a woman who gave her name as 'Davinia', had her head and neck bound in bandages. It emerged that she had been near the front of the train when the blast hit. One survivor who spoke to her said: 'All she could remember was a fire-ball coming towards her. She said it felt as if she had hit a wall' (ibid.). People were being affected in ways that remained unspeakable. They had been shocked by what had happened to them, or what they had been forced to witness.

The explosion on the number 30 bus – which, for a while, had been reported on the television as a tourist bus, happened 30 minutes after the attack on the Piccadilly line train around the corner at Russell Square. The bus had been diverted and the driver had just pulled to the side of the road to get help in navigating through the unfamiliar streets of Bloomsbury when the bomb detonated. The bomb seemed to have been placed somewhere near the back of the bus's top deck. 'There was what seemed like a muffled bang and a huge plume of smoke,' said Neil Courtis, 34, a financial journalist.

> I went towards the blast and saw a woman with her left leg blown off. She looked in a bad way.
>
> I could smell cordite. The bus looked as if someone had peeled off the roof and there seemed to be bits of people around that had been blown through the windows.
>
> (Ibid.: 5)

But Mr Courtis said the scene was strangely calm, 'The pavements were filled with pedestrians but there was no panic and no screaming. People were calling for anyone who knew first aid' (ibid.).

George Psaradakis, 49, who was driving the bus, had worked for Stagecoach for three years. He said his first thoughts were for his passengers: 'Suddenly there was a bang, then carnage. Everything seemed to happen behind me. I tried to help the poor people, there were many injured and at first I thought, "how am I alive when everyone is dying around me?"' When he was interviewed for the *Independent*, he said: 'Myself and other drivers in London have an important job and we are going to continue to do that the best we can. We are going to continue our lives. We are not going to be intimidated' (*Independent*, 9 July 2005: 11). I heard that, after having tended to the injured, he walked all the way to Acton in a state of shock, unsure of where he was going.

Aftershock

Angela Pelzl really wanted to get on the number 72 bus, but time was marching on and she was going to be late for work, so she got on the number 30 when it arrived at her stop at Highbury and Islington. Exactly 24 hours earlier, she had done the same thing, boarded the same bus to take her to her office in Bloomsbury. Thankfully for her, she had got off when it became snarled in traffic around the King's Cross Thameslink station. As Jonathan Brown reports:

> Despite thinking about it all day yesterday, last night and again this morning, she still could not be sure if it was her bus that had been blown up a few minutes later on Tavistock Square. Its roof peeled away like a tin can, 13 of its passengers killed and many more horribly maimed.
>
> 'The one I saw on the news had a "Love Coca-Cola" sign on it. I've been trying to remember if mine did but I just don't know if it was my bus. It is such an odd feeling," said Angela, 33, graphic designer, as the bus made its way down Pentonville Road, noticeably less full than normal.... On Thursday, which No 30 you took became a deadly lottery. Life and death separated by a few seconds, dictated by the capricious London traffic.
>
> (*Independent*, 9 July 2005: 11)

Sitting downstairs at the back as the bus crawled along Balls Bond Road on that Friday was Claire Hicks, 38. The accountant makes the journey westward every day to Marble Arch. She had just missed the bus targeted by the terrorists, watching it drive off without her:

> I thank my lucky stars. But now we have to get back to normal. I will deal with the fear. I will look out for any strange packages, take notice of who gets on. But you can't judge people by their appearance. That is unfair to the one that are innocent and that is the vast majority of people.
>
> (Ibid.)

At least for the time being, her mode of perception has changed and she has become sensitive to what is happening around her, in ways she might not have felt she needed to before. Like others on the bus, she felt 'there but the grace of God'. Yesterday at this time, as the bus was itching around King's Cross Junction, people were dying in the tunnels below.

Mr Margolis, 29, a project manager at Digiterre Software Company in Hammersmith, had been in the first carriage, close to where the bomb was detonated in the King's Cross tube blast that claimed at least 21 lives. He was among the first survivors to walk the track and emerge at King's Cross station. He was determined not to let the attack destroy his life. He said:

> My first reaction was, 'I'm never getting on the tube again' and I was petrified. But then I wanted to make sure this thing does not get the better of me or disrupt my life. I took the day off and my wife and I

got a taxi to central London but decided we would get the tube home on the Victoria line from Euston.

I went quiet as I went down the escalator. I thought I'd be very afraid but it felt normal. I talked to my wife through the journey and felt fine but I don't know how I will be by myself. The next milestone is to get the tube on my own on Monday and not getting scared when it jolts.

(Independent, 9 July 2005: 11)

After the blast, Mr Margolis had head injuries. He was given water and phoned his wife Sarah and other relatives. She is a producer in an interactive agency in Central London. She said she barely recognised her husband. 'His face was black from soot, he had blood running down his face, neck, chest,' she said. 'His white shirt was covered in blood. I ran up to him and gave him a hug' (ibid.).

Hiten Shah, a lighting shop manager, who had just stepped off his train at Baker Street when it exploded into a mangled wreck of glass and metal, insisted, against the advice of his heavily pregnant wife Sweatel, on returning to work. He had commuted to Edgware Road for six years, but on Friday he abandoned the Circle line and walked to his office. The day before he had spent the rest of the day concentrated assiduously on his work: 'I didn't want to see what had happened. I was afraid of what I would see. That could have been me.' For Mr Shah, like so many caught in the terror that rocked London, there is a strong sense of survivor's guilt. 'I was selfish,' he said bluntly.

You try and go back and help somebody but I was not allowed to go back. I just tried to get out. Everyone tried to get out. I just can't stop thinking about it.

I can remember this man shouting 'please open the barriers there is something wrong underneath.' People were looking into the tunnel but you couldn't see anything. Everybody panicked and tried to get out. I was on a train that went through King's Cross just before the fire in 1987.

This is my third life.

(Ibid.: 10)

Being affected

On Friday morning, the day after the day we had all been expecting in London ever since 9/11, the streets were unusually still. I was making my way to Paddington to take a train to Bristol. I did not feel ready to take the tube and in any case they were not working around Paddington so I had taken a taxi. I felt tense as we made our way across the town, though I was trying to tell myself that I was feeling fine. My day had been disturbed and I had not been able to make it to work, so I felt that I 'should not' feel so affected by what had happened, even though on another level it touched all those fears as somehow embodied whenever the trains had been caught in the tunnel and I was left unsure of what was going on. I kept telling myself that 'I should not feel so affected because there was no reason to feel endangered'. I felt disturbed for most of Thursday and could feel the tension in my bones, unable to really identify or name my fears. I knew that 'it could have been me' in that, like so many other Londoners, I commute most days into work and pass through King's Cross. Of course the Northern Line had not been directly affected, but then it is hard not to feel that it so easily could have been. It was just they made different choices of what lines to take out of King's Cross, and so where to place their bombs.

As I was trying to copy the code that I had written on a piece of paper so that I could retrieve my tickets from the pre-paid machine I realised that I was not getting the code right. My behaviour was allowing me to recognise just how tense and unsure I was really feeling, whatever control I might have wanted to assert. Like the day before as I was in Golders Green, I had to recognise that I was not 'in control' and that, even if it had been important for me to make it into work, I was not going to be able to do so. This questioned the ways that an identification of masculinity with self-control is so easily activated in times of uncertainty. As men, we can so easily feel that we need to be strong for others so that it is important for us to be able to affirm control over our own experience. It is difficult not to feel that emotions are signs of weakness, even if we have learned otherwise.[6] We find ourselves trapped within a rationalism we can question intellectually only to find that it is our behaviours that let us know the tensions, fears and uncertainties we are living with. I had to accept that I was *affected* by the events in London in ways that I was not really prepared for. It was not simply a matter of routines being disturbed, but of the embodied fears and the intense sufferings that were perpetrated by the terrorist bombs in London.

It is easy to judge ourselves negatively when we feel that we should 'not feel fear' or that it is somehow 'irrational' because we were not directly affected and so should be feeling relief for ourselves and families, and sympathy for those who have not been 'so lucky' but somehow found themselves as innocent civilians in the middle of these unspeakable horrors. As Diana Evans wrote in the *Independent* special section on 'London Voices', 'For months, even years, Londoners have boarded the Tube with a sense of quiet recklessness; it could be today, it could be tomorrow. The rescue services have waited in the wings' (*Independent*, 9 July 2005: 29). Although the attacks of that Thursday are hardly comparable in scale to the destruction of the Blitz, the fact that the sixtieth anniversary of the end of the Second World War was being celebrated at the weekend may have encouraged talk about the stoicism and resilience of the British people at the same time that the transformations of London into a diverse and multi-cultural city was also being acknowledged as a source of strength.[7] But, for Diana Evans,

> It feels much like another world war. How could there not be sto-icism? And how could there not be kindness?
>
> On Thursday evening, I walked in the fading light. The streets were quiet, There was a sense of hurt and humility in the air. In the newsagent, as the woman at the counter gave me my change, she said quietly: 'Take care.'
>
> (Ibid.)

Writing in the same section, Paul Barker talks about the resilience of London as a wounded capital as proof 'that a great metropolis is a more resilient organism than the terrorists might imagine.... This resilience is, I suspect, an unknown quantity in the minds of those who seek deliberately to destroy it, physically or morally' (*Independent*, 9 July 2005: 29). He also recognises that

> Cities such as this have an enduring character: almost a sort of histor-ical memory, built into their streets and their inhabitants. New York was not destroyed by the 9/11 assault, though so many died. The row over what should replace the World Trade Center proves that New York and New Yorkers remain as tough, and as quarrelsome, as ever.
>
> (Ibid.)

He recalls:

> At the height of the Second World War blitz, and trying to pin down just what Englishness meant, George Orwell said in an essay: 'As I write, highly civilised human beings are flying over-head, trying to kill me.'[8] As I write this, I suppose other human beings, also in thrall of an apocalyptic creed, are trying to kill me and other Londoners and their families.
>
> (Ibid.)

But this time, the danger comes from under the ground. For a while, it seemed as if we would never be able to *see* what happened, as we did on the attack on the Twin Towers but, because technological advances, images arrived, even if we were spared the sounds that would otherwise have accompanied them.

Reflecting on his experience in London, Euan Ferguson wrote:

> You do, as they say, find yourself looking at your neighbour differ-ently. For many hours on Thursday and a strange number on Friday, I

did. Not looking at them with suspicion: not casting quiet second glances at unsettling combinations.... Looking at them, instead, with fresh, new and very un-London eyes, seeing them as people.

(*Observer*, 10 July 2005: 18)

He questions those who suggest that this sudden coming together is related to a new spirit engendered by the Olympic win, saying:

I think it goes back further than that. We did know it was coming. We may have forgotten, for a while, but inside we still knew the bad stuff, like a smoker's relationship with his lungs. No one in this city can forget New York's reaction to 9/11; and a quiet part of Londoners – by which I mean, simply, people living in London – had been preparing for theirs.

(Ibid.)

Uncertain future(s)

Mary Riddel recognised that, in the days after the horrors of that Thursday,

Sirens sound different now. The blare of a police car or ambulance is no longer the familiar, 24-hour background noise of inner London but a jolt back to the moment they bombed London. Then there is the quieter descant of grief.

(*Observer*, 10 July 2005: 28)

The disappeared have also acquired names and faces. She recognises that some of the people in London who were bystanders to the events could have

mustered up some of the Blitz spirit lauded in the past days, but their faces reflected mainly puzzlement. How do you react when the unthinkable becomes the overdue? This was a story of death foretold, predictable in all but the bitter scheduling.

(Ibid.)

As she says:

It was always going to happen this way. Everyone had heard the sirens, smelled the smoke and seen the tears roll down long before it all began. Somewhere in a landscape as familiar as the Monopoly board, the recurring nightmare would become reality.

(Ibid.)

But she also warns about the future, particularly in relation to freedom and human rights that so often get curtailed in the wake of atrocities: 'Already some commentators are calling for justice to be 'tilted' to protect the innocent from butchers who will stop at nothing' (ibid.). She recognises that

> Somewhere in the wake of 9/11, we became a more intolerant country, fearful of our children and mistrustful of our immigrants. One of the first result of last week's bombs was the 30,000 hate-filled emails sent to the Muslim Council of Britain.
>
> Do not let us go down the sterile route of clashing civilisations. Of the 1.6 million British Muslims, the vast majority abhor violence; besides, Islam has no stranglehold on brutishness. Europe pioneered political terror and its sideshoots of state torture and genocide. Then there is terror by omission.
>
> (Ibid.)

John Gray also insists:

> The threat of indiscriminate terror will be with us in any future we can realistically foresee. Terror has causes and it is right that they should be investigated. The war in Iraq has given al-Qaida a major boost, enabling it to link its extremist agenda with grievances that are widely felt in Islamic countries.
>
> (*Observer*, 10 July 2005: 29)

Gray argues: 'Western governments have helped to make al-Qaida what it is today, but it would be folly to imagine that any shift in their policies can neutralise the threat it now poses.' He acknowledges changes in the structure of al-Qaida whereby it is no longer the semi-centralised organisation it was before the destruction of the Taliban in Afghanistan, having transformed into a much looser network of autonomous groups sharing an apocalyptic version of Islamist ideology.[9]

Gray wants us to acknowledge that some of the most advanced Western societies have produced terrorist groups that insist that the existing world is on the brink of an imminent, total and violent transformation. The worldview of Timothy McVeigh, for instance, who was found responsible for the Oklahoma bombing of 1995 that killed more than 160 people, was part of a world of right-wing militias in the US that believed the country was on the brink of a huge conflict in which it would be partly destroyed, racially 'purified' and then reborn.

However, I would question Gray's idea that 'In terms of its apocalyptic mindset, al-Qaida is not unique, nor it is peculiarly Islamic. It is the most recent expression of a tradition of terrorism which has deep roots in Western religious beliefs and in modern revolutionary politics.' I think this can be an unhelpful insight if it means that we do not explore the particular Islamic sources from which these traditions emerge. But it allows Gray to make the point that

Terror is not now, if it ever was, something that comes to us from outside. It is part of the society in which we live. Both liberals and neoconservatives believe terrorism can be dealt with by removing its causes. The truth is less reassuring. Al-Qaeda has mutated into a decentralised, often locally based type of apocalyptic terrorism and in its new guise, seems to be acquiring a formidable momentum. We are going to need all our resources of wisdom, guile and determination to deal with it.

(Ibid.)

3   Urban dreams, fears and realities

Urban moods

How precarious lives can seem within the material culture of urban spaces is partly shown through the speed with which 'events' can impact on the feelings people can have for everyday life and the different kinds of narratives they prepare for themselves. Writing in the immediate wake of the bombings in London, Ian McEwan remembers that

> The mood of a city has never swung so sharply. On Wednesday there was no better place on earth. After the victory in Singapore, Londoners were celebrating the prospect of an explosion of new energy and creativity.... The echoes of rock 'n' roll in Hyde Park and its wave of warm and fundamentally decent emotions were only just fading.
> In Gleneagles, the summit was about to address at least – and at last – the core of the world's concerns, and we could take some satisfaction that our government had pushed the agenda.
>
> (*Guardian* 2 8 July 2005: 3)

These were events that so many people in London witnessed and somehow embodied through what was turning out to be a historic week for the capital city. He also recognised that

> London was flying high and we moved confidently about the city – the paranoia after 9/11 and Madrid was mostly forgotten and no one had second thoughts about taking the tube. The 'war on terror', that much examined trope, was an exhausting rallying cry, with all the appearance of a moth-eaten regimental banner in a village church.
>
> (Ibid.)[1]

But we were to awaken with a shock as we gradually took in what was going on in the city on Thursday morning. As McEwan realised, 'now the disaster was upon us, it had an air of weary inevitability, and it looked familiar, as though it had happened long ago.... How could we have for-gotten that this was always going to happen?' He recalls:

> The mood on the streets was of numb acceptance, or strange calm.... Groups gathered impassively in the road, among the gridlocked traffic, listening through open windows to car radios.
>
> On a pub TV the breaking news services were having trouble finding the images to match the awfulness of the event. But this was not, or not yet, a public spectacle like New York or Madrid. The nightmare was happening far below our feet. Everyone knew that if the force that mangled the bus in Tavistock Square was contained within the walls of a tunnel, the human cost would be high, and the rescue appallingly difficult.... no one seemed to want to talk about it.
>
> (Ibid.: 4)

On the streets, life was also going on as normal. Life simply refused to be disrupted, as Auden appreciated of the Blitz. McEwan continues: 'While rescue workers searched for survivors and the dead in the smoke-filled blackness below, at pavement level men were loading lorries, a woman sold umbrellas in her usual patch, the lunchtime sandwich makers were hard at work.' McEwan also seems sure that 'once we have counted up our dead, and the numbness turns to anger and grief, we will see that our lives here will be difficult. We have been savagely woken from a pleasant dream' (ibid.). So many people who travelled in London after 9/11 carried the feeling that the city would inevitably have its turn. But now that it has happened, there is a fear that it can always happen again. We might want to think that once the attack has been done, attention will move elsewhere and London will be safe again. But we know from Madrid that the bombers were planning other action and if they had not been caught and taken their lives, they might well have tried again. They might have felt that if they had been successful once and not been caught, they could try again and cause further disruption and loss of life.[2]

James Meek was a Londoner who, like so many others, woke up on Thursday 5 July still basking in the warm glow of the Olympic triumph when the news they had dreaded and half expected since 9/11 slowly dawned. He was walking down the Essex Road towards King's Cross and the western edge of the City

> everybody was talking; sometimes to each other, mostly to their loved ones on the mobiles. The networks were strained but just about coping. You kept hearing snatches of conversation as the news spread and people confronted the sudden reduction of London to a pedestrian city. '... bus is blown up ...' '... really nasty ...' ... Even those who weren't speaking in their mobiles were holding them in their hands, expecting them to ring, waiting for a signal, or just as talismans of the

idea of order, of the idea that this last electronic totem of technology and civilisation would lead them through a rude intrusion of chaos.

(*Guardian 2*, 8 July 2005: 4)

But it was only when he got 'to the shuttered gates of Angel tube station that the full sense of a capital in the grip of an emergency began to sink in' (ibid.).
    Meek recognises that

> For anyone who has lived in London for more than a few years, the tube map is more than a map on the wall. It burns itself into the brain, like the circuit diagram its design is based on. At news of any disruption, little stretches of it flash red, and almost without thinking, you try to chart a way round the obstruction. For the whole system to be sealed up without warning is to find the ground beneath your feet, paradoxically, to be not so solid as it was.'[3]

(Ibid.)

I confronted the closed gates with the line of London Transport police standing outside at Golders Green. They said there had been some kind of explosion in Central London and there was no way of getting through. It was a moment of powerlessness that showed the different possibly routes I had worked out in my head were not even worth attempting. They advised us to go home unless it was absolutely necessary.
    In the last century and in two world wars, the Underground was a place where Londoners sought refuge and protection from the bombs that were coming from the air. Henry Moore's images of people sleeping on the floors of Underground stations were some of the defining images of London during the Second World War. But, as Meek knows, 'In this century, in a war without clear aims, ends or sides, it has become – as, for four years, we have more than half expected – a place where bombs go off.' Many people taking the tube since 9/11 have carried with them an unspoken sense of fear and anxiety. Though as time went on we did our best to forget the fears we still silently carried, we all knew that there were risks involved in 'going underground'.
    Although we probably did not discriminate between the different Underground lines, after the London bombings people are suddenly aware that there might be different kinds of dangers travelling on the different lines. Two of the bombs – at Aldgate and Edgware Road – were in trains just below the surface, on so-called 'cut and cover' lines, so the force of the blast was dissipated into a relatively wide tunnel. It seems as if seven people died at Edgware Road and seven at Aldgate in these terrible calculations of death. But the bomb on the Piccadilly line near King's Cross exploded in one of the Underground's deep tunnels, some 100 ft below the surface. There the blast had nowhere to go and many more people are known to have died.

As George Psaradakis drove the number 30 bus past the Angel station and towards King's Cross, there were already signs that something was wrong. The city's traffic – never easy – was in a state of chaos. Thousands of commuters had left Underground train stations and were milling about the streets looking for alternative ways of getting to work. Few of them had any idea of the scale of the devastation and horror below, where three bombs had gone off in the space of a few minutes at different points in the network. The images of what was going on underground only became available as people escaped from the terrible scenes of horror. The focus was on the destruction of the bus because those horrors were immediately visible above ground. Images from beneath ground were eventually to come from cameras on passengers' cell phones, the latest innovation in the grim art of terrorism documentary.

Nicolas Thioulouse, 27, a French architect, was in the train under Edgware Road station when the bomb exploded on a train on the adjacent track. 'I had the feeling I was in a fish tank,' says Thioulouse, 'seeing people in the opposite car with their faces completely covered in blood.' He recalls, 'Our first reaction besides checking casualties and being in shock was looking at ourselves and trying to understand.... The sound of people crying and shouting for help was just horrible. I never felt so unpowerful in my life' (*Time*, 18 July 2005: 20–21). This might be one reason why he used his cell phone to record the panic at Edgware Road station as it unfolded. The images give some kind of impression of the horror, but there is also a sense that we should *not* really be able to see these moments as people are covering their mouths and struggling for breath. We might feel a need to imagine ourselves into the situation, knowing that it could 'so easily have been us'. But we also know that it would have been terrible to 'be there' and that we would still be living with the shock, unsure of how we might have responded to the trauma, or we might never have survived if we had been unlucky enough to choose the 'wrong' carriage.

James Meek reminds us:

> There was another transport network. Even before Madrid, there was a claustrophobic unease about the tube, and even more Londoners were acquiring another mental transport map, the complex map of the city's bus routes. There was a certain pride in knowing how to go from route to route to get where you wanted without ever going underground.
>
> (*Guardian 2*, 8 July 2005: 4)

You could feel safe looking down from the upper deck of a red double-decker bus, looking down on the traffic and bustle in the streets below. But this conviction has also been shown to be naive, for as Meek realises, 'In retrospect, a London bus was an obvious target, a symbol of the city.'

Even if it was not intentionally chosen and the bomb went off in transit to another tube destination, buses will never feel safe again in the same way.

Meek confesses, 'Yet deep down, I suppose, I never really believed a bus would be a target either honourable enough, or justifiable enough for a terrorist. It is still a poor person's means of transport' (ibid.). He also knew that London buses,

> particularly the buses between Hackney and the centre, are also filled with immigrants, and it is very possible that if a bomb exploded in any one of them, it would kill and maim at least one person from every continent or of every major faith.
>
> (Ibid.)[4]

Urban anxieties

As Oliver Burkeman recognised:

> Across London the sense was the same: a barely comprehensible lurch from limitless jubilation to a very provisional emotion, mixing horror and bafflement in equal measure. Starved of information about what was happening, Londoners and out-of-towners alike spent much of the day in near-silence, pacing the streets and pounding the call buttons on their mobile phones in the hope of making a connection – just to stay busy.
>
> (*Guardian*, 8 July 2005: 2)

Few signs remained of the celebrations the night before, as most of the bunting from Trafalgar Square had been removed as well as the boards saying 'Thank You London' from the foot of Nelson's Column. Burkeman recalled, 'Only the occasional "Back the Bid" banner flapped from a lamp-post in the worsening rain while copies of the first edition of yesterday's celebratory *Evening Standard*, already long out of date, lay abandoned in gutters' (ibid.).

The broadcasts kept explaining that London was in chaos but, as Burkeman remembered,

> even yards from the blast sites, it was a quiet kind of chaos.
>   Only snippets of conversation revealed an undertone of panic:
>   'I'm never travelling in the tube again.'
>   'Are there people still trapped underground?'
>   'I've got my family in Greece giving me more information than I'm getting here.'
>   … With swaths of the capital cordoned off, the surrounding streets were eerily quiet where they should have been noisy and packed … there was little to do but wait, and to speculate about the future.

'These guys, they don't care who they kill – Muslim, Christians, black, white,' said an overground train manager from Manchester, who declined to give his name, but said that he came from a Muslim background. 'I was born and bred here, but when people in this country start feeling threatened, you don't know what's going to happen. Maybe they lash out. Maybe they start to look for people they can blame.'

(Ibid.)

Ed Vulliamy took the Central line towards Liverpool Street from Bethnal Green almost exactly 24 hours after the first of Thursday's bombs and 'the passengers' mood did not match the surge of testosterone and fear running through the tabloid papers they were reading' (*Guardian*, 9 July 2005: 9). Rather, it was a muted, phlegmatic – if eerie – affair as he described it: 'Across the network, there was an entwinement between apparent normality and some exhausted emotional hangover – the morning after' (ibid.). Reflecting upon why people did not seem to be scared to be on the tube, Ronald Brotherton, a retired dentist alighting at Mornington Crescent, said: 'Well it's hard to put your finger on it. Maybe because London is used to this sort of thing with the IRA. We've had bombs before, and didn't stop doing what we do.'

'Perhaps,' said Jennifer McLean, a social worker, 'because we didn't actually see very much of what happened yesterday, just a few pictures. And, when you think about it, it could have been so much worse. I think we've absorbed it and want to get on.'

'Fact is,' said Dave Welland, a graphics student, 'that London puts up with so much shit, we can handle this' (ibid.).

Technologies

The few images people did see from the horrors that happened beneath the ground were often grainy and immediate, captured by people caught up in the bombings on their mobile phones. We also saw images of the Tavistock Square bus seconds after the blast. By the end of the day, as Kirsty Scott reported, about 1,000 mobile photographs and 20 amateur videos had been sent to the BBC. Countless others appeared on websites across the world. As Vicky Taylor, editor of interactivity for the BBC website, acknowledges:

> what it does do is put you in places that you can't possibly be as a broadcaster.
>
> You are really getting such impact from this. It is such a personal event.
>
> They are not just sending an image. They are telling you what has happened to them at the time.

(*Guardian*, 9 July 2005: 11)

Some of the images that arrived at Sky News were so graphic they had to be pixelated before they could be aired. 'Most of the time TV news or print journalists turn up, sometimes very quickly, but after an event has happened,' said John Ryley, executive editor of Sky News.

> The difference that mobile technology makes, it empowers ... ordinary people to show what happened as it happens, not a minute later or an hour later. So you are seeing the drama, the story unfolding.
> The technology takes you one step further. It will change the nature of the way events and stories are perceived.
>
> (Ibid.)

At the same time, he wondered how those caught up in the blasts thought to reach for their phones. 'I think I would have wanted to get the hell out of there,' he said. But of course many were just stuck where they were, just waiting for others to rescue them. Cynthia McVey, a psychologist interviewed by Kirsty Scott also said that the act of recording what was happening may have been reassuring:

> Some people can show remarkable presence of mind in life-threatening situations and doing that can afford them some control.
> The things about these situations is that you have no control.
> I wonder, too, if it hasn't become second nature to people. If anything happens it's almost an automatic response; you get your phone out and record it.
>
> (*Guardian*, 9 July 2005: 11)

For many of the 7.5 million people who live in the capital, it was only later in the afternoon, as they were deluged with text messages and emails from around the world, that they realised the scale of the terrorist attack. We had phone calls from family around the world who were worried because of the images they had seen and the news they had heard. There was a need for people who knew each other to make contact across space and so 'touch base' with each other. As the mobile networks came back to full strength later in the afternoon, texts and voice-mail messages from earlier in the day started to filter through. Technology might have made the world a smaller place on Thursday, but it also made it more desperate. The unsent text message or the unanswered phone call suddenly took on potentially alarming connotations. Through new forms of teletechnologies people were able to reassure each other and share images of what they had seen. New technologies profoundly shaped the social and psychic context in which 7/7 and its aftermath were played out.[5]

If people could not get into contact, they often imagined the worst and could feel quite desperate for news from friends and 'loved ones', as we are learning to call them. With mobile networks overloaded and, in some parts of Central London, shut down altogether as resources were diverted to emergency services, it was often impossible for people to reach others they wanted to hear from.

As Owen Gibson reported:

> Around Russell Square and King's Cross, a crowd of people could be seen with their phones clamped to their ears, frantically dialling and redialling. Others asked passengers for change, reluctantly joining the anachronistic queues for phone boxes and struggling to remember landline numbers long since jettisoned for their mobile equivalents.
>
> (*Guardian*, 9 July 2005: 11)

Vodaphone said it had experienced a 250 per cent increase in attempted calls in Central London. Double the average number of text messages were sent in the few hours after the attacks. Unable to get through on mobile phones, many people took to sending round-robin emails with optimistic subject headings: 'Everyone OK?', 'All OK?', 'Have your heard from … ?' Email-routing firms also reported a doubling of traffic in the 24 hours that followed the blasts. People turned to email when they could not get through.[6]

Fears

As happened after September 11 and the Madrid and Bali bombings, Web communities were rapidly established. Lists of those missing and those reassuring others that they were safe were aimed not only at families and friends, but an extended network of virtual communities that was being built up on the Internet. With news so slow to filter through to official outlets, the Internet became the main source of information for many people stuck in offices across the country. As Owen Gibson reported: 'The BBC, Sky and Guardian Unlimited received hundreds of witness accounts within hours of the explosions, with more informal reflections, practical information and pleas for families and friends to get in touch spread across scores of other Websites' (*Guardian*, 9 July 2005: 11).

However, some people were to remain unable to contact their families and friends. Curling in the wind outside King's Cross Underground station on Saturday 9 July were posters pleading for information on the whereabouts of the missing that told stories of loss and devastation:

> Missing since the terrorist attacks in London on the 7th July 2005: **Rachelle Lieng Siong Chung For Yuen.** Her family and friends fear that she might have been caught up in the King's Cross tube station explosion on the Piccadilly line. We have been looking for her endlessly since the incident but to no avail.
>
> (*Observer*, 10 July 2005: 13)

If the scene was reminiscent of the Wall of Tears that appeared in Manhattan after 9/11 and in Thailand after the tsunami of Boxing Day 2004, for most Londoners these were tragedies that took place in far-away places understood via television. Now death had come to London, and others looked on with sympathy and understanding from around the world.

For Pilar Manjon, news of the attacks in London were a cruel reminder of what had happened in Madrid 15 months earlier. 'This is London's 11/M,' she said, using the shorthand that Spaniards apply to their own day of death and terror – 11 March 2004 – when 191 commuters were killed on early morning trains as they travelled into the city centre. Her 20-year-old son, Daniel, had stepped on to one of those trains three minutes before the bomb went off. He hadn't turned up at university, where he was reading engineering. 'We know how it feels to be desperately looking for someone who has disappeared,' she said. Watching scenes of the injured and the response of the London emergency services meant reliving her own tragedy: 'It is not easy for any terrorism victims, but for the 11th March victims it is specially bad. We feel the pain as if it were our own' (ibid.: 15).

It started innocuously enough in London, with reports coming through that there was some kind of small-scale explosion on the Underground, probably due to a power surge. As Sir Ian Blair, Metropolitan Police Commissioner, admitted, 'Like everyone else my first thoughts were, "Well maybe this is a bomb, but maybe it isn't"', but as news of the second blast reached his office, 'With the second one, it began to feel pretty clear what was really happening' (ibid.: 14). As, above-ground, the capital was still basking in the glory of having won the bid to host the 2012 Olympic Games, underground a horrific narrative was beginning to unfold. An explosion had ripped through the floor of the third carriage of a tube train as it was coming into Liverpool Street station. George O'Connell, 16, was on his first day of work experience in the City of London and he was travelling on the Circle line from Aldgate station:

> I remember the moment the blast happened, I saw white light, I thought I was dead. I heard a massive bang, I was covered in blood, The doors flew from the force of the blast. People were screaming get us out.
>
> (*Observer*, 10 July 2005: 13)

'We felt the train shudder,' said another passenger, Terry O'Shea. 'Then smoke started coming into the compartment. It was terrible. People were panicking, but they calmed down after one or two minutes.' Later, she recalls, 'As they led us down the track past the carriage where the explosion was, we could see the roof was torn off, and there were bodies on the track' (ibid.).

Meanwhile, just over a mile away, another subterranean nightmare was unfolding as a second device exploded in the first carriage of a tube train travelling on the Piccadilly line between Russell Square and King's Cross. Allice O'Keeffe, 25, a freelance journalist, was caught up in the blast:

> When the train slammed to a halt and the carriage flooded with thick black smoke, I thought, "that's it, this is how I am going to die". The train's on fire and we're all going to asphyxiate slowly. I heard screams from the carriage in front. Beside me, a woman was moaning, "Jesus, Jesus", which seemed appropriate, although I'm not a believer. I wanted to pray too but couldn't quite let myself.
>
> I'm claustrophobic, and if anyone had asked me to describe hell, this would have been it. I felt myself shutting down. I curled up against the glass partition and wrapped my coat around my face, trying to keep my breathing under control.
>
> The first five minutes were the worst. After that, it became clear that the smoke wasn't getting any thicker and some air was still circulating. Somewhere, a woman was still screaming hysterically, much to the annoyance of everyone around me. There was a feeling that if anyone lost their nerve, the situation would become impossible. I didn't let myself imagine the screamer was in a carriage full of corpses, as I now realise she probably was.
>
> It was 30 interminable minutes until we were evacuated. As we straggled towards the bright lights of King's Cross I saw the injured for the first time: one young man staggering and soaked in blood, whose staring eyes are still imprinted on my brain; a middle-aged women with her eye a sticky mess. I realised that I had been one of the lucky ones. I was crazed with shock when I got out of the station. I got through to my mum on the phone. She told me that there has been several incidents across London, but neither of us knew that my train had been bombed. I decided to try and get to her office in Old Street. I was still so confused that I walked in the wrong direction and found myself lost in the scrum of commuters. Nobody seemed to notice that my face and hair were black with soot. After wandering in circles for awhile, I found a black cab.
>
> My mum didn't recognise me, as I was blackened and my eyes were still goggling with shock when I arrived in her office. I then watched events unfold on television. Now it seems like a bad dream.
>
> (Ibid.: 14)

Another young woman, who declined to be named, and who was on the same Piccadilly line train, told the *Observer*:

> I remember the moment the explosion happened, the train was packed as usual, the explosion ripped through the carriage, the blast ripped through the guy in front of me. I would not be here if he was not

there; it still has not sunk in what happened. I wonder if he had children, his guts were spilled out. It was worse than anything imaginable.

(Ibid.: 14)

The third incident at Edgware Road station in West London was also initially blamed on a probable power surge. Below ground, commuters knew otherwise. The blast in the first carriage of a tube on the Circle line train leaving for Paddington had blown through a wall and hit two other trains on an adjoining platform. Carol Miller, 35, from Oxford, who was on a Circle line train travelling in the opposite direction from those hit said:

I saw one lady who was ripped to pieces, lying between the two trains. People were trying to help her. It was the most horrendous thing I've ever seen in my life. People were screaming out, there was debris everywhere. We were trying to open doors to let in air but we couldn't. There were two tubes crossing in different directions. As it [the other train] got to our carriage it exploded. It was a massive explosion and immediately everything filled up with smoke.

(Ibid.: 15)

Survivors were trapped for up to 30 minutes before being led to safety through the tunnel. They had been evacuated from the back of the train and along the rails. Tony Dodd, 39, who works for Metronet, a company responsible for part of the tube line, was one of those who went to help: 'It was pretty awful down there. There were bodies and people were very badly burned' (*Guardian*, 8 July 2005: 5). Then, into the daylight stumbled the walking wounded and West London's café society was transformed into a giant makeshift emergency hospital as double-decker buses were used to ferry the injured to nearby St Mary's hospital. At first they had been taken to a Marks and Spencer store but, by 10 am, as more casualties arrived and the scale of the attacks became clearer, they were evacuated to the Hilton Metropole Hotel on the opposite side of Edgware Road. Shopping trolleys filled with medical supplies were in the lobby.

Several people were still bleeding from the cuts and burns to their heads. Paul Dadge, 28, a project manager, helped one of the most seriously injured, a woman who gave her name as 'Davinia'. She was seated in the lobby with the bandages and face mask he had helped her with. Like many others, she was too traumatised to speak. The image of Paul helping her across the street was captured on the front pages of many newspapers. It became iconic of the tragedy, reflecting both the help that was being offered as well as the fear of the burns and the trauma that remained unseen beneath the mask.[7]

Traumas

Paul Ward, a senior nurse in charge of accident and emergency at University College Hospital, also dealt with the injured. In an interview, he said:

> I saw them as they came in, and assessed them with my colleagues. Some had smoke inhalation and burns, and a lot of them were covered with soot which makes it difficult because you can't immediately see how injured they are.
>
> Personally, I can deal with every kind of trauma, but there's always an emotional after-effect. When someone comes up to you with no injury, but they are trembling head to toe with fear, and you touch them, then you can feel the horror of what they've been through. That really brings it home to you.
>
> I'm Australian, and I'm so impressed by the way people here have coped. The response was fantastic with strangers coming in to offer their help. I've been left most of all with this huge sense of solidarity.
>
> (*Observer*, 10 July 2005: 16)

With so much of the horror contained underground, the scenes at Tavistock Square where the bus had exploded became the focus of the world's television cameras. The bus looked grotesque. Blood was splattered up the walls of the BMA building. Along one side of the bus, an advert for a forthcoming film could still be made out: 'Outright terror, bold and brilliant', it said. The rest of the ad had been blown away. The carnage contrasted brutally with the tranquillity of the nearby square with its dedications to peace – a statue of Mahatma Gandhi and a cherry tree marking the bombings of Hiroshima and Nagasaki.

Among all the memorable images of horror shown on television in the evening following the bus blast, one stands out for depicting the urgency and the terror of the passers-by in Tavistock Square. It is of a young couple holding hands, running away from the explosion. You can see the terror in their eyes as well as the sadness at what they had witnessed. Jo Bor had been standing 20 yards from the bus as it slowed down. He was on his mobile to the film production company he works for, saying he would be late. His girlfriend Vicki Dokas was standing next to him.

'Nothing was really moving, and there was a lot of traffic, a lot of people like us who had started walking from Euston or King's Cross to try and get to work,' Bor recalled.

> As I put the mobile phone down, I heard a massive bang and felt this enormous power hit me in the face. All I could see was white smoke and then the top of a bus, which was opened up like a tin can. I didn't know what to do. I froze, but my girlfriend shouted out, 'Run'.
>
> (*Observer*, 10 July 2005: 16)

Bor obeyed, and then he looked back in order to grab her hand. He saw something he will never forget:

> As the smoke died down, there were bodies everywhere. Everyone I could see in front of me looked dead. Suddenly, after all the noise of people trying to get to work, it was very, very silent. There was blood spattered everywhere, but strangely people seemed quite calm.
>
> (Ibid.)

He found himself caught in a moral dilemma created through these new technologies about whether to record the moment, but decided against it. As he explained:

> I wanted to take a photo, to document it, but then I didn't want to, because it seemed wrong. Then people started crying, my girlfriend was hugging a woman who was very distraught. Many people started to shelter in doorways, I don't really know why. We tried to, but the doorways were full up, so we just walked away.
>
> (Ibid.)

Had they been just a little closer, they too might have been casualties. Like so many people who heard about what had happened, their story is one of 'near misses', a haunting sense that 'there but for the grace of God, or just luck, I too could have been caught in an explosion on the way to work'. As Robert McCrum wrote: 'Fate, like love, is all around us. Everyday life in an age of terror is composed of thousands of life-and-death decisions. It takes a terror attack to remind us how contingent life can be.' For the Greeks 'the best you could do was to make the most of the present (carpe diem) and accept your fate with dignity and stoicism. "A man should be ready for the journey to the world below," said Socrates, "ready to go when the Fates call him."' (*Observer*, 10 July 2005: 31).

One fortunate survivor who happened to shun his regular carriage (the one with the bomb) on the Piccadilly line told the BBC: 'I just feel incredibly lucky.' As McCrum recognised: 'Luck, not fate, is what we now believe in. But luck still carries connotations of supernatural reward' (*Observer*, 10 July 2005: 31).

4   Missing, loss, fear and terror

Narratives

In order to make sense of events that unsettle and threaten the ways people understand their everyday lives, so giving them some kind of handle on what is unfolding around them, the mass media often focus on the fate of particular individuals that quickly assume the status of local, national and sometimes even global icons. It is through the fate of these individuals that people are encouraged to make sense of those larger forces that have suddenly and shockingly broken into their everyday lives and routines. Sometimes people are encouraged to *identify* with these individuals, so feeling some resonance with their pain and a sense of relief that they could so easily have been caught up in that event.[1]

At other times there is a focus upon the diversity of different peoples who share the urban space of London and who have somehow been caught up within a shared tragedy. Through their individual narratives and expressions of loss and lamentation, the city can suddenly recognise itself through its complex everyday multicultural realities.[2] Through a process of shared grief, an urban space can come to redefine itself as a complex multi-culture as the diversity of its population is made visible, possibly for the first time. This is what happened in London, where there were immediate comparisons made with New York and Madrid where similar atrocities had taken place. There was a sense of connection between different cities that found themselves on the same roll call of terrorism.

Through these individual narratives, connections are made between the individual and the larger society, and through the fate of individuals, others find a way of relating to events they might have only witnessed on television or on the Internet. This seems to be a way of giving a sense of control over events that otherwise seem, at least for awhile, outside of control, so creating a source of fear and uncertainty. There seems to be a sense of urgency to *share* the narratives of individual lives, for it is through their stories and a sense of how they came to be at a particular place at a certain time that people identify with 'events' that otherwise seem beyond their comprehension. Through these personal stories, 'events' become more comprehensible, as often it feels impossible to grasp why people might have perpetrated such harm and terror against fellow human beings. Through being able to focus and channel grief and anger at what has befallen other people in the city, a sense of solidarity can be produced as people come together through acts of mourning. This extends Weber's notion of '*verstehen*' by which we might come to place ourselves in the position of others through some form of sympathetic identification. Often it is through hearing the stories of others and coming to know 'how they came to be where they were' that we can identify with their fate.[3]

With the bombings in London, this allowed for identification across cultural, ethnic and racial differences. Paradoxically, it allowed the city to recognise itself, possibly for the first time in London's history, in more complex terms as it gave people a *living* sense of its urban multiculture. But it also recalled earlier moments of crisis in the life of the city; for example, the Blitz in London was quickly invoked through historical memories and narratives in the media, partly to make sense of public responses in the present while at the same time making visible how London's population had transformed in its composition. Through contrasts with earlier moments of crisis, it became possible for some to clarify what was different in the present and so secure a firmer grip on the event they were living through.

Missing

The *Independent* on Saturday 9 July, two days after the bombings in London, carried an image of Shahara Akther Islam and the following words that covered its front page: 'Shahara Akther Islam was a lively 20-year old, a devout Muslim with all her life before her.' In slightly smaller print it went on:

> On Thursday, she had to attend a dental appointment before going to her job at the Co-operative Bank. So she said goodbye to her younger brother at their home in Plaistow, east London, and headed off on the Underground. It was a day like so many others.
>
> She never arrived. And now this young woman, who so confidently straddled the twin cultures of her mosque and her city, is missing, She is feared dead, a victim of the horrific violence wreaked on London this week, almost certainly by the terrorists of al-Qa'ida, murdering and maiming in the name of her faith.
>
> (*Independent*, 9 July 2005: 1)

Her family feared that she was caught up in the explosion that wrecked the Circle line train at Aldgate. Like other families, they had spent much of the day desperately trawling hospitals for news of her, and when the article was published on Saturday they did not know for sure. As Maxine

Frith and Elizabeth Davies reported for the *Independent*, 'It seems an unspeakable cruel fate for them and for a young woman who could have been a poster girl for young British Muslims today' (ibid.: 2). Shahara has been born in Whitechapel to a family who came to Britain in the 1960s from Bangladesh and we are told 'has been going to the mosque every Friday with her close-knit family, but she also loves designer handbags, designer clothes and going out with friends' (ibid.).[4]

She went to Barking Abbey School near her home and took A-levels before leaving school to work at the bank. For the *Independent* at least, as they chose to figure her in this prominent way, 'Shahara embodies as much as anyone multicultural Britain and the way in which younger generations of Muslims are embracing both their own and Western cultures.' But as we know, this is only part of the story and represents only one of the ways of embracing cultural differences. This was sharply presented as I wrote this on Wednesday 13 July 2005, a day after the police reported that four British-Muslims were suicide bombers.

Her uncle, Nazmul Hasan, helping in the search for her, said:

> She's one of those people who just makes friends wherever she goes. She's a lovely girl, really feminine. But she didn't want to go to university – she just wanted to start working so she could spend money. She loves her Burberry and Gucci handbags. She doesn't wear a hijab, she wears Western clothes, but she is very close to her family, her mother especially.
>
> She doesn't have a boyfriend. She is a lovely well-behaved girl – she has her own opinions and she can hold her own in any company, but she's not a ladette, and we all absolutely adore her.
>
> (Ibid.)

In part this reflects the views of an older generation and we do not know what kind of account she might have given of herself. We can hear the balance that is being struck in his words and also the impressions that he wants to avoid giving. He is walking a thin line in an emotionally desperate situation.

Mr Hassan went on:

> She doesn't think that much about politics – she likes hanging out with her friends, talking and laughing a lot. We just want to bring her home – whether that means she's one of the fatalities or not, we just want something to bring home.
>
> The whole family is just completely devastated. If we had a body, if we knew she was dead, at least we would be able to start mourning, If she was injured really bad, at least we could be there for her in hospital.
>
> What tortures us is the fact that the police say that there are still

bodies in the tunnel. I keep thinking, what if she is lying there, still alive, still just breathing, but needing help, and nobody is coming for her? This is the worst situation to be in.

(*Independent*, 9 July 2005: 2)

Shahara's father, Shamsul, 44, a bus supervisor with London Transport, made an appeal for information at East London Mosque, a few hundred yards from the scene of the Aldgate attack. 'We have no other words to say other than we hope she will return home, I just hope that everyone is praying for her well-being and that she will return home in good health,' he said.

'My prayers go to every other family and I hope that they too pray for my daughter.'

Asked what he thought of those who committed the attack, he said: 'These people are not human beings, they are not doing anything for Islam. They may call themselves Muslims but there is no such thing as a Muslim killing people.'[5]

The family had gathered with thousands of others at the East London mosque to pray for those caught in the attack. Her mother, Rumena, 40, is a housewife who looks after her 17-year-old brother and 13-year-old sister.

Shahara's uncle said: 'Her father is trying to hold it together but her mother is just completely devastated by this' (ibid.).

As Terry Kirby reported in the *Independent*:

They hoped for the best but feared the worst. For many relatives and friends of those still missing since the London bombs exploded on Thursday morning, yesterday turned into a desperate and anguished journey from hospital to hospital, seeking news of their loved ones.

(Ibid.)

Seven people died at Edgware Road and seven at Aldgate, and another 13 on the bus that exploded in Tavistock Square. At least 21 bodies were recovered from the Piccadilly line train outside Russell Square, but this figure was always expected to rise as the single tunnel was so much deeper, more difficult to access and the blast greater because it had nowhere to go. The family of Rachelle Chung For Yuen, 27, an accountant from Mauritius, living in Mill Hill in North London, believed she may have been among those who died on the Piccadilly line. They had visited all the hospitals that had taken casualties and were beginning to lose hope. 'I am really frustrated,' said Jeffray Yeun, her brother-in-law, 'I don't know what else I can do' (ibid.).

Also criss-crossing London at the time was Yvonne Nash, partner of Jamie Gordon, 37, an office worker from Enfield last heard of on Thursday morning boarding a bus in the Euston area. On Friday morning, Yvonne, who works for Orange, the mobile-phone operator, managed to trace his phone and found it at the site of the bus explosion in Tavistock Square. She said: 'I just have to find him, I have to know what happened. You cannot sleep, cannot eat when you are that worried about somebody. We don't know where he is and we are just desperate to find out' (ibid.). She and his colleagues were putting up posters around Tavistock Square. I listened to the ITN news on Wednesday 13 July as his death was officially confirmed.

The pictures of most of the people who had died were placed on the front page of newspapers so that they became familiar in the intense emotions of the days following the bombings on Thursday 7 July 2005. They became familiar and their names became so well known that when, each day, a couple of people were officially confirmed dead by the police, we could often recognise who they were and feel we knew some of their personal stories. Suddenly the multicultural nature of London was made visible through loss – though if you regularly used the Underground to get to work, this was not really a surprise. From that Thursday, home-made posters were being stuck to lampposts around King's Cross and Tavistock Square, appealing for news about family and friends, showing faces almost too carefree to bear. On the Friday, David Webb stood outside King's Cross Underground station clutching a framed photograph of his 29-year-old sister Laura Webb who took the tube to work and had not been seen since. I saw him being interviewed with his brother on *Channel 4 News* on Tuesday 12 July 2005, where they were both insisting that they owed it to Laura to continue believing that she was still alive. Until they were given firm evidence, they would insist that she was alive.

There were so many faces and so much loss, but given that there were not the numbers that we saw in New York, Bali or Madrid, there was a feeling of familiarity, as if the losses were being experienced personally. They were a loss to London but since we were beginning to feel easier in identifying ourselves as 'Londoners', they felt like more personal losses too. But this also meant that certain losses somehow reflected the story of a multicultural London where diverse communities would discover their strength and where the bombers would fail to divide a tolerant city. As Tony Parsons frames it in the *Daily Mirror* (11 July):

> The victims, the survivors, the missing – they represent every creed and colour on the planet.... But one face haunts the pages of our newspapers.... It is the face of Shahara Akther Islam – a true Briton, a young East Ender and a devout Muslim. Shahara is missing ....
>
> To those who talk about 'effing Muslims', I say: How can you hate this girl? How can you hate her family? Their pain is beyond our imagination, and their suffering is our own. Shahara was 20 years old, and her faith meant nothing to the bombers. They were indiscriminate in their murder.... Do not hate Muslims because of bloody Thursday. Save your hatred for those who have surely earned it.

The sense of outrage at the attacks and a determination that London's multicultural tolerance would be sustained was also expressed by London Mayor Ken Livingstone, who heard about the bombings in Singapore where he had been celebrating London's successful Olympic bid:

> This was not a terrorist attack against the mighty and the powerful. It was not aimed at presidents or prime ministers. It was aimed at ordinary, working-class Londoners, black and white, Muslim and Christian, Hindu and Jew, young and old.
>
> It was an indiscriminate attempt to slaughter, irrespective of any considerations for age, for class, for religion, or whatever. That isn't an ideology, it isn't even a perverted faith – it is just an indiscriminate attempt at mass murder and we know what the objective is. They seek to divide Londoners. They seek to turn Londoners against each other.[6]

> (Ibid.)

Mourning(s)

I am writing this exactly a week after the bombing, on Thursday morning. Somehow writing seems to be a way of coming to terms with the shock that I felt and carried through the day, a sense that I could so easily have been involved in some way given that my route to Goldsmiths on the Northern line passes through King's Cross and that I was travelling late on that day. Writing has always been my way of trying to 'make sense' of what is going on, as if it is through the writing that I hope to find a language that feels more *adequate* to the situation. It is partly because I feel let down by prevailing ways of thinking within social and political theory, which is exposed by the emptiness of prevailing discourses in the face of these events, that I hope, through writing, more adequate terms of thinking and feeling will somehow become available.

I suppose that writing is also a form of mourning for me, since there was so little communication about the losses our own family had suffered through the Holocaust. As a child I found it bewildering to know that so many members of my own family had been murdered by the Nazis, but only to be told that this shows 'what Hitler did to the Jews'. As children growing up in post-war London we were to be protected from these traumatic histories in the hope they would not unconsciously impact upon us. As I explored in *Shadows of the Shoah: Jewish Identity and Belonging*, our parents wanted to believe that these traumatic histories and memories could belong to them alone and they could create firm boundaries around them.[7] They wanted us to grow up to 'become English', whatever this meant at the time, in the 1950s, and they sensed that if we were connected to these traumatic histories this would mark us out as different and so make it impossible to belong. As second-generation children of refugees, we were to be encouraged to forget the traumatic histories that had displaced our families and brought them to London as refugees from Hitler's occupation of continental Europe, so that we could create our 'English' identities in the present.

Growing up in London in the 1950s, there were far fewer immigrants, and those that were here were made to feel that it was through assimilating into the dominant culture that they could make themselves belong – by becoming 'like everyone else'. This was at the beginning of large-scale migration from the Caribbean and the Indian sub-continent.[8] Possibly this helps to make clear my own motivation in writing about these events, and explains why I felt drawn to write as a way of attempting to grasp events that prevailing social and political theories seemed unable to illuminate. I felt we needed to reach for new ways of thinking and feeling that could hopefully help to illuminate the very different social realities that were being made visible by events of such a traumatic nature.

As the days passed, more people were officially declared dead. On Tuesday 12 July 2005, they announced two more victims – Jamie Gordon and Phillip Stuart Russell. Friends and family of Mr Gordon, 30, who came from Enfield, North London and worked for City Asset Management in Old Street, had been searching for him since the blast. His family and his partner, Yvonne Nash, released a statement saying:

> Jamie was a kind, caring person who always put other people first. His great sense of humour and personable nature put him centre stage with family and friends.
>
> He loved life – but didn't take it too seriously. He was very much in love with Yvonne and finally settling down with plans for a wedding and family. Jamie comes from a large and close family, and spent his formative years in Zimbabwe where he developed his love for horse riding and tennis.
>
> Jamie enjoyed family ski holidays, and was an accomplished guitar player and singer. Jamie touched many people's lives and the response to this tragedy is overwhelming ...'
>
> (*Sun*, 13 July 2005)

Jamie had phoned his office before boarding the bus – which he only caught because he had stayed the night at a pal's house. Yvonne told Virginia Wheeler of the *Sun*: 'It wasn't his normal route to work. It is shocking to think he went through something that traumatic and we couldn't be with him' (ibid.). She had spent days outside King's Cross station clutching a photograph of them together in the hope someone had seen him alive. It was not to be.

The family of Elizabeth Daplyn, 26, who was last seen catching a Piccadilly line train to King's Cross, but had been missing since the blast, told Wheeler that they had 'given up hope' of finding her alive. Her uncle, the

Reverend Tim Daplyn, of Harptree, Somerset, said Elizabeth's parents, Mike and Pam, were waiting for her death announcement. He said:

> We're waiting to hear what we already know in our hearts to be fact.
>
> The tense of the language we are using to describe her has changed to 'was' rather than 'is'. Miracles do happen but we are not expecting one.
>
> (*Sun*, 13 July 2005: 7)

Mr Russell's parents, Graham and Veronica, were being comforted by friends and family at their home in East Peckham, Kent, as they waited for the official confirmation of their son's death. 'I am just trying to mourn and grieve his loss,' his father said. 'He's a wonderful kid who was in the wrong place at the wrong time' (*Guardian*, 12 July 2005: 4).

On Saturday 9 July, the mother of Anthony Fatayi Williams flew in from Nigeria, like many other relatives, to join the search for her son, Anthony, from Hendon, North London, an executive with the Amoco oil company. Delays on the Northern line prevented him from getting to his work and it was thought that he may have been on the bus that exploded in Tavistock Square. His close friend Amrit Walia attempted to call his mobile at 8.39 am but he had missed the call. 'He has not contacted a single one of his friends since yesterday morning and his mobile is constantly on voicemail,' Mr Walia said. 'He is usually very conscientious and would have called if only to check everyone else was OK.' With friends, he had driven round London and checked the ten hospitals. He said: 'We understand the police have a job to do, but it is agonising to sit and wait, which is all they have advised us to do' (*Independent*, 9 July 2005: 5).

On Saturday the family had still not heard. His cousin, Yomi Williams, 23, from London said:

> We still haven't heard anything. We sent his pictures to the newspapers, posted them on the internet, we did a lot of TV interviews, we've put posters everywhere, checked all the hospitals about four or five times and we still didn't get anything. He called his workplace and said he was being evacuated and he was going to get a bus. We think he was on the No 30. I feel terrible. I haven't eaten or slept for two days, I'm just hoping and praying that he's OK. He's a very nice, loving guy, very straightforward and loved by many. He has a lot of friends and always tries to help people. He's a good person with a good heart.
>
> (*Independent on Sunday*, 10 July 2005: 3)

On Monday following the bombing, Marie Fatayi Williams, surrounded by family and friends, stood near Tavistock Square, where her son Anthony was feared to have been killed. She delivered a lament for her lost son that touched so many and somehow was able to express the grief, anger and bewilderment that so many were still feeling in the wake of the bombings. Somehow she was able in her words to express and give form to complex emotions and questions that had been around for so many. The language echoes verses from the Bible as well as the Koran. It was a direct expression of the pain of a mother who was lamenting the loss of her son. It was an expression of grief and loss as well as a direct questioning of the terrorists who could carry out such acts.

Like so many in multicultural London, Anthony had travelled from Africa, as others have travelled from so many different lands to make new lives in London, while carrying the hopes and dreams of his family. Standing near to the double-decker bus, itself a wrecked icon of the city she said:

> This is Anthony, Anthony Fatayi-Williams, 26 years old, he's missing and we fear that he was in the bus explosion ... on Thursday. We don't know. We do know from the witnesses that he left the Northern Line in Euston. We know he made a call to his office at Amec at 9.41 from the NW1 area to say he could not make [it] by the tube but he would find alternative means to work.
>
> Since then he has not made any contact with any single person. Now New York, now Madrid, now London. There has been widespread slaughter of innocent people. There have been streams of tears, innocent tears. There have been rivers of blood, innocent blood. Death in the morning, people going to find their livelihood, death in the noontime on the highways and the streets.
>
> (*Guardian 2*, 13 July 2005: 3)

Then Marie's speech turns to talk directly to the bombers or those who might identify with their actions. She calls for reflection. She insists that terrorism is not the way:

> They are not warriors. Which cause has been served? Certainly not the cause of God, not the cause of Allah because God Almighty only gives life and is full of mercy. Anyone who has been misled, or is being misled to believe that by killing innocent people she is serving God should think again because it's not true. Terrorism is not the way, terrorism is not the way, it doesn't beget peace. We can't deliver peace by terrorism, never can we deliver peace by killing people.
>
> (Ibid.)

She then offers a history lesson that opens up different paths to peace and justice, whatever the hurt and identification with suffering people might be carrying:

Throughout history, those people who have changed the world have done so without violence, they have [won] people to their cause through peaceful protest. Nelson Mandela, Martin Luther King, Mahatma Gandhi, their discipline, their self-sacrifice, their conviction made people turn towards them, to follow them. What inspiration can senseless slaughter provide? Death and destruction of young people in their prime as well as old and helpless can never be the foundation for building society.

(Ibid.)

Then, more personally, she shares her grief for her son:

My son, Anthony is my first son, my only son, the head of my family. In African society, we hold on to sons. He has dreams and hopes and I, his mother, must fight to protect them. This is now the fifth day, five days on, and we are waiting to know what happened to him and I, his mother, I need to know what happened to Anthony. His young sisters need to know what happened, his uncles and aunties need to know what happened to Anthony, his father needs to know what happened to Anthony. Millions of my friends back home in Nigeria need to know what happened to Anthony. His friends surrounding me here, who put this together, need to know what happened to Anthony. I need to know, I want to protect him. I'm his mother, I will fight till I die to protect him. To protect his values and to protect his memory.

(Ibid.)

Connecting to the grief of others, she laments and cries out for understanding and explanation. She needs to know, and also Anthony needs to know, why this has befallen him:

Innocent blood will always cry to God Almighty for reparation. How much blood must be spilled? How many tears shall we cry? How many mothers' hearts must be maimed? My heart is maimed. I pray I will see my son, Anthony. Why? I need to know, Anthony needs to know, so do many others. unaccounted for. innocent victims, they need to know.

(Ibid.)

Then a pause for reflection within the present of a multicultural London:

We cannot live in fear but need to find another way. Hatred only begets hatred.

It is time to stop and think. We cannot live in fear because we are surrounded by hatred. Look around us today, Anthony is Nigerian, born in London, worked in London, he is a world citizen. Here today we have Christians, Muslims, Jews, Sikhs, Hindus, all of us united in love for Anthony. Hatred begets only hatred. It is time to stop this vicious cycle of killing, We must all stand together, for our common humanity. I need to know what happened to my Anthony. He's the love of my life, my first son, my first son, 26 ... he was making me happy. I am proud of him but I need to know where he is ... I grieve, I am sad, I am distraught, I am destroyed ...

(Ibid.)

Memories

Ken Livingstone thanked the emergency services and the transport staff in the name of the city, for their 'acts of selfless dedication', and Londoners for their stoicism and courage: 'There are places where such things could have unleashed internal strife and violence. In London the city stood together' (The *Independent*, 9 July 2005: 30). But there were also incidents of reprisals against Muslim communities in different parts of the country, even before it was announced the bombs had been left by British Muslims who had been born and educated in Britain. At Friday prayers, the day after, Muslims were urged to stay calm and vigilant amid fears of reprisals. Johann Hari had walked to the East London Mosque to watch afternoon prayers on the Thursday. He heard Chairman Mohammed Bari saying from the podium:

Only yesterday, we celebrated getting the Olympics for our city and our country. But a terrible thing happened in our country this morning.... Whoever has done this is a friend of no one and certainly not a friend of Muslims. The whole world will be watching us now. We must give a message of peace.

(Ibid.)

Many people made a point at smiling at him, an obvious non-Muslim in their midst. Yassin Dijali, 31, said to him, 'It could have been our children on those trains too. This is where we belong. These people are insane' (ibid.).

Hari recognised that

London's response to the attacks is subtly different to that of other cities. Like New York, we have our pictures of the missing-presumed-dead, but there is none of the visceral nationalism and I have yet to see a single Union Jack. Unlike Madrid, I could find no backlash against our political leaders (or at least, not yet); people seemed to react as if this was not a political act but a natural disaster, with no deeper causes than the tsunami.

(Ibid.)

On Friday morning, sitting outside a café on Whitechapel High Street, Hari talked to one of the lingering Jewish residents of the old East End, an 86-year-old called Henry Abelman. He was drinking tea as he does every morning. He said he was here the last time fascists attacked London and, he said with a laugh, he expects to be here the next time they toss some bombs at us too.

> Not so long ago, we had bombs like this every day for six years coming from an army backed by twenty million people. That didn't destroy or divide us, so what do you think a few spoilt brats with home made bombs are going to do?
>
> (Ibid.)

Paul Baily, writing in the *Independent*, makes similar connections. He recalls that he was born in 1937 in a terraced house that was razed by a German bomb three years later.

> The Jerries, as we in south London called the Germans, were our enemies. They were led by a man who wanted to rule the world. We knew nothing of the concentration camps and Hitler's determination to extinguish the Jewish race.
>
> (*Independent*, 9 July 2005: 31)

He points out that

> Those who support Islamic fundamentalism are as anti-Semitic as the Nazis but with a terrifying difference. They have Allah on their side. There are virgins on hold in Paradise to give male suicide bombers the time of their afterlife. And I am not surprised they have turned their diabolic attention on London, a bastion of the materialism these spiritual fanatics wish to expunge from the earth.
>
> (Ibid.)

Baily goes on to say:

> I believe, along with millions of my countrymen, that the Bush-inspired war on terror is bound to inspire more terrorism. If you declare war, you get the same back in spades. We should never have invaded Iraq. I saw, through a child's eyes, the wonderful city of my birth reduced to rubble. I can remember the first death of my childhood. It was the same night my parents' house was bombed. In one of the neighbouring houses hit by the blast, a small boy died when the pillow on which his head was resting burst. He was suffocated by the feathers from it. I thought of him yesterday, an innocent among innocents, as other innocents were killed and injured. In that far-off Bat-

tersea, everybody was born and raised in Britain. Our landlord was Jewish, and tenants called him 'Shylock', although they had neither read nor seen *The Merchant of Venice*. The first Jamaicans, known as 'darkies', arrived in the 1950s.... This was a closed society, in which all foreigners – from near or far – were suspicious.[9]

I moved to Shepherds Bush in 1972, and in the three decades since, the borough has welcomed Serbs, Croatians, Turks, Armenians, and thousands of Muslims from the Arab states, Pakistan and Eastern Europe. They, and their friends and relatives, were among the victims two days ago. And those outraged people now defacing mosques and spitting at Muslims in the street and hurling abuse at them should remember terrorists are indiscriminate, 'The more dead, the merrier' could be their appalling motto.

(Ibid.)

Different generations will call upon different histories and memories that need to be listened to. They will find that different fears and connections are brought to the surface of their minds. Rowan Pelling, talking from a different generational perspective, wrote:

It was bound to happen – talk of doughty Londoners showing the Blitz spirit in the face of terrorist outrage. The reference springs all too readily to mind with this weekend's 60th anniversary commemorations of the end of the Second World War.

(*Independent on Sunday*, 10 July 2005: 29)

But she thinks that it is an

inadequate analogy, all the same. Do this week's detonations, however horrifying, come close to the sustained blanket bombings of the East End? In the Forties the British knew who the enemy was, and why the blood sacrifice was a price worth paying. We knew Hitler's aims, could appraise his logic and abhor it.

(Ibid.)[10]

She recognises that 'Today, many Londoners believe that Britain's participation in the Iraq war was unwise, if not unjust, and would provoke dire consequences.' At the same time, Pelling says,

But only the most blinkered would deny that such outrages may have occurred anyway. In 2005 it's hard to be united against a common foe when you don't know who he is, where he lurks or his strength. It's difficult to unite in patriotic fervour when London is now, blessedly, one of the most diverse cities on the planet.

(Ibid.)

As she goes on to say:

> It may help many people to cloak the necessity of living and working in London as an act of 'defiance' – and good luck to them – but in my experience the majority of those people are men, for who a sense of impotence is the most corrosive emotion. It is as absurd to talk about bravery in relation to public transport as it is to talk about it in cancer patients: in both cases you have little viable choice.
>
> (Ibid.)

As Rowan Pelling understand it:

> What various people have invoked as 'London pride' I believe to be a different sort of resilience based in pragmatism – which I have observed in other cities used to bloodshed. But it's just as admirable in its calm acceptance of life's adversities. Londoners know that their city can survive a variety of assaults and yet prosper, so there's no point in hysteria: some will die, many, many more will live.
>
> (Ibid.)

We should also appreciate people dropping their reserve and communicating with each other in a time of need: 'It's only now I learn how many commuters have, like me, stepped off a tube or bus after observing a suspicious passenger. But we were too afraid of appearing foolish to share our concerns' (ibid.). Whether this will change we can only wait and see, but I heard – though it might be one of many urban myths circulating – that some people on the number 30 bus got off because they thought there was a bomb aboard but others refused to believe it.

5 Risks, traumas and insecurities

Landscapes of fear

How did the landscapes of fear, risk and insecurity shift so quickly in the light of the London bombings of 7/7? Since the attack on the Twin Towers on 9/11, London knew that it was going to be a target. It was not a matter of whether they would be hit, but 'when?' and 'how?' This meant that people living in the capital city were used to living with an undertone of anxiety and expectations. They were convinced that an 'event' would happen that would be shocking and would be likely to kill many innocent people. This was their understanding of terrorism. They knew that something 'terrible' was going to happen, but they were unsure of how they could really protect themselves. Living and working in London meant that you were living with an *endless threat*, but you were unsure of where it was coming from and where it might hit. This is what created a landscape of urban fear that was difficult to identify or to really appreciate what difference it was making to your everyday life. Instead, people had become accustomed to living with this sense of threat and so used to moving around the landscape of the city that they began to believe that possibly it would not happen at all. It was the experience of living in these different registers that made life different in ways that were hard to identify.[1]

The fear of terrorism had somehow become a feature of everyday life. People learned to live with their own anxieties, learned how to ignore what they feared and live life 'as if it were normal'. At some level this meant that people were constantly *on guard* without really appreciating how they held tension in their bodies and how it had made them wary and suspicious of others. Some people learned to withdraw into themselves as they used their technologies to create what felt like a familiar sound space in which they could move across the landscape of the city. As the Walkman gave way to iPod, so people moved through space listening to familiar sounds that could help them feel easier emotionally with themselves. But these technologies also cut people off from those strangers they were travelling with, and shut them off in a sound world of their own. It was part of an individualisation as security that was taking shape. People were learning how to fend off their fears and treat them as interferences they had to learn to control.[2]

After New York and Madrid, it seemed as if London would be the next target. It was also pretty likely that the London underground would be a target, so that when the attacks happened people felt that 'this was it – this is what we have all been expecting and waiting for'. It was bad, but there was a sense of relief for those who were not directly affected and a sense that it 'could have been so much worse'. But there was also a sense of diverse transnational communities coming together in the face of terrorism and the creation of a sense of belonging that transgressed traditional ethnic and racial boundaries. As people witnessed the diversity of backgrounds of those who had been directly caught up in the bombings, they were confronted with representations of a capital city that had changed radically in the last 20 years, transforming itself into a global multicultural city in which so many communities lived next to each other, if not always relating well with each other.[3]

But the identification of the bombers as Muslims, especially when it became clear that these were young Muslims brought up in Britain, also placed strains on community relations. Assumptions in relation to marginality, citizenship and belonging were shifting rapidly as people found themselves trying to make sense of these terrifying events within a new landscape of fear and uncertainty. People outside Muslim communities were often made suddenly aware of how little they knew about Islam and how different communities seemed to live in relative isolation from each other. They also had to confront the strength of religious feeling in a young generation that had been expected to make familiar moves from religious to secular, as the second-generation immigrants were experienced with state schooling in Britain. But where an earlier generation has defined itself in relation to countries of origin, their children, often born in this country, were looking towards their Muslim identity to establish a sense of identity and belonging.

But, at the same time, they shared generational memories and anxieties.[4]

Ruins

Ian Sinclair, a week on from the terrorist bombings in London, remembered that

> The ruins we remember from another era – shells of churches, despoiled libraries – survive in romantic monochrome: the comforting lie. Stoic architecture, chippy humans, the Queen Mother like a Pearly Queen visiting the East End. Tumbled masonry, wrecked teeth. War photographers pick their way through the rubble of the new morning making art, framing statuary against a lowering sky.
>
> Now the horror comes in the muted register of the universal

mobile-phone greeting. I'M FINE RU OK is the text we receive before we know anything is wrong. Fast-twitching technology anticipates disaster. The latest gizmos mediate between the ugly truth of the streets, dirt, danger, noise – and the computer generated cyberspace of the world as it ought to be – blue water, green trees, Barratt homes. Contemporary ruins are never quite finished: shamed vanity project hospitals, state-of-the-art pools that don't actually open.... Then suddenly, from nowhere, news reports blow such feeble strategies apart, presenting us, in unforgiving full colour close-up, with real damage, actual bodily harm.

(*Guardian 2* 14 July 2005: 6)[5]

Sinclair reminds us:

We shouldn't be familiar unless we work in hospitals, in casualty departments: cooked flesh pitted with dirt, second-degree burns, hands in plastic bags. This, as we eat or slump in our homes after the daily battle with an overstretched transport system, is news from elsewhere. But that elsewhere is strangely familiar. We've grown used to out-of-synch video-phone quiver from deserts, shanty towns, wrecked tourist hotels. Such sights do not belong in Aldgate East, Tavistock Square. They hurt.

The victims speak with our own voices. They make sense of trauma, placing it in a framework of everyday concerns. Interviewed, the walking-wounded fix on certain details, the insensitivity of being led back from the smoke-filled, wrecked carriage past the bodies of the dead. This, they acknowledge, is the Theatre of the City. It is democratic, anyone can join in. The writer Derek Raymond used to call it the 'general contract' – morality. Shit happens. You don't have to fill in an application.

(Ibid.)

If Sinclair is right that we have to 'recognise that anxiety is now a permanent and irreversible condition. It will happen again and again' (ibid.), there are different anxieties and they fall differently on different communities in London. Soon after the bombings, and days before it was confirmed that this had been the work of 'home-grown' British Muslims, there was already a backlash and Muslim leaders were warning of mounting Islamophobia after attacks on mosques. Abdul Munim sat amid the charred walls and smoky stench of his mosque, the Shajala mosque in Birkenhead, in the Wirral, that had been attacked by two white men who poured petrol through the letterbox and ignited it, days after the attacks in London. The assistant Iman, Boshir Ullahm, was trapped in his upstairs bedroom, as fire raged on the landing outside. Fire crews pulled him to safety from an upstairs window and extinguished the blaze. Abdul Munim reflected on levels of religious and racial intolerance that were even worse than when he made Britain his home, 40 years ago:

> We've had some hard times and thought they were all in the past. ... But now, because of what is happening in the world, it is far less safe. We say to anyone who doubts us, 'The London bombings were wrong.'
>
> (*Independent*, 12 July 2005: 1)

The grills on the windows outside the mosque show it has been a target of violence before. They had been installed after 9/11 when firebombs were pushed through the letterbox.

Muslim leaders throughout Britain called for calm after a series of attacks on mosques in the wake of the London bombings. The Mazahirul Uloom mosque in Mile End Road, East London, had nearly every window of the mosque broken. The attackers, who struck early on Saturday 9 July 2005, used crowbars and a hammer to shatter 19 windows. Faruk Ahmed, the mosque's general secretary, said:

> We did not expect this to happen in our mosque, at the heart of a peace-loving Muslim community. This is a place of worship and all humans should respect that, whether it is a church, a synagogue, a temple or a mosque.
>
> (Ibid.: 2)

In Nottingham, a 48-year-old man from Pakistan died on Sunday 10 July 2005 after what police are treating as a racially aggravated attack. Six people were arrested in connection with the attack. Police were investigating several other attacks. By Tuesday 10 July 2005, arson and criminal damage had been reported in Tower Hamlets and Merton, both in London, Telford, Leeds, Bristol and Bradford. There was growing unease within the Asian community more generally.[6]

Kashied Dunbar, 40, a gym sales and marketing manager, was reported in the *Independent* on Tuesday 12 July 2005, before the police announcement about the investigations in Leeds the following day, as saying:

> London in the aftermath of the bombing reminds me of Cape Town during apartheid. All those years of racial hatred are coming back to me. I have been living in London with my wife for three years but I remember how it felt to be persecuted for the colour of my skin.
>
> (Ibid.)

People carry their own emotional histories, and these will often be activated in times of unease. As Furkan Sharif, 24, a trainee lawyer from Hackney, said:

being from a Muslim background you've now got eyes looking at you as you walk down the platform. I feel as British as anyone but in some people's minds that doesn't matter. It's natural to be more suspicious at a time like this but it isn't an excuse for prejudice.

(Ibid.)

Shalim Miah, 28, who works as a train announcer, from Manor Park, says:

I am a fundamentalist Muslim and by that I mean that I believe in the original lessons of Islam – those which teach peace and harmony among men. I condemn these senseless acts of violence. The terrorists are not Muslims – they are misguided, misled and brainwashed. The media should stop using the term Islamic terrorists – the two are totally separate things. Londoners won't change, they've seen it all before.

(Ibid.)

A sense that people are being 'watched' in different ways as part of the anxiety created in the wake of the bombings is also expressed by Pramod Penceliah, 21, a security guard:

I am from South Africa and of Indian origin but I can tell people are looking at the colour of my skin and thinking 'he's a Muslim'. I was in a bar and a white guy was staring at me. I could tell he was stereotyping me. I don't blame people for doing this but I wish they could see I am as against the killings of innocent people as they are and now I feel just as scared as they do on buses and trains.

(Ibid.)

Sangit Patel, 23, a student from Finchley, feels similarly:

I have been apprehensive about taking the bus or tube. I'm concerned that I will be viewed suspiciously if it turns out that Muslims were behind the attacks. But you have to trust others to be fair. I will carry on as normal.

(Ibid.)

These fears also affect the ways different ethnic minorities begin to see each other, at least for a while, and possibly more long term. As Waheed Araf, 27, from Hackney sees it:

These attacks are giving all Muslims a bad name. Now, I am looking at other Asians who look like me and think maybe it could be them. Some people will see all Muslims in the same light. I haven't done anything wrong but all Muslims have been dragged into this.

(Ibid.)

These are sentiments that other ethnic minorities can also appreciate. Jewish people have long feared that they will be held in some way responsible for the crimes and misdeeds of their co-religionists as if responsibility has somehow to be shared. In the wake of 9/11 and 7/7, different Asian communities in Britain can be fearful that they will be identified as 'Muslims' and that their own religions and cultures will also be feared.

Reflections

In the *Guardian* on Saturday 9 July, following the bombings in London there were edited responses from the *Guardian*'s Muslim youth forum that meets annually for discussion and debate. This allows us to hear the voices of young people who are so often spoken for or generalised about in sociological discourses. It allows us to hear how they are making sense of the disturbing events through their own narratives and how these narratives can also change over time. For some, it might have been tempting to deny that it was really Muslims who were involved but, as the evidence mounts, they might have to think differently. This shows the impact of events but also the ways they potentially disturb 'common-sense' understandings people might feel attached to.[7] They might be called upon to give a response as if they carry some kind of responsibility because they happen to be Muslims themselves. This shows the *complexity* of migrant identifications and the differential pressures placed on people through particular events. It also helps to question a Weberian tradition that fosters a belief that people are somehow free to 'make sense' of their experience through assigning whatever meanings feel appropriate.[8]

Intissar Khreegi in the first contribution is reported as saying:

> I may be blamed for something of which I could easily have been a victim. At first I dismissed this – surely people would realise that not all Muslims were to blame for this? But my heart sank as I read that in the few hours after the attack, the Muslim Council of Britain had received thousands of abusive emails. The two that I read chilled me. I've been lucky never to have been seriously abused because of my religion but the emails made me realise what Muslims might face in the days to come.
>
> The irony of it – the fact that I, a Londoner who was just as appalled and shocked by these attacks and who had an equal chance of being a victim, might be blamed for the action of criminals who have nothing to do with me – depressed me and leaves me feeling frustrated and helpless.... I don't know what more we can do to make people realise we are just as appalled and disgusted by these acts ... they threaten to destroy everything we've done to establish

normal lives for ourselves and build a common understanding with others.

(*Guardian*, 9 July 2005: 23)

This was a commonly expressed sentiment. Muslim leaders and politicians stressed that these acts had 'nothing to do with Islam'. It was something completely separate rather than a 'perversion' of Islam, which remained a peace-loving tradition that could not be interpreted to justify forms of jihad. A complete distance was to be established, at least in the early days, as expressed by Dr Sacranie, secretary general of the Muslim Council of Britain. In his letter to British imams, he wrote: 'Let us be absolutely clear: those who planned and carried out these heartless attacks – whoever they are and whatever faith they may claim to profess – are surely the enemies of all of us, Muslims and non-Muslims' (*Independent*, 12 July 2005: 2). But this position became harder to sustain with the police revelations that the London terrorists were young, British-born Muslims who had been raised in the suburbs of Leeds. Rather than draw a line around Islam as if it were a homogeneous religion, questions were raised about different kinds of traditions, different traditions of interpretation that might have encouraged and sustained militant Islamist beliefs.

Ajmal Masoor draws a clear distinction:

> 'Islamist terrorists' is what many are calling them; I am afraid there is no Islam in terrorism; therefore a terrorist cannot be an Islamist. To be a Muslim one has to accept Islam and Islam does not call for terror.... Prophet Mohammad said, 'He is not a Muslim from whose hand and tongue his neighbour is not safe,' and 'The one who is not merciful to the people of this earth, the one who is in the heavens [God] will not be merciful to him.'

(Ibid.)

Though he might agree with this sentiment, Ehsan Masood insists that theological questions still have to be opened up as well. He says:

> There's an uncomfortable question that we in the British Muslim community need to face up too – a theological one. Every time a group linked to al-Qaida commits an act of terrorism, it justifies this by whipping out a verse from the Qur'an. This is a dishonest use of religion; and at the same time it is a gift to groups like the BNP. Why? Because they, like al-Qaida, also like to draw out isolated verses of the Qur'an to 'prove' that British Muslims can never be trusted to live as true citizens of western countries.
>
> So far community organisations such as the Muslim Council of Britain have been reluctant to promote a debate on Islamic theology

because of a fear that it could harm the fragile consensus on which the MCB is based. This debate needs to happen ... '

(Ibid.)

But there are other voices that insist it is not an issue of theology alone, since so many young people feel a sense of identification at the suffering that they see perpetrated on their Muslim brothers and sisters in other countries, particularly in Palestine, Afghanistan, Chechnya and Iraq. Since Islam is a universal religion, people learn to identify with sufferings that cross national boundaries, especially if they feel that their own government is somehow responsible for the killing of innocent people in Iraq. They come to experience it as if they themselves are responsible for this suffering and therefore have an obligation to do something about it.

This is something an older generation brought up within the national histories of Pakistan or India might not appreciate since they carry different aspirations of belonging. There might also be a sense that the suffering that was produced through the partition and the million people who lost their lives at that time have never really been mourned, so the grief has been held within families and unconsciously passed on to the second generation who might feel uneasy about some of the sources of their own grief and anger. Unlike the Holocaust, there have been far fewer communal narratives to help communities come to terms with these tragic losses. Rather, as the generation that immigrated have been so concerned with earning a living, there is often a break between generations.

In the *Guardian*'s Muslim youth forum there are voices that help to illuminate the lines of identification that young Muslims feel with the sufferings of their Muslim brothers and sisters. This is a sentiment that many people in the West find hard to understand since Western rationalism has been predominantly framed with the terms of the European nation state. Since there can be no 'reason' that might justify terrorist violence, it is a matter of looking for 'causes' and recognising that young people who perpetrate violence are 'beyond reason'.

This was a position that Conservative spokesperson Oliver Letwin took on the *Any Questions* programme on Radio 4 on Saturday 16 July 2005. It was a position that was familiar after 9/11 where any attempt at understanding was somehow accepted as necessarily a form of justification. It is a matter, then, of tightening security measures to deal with 'senseless' violence and making sure that these people are apprehended in time. This is to assume in advance that the political sufferings of others, and the injustices they might feel perpetrated in their government's name, can never really help to understand how young people might feel so desperate that they act in these terrible ways. We are left with a sense that little can really be done to understand their motivations. Since these terrorist acts are 'senseless', they cannot be understood rationally.

On *Any Questions*, the MP George Galloway insisted that there was
what he called a 'swamp of deep resentment and anger' that had been
fuelled by government policies towards the Arab world over a long period
of time. He questioned those who said that since 9/11 took place before
the wars in Afghanistan and Iraq, the political actions of governments
could not be held responsible in any way. He pointed out that there had
long been resentment at Western policies after the first Iraq war. A refusal
to acknowledge political factors was to turn attention towards the Muslim
community and the 'evil ideology' that Blair was to talk about as needing
to be uprooted, presumably from the fringes of the community. This was
to turn responsibility back onto the communities themselves as they were
now being expected to co-operate with the police and inform on people
who might be preaching 'extremist' versions of Islam, ideas that we were
assured had 'nothing to do' with Islam itself. But the situation is more
complex and we need to listen to more young voices to appreciate the different identifications across national boundaries that Islam in the younger
generation can foster.

Shabbir Ahsan insists:

> I pray for all those innocent families who have been caught up in these
> events so unexpectedly. In the same way we must also remember those
> innocent families who have also suffered under the bombs of the US
> and the UK in places like Afghanistan and Iraq, who – like the Lon-
> doners on Thursday – were just going about their daily business. It is a
> sad time for all concerned.
>
> (*Guardian*, 9 July 2005: 23)

This is a sentiment that seems to be shared by Salman Yaqoob, who says,
again before we knew who was responsible for the London bombings:

> If we bomb other people's countries, it is only a matter of time before
> they bomb ours in return. The people who carried out these acts are
> obviously responsible, but it is impossible to understand these actions
> without the context of George Bush and Tony Blair's war on terror
> and its impact on the people of Afghanistan and Iraq. Tens of thou-
> sands of innocent people have lost their lives in both countries since
> we invaded, yet not only is their pain not recognised, their deaths are
> not even recorded. Such are the double standards of our foreign
> policy.
>
> To simply attribute 'envy' or hatred for our 'freedoms and way of
> life' here in the west to the terrorists ... is a deliberate device to side-
> step any real discussion on the vital questions: why? Why now? Why
> us? The consequences are a terrible self-fulfilling prophecy of people
> who have had violence inflicted on them inflicting violence in return.
>
> (Ibid.)

Of course it might be a small minority, but many young Muslims seem to identify with their brothers and sisters in these spaces that make it difficult for them to identify with the British government as their own. The fact that the Blair government seemed to ignore the wishes not only of the Muslim communities but of so many who marched against the war in London, can assume a particular meaning for young Muslims. It works to undermine their sense of British identity and citizenship since it becomes intolerable to feel that if they identify with 'being British' they are thereby responsible themselves for causing so much pain and suffering to other Muslims. This means it is not a matter of explaining why so many other communities who were against the war do not resort to violence, but of grasping that Islam as a universal identification can separate the second generation from their parents.[9]

The older generation might care equally but they separate religion from politics, in ways that no longer feel tolerable to the young who have shifted from an ethnic identity towards a religious one. They might not feel that Pakistan or India is 'home' in the way it remains for their parents. Rather, they feel uprooted from place, as if unable to identify with any space as their own. This gives a religious identity a particular significance since it has to carry so much *emotional weight*. There was also the self-rejection involved in rejecting their histories and education in Britain.

Shock

Though there had been suicide bombers who had been brought up in Britain, the shock was that the bombings would be turned against citizens on the tube and on the buses in London. There was sometimes a readiness to support bombings in Palestine that was deemed to be a very different context since the Palestinians were suffering from an occupation they could not shift through expressing their views in a democratic state. I watched a *Newsnight* programme on BBC 2 where Muslim community leaders and scholars fiercely condemned the bombings in London while at the same time insisting that Palestine afforded a radically different 'context' where, they seemed to believe, suicide bombings against civilians in Israel could somehow be justified. They did not seem ready to condemn the employment of suicide bombings in any context or worry about the morality of these justifications on a younger generation.

When the police announced that they had evidence that the London bombings were carried out by three, or possibly four, young Muslim men who had grown up in Leeds, it was, as Madeline Bunting recognised, 'an agonising moment to be a British Muslim. This has been their worst nightmare come true: British born young men from families well established in this country carrying out a suicide attack.' They did not live in ghettos but in ethnically mixed suburbs. As she says, 'until July 7, they seemed to illustrate, with thousands of other young Muslims, Britain's pragmatic multi-

culturalism' (*Guardian*, 14 July 2005: 24). This makes the 7/7 atrocities a
different narrative from those of Madrid or New York because 'our enemy
is in our midst'. This will inevitably put the British model of multiculturalism under scrutiny – 'It's hallmark, a kind of British indifference, often
indistinguishable from tolerance that leaves people to get on with things in
their own way ...'

Bunting recognises that Muslims are being charged with an almost
impossible task; as one Muslim said to her, 'If even the mother of one of
the suicide bombers did not know what her son was doing, how can the
rest of the community be expected to know?' As another Muslim told her,
somewhat bitterly, 'It's no longer enough that we condemn terrorists,
we've now got to flush them out.' But this also connects to a wider soul
searching within the community, which one imam expressed as 'Why has
the Muslim community failed in reining in their own youth and shaping
their future? Why have the mosques failed to provide rigorous leadership?
We must acknowledge our failure.' As one anguished Muslim put it to
her:

> What is it about Islam that makes people suicidal? Plenty of people are
> really angry about Iraq, but they don't give up their life at 19. There's
> a missing link here – what makes a boy commit suicide? It can only be
> if he thinks that what lies in store for him is better than life – and
> that's got to be Islamic theology.
>
> It will have to change, In particular, the references to violence in the
> Qur'an have to be contextualised; in a global village, this has to be
> reinterpreted and that has to be done by our Islamic scholars. New
> thinking is desperately needed.
>
> (*Guardian*, 14 July 2005: 24)

But alongside the heartfelt self-criticism, Madeline Bunting also heard
that British foreign policy was being cited as being just as important. She
heard that it was corroding trust in the British political system and poison-
ing the youth: 'You cannot ask us to contain the anger within our
community caused by this country's foreign policy.' The honesty and new
thinking required of us, say Muslims, must be mirrored by a government
that can no longer pretend that Iraq and Palestine are irrelevant. She
sensed an anxiety among Muslims that government would feel that, to
avoid terrorism, they must know more about the Muslim communities
and that this 'integration' agenda would involve, as one commentator
expressed it, that the government should 'tear into those Muslim ghettos.
Force them to open up. Make the imams answer.... they must become
more ordinary.' This could involve the state being involved in monitoring
every aspect of Muslim life. But, Bunting warns, 'We – Muslim and non-
Muslim – have be much cleverer than that. There is no point alienating
another generation of Muslim men with an intrusive, aggressive state; that

will only push more of those poised on the margins into secretive extremism' (ibid.).

Bunting knows that much of the talk about radical imams is misplaced since most UK mosques are cautious and have lost touch with the young, who often look to the Internet for inspiration, not the local imams, as is clear from the interviews in Leeds. We have to rely upon the Muslim communities' own capacity for reform and renewal which was why, according to Bunting, it was so inexcusable that the *Sun*'s front page on Tuesday 12 July 2005 demonised the Muslim thinker Tariq Ramadan, a man who commands respect across the Muslim world and one of the thinkers who can potentially reach young Muslims and help them to create a way forward for a self-confident Islam securely based in Europe. Rather than others listening and learning, young Muslims could watch him being demonised in the press.

Learnings

In an article entitled 'Living together takes effort' already published by the *Guardian* on Saturday 9 July, days before those responsible had been named by the police, Tariq Ramadan argued:

> The message of the criminals who attacked London is plain: 'We can strike Western societies from within; no one is safe from terror; we have the means to chose the right time, the right places, the right symbols.' We must acknowledge that their message, coming the day after the announcement of London's victory to host the Olympic games in 2012, was strong and terrifying.
>
> (*Guardian*, 9 July 2005: 23)

He goes on to say: 'The objective of these attacks is to make us realise how fragile our societies are. From this feeling of fragility arises fear – for oneself and of the Other.' But he also knows that 'The proponents of the "clash of civilisations" theory will have won if we allow ourselves to become suspicious towards people of other faiths and cultures' (ibid.).

Ramadan argues that to condemn is not enough and that 'Our values, our societies, our common future requires that we become aware of our shared responsibilities'. He argues that we can preserve London as a multicultural society and 'preserve its pluralistic equilibrium only through the personal engagement of every individual in their daily life, within their own neighbourhood'. This means that everyone, whatever their background, must be prepared to respond to terror by showing in our everyday lives and contact with others that 'our experience of human brotherhood and mutual respect is stronger than their message of hate. Our lives are fragile, but our commitment to our ideals is strong' (ibid.). He understand that 'The strength of democratic societies relies on their capacity to know how to stand firm against extremism while respecting justice in the means used to fight terrorism'. We have to understand that 'a pluralistic society requires the personal and daily commitment of every citizen'.

This means we can achieve this balance only if every citizen

> after the shock of this attack, makes the effort to get to know his neighbour better – his difference, his complexity, his values and hopes. It is not enough for progressive, open-minded people to say 'This is not Islam!' It is urgent that such people meet and act alongside Muslims – practically, concretely, daily.
>
> (Ibid.)

For Muslims this means they

> must speak out and explain who they are, what they believe in, what they stand for, what is the meaning of their life. They must have the courage to denounce what is said and done by certain Muslims in the name of their religion. They will not reassure their fellow citizens by pretending to be 'like them', saying only what they want to hear and becoming invisible. They have to assert their identities, refuse simplistic discourses, promote critical, and self-critical understanding and get out from their intellectual, religious and social ghettos. European societies need to see European Muslims involved in society's questions of the day: citizenship, school, unemployment. Their strength must lie in refusing to be victims and in becoming active citizens, politically engaged both domestically and internationally.
>
> (Ibid.)

But this vision of multicultural Britain talked of by the Home Secretary Charles Clarke, as M.R. Heylings pointed out in a letter to the *Guardian*,

> is not the Britain of the Yorkshire bombers. Despite pockets of intermingling, the scene here is more of a bipolar society with English and Pakistani in highly segregated areas. The home counties' view based on London's mix of many does not translate to urban Yorkshire and Lancashire. The parallels with Northern Ireland are more informative, with English–Asian contrast as stark as, or even starker, than the Protestant–Catholic.
>
> Evidence of a strong indigenous feeling against 'otherness' is clear. Note the recent general election showing in Dewsbury with the highest number of votes in the UK for the British National Party, an estimated one in five of white voters. Read the surnames in the local press of cricket teams and note the bipolar nature of cricketing society. … Yes,

let's 'root out those who preach and practice hatred'; but it's not one-way traffic.

(Guardian, 15 July 2005: 25)

Salma Yaqoob agrees when Tony Blair describes the London bombings as a perversion of Islam, but also questions the simplistic version offered by Blair that seems to be setting the parameters of debate. According to him, as Yaqoob explains it, 'the "perversion of Islam" driving a minority of Muslims boils down to this: hatred of the Western way of life and of freedom means that Muslims (wherever they live) should kill and bomb people for force them to be Islamic.' Salma argues, 'This formulation ensures that any contextualisation will remain absent.' This may protect Blair, who does not want to concede any links with the sufferings in Iraq and Afghanistan, but it makes it harder to grasp that 'what is undeniable is that the shoddy theology – no matter how 'unIslamic' ... is driven by political injustice. It is the boiling anger and hurt that is shaping the interpretation of religious texts into such grotesque distortions' *(Guardian*, 15 July 2005: 23).

But this leaves British Muslims in a very difficult place:

> To bring in these wider questions requires them to dissent from the government line. This is difficult for them, keen as they are to avoid further marginalisation. However, if Muslim leaders succumb to the pressure of censorship and fail to visibly oppose the government on certain foreign policy issues, the gap between leaders and those they seek to represent and influence will widen, increasing the possibility of more dangerous routes being adopted by the disillusioned.
>
> (Ibid.)

In some ways this resonates with a letter by Irfan Hussain from London who insists: 'It's time we looked at ourselves critically and saw where we have failed the country and our community.' Enough of this 'victim syndrome' of Muslims apologising and trying to explain their religion. Enough of the talk that this is not Islam.

> The older imams have failed us. They are supposed to be leaders of the community, but have been too soft on extremists. They have nothing in common with the younger Muslims and no understanding of the issues. Is it any wonder that an eloquent extremist is able to recruit when he is able to connect with the young? ... From the government we need socio-economic and political factors to be addressed – deprivation, isolation and the Middle East – to get rid of this sense of injustice.
>
> *(Guardian* 14 July 2005: 25)

6   Young masculinities, Islam and terror

Re-visionings

This chapter explores the changes in Muslim communities since 9/11 and the changing nature of urban identities, as young Muslim men and women define themselves in more religious terms. This involves questioning traditions of secular rationalism that have shaped ideas of secularisation and the transitions from faith to reason. These assumptions have accompanied ideas of industrialisation and the progress from tradition to modernity, as well as the process of integration of migrant communities. Traditionally, migrants into the West are assumed to have come from more religious cultures that would often be deemed to be traditional and implicitly defined as 'backward'. From the perspectives of secular traditions of social theory that tend to identify history, progress and freedom, these cultures from which they migrate are yet to fully benefit from the advances of modernity and industrialisation that are so often figured within the terms of a Western Enlightenment rationalism. As diasporic communities settle in the West, it had generally been assumed that, if not the migrants themselves, at least their children would make the transition from 'religious faith' to secular beliefs.[1]

Though there were discussions around issues of religious fundamentalism, particularly within anthropology, these tended to be treated as aberrations within an assumed general trend from tradition to modernity. It was tempting to think of religious belief as a reaction to the pace of modernisation and the difficulties that sections of the community had in 'keeping up' with the pace of change. Within the terms of Durkheimian social theory, this was an issue that largely had to do with timing and the pace of change. With time, these reluctant or oppositional sectors would also come to appreciate the gains of capitalist industrialisation and the material opportunities it promised.[2] They would also hopefully be impressed with the fruits of freedom and democracy that were supposed to come in the wake of this industrialisation. It was partly because of the depth of these assumptions within social and political theory that it was difficult to appreciate the significance of the Iranian Revolution and the coming to power of Ayatollah Komeini. It was tempting to see this as an exceptional situation due to the excesses of the Shah's regime, rather than a call on the West to rethink the philosophical frameworks that had shaped the identification of modernity with secularisation. This was an example where 'events' of historical significance were squeezed into prevailing intellectual frameworks, rather than acknowledging the disruptive challenge presented by these events.[3]

Relatively few intellectuals in the West acknowledged their ignorance of different religious and spiritual traditions as a result of the Iranian Revolution. But, with the 9/11 attacks on the Twin Towers in New York and the Pentagon in Washington, there was a recognition that Western philosophical frameworks that has so readily assumed a transition from religion to secular, from faith to reason as a consequence of industrialisation and capitalist development, needed to be (re)imagined. It was these 'events' that initiated a widespread *disturbance* to the 'common sense' understandings that shaped the ways so many people in the United States understood their relationship to the world. They also helped to frame the question, 'why do they hate us so much to want to kill so many innocent people?' This was such a challenging question because so many people in the United States still believed its self-representation that they were only bringing the good news of freedom and democracy to the rest of the world. This meant that, for Bush's administration, it had to be either because the attackers were 'evil' or had been misled by an evil philosophy, or because they were envious of the 'good life' we were willing to spread that they had to attack us so violently.[4]

But 9/11 presented an intellectual challenge to the West more generally, not just because it reminded the West that others would be prepared to kill themselves for their beliefs, but also because the philosophical traditions that informed disciplines in the West had refused to acknowledge the significance of Islam within the historical experience of the West, but had learned to treat it as historically 'other'. This is the way it had learned to treat other religious traditions that were to be taught in separate departments of religion and so separated from the shaping of intellectual and philosophical traditions within the West. Because academic knowledge was defined as inherently secular, and because Western modernity was shaped through a radical split between science and religion, there were few paths open that could, for example, acknowledge how vital Islam and Judaism has been in returning a Greek philosophical inheritance to the West. At least Simone Weil, in *The Need for Roots*, had recognised some of the implications of the tradition of Western Humanism framing such a radical distinction between the humanities and the sciences that worked to expel ethical concerns from the search for scientific knowledge.[5]

The events around 9/11 not only encouraged Western intellectuals to learn more about Islam, as they felt shamed for knowing so little about the Qu'ran, but also to rethink some of their philosophical presuppositions that had not only made it difficult to predict that such terrorism could strike, but which often rendered them speechless in the face of it. It was much easier to treat it as an aberration that had to do with an irrational fundamentalism that necessarily fell outside the frameworks of intellectual knowledge. It could become an 'object' of investigation only if it was assumed that these were 'irrational' responses that could only be explained within a discourse of pathologies. But, as Weil recognised, this was what made it so difficult for Western modernity to come to terms with the philosophical crisis marked by the catastrophic events of the Holocaust and the dropping of nuclear bombs on Hiroshima and Nagasaki. These were events that *should* have stopped Western intellectual traditions in their tracks, and you might have expected the response to be even more intense than after the First World War, which had precipitated an intellectual crisis.[6] But what was striking was that it seemed much easier to treat Auschwitz, at least for a long time, as an aberration that had to be understood as a consequence of Hitler's madness and irrational desires to exterminate European Jewry.

After 9/11 social and political theories need to recognise, as we shall explore later, that we need to revision the philosophical frameworks that inform intellectual disciplines constructed through a radical split between faith and reason. We need to draw upon intellectual sources that in some way anticipated a crisis in European modernity, for example in the writings of the later Wittgenstein, Heidegger, Adorno and Weil.[7] But we also need to follow the responses in Muslim communities, particularly the radicalisation of young men, so that we begin to appreciate the ease with which they can feel marginalised and hidden as religious seekers and so can feel pushed to the extremes.

Backlash

A recent report, 'Intolerance and Discrimination against Muslims in the EU', by the International Helsinki Federation for Human Rights, points out that earlier atrocities – from 9/11 to Bali and Madrid – have produced a direct backlash against Muslim communities in Europe. Every incident led to incidents of abuse of Muslim women and general harassment of bearded men, desecration of mosques, negative sentiments against Islam and attacks on Muslims. But the changes in Britain since 9/11 that have produced mutually respectful relations within civil society and with police and government means the backlash after the London bombings will occur in a different landscape. After the tragedy of 9/11, Muslims, as Ziauddin Sardar recalls, 'found themselves alone. Apart from loudly denouncing terrorism, they had to distance themselves from extremists while simultaneously apologising constantly for their existence' (*Independent on Sunday*, 10 July 2005: 28). This time around, Muslims are not isolated. The peaceful nature of Islam at large is being upheld from all sides. The Archbishop of Canterbury, attending an interfaith meeting at the time of the London bombings, broke off his meeting to show respect by making a public statement asserting faith communities have to 'continue to stand and work together' for 'our shared understanding of the life that God calls us to' (ibid.).[8]

As Ziauddin Sardar recognises, since 9/11, 'The Muslim community has changed: it has been energised and alerted by events. It has not completed a generational or intellectual refashioning. There is still much to do. But the sense of victimhood is evaporating.' He also insists:

> After the atrocity in London, Muslims have to try even harder to change how the 'war on terror' has been defined and conceived. What Britain has to learn at home will be the best yardstick of how its policy needs to change abroad. Can you on the one hand talk community engagement and inclusion while promoting draconian legislative measures that have caused a 300 per cent increase in stop and search of Muslims in London and while the fear of Belmarsh lurks?
>
> (Ibid.)[9]

Kishwer Falkner, a Liberal Democrat peer from a Muslim background, acknowledges that since 9/11 'many of us have been grappling with how and why British Muslim youth – usually second or third generation – have found extremism, and, in rare cases, Terrorism, so compelling' (*Independent*, 12 July 2005: 27). Having visited many communities, she recognises the answers are complex and that socio-economic issues are part of the problem: 'The levels of social deprivation of Muslims living in Burnley, Bradford or Leeds tell the story of years of neglect, ignorance, poor upward mobility and segregated communities, hence alienation from the mainstream' (ibid.). This raises difficult questions we have long avoided; for instance, whether, if we are to tackle extremism in our midst,

> Should segregation and its isolation from the mainstream be tolerated under the guise of multiculturalism? How far should the secular state and its bedrock of shared values be stretched to accommodate religious pluralism, when religion is twisted by extremists on all sides?
>
> (Ibid.)

Falkner was writing before the police announcement of the responsibility of British Muslims, saying:

> Since last Thursday, many British Muslims have been united by similar sentiments: the hope that the terrorists are not 'ours', and if they are from Muslim backgrounds at all, the hope that they are clearly identified as foreign al-Qa'ida operatives.
>
> (Ibid.)

But this hope for 'some distance between them and us' was not to be. Her questions about segregation, that are too easily missed within a more multicultural London, are given an added urgency. Segregation, she recognises, makes it difficult to 'test' values and ideas against competing norms. Drawing on her own experience, she writes:

> The experience of racial difference, and most Muslims are not white, sits differently within our skin at different stages of our lives, but is most difficult in youth. When religious and cultural difference is added and reinforced through very tight knit family structures where integration into the wider British community is rare, then mainstream values do not easily transfer across.
>
> (Ibid.)

Although she does not interrogate the state of 'mainstream values', she does appreciate that many Muslim groups that have developed on the margins of the Muslim establishment feel 'that their leaders either do not speak for them or are impotent to bring about change. For them the internet and travel becomes the tools of building solidarity and recognising identity. Each man truly becomes an island.' I was struck by this last sentence, wondering what it really meant to convey. But again she helpfully shares some of her own experience, going on immediately to say with little explanation:

> The perception of injustice runs deep. In Muslim seminars or on the doorstep, all too often one hears of condemnation not only for the Iraq war, but of the war against Afghanistan as well. The West is routinely criticised for waging an attack on the Muslim world, not states which are a threat. When pressed for an answer as to what should have been done with a Taliban-run, al-Qa'ida-embracing Afghanistan, one is met with silence at best, or a simple denial that al-Qa'ida was a threat.
>
> As one tries to bring shades of grey into a black-and-white world view, eyes glaze over and the argument is lost.... When extremism culminates in terrorism, the refrain from the leaders is that these are not 'real' Muslims. While almost all Muslims would not condone terrorism, it is now evident that there are some who conflate justice for the Muslim ummah with justification for murder. These people do not see themselves as outside our faith, indeed they see themselves as representing its unsullied purity. What is more, the boundary between these apologists and the mainstream is not always clearly identifiable.
>
> (Ibid.)

Voicing shock

The *Sun*'s front page on the morning after the day the news broke (Tuesday 12 July 2005) ran the headline 'THE BRIT BOMBERS' without mentioning they were young Muslim men. It went on to say:

> * All 4 were suicide killers * Gang came from Yorkshire
> Two were aged 19 and 22 * Disguised as hitchhikers

The story, by Mike Sullivan, with 'Crime Editor' on the side in much smaller print, said:

> Four young Britons carried out the London suicide bombings which killed 70 commuters.
>   Police said last night one was 19, one 22, and another 30. The fourth is believed to be a teenager too.
>   They drove from West Yorkshire to Luton. They were met by an accomplice and boarded a train to King's Cross where they were caught on CCTV cameras smiling and chatting, with rucksacks on their backs ...

It is these last words that catch you by surprise. How can people going to their deaths be 'smiling and chatting'? But this is in line with other suicide bombings in Israel/Palestine that show young people finally on a mission that will bring them to a heavenly reward. This is part of a process of readiness that needs to be explained.

The tone immediately changes on the inside front page, where we have the large headline 'BACKPACK BUTCHERS', then in smaller print 'Terror mob had bombs in rucksacks'. The piece begins with the front-page mutation of 'Four Young Britons' into 'Four young British Muslims dressed like backpackers were the butchers behind London's first suicide bombings'. But there is quite a different tone in the writing of Anila Baig, a Muslim journalist who writes for the paper. Under a heading of 'All of us must pull together' she writes:

> Today it feels as if my world has been blown apart, even though I was nowhere near the London bombs.
>   The war on terror has finally made it into my own back yard.
>   Four possible suicide bombers. From Yorkshire. Leeds has been cordoned off. Streets are closed in Dewsbury.
>   It defies belief, certainly my belief.
>   How did these four men think they had the right to take innocent lives?
>   What would have been going through their minds knowing they were about to unleash such carnage in our capital?

I know from experience that Muslim youths do feel alienated, torn between their duties to God and the conflict of having been born and raised in Britain.

Most of us are well-adjusted and feel blessed that we can move confidently between our Eastern and Western roots.

But for some, it is not the way. These men and boys feel they don't belong, even if they are successful members of society. That isolation is exploited by those with a political agenda. The 'outsiders' learn a culture of hate.

(*Sun*, 13 July 2005: 4)

It is striking how this becomes an issue of *gender* as she slips into talking about 'these men and boys'. It is as if male Muslims feel a particular sense of responsibility that falls upon men within the tradition that means they feel 'torn' in particular ways 'between their duties to God and the conflict of having born and raised in Britain'. At some level there is a haunting sense that they could not really have been 'born and raised' in Britain. Somehow it had all been a terrible mistake because they did not come to feel any sense of belonging, and when they reflect on their childhoods, they might confront a sense of individual isolation that remained largely unspoken. This might be the 'island' that Falkner referred to, almost in passing.

Anila Baig goes on to question some of her own assumptions, saying:

We expect the bombers to be dropouts but they aren't – and what possible excuse does that leave us? The horror is that, yes, they are like us.

The people of my community were just getting their heads around it.

Most were unwilling to accept the bombs were anything to do with us. It would be some foreign extremist group.

But with slow and unmitigated horror it sinks in. These were probably boys like my brothers – probably young, probably devout, probably a mix of East and West.

Things were bad enough for Muslims in the wake of the attack last Thursday.

(Ibid.)

Baig goes on to share her own experiences and the ways it was already shifting her own beliefs:

'When people made claims about Islamophobia, I laughed it off as a persecution complex.

But yesterday I was abused in the street for the first time. I have tasted contempt first hand.

> Will people not sit next to us on the bus? Will they stop saying hello? The little things. Will my friends see me differently?
>
> It is like a horror film where the everyday becomes grotesque and that panicky feeling in our stomach won't go away. For the first time in my life since the neo-Nazi marches of the 1970s, I taste fear.
>
> (Ibid.)

She is also determined in a way that recognises the anger and hurt the community feels about their country's foreign policy, an anger that Blair has sought to displace through talking about an 'evil ideology'. She says:

> Of course Muslims should not be silenced for speaking out against the injustices against Muslims. The more we feel our voices are being hushed, the more extreme people become.
>
> Feeling sorrow for Palestinian orphans or Muslim victims in Bosnia does not make us complicit in terror.
>
> Many in our community feel sorrow for those who lost their lives in Iraq, Kashmir and Chechnya and wish Blair and Bush had not gone to war. Millions of Westerners made the same point, yet they will never be eyed with suspicion.
>
> (Ibid.)

Possibly in these tense days it is easier to talk about sorrow than about the anger that is so widespread, about how people do not seem to care about the innocent civilians that are being killed on a daily basis through suicide bombs in Iraq. But Baig is clear that

> Shock does not begin to even start to describe how we feel. We feel bereft. Mothers will wail, fathers will cry. These boys have not done this with the blessings of their families.
>
> But we have been kidding ourselves when we said 'It can't happen here'. This is the wake-up call.
>
> (Ibid.)

Young British Muslim men

Shehzad Tanweer – known as 'Kakato' by his chums – was one of the London Underground bombers. He was responsible for the explosion at Aldgate. He perished along with the innocent victims and his driving licence and credit cards were found in the wreckage, strangely along with documents belonging to the young man responsible for the bombing at Edgware Road. His friends in the Leeds suburb of Beeston in Leeds, where the 22-year-old sometimes helped out with his father's chip shop, were stunned at the news. They insisted he had no connection to any radical group. Azzy Mohammed, 21, said:

'He's the kind of person who gets along with anyone.

'His sense of humour is very good. He's a sweet lad.'

Another pal said, 'He had become very religious and quite devout and would pray five times a day but I never imagined he would get caught up in anything like this.

(*Sun*, 13 July 2005: 4).

On the eve of the bombing, Tanweer casually played football with pals at Cross Flatts Park – 50 yards from the family chippy. Another shocked pal, Mohammed Answar, 19, added: 'It is not in his nature to do something like this. He is the type who would condemn it.' Friends told how he had recently completed a sports science degree at Leeds Metropolitan but seemed happy enough frying fish at his father's takeaway.

One said:

'His family reported him missing last week and have been unable to get hold of him.

'I knew Khaka personally. He was a lovely lad. There was no indication of any extremism. The family are decent, hardworking people.'

Another friend said: 'His dad is a successful businessman owning properties in the area. He used to work for the West Yorkshire Police. He is a pillar of the community.'

Another friend added: 'They are not extremists. If he's caught up in this it is because he has been misled'.

(Ibid.)

This was a theme that was to develop over the following days, that the boys must have been 'brainwashed' and so could not really be held responsible. Rather, they must have been under the control of a 'Mr Big', as the *Sun* came to talk about him. A friend of the Tanweer family said: 'Mum and dad will be devastated. I just can't take it in that he would have done such a terrible thing as this. He was working in the chip shop smiling and laughing two days before the bombing' (*Sun*, 12 July: 4).

People who knew him were shocked at his involvement in the bombings. Tanweer, 22 – described as a 'super intelligent' science buff during his school days – kept his views hidden even from his family. A former school friend said:

Nobody can believe it. When he was at school his hero was Mike Tyson, not Osama Bin Laden. He was quite religious but had little interest in politics. He loved sport. He was cricket mad and a good fast bowler.

He loved boxing and American wrestling. He played football for the school and was brilliant at triple jump and long jump.

(*Sun*, 14 July 2005: 5)

Another ex-pupil from Wortley High School in Leeds said:

> He would have been the last person you would say would get involved
> in something like this.
> He was kind, polite and respectful at school. He was super intelli-
> gent. We used to struggle to get good grades but he seemed to find it
> all easy.
> His family were very strict about him doing his homework though.
> He was a really quiet lad but also had a great sense of humour and
> was always smiling. He was a teacher's dream. He always got on with
> any work he was set and was always extremely polite.
> I can't believe he's done this. He was so English in his beliefs and
> very westernised in the way he dressed. We knew he had his religious
> beliefs and that he read the Koran. But there was no way you could
> accuse him of being an extremist.
>
> (Ibid.)

Late in 2004 he had visited Pakistan to study the Koran. He had originally planned to spend a year in Lahore, but he was back within three
months, telling his family, 'I didn't like it. I didn't like the people.' He
seems to have made contact with different religious groups in Pakistan but
did not tell his parents about it. They might have shared the same house in
Beeston, but they lived in different worlds. This generational divide is quite
common. Children behaved as they were expected within their strict families, but lived quite different lives away from them. His uncle Bashir Ahmed
said:

> His parents were very proud of him and very pleased he was taking his
> religious studies seriously when many parents are worried about their
> children going to the pub.
> … He was just a good British boy when he was growing up, a
> young sports fan from a good family. It is hard to accept what must
> have happened to him.… Shehzad would not have been capable of
> this bombing unless his mind had been poisoned.
>
> (Ibid.)

In a personal testimony, the cousin of Shezad Tanwer – who on the
Monday after the attacks was boarding a London bus in defiance, just like
thousands of other communities across the city – on the Tuesday

> heard something beyond imagination. Something that would test my
> community and shatter my family. One of the bombers was my
> cousin.
> I had seen him days before the event, but I hadn't seen what was
> coming.… Shehzad's parents taught him that violence didn't solve

anything, and that violence isn't accepted in Islam. My parents would always remind me that the meaning of the word Islam – peace.... Shezad grew into a calm and peaceful young man. Nothing could anger him. I cannot remember the last time I heard him even raise his voice.

(*Guardian*, 18 July 2005: 4)

Although she never discussed politics with him, she is sure

he would have felt very strongly about all those things, just as most Muslims in Britain do. I certainly do. I believe the Iraq war was not justified. I believe the treatment of alleged war criminals at Guantanamo Bay is a gross misconduct of human rights that every citizen on this planet should be ashamed of. And of course there should be a fair two-state resolution in the Middle East.

My beliefs are strong but I do not believe they are justification enough to kill innocent people. Whatever the reasons for Shehzad's actions, he took them with him. Nobody will ever have the answer, not even his family.

(Ibid.)

She insists that 'relatives of the bombers do not want to see any more of their children being used as the tools of somebody else's evil ideology', so accepting the terms that Blair has wanted to establish, even if she seems to recognise otherwise. We can learn from these tensions in her discourse.

She questions that the *Sun*

branded George Galloway as a 'traitor' for questioning the role of the Iraq war in motivating Thursday's attacks. In doing so, they sent a perilous message to every disillusioned Muslim in this country. They made it clear dialogue is not an acceptable way to vent our anger at the treatment of Muslims across the world.

If you silence those who have grievances to air, what tools do you leave them with?

(Ibid.)

At the same time as she raises these questions, she concludes with a firm belief: 'I have no doubt in my mind that Shehzad was merely a tool of somebody else's evil ideology. I am certain somebody got to him, and duped him ... ' Of course this is an understandable response from someone so close, but it can so easily deny him a sense of responsibility for his own actions, however terrible the consequences have been for so many.

Mohammad Sidique Khan, 30, from Lees Holm, Dewsbury, and born in Leeds, was named by the police as being responsible for the bombing at

Edgware Road. He is the father of a 14-month-old daughter, Maryam, and had recently separated from her mother who is expecting their second child. For a while he had worked as a mentor for children with learning difficulties at Hillside Primary School and the head teacher and many parents spoke with appreciation about the work he had done. He said of his work with children aged five and upwards: 'A lot of them have said this is the best school they have been to.' Staff described Khan as gently spoken, endlessly patient and hugely popular with the children. One child who had been taught by him at Hillside said:

> He seemed a really kind man, he taught the really bad kids and every-one seemed to like him. He was there about three years and then he went on holiday and never came back. We just knew him as Mr Khan.
> (*Guardian*, 14 July 2005: 3)

Khan was born in 1974 at St James's Hospital, Leeds. His father, Tika Khan, who had migrated from Pakistan, worked in a foundry. His mother was Mamida Begum. His family moved from Leeds to Beeston where he attended the Mathew Murray high school. He did well enough academi-cally to get a place at the University of Leeds where he met his future wife, Hasina, an Indian Muslim whose family lived in Dewsbury. She also worked as a Community Enrichment Officer, working in schools alongside special needs pupils. She gave up her job after the birth of their first child, but Khan continued working several days a week. Neighbours spoke of the Khans as a 'quiet couple'. One woman, who did not want to be named, told Andrew Parker of the *Sun*:

> They seemed like a really happy family. Hasina was from an Indian family and there are not often mixed Pakistani and Indian marriages but they didn't mind.
>   But they were both Muslims, she sometimes wore a veil, he had a beard and they shaved their baby daughter's head.
>   There were lots of Muslim men who visited their house but they had only lived here for six months and were not regulars at the mosque and hadn't yet become part of the community.
> (*Sun*, 14 July 2005: 3)

Investigations revealed that Khan was respected as a mentor by other young Muslim boys in the area. He played football with lads in the park and opened up a gym in the basement of Jamia mosque in Hardy Street in 2000. Apparently it was a space with gym equipment bought through an EU grant intended to get youngsters off the street and away from the temptations of crime. Among his earliest intake were Shezad Tanweer, then aged 17, and 13-year-old Hasib Hussain. It seems that all the young men involved in the bombings were fitness fanatics skilled in different martial arts. The uncle of Shehzad Tanweer said that, when stories about the gym were beginning to circulate:

> We consider Shehzad to have been a victim of Khan because of a grooming process in the gym.
> It was below the mosque and the only adult allowed inside was Khan, At the time, no one had a problem with that because he was a respected teacher.
> But since Shehzad's death his friends have told us that Khan was using the gym to poison the minds of the youngsters.
> (*Mail on Sunday*, 17 July 2005: 6)

Apparently Khan also used a building in Lodge Lane, an annex of the nearby Hamara Healthy Living Centre on Tempest Road, a government-funded scheme opened two years ago by Hilary Benn, the local MP. Hamara is an Urdu word meaning 'ours'. Khan used the building as a centre for voluntary work and it became a place where young Asians congregated. It seems as if the older Khan might well have played a critical part in getting people together. A youth worker at the Leeds City Council-funded centre said it had been causing concern for some time because of fears that one of the staff was 'radicalising and recruiting' young Muslim men. 'Rather than the mosque this was the place that people went for radicalism', the worker said (the *Guardian*, 14 July 2005: 3).

Sadiq Khan, Labour MP for Tooting and former civil liberties lawyer, has warned against treating the Muslim community as something separate from wider society. He insists:

> There needs to be an examination of how we deal with the atmosphere and conditions that lead to educated middle-class men and disenfranchised, disillusioned young men doing these things.
> One place we know all these people went to is not youth clubs or madrasas. They all went to our schools from 4 to 16. So why aren't our schools giving positive role models or teaching them about the history of Islamic mathematics and artists? Why are their role models the mujarideen in Afghanistan? The loss of identity does not happen when you are 16, but over a period of years.
> (*Guardian*, 14 July 2005: 4)

These themes were echoed by Lord Ahmed of Rotherham, who wrote:

> For too long we have turned our back on Britain and what it means to be British. We have, both by force of circumstance and by choice, lived in our own parallel universe – living in this country but not truly a part of it.
> The reasons for this are historical, political and economic. In the

Seventies, when my family and thousands of other Muslims came here from India, Bangladesh, Pakistan, most never believed that they would stay.

They lived where the work was, where they had friends and where they felt they had the safety of numbers. Many sent money back home to build a house, perhaps, or help support a family. They kept their language, customs, traditions and style of dress, and insisted their children were brought up in their image.

They didn't embrace English culture and didn't stress to their sons and daughters the crucial importance of education. Why would they, when they never planned to stay? No doubt they had the best intentions. But most never did go home, and as a result many of their children, the second and third generation of British Muslims were betrayed.

They were condemned to live their lives in the grip of an identity crisis – neither Indian, Pakistani, Bangladeshi nor properly British.

(*Mail on Sunday*, 17 July 2005: 25)

Although many people have achieved great success and made it into a variety of professions, there are 'far too many with poor qualifications ... and little chance little chance of well-paid work. They live in deprivation and isolation and see no way out.' They feel pressure from their parents to speak what, for them, is a 'foreign' language, wear traditional dress and show interest in things that seem to have little relevance to their own lives. They can feel obliged to participate in arranged marriages while they see the freedoms that English children have and want the same for themselves. Many young people were left feeling *estranged* both from Britain and from their parents' culture. The mosques and older generation mistook their children's protestations for the noisy and vocal teenage culture of the West. As Ahmed explains it, emphasising an external responsibility:

over the past decade a new breed of politically motivated ideologues, mainly from the Middle East, recognised these disenfranchised young people as a fertile recruitment ground. They urged them to compare their suffering with those of Muslims in Palestine, Chechnya, Iraq and the Balkans and to rise up against what they described as 'infidels'.

(Ibid.)[10]

British Muslims are experiencing the crisis wrought by the attacks in vastly different ways. The most pronounced differences seem to be between young and old. Many of the older Muslims are speaking of their children as having been 'brainwashed'. Qurban Hussain, deputy leader of Luton council, is sharply conscious of the extremists. He received death threats for standing for a 'western' political party in the May elections, even though it was the anti-war Liberal Democrats. He emphatically denounces the suicide bombers and speaks of an intelligence failure, but he is also willing to scrutinise his own community:

> This is another tragedy: the generation gap between young and old in the ethnic minorities is much greater than in the indigenous population. Our elder generation were law-abiding and hardworking. Where they failed was they put all their God-given hours into work and didn't spend time with their children. When these people are brainwashed, they are brainwashed to an extent that they don't talk to their parents.
>
> (*Guardian*, 16 July 2005: 6)

Generations

Patrick Barkham meets some younger pupils after their lessons. They are driven to their classes by parents in VW Passats to study Arabic and the Qur'an five evenings a week. 'We want them to be proud Muslims and proud British citizens,' says Ibrahim Mogra, their teacher.

> This is our country, this is home. There is no reason for them to feel second-class or alien. If you ask them who they are, they would say Muslim and I think that's right. As a person of faith, for me, God comes before everything. But there is no contradiction. I'm Muslim, I'm British, I'm Asian, I'm an Imam, I'm a teacher.
>
> (Ibid.)

But for others as they grow up, things are often not so easy, and the idea that 'God comes before everything' can be interpreted in different ways, especially if you identify with the sufferings of others. The young people Barkham meets point out double standards in government and media treatment of their faith. Of course the bombs were wrong and destroyed innocent people's lives, but look at what fuelled it: Iraq, Afghanistan, Palestine.

'In Afghanistan people die every single day but that's never mentioned,' points out Irshad, 14. 'Nobody is there to help the people in Palestine.' Arshad, also 14, finishes the argument: 'It's not a war against terrorism, it's a war against Islam. That's how some people see it.' These are young voices that talk in different tones from their teachers. They are making connections that can so easily leave them with a feeling of estrangement when they think it is 'their country' that is killing innocent Muslims in Iraq, but how can it be 'theirs' if it is really their Muslim brothers and sisters that are being killed as innocent civilians? This can make it hard to think of themselves as 'British', even if they would otherwise want to. It can also be that young men carry a particular sense of responsibility within the religious tradition that can leave them feeling that it is somehow 'up to them' as young men to do something about this suffering. It cannot simply be allowed to go on.

It is wearily routine, Barkham acknowledges, for reporters to rush to mosques whenever there are outbreaks of extremism. As Mo, a young Muslim who works at a BT call centre, points out to him, reporters didn't swarm around Catholic churches whenever the IRA blew something up. Mo buys him a soft drink from a local kebab shop. 'Stay here, I've got something to show you.' He returns with a sheet of typed paper that his sister stuck to her bedroom wall. It reads:

> Former heavyweight boxing champion Muhammad Ali visited the remains of the World Trade Centre. When reporters asked how he felt about suspects sharing his Islamic faith, Ali responded pleasantly, 'How do you feel about Hitler sharing yours?' Ever wondered ... why a nun can be covered from head to toe and she's respected for devoting herself to God, but when a Muslimah does that, she's considered oppressed?
>
> (Ibid.)

Mr Akhter, 38, who sells Islamic books and shalwar Kameez in Derby came to Britain from Kashmir ten years ago, believes the generation gap is based on the language barrier between English-speaking young Muslims and their elders.

> It doesn't matter what the imam says inside the mosque because young people don't understand. The real education goes on outside. In mosques our religious leaders are speaking in Urdu. The only people speaking in English are extremists like Abu Hamza and Bakri Mohammed. Youngsters do not get the real message of Islam.
>
> (Ibid.: 7)

Al-Muhajiroun, an organisation that is now defunct but was led for a while by Bakri Mohammed, was accused of recruiting Derby resident Omar Khan Sharif, who was found dead after a suicide bombing in Israel two years ago in which four people died. But Akhter also argues that the extremists are a 'reactionary product of this country' and not produced by Muslims alone. Hamza and Bakri Mohammed were 'given enormous and disproportionate media time to say poisonous things. Why did you make them our heroes? Why did you give them airtime?' (ibid.).

In Beeston, on the outskirts of Leeds, behind the police tape set up around selected buildings, Ima gathers with a group of mates. The 27-year-old knew Shehzad Tanweer pretty well. For him, there is a 'cultural gap' between the generations: 'The generation that did the bombings have had a free rein. They've been given a good education and been able to do whatever they like. The older generation haven't tuned in. They don't know Tupac Shakur or Steven Gerrard' (ibid.). Like many younger Muslims, Ima wants to see not just his elders but also wider society trying harder to understand modern British Muslims. Nobody has been interested in listening to them. 'We need a close examination of what the youth of today are thinking and doing,' he says. 'Any young person is vulnerable to any form of extremism. You have to open the doors a bit. Lack of information breeds misinformation. The less we are told, the less we feel this is our country' (ibid.).

7   Young men, Islamic cultures and belonging(s)

Young Islamic masculinities

In tracing the background of the second-generation young men who were involved in the London bombings and the influences shaping their particular masculinities, I invoke a notion of generational (dis)placement to explore how they find themselves in a world very different from anything their parents knew. Often unable to communicate with their parents, young Muslim men may feel obliged to show signs of respect to their fathers, but at the same time can feel internally estranged. They might show these outward signs of respect, and so learn to behave *appropriately*, while shaping very different kinds of lives for themselves with their friends and on the Internet in the privacy of their rooms. This is not so different from other second-generation young men who have grown up in migrant communities, but we require forms of qualitative research that can appreciate the need to listen to the particular cultural narratives and ways particular traumatic, including the unspoken traumatic, histories of exile and displacement find an echo in future generations.[1]

When young men born in this country visit the mosques, they sometimes cannot understand the sermons given in Urdu, so they can also feel estranged through the English they speak with their mates. They might feel torn between different worlds with pressures to define a sense of their own generational experience in contrast to their parents' generation, who might look to home in ways the younger generation feel unable or unwilling to. With access to global media, they learn to create transnational virtual spaces in which they can communicate and find resonance with their own lives and a sense of belonging that can easily transgress boundaries of geography. They can create *complex identifications* that can be difficult to explain to those, even their close mates, with whom they share everyday lives. This is why it is so vital to craft social theories that can value the narratives these young men are creating for themselves, framing their masculinities in ways that affirm the anger, disappointments, frustrations and injustices they often feel at the world.[2]

Hasib Hussain lay sprawled upon the grass of Cross Flatt's Park that borders the red-bricked houses of Beeston. The 18-year-old was smoking dope with his friends four days before the London bombings. 'When you grow up with someone and smoke weed with them it normally means you're close,' said a lifelong friend of Hussein's after hearing about the bombings. The imposing frame of Hussein had been toughened by his time at the nearby Mathew Murray High School, which is described by those who shared a classroom 'as a violent place, where police were often called. The fights were always between whites and Asians'. Like Shehzad Tanweer, Hasib could also 'handle himself'. They both idealised Khan from his days as a youth worker in Beeston when he had nurtured their love of cricket and football. He was the person who took them on canoeing and camping trips to the nearby Yorkshire Dales; the man who bought them 'loads of extra bullets' when he took them paint-balling.

According to a report in the *Observer*, 'Yet last summer Khan changed. It was following his final trip to Pakistan. Those who knew him had detected a mood change.' He resigned from his position as a popular teaching assistant at the Hillside Primary School in Leeds. The same report states:

> In the same period, Tanweer too was undergoing a profound personal transformation. Last December, he met militant groups linked to al-Qaeda north of Lahore. Days after returning to Beeston, a man he met was arrested for an attack in 2002 on an Islamabad church near a US embassy.
>
> (*Observer*, 17 July 2005: 13)

'It was during this period that clerics in south Leeds also detected the first signs of a growing radicalisation in Hussain' (ibid.). Despite his age, Hussein had travelled extensively to increase his understanding of Islam. He had visited Pakistan as well as Saudi Arabia, twice for the pilgrimage Haji and three times to visit the holy city of Umra. Known as a gentle giant to his school pals, he became increasingly interested in Islam after a visit to relatives in Pakistan two years ago. He started wearing traditional Muslim dress and growing a beard. According to a neighbour, he started to stay in his room all the time. His older brother Imi was far more outgoing, while Hasib was more reserved. Despite a good attendance record at school, he was withdrawn by teachers from most of his GCSE exams. An ex-classmate said Hussain was known as a quite boy – but could fight back if provoked. He added 'He was very tall and very fit and he got into a few fights – which he usually won. I don't think there were many people at school of his own age who would have a go at him' (*Sun*, 14 July 2005: 4).

Just before Khan resigned from his teaching jobs, elders from Beeston's Stratford Street mosque apparently told the radicalised young men that their 'inappropriate teachings' had no place in the prayerhouses of south

Leeds. According to the report, far 'from the preconception that those who commit terrorist acts are often privileged, the suicide bombers lived in humdrum terracing with their career prospects already in decline' (*Observer*, 17 July 2005: 14). Tariq Panja appreciates that even if the assessment of one of Hasib Hussein's friend was 'He must have led a double life', it is abundantly clear that in the predominantly working-class area of Beeston,

> there are many double lives led here. Alcohol, drugs and girls may be taboo subjects at home, where they are always conscious of their Muslim faith. But, like most young British men, away from home, it is a different story.
>
> (Ibid.: 17)

Thinking of Hasib, he says: 'That the radicalisation of a young man such as this points to someone who is uncomfortable in his own skin.'

They can be 'uncomfortable' in their skins in so many different ways. For many, though they might be able to read Arabic, the Koran remains incomprehensible to them. The sermons on Friday will be given in the language of the founders of the mosque, which in Beeston means they are delivered in Urdu. The content rarely considers the lives of the scores of young men present. Rather, both in the mosque and at home they are expected to behave appropriately, even if they do not understand the purpose of what they are doing. Little is said in either place that can possibly help young Muslim men come to terms with their *ambivalence* towards their identities. This leaves many young men vulnerable to radical groups that seem able to recognise and speak to their spiritual yearnings and sense of social and cultural displacement. Speaking in a language they can understand, the groups 'come to the rescue', filling in the gaps with certainties.

As Panja understands it for himself:

> Coming across as thoughtful and coherent, it is easy for such movements as Hizb-ut Tahrir to get into the minds of youngsters who are to a certain extent empty vessels. The information is easily accepted because of its seeming coherence and, more importantly, because many of those they seek to indoctrinate have nothing to offer in return. This is not discovery through the exchange of ideas. This is writing onto a blank page.... It is us against them. It doesn't matter where we are, or what the laws of the land are, the only laws we should follow are those of the Koran.
>
> (Ibid.)

The uncertainties and ambivalences of second- and third-generation migrant identities are replaced by the singular authority of the Koran. As Panja says:

Though many groups claim to be non-violent, the impact they have on the consciousness of the vulnerable lives they influence can be catastrophic.' 'I fear' ... that until we enjoy a cultural shift in modern British Islam we are in danger of creating more lost souls like Hasib.

(Ibid.)[3]

The 'fourth man' already mentioned was named as Jermaine Lindsay. He knew some of the others from having lived in the Huddersfield suburb of Dalton in Holays. He went to a local church junior school, Rawthorpe Junior, and then on to Rawthorpe secondary school where he was also known for a love of sports, particularly athletics. Theresa Weldrick, who was in the year below at secondary school, was stunned to learn of his part in the London atrocities: 'He was really nice. He was one of those people you never expected to get into trouble. He was just so good. What possessed his soul?' (The *Mail On Sunday*, 17 July 2005: 7). Similar themes seem to emerge from other biographies, as if they were 'too good to be true'. Sally Lewin grew up a little awed by Jamal: 'He did all his exams and was in the top group. He was dead brainy.' He was the son of a single parent, Mary McLeod, a 39-year-old British social worker, who, speaking from her mother's house in Jamaica, said he was converted by Muslim friends when he was 15 and he persuaded her to convert against the wishes of her Christian family.[4]

'After September 11, I was devastated and so was Jermaine,' she said. 'We cried for all the people who died and wondered how Muslims could do this.' Ms McLeod gave birth to Jermaine in Jamaica before moving to England. His father was largely absent during Jermaine's youth. As her mother explains:

Then Mary fell in love with a man from England and he took her and Jermaine there but she claims he did not treat her well. After having one daughter by him, she left him and had another daughter by someone else. Somewhere in that period, she got into this Muslim thing.

(Ibid.)

She had hoped that Islam's strict prohibition on alcohol and extra-marital sex would keep him out of trouble. Towards the end of his secondary school, he started wearing traditional Islamic dress. His younger sister Lauren also began to wear the traditional headscarf. His mother was delighted when he married a young white British Muslim convert, Samantha Lewthwaite, now 21. They have a 15-month-old son Abdullah and she is pregnant with their second child. Last year they moved south to Aylesbury, where Samantha was originally from. He was very involved in physical fitness training and martial arts. It seems as if he broke off the relationship in the months before the bombing in London.

Timings

Munir Akram, Pakistan's UN ambassador, advised against trying to shift responsibility to his country, and blamed Tony Blair's policies in the Middle East. He said: 'It is important not to pin blame on somebody else when the problem lies internally. Your policies in the Middle East, your policies in the Islamic world, that is the problem with your society...' He insisted that even if Tanweer and his accomplices had visited Pakistan, they had not been there long enough to be turned into bombers by al-Qaida or at the madrasas. In an interview on BBC World, Sunday 17 July 2005, he said:

> Brainwashing is a long process. You cannot brainwash somebody instantly, unless he is inclined to be brainwashed. Rather, it was the years spent in Britain that transformed them into the UK's first suicide bombers.
>
> They were born in Britain, bred there, lived there, were by all accounts British lads. What motivated British lads to do this? It is not because their blood was from Pakistan. Whatever angst they had was a result of living in Britain.
>
> (Quoted in the *Guardian*, 18 July 2005: 5)

As Jonathan Freedland says about the image that was released of the four men entering Luton station with their backpacks:

> The killers are not terrifying monsters, but the kind of lads you see on the streets of any British town any day of the week. They do not carry guns or knives – the things we have been conditioned to fear – but backpacks, like students or tourists.
>
> And this is not Baghdad or Basra but Luton, a town whose name could be a byword for nondescript averageness. The lesson of this picture is, change our nightmares – your fears are out of date. For scenes of bland normality, like this one, can contain devastation.
>
> (*Guardian*, 18 July 2005: 5)

As Freedland says: 'It could be the most banal photograph in the world.... And yet you could stare at it for hours.' But this is because 'what we see most in this image is not what's in it, but what we put there. Because we know what happened next, we detect a purpose in the men's steps, like gangsters about to stage a job' (ibid.).

If we want to understand some of what might have driven these men, we need to appreciate, as Madeleine Bunting argues, that three of the Leeds-based bombers probably came from Mirpur, part of Pakistani Kashmir. Coming from subsistence farming communities with little or no schooling, 'They made a huge cultural and geographical leap to settle in the UK – the dislocation is hard to imagine.' As she explains, 'One of the things they brought with them was the perception of a long history of dispossession and marginalisation. Partition brought terrible bloodshed and the division of Kashmir between Pakistan and India' (*Guardian*, 18 July 2005: 17). Often these traumatic histories, like the history of the Shoah in refugee Jewish families, remained unspoken. There were often few narratives available, only a sullen and sometimes bitter feeling of loss that shaped the atmosphere in families.[5]

In the 1980s, the remittances began to flow into this traditionally poor region, bringing computers, televisions, the Internet, satellite dishes, microwaves and fridges. One of the strongest Mirpuri traditions is that you marry your first cousin, so there is a constant exchange with the UK to renew the Mirpuri influence for the next generation. As Bunting explains, 'Mirpur has been an example – and there are others the world over – of the painful disruption in deeply traditional communities of a sudden influx of wealth and interface with modernity' (ibid.). Some of these conflicts showed themselves in unresolved tensions between generations within families. Often there was a *painful silence* and relatively little communication. A younger generation gave up thinking that their parents could ever grasp the conflicts they had to deal with in their everyday lives in school. They learned to live a double life, never thinking that it might be possible to communicate what was going on for them with an older generation.

Dispossession

According to Bunting:

> The narrative of dispossession gained new force in the 80s amid the collapse of the industries in which the first generation had come to work. Men who had worked long hours in the textiles and steel industry – and had been, arguably, more integrated into white workforces than their taxi-driver and curry-house sons – found themselves redundant.
>
> (Ibid.)

Redundancy can be difficult for families to confront since it undermines the traditional patriarchal authority of fathers who lose the status that comes from working and being the provider for the family. Sometimes this can encourage fathers to be harsher in their discipline, unsure of their own position. They are concerned to insist upon the respect that is still owed to them by the younger generation, who might feel even more alienated and distant from their own families.

It is also significant that the vast majority of Mirpuris adhere to a tradition of Sufi Islam called 'Badawi' that revolves around holy elders known as 'pirs' whose graves becomes shrines and places of pilgrimage. The problem, which has been well known within Muslim circles, is that Barel-wism has particularly struggled to translate itself effectively into British urban life. They are often treated with disdain and this can create its own hurts. The communities have steered clear of the national organisations such as the Muslim Council of Britain. One wry comment at a weekend gathering of young Muslims (16–17 July 2005), repeated by Bunting, is that if Sacranie, a Malawi-born Indian Muslim and a leading figure of the MCB, was visiting the Leeds Barelwis, it is great, but it's probably for the first time. The kids who come to prayers find themselves tightly controlled by the old patriarchal elders, who hire their Urdu-speaking imams from the home village. They do not understand much of what they see or hear, and so drift off to find an Islam that can answer their questions.

As Bunting recognises from her conversations with young Muslims in London:

> A profound disconnection has opened up between the communal experiences of political and economic dispossession and the pious, otherworldly Barelwi traditions. As one Yorkshireman from a Barelwi background, Azhar Hussain, said: 'When I was 17 and went to university and began to take religion more seriously I went to hear the Islamic groups to see which one made the most sense. The Barelwis are not on university campuses; they can't answer those questions.' In the early 90s Arabs told Navid Akhtar, a broadcast journalist from a Barelwis background, that they had spotted a constituency in these disaffected young Muslims; 'They called them the "orphans of Islam",' Akhtar says.
>
> (Ibid.)

Does this suggest that young men brought up with this tradition can feel more *displaced* within their own families, unable to receive the kind of counsel they might need from their parents? With fathers who demand respect and will readily impose their authority on their boys to behave, they might feel themselves identified with fathers they have hardly any relationship with. Not only were their fathers out working all hours when they were young, but they demanded respect and obedience when they were home. This could mean that boys were often left more isolated and alone, unable to ask for help or to show their emotional needs within a strict religious culture where emotions would too easily be regarded as a sign of weakness.[6]

Rather, boys were expected to 'look after themselves' from an early age, as well as provide protection for their younger sisters. Often sisters in the West Yorkshire towns stayed in closer relationship with their mothers, though they had their own issues of language and understanding, especially when they wanted to enjoy some of the freedoms of other girls they knew at school, only to find themselves largely confined to domestic work, helping out with their mothers. The boys were often given a different kind of space for themselves, and were also burdened with a sense of responsibility. They might have had to witness their fathers' subservience and felt that they conceded too easily to the demands of the white culture. They might have been determined to speak out if they were condescended to and used their schooling to affirm a sense of their Muslim masculinities.[7]

As Bunting frames gender issues, putting more stress on the opportunities some young women have been able to claim through education (though this is probably more valid within larger cities):

> To compound the crisis of identity for male teenagers, Muslim girls are thriving with their new-found opportunities in the UK as they pull steadily ahead of their male counterparts at GCSE level and in the numbers going on to higher education.
>
> (Ibid.)

Some young men have found their way through, but often from families that have, for some reason, been able to value education, perhaps because they might have come from more middle-class backgrounds. But often education opportunities were sacrificed for boys who felt they had to earn money to help support their families. At the same time as they feel estranged from their fathers, they can also feel responsible for bringing in money to the family. But it is the *dislocation* they feel, possibly because their families had lived with a myth of return, so that they got used to living in a constant state of impermanence. Though the years went by and parents did not return to their homelands, the stories of return often framed their childhoods. This often discouraged people from learning English so that children often found themselves having to interpret for their families, and so carrying a responsibility that was beyond their years. They knew a different world because they moved between home and ethnically divided schools.[8]

An older generation have been well aware of the threat of extremism. Bunting was told by a Muslim living in a northern town:

> We've been too afraid. There are so many frustrated, angry men who tell me, 'They're doing it in Iraq, why can't we do it to them?' They convince themselves that this is Islamic. I find it frustrating that our community hasn't tackled this. We have to talk to them about these issues – let them get their anger out.
>
> (Ibid.)

This man, who works as a voluntary community worker, will be on the frontline and, as Bunting realises, 'It will be his judgement call as to when he can guide a disorientated, angry young man or whether he has to shop him to the police' (ibid.).

But even if this becomes a matter of individuals, the community worker makes clear that there are so many young men who feel this way that we have to reflect upon the features of uprootedness and displacement that mean that so many seem to identify with other Muslims who are suffering as innocent civilians in Iraq; and so identifying with the victims where 'them' seems to become the British or the whites. Growing up in towns and cities where 'British' is often identified with whiteness, and where 'Asian' and 'Muslim' are framed as *oppositional identities*, young men seem to rarely acknowledge that they can be 'Muslim', 'Asian' and 'British'. When it is pointed out to them that they might eat fish and chips and burgers as much as Asian food, or that they take for granted freedoms that they only have in this country because they were 'born here' and claim to be 'British' – and, in any case, they often feel easiest speaking English, more so than Punjabi – they often resist concluding that this means they are 'British' in any way. Even though they might sometimes define themselves as 'British Muslims', this is not recognised as a way of defining a particular way of 'being British' but often as a way of refusing to acknowledge that they can identify with 'British' at all.[9]

Belongings

For his contemporaries on the street, 22-year-old Shehzed Tanweer, known as 'Kaki', was well-known and well-liked. They did not see him as 'different' in any way from the rest of them, at least as far as they knew. As one man in a group outside the King Kebab takeaway said: 'He was the best lad. Everybody liked him.' 'He was gentle' and 'he got on with everybody'. Ameer, a younger boy in a nearby park, could 'definitely not believe it was Kaki' (*Time*, 25 July 2005: 33), although the evidence suggests otherwise. But if these young people had no suspicion of what had been going on, they understood and identified with so many of the angers and frustrations that their parents had little understanding of. Understanding had been in short supply, even within families. Khaliq Ahmed, a taxi-driver in Leeds, mused: 'I'm British, you know. I live here. If I had to fight, I'd fight for my country. But my son, he's 18, and you know what he did? He had the word 'Pakistan' tattooed on his hand' (ibid.: 34). He went on to say: 'There is definitely something about the younger generation. They feel under attack and I don't know why.'

This marks a rift between generations, for supposedly his son would not say 'I'm British' and, even though he might say that he 'lives here', he would not feel, in the way his father does, that this means he in any way belongs here. Rather, he is more likely to identify as a 'Muslim', even if he is not particularly religious, who identifies with 'brothers' and 'sisters' of the wider Muslim community of the Uhman. But if he does not believe that he belongs in Pakistan, which might be where his father comes from, he identifies with it in a way that shocks his father, who cannot understand the tattoo on his hand. It is a bodily marking that is permanent and which shows a commitment in an otherwise uncertain world of belongings. It is not as if the younger generation wants to belong here, even though they acknowledge they have been born here and are living here. They feel as if they have long been ignored within their own Muslim communities, let alone within the larger world where they witnessed so many people marching against the war. Now they are ignored by Blair's government that was determined to go ahead with a war that has cost the lives of so many Muslim brothers and sisters, where they were ready to lie about WMD to persuade people to support the war effort and do not care enough to have detailed figures about the numbers of innocent civilians who have died in Iraq. Their experiences seem to *prove* that the lives of Muslims are definitely worth less than the lives of whites. How can they 'belong' to a country that is ready to do this?[10]

For the friends of Tanweer on the street, such actions just confirm their diagnosis of the ills of Western society. It is as if they have decided some time back that they did not want to have anything to do with it. Rather, they often feel that the West has been at war with Muslims since 9/11 so that, in a sense, it is at war with them too, since they identify themselves as Muslims. They might be bewildered by Tanweer's actions, but they will readily speculate about what motivates him. They understood too easily what might have led young people like themselves to do such terrible things. One young man in Beeston thought the roots lay 'in the persecution of Muslims worldwide' and the slaughter of innocents in Palestine and Iraq. 'Wouldn't you want to fight if you saw your brotherhood, children and babies attacked?' he asked (ibid.: 35).

This view is not limited to Leeds and the northern towns. In Southall Broadway, West London, Sarfraz Hussein, 24, who helps his uncle run the Kashmir Karahi restaurant, explains that

> People here are getting angry because of what's happening in other countries, such as Afghanistan and Iraq. For years now, no one has been listening to the Muslims. They're trying to get out a message because they've suffering so much and no one is listening. And that's why [the bombers] probably thought, 'We've got no other way to get our message across'. Ordinary people just got caught up.
>
> (Ibid.)

But Hussein knows this cannot be the answer. 'You have to think what has the bombing changed? It hasn't driven the Israelis out of Palestine, it hasn't solved anything in Iraq. It's just made it worse for the British people,' he says. 'Now if I go and apply for a job, employers might think, 'We don't want this person, he's a terrorist' (ibid.).

It is the nature of the suffering that comes through an identification with Muslim brothers and sisters in other lands that is difficult for a rationalist modernity, shaped within the terms of the nation state, to comprehend. Why should young people care so much for their co-religionists, especially when they are living lives as British Muslims who should be thinking about ways they can integrate into a multicultural Britain? Surely if you are 'British', you should identify with the freedoms that you have in your own country and appreciate the responsibilities of citizenship?

It reminds me of people in Britain during the war who thought it somehow irrational for British Jews to be so worried and concerned about the fate of Jews within Nazi-dominated Europe. They felt uneasy about these feelings, as if it were a threat to the loyalty they 'should feel' to the country they were living in. They wanted to insist that they have nothing more in common with their 'co-religionists' than Christians might have with Christians in Europe. They could not accept a notion of 'peoplehood' that could cross national boundaries and so amount to a transnational identity. They also knew that, in the First World War, there were German and British Jews fighting against each other in different armies. They wanted to feel that your primary identification is with your country and that 'religious' identities within a tradition of Enlightenment rationalism were a matter of individual belief alone. In the modern era, religion is largely treated with anxiety and suspicion, because it is seen as a potential source of division and conflict. This is why it is often safest if regarded as a matter of private concern.[11]

Identifications

A younger generation of Muslims have learned to identify with the sufferings of Muslims at the hands 'of the West' in Afghanistan, Iraq, Chechnya and Kashmir. They have learned to identify across the boundaries of the nation state that no longer define the shape of their care and concern. Rather, it was because of the wars they see the West being engaged in against Muslims that they find it impossible to identify with the towns and cities where they live. As far as they are concerned, these spaces are where they live and make their lives, but in so sense define who they are or what sufferings they are concerned with. Rather, they feel guilt and shame because of the sufferings that are caused by their own governments in the West, so they can feel a special sense of *responsibility* to do something about it.

Since they feel nobody is listening to what they have to say, they take action against the 'infidels' in order that governments in the West realise they are not invulnerable but can be made to suffer too. Young people can get drawn into taking actions against 'an enemy' of Islam where they are doing things for the sufferings of other 'brothers and sisters'. They are focused upon hurting others defined as 'infidels' so that they can make people realise the suffering that their governments are causing, without recognising that it is people who will die and suffer. They enter an imaginary space where they are also sacrificing their own lives so that, if others are also made to suffer, so be it – but at least they recognise what so many other innocent Muslims are being made to suffer.[12]

As Jonathan Freedland recognised: 'the suicide bomber represents a unique kind of threat; an enemy that does not fear being captured or killed is always bound to be more potent' (*Guardian*, 13 July 2005: 21). Once an example has been set and a barrier broken, others can surely follow in their wake. The fact that their property and identity cards were discovered at the sites suggests they *wanted* to be known and that they were somehow proud of what they are doing. This should hardly be surprising since the suicide bomber aims to be a martyr who, in Islamic traditions they hold to, will go directly to heaven to be rewarded there. If it had been a foreign cell, like that responsible for the Madrid bombing, we could have comforted ourselves that this was an external phenomenon, an alien intrusion. But since the threat has come from within, from young people who on the surface of things seem no different from their friends, it feels so much more threatening. It will not be so easy to draw lines between 'moderates' and 'extremists' as authorities hope.

As Freedland wrote: 'Of course, this burden cannot fall on Muslims alone. The realisation that Britons are ready to bomb their fellow citizens is a challenge to the whole of society' (ibid.). But it is not clear that this younger generation of young Muslims regarded themselves as 'fellow citizens'. Dlpazier Aslam, who describes himself as 'a Yorkshire lad, born and bred', insists that we should do ourselves a favour and not act shocked, because we have been warned many times that an attack was inevitable:

> Shocked would be to suggest we didn't appreciate that when Falluja was flattened, the people under it were dead but not forgotten – long before we had moved on to reading more interesting headlines about the Olympics. It is not the done thing to make such comparisons, but Muslims on the streets do. Some 2,749 people were killed in the 9/11 attacks. To discover the cost of 'liberating' Iraqis you need to multiply that figure by eight, and still you will fall short of the estimated minimum of 22,787 civilian Iraqi casualties today. But it's not cool to say this, now that London's skyline has also has plumed grey.
>
> (Ibid.)

Blair has insisted – and the government has generally followed his line – that the London bombings could have nothing to do with the sufferings and injustices in Iraq. Rather, it has to do with an 'evil ideology' that has somehow taken over the minds of young people and needs to be 'rooted out'. But Aslam suggests:

> Shocked would also be to suggest that the bombings happened through no responsibility of our own. OK, the streets of London were

filled with anti-war marchers, so why punish the average Londoner? But the argument that this was essentially a US-led war does not pass muster. In the Muslim world, the pond that divides Britain and America is a shallow one. And the same cry – why punish us? – is often heard from Iraqi mothers as the 'collateral damage' increases daily.

(Ibid.)

Also speaking of shock, Robin Cook, former Foreign Secretary in Blair's government, recognised that

one day of terrorist atrocity shocked our nation, altered our political priorities, and has dominated comment.
   Yet it is an awful fact of life in Iraq that every day brings a comparable toll of violent death and broken families. In the 10 days following the London bombings there have been no fewer than 30 suicide bombings in Iraq. In one single attack, a hundred people were killed when a fuel tanker was blown up near a crowded market.

(*Evening Standard*, 19 July 2005: 13)

He added:

It is plain to all but the most blinkered that the US military are deluded in their faith that they will win if only they can bury enough insurgents beneath the rubble of Iraqi homes.
   The Iraqi health ministry reveals that as recently as January deaths from US military were still running at almost double the rate from suicide bombers. The more Iraqis are killed by occupying forces, the greater are the recruits of the insurgency.

(Ibid.)

Dilpazier Aslam says that young Muslims understand all this, and therefore we should not be shocked to discover that 'in the green hills of Yorkshire, a group of men given all the liberties they could have wished for could do this'. He wants us to understand the Muslim community is no monolithic whole, but that generally 'Second-and-third generation Muslims are without the don't-rock-the-boat attitude of that restricted our forefathers. We're much sassier with our opinions, not caring if the boat rocks or not.' This explains why the young so easily get angry with that breed of Muslim 'community leader' who remains silent while anger is seething on the streets. He recalls:

I prayed my Eid prayer in a mosque in Sheffield and, though most there were sickened and angry about events in Iraq, the imam chose not to mention Falluja either. We 'youngsters' – some now in our 40s

– had seen it before. This was deliberate silence, in case the boat rocked.

Perhaps now is the time to be honest with each other and to stop labelling the enemy with simplistic terms such as 'young', 'under-privileged', 'undereducated' and perhaps even 'fringe'. The don't-rock-the-boat attitude of elders doesn't mean the agitation wanes; it means it builds till it can be contained no more.

(*Guardian*, 13 July 2005: 21)

But what does one say to young Muslims whose anger is understandable and justified? It is not enough just to say that they have misunderstood Islam or that they have somehow been brainwashed because they do not know their own minds. Nor is it enough to say that this is not Islam. Issues remain about how they can channel their anger into political action within a democratic politics and how they can feel their voices are being understood in all their diversity. We have to recognise and validate their sense of injustice rather than to minimise it through categorically denying that the London bombings have nothing to do with the injustices people feel about Afghanistan and Iraq. We have to recognise and learn to respect the diverse transnational loyalties citizens carry within a cosmopolitan polity in ways that help to redefine the nation state and its traditional conceptions of national politics.

At the same time, we also have to understand the impact of globalisation and transnational politics in the remaking of political identities and identifications within complex urban multicultures and postmodern societies. As part of a critical multiculturalism we also have to appreciate the place of new religious identities that cross national boundaries and create identification and anger that question traditional political frameworks of the nation state and so transnational notions of citizenship and belonging. Not only does this question ways traditionally secular modern societies have engaged with religions as a private concern to do with individual subjective belief, but it forces disciplines in the social sciences and humanities to rethink the relationships of religion, migration and diasporic difference(s) and diversities within a new global democratic politics. Not only does this mean learning how to think transnational affiliations across boundaries of local and global, but it involves learning how to engage in transcultural conversations across religious and secular civilisations in ways that call for new philosophical frameworks.

8 Global terror, Islam and citizenships

Global terror

Globalisation and the 'war on terror' pursued in the wake of 9/11 oblige us to rethink the frameworks of classical social theory set within the terms of the nation state. It also forces us to revise the notion of the 'international' that has so often been imagined as a relationship between nation states. Following through different identifications of a 'war against terror' as a 'war against Islam', this chapter explores different explanations of the London bombings as a response to global injustices. In his first interview since the London bombings of 7 July 2005, Shiek Omar Bakri Mohammed, who had until recently led the al-Muhajiroun group in Britain, denounced the London bombings but insisted that Britain had brought the atrocity on itself:

> The British people did not make enough effort to stop its own government committing its own atrocities in Iraq and Afghanistan.
> They showed Tony Blair full support when they elected him Prime Minister again, even after he waged the latest war against Iraq.
> (*Evening Standard*, 19 July 2005: 1)

He said Britain had failed to learn lessons from 9/11 and from the Madrid bombings last year. He suggested that, if they had not supported the US, they would not have been such an obvious target themselves. Mr Choudary, a close associate of Bakri Mohammed, told the *Evening Standard* that the 'real terrorists' are the British 'regime' and police for trying to divide the Muslim community into moderates and extremists. He said no such distinction existed in Islam, adding: 'Either you are a practising Muslim or a non-practising Muslim.' He added: 'I believe another 7/7 is a very real possibility. The concept of self-sacrifice operations is as old as the divine text' (Ibid.: 1, 4).[1]

He also seemed to blame the country's mainstream Muslim leaders for seemingly failing to distinguish between the rights and wrongs of suicide bombings at home and abroad. This is a theme that has been at the edge of discussion in the wake of the London bombings, as some Muslim activists seem reluctant to morally condemn suicide bombers in Israel/Palestine where they say there is a different 'context' that needs to be appreciated. This seems to be the position of Al-Qaradawi, who was invited by Ken Livingston to City Hall last year. The Mayor said Al-Qaradawi had called the London attacks 'evil acts characterised by barbarity and savagery which are condemned in Islam'.

Mr Livingston said, 'You couldn't be stronger in your condemnation.' He said it would be wrong to say Al-Qaradawi supported suicide bombers, adding:

> Given that the Palestinians don't have jet fighters and don't have tanks, they only have their bodies to use as weapons. In that unfair balance, that is what people use. I don't think he is urging people to go out and become suicide bombers.

He added: 'The consistent double-standards about the Middle East has created disaffection with youths' (*Evening Standard*, 19 July 2005: 4). If this is true about disaffection, it remains open whether people should be taught that suicide bombings against innocent civilians is never morally justified, even if it is what people might feel obliged to do in particular conflicts. This was the position supposedly endorsed by Islamic scholars across a range of traditions who declared on 19 July 2005 that suicide bombing is not martyrdom, but a criminal act. But it is unclear what status such a declaration might have and how it might be interpreted by different generations. Al-Qaradawi might take the position that British Muslims are in a very different political situation from Palestinian refugees, but for many it will be his vindication of suicide bombing that counts.[2]

Tony Blair has pressed upon Muslim communities to confront the 'perverted and poisonous' doctrines of Islamic extremism that he wants to insist has 'nothing to do with Islam'. He warned MPs on Wednesday 13 July 2005 that international cooperation would be needed to 'pull up this evil ideology by its roots'. So it seems the position is to declare an 'evil ideology' that can somehow be dealt with separately and independently of the reformation of different traditions of Islam. Mr Blair repeatedly stressed at Question Time that most Muslims shared the wider society's disdain for terrorists acting on a 'perverted and poisonous misrepresentation' of Islam. He had told the Commons that the bombers had emerged from 'a small group of extremists. Not one that can be ignored because of the danger they pose. But neither should it define Muslims in Britain who are overwhelmingly law-abiding, decent members of our society' (*Guardian*, 14 July 2005: 3).

This was a sentiment widely shared in the face of the bombings, as communities in London insisted on coming together in Trafalgar Square to express their insistence that they would not be divided or turn against each other. At the vigil held exactly a week after the bombings, in an evening that followed a widely supported two minutes of silence at mid-day across European cities, Ken Livingstone, visibly moved by the scene, said in London: 'you see the world gathered in one city, living in harmony, as an example to all.' Around him were banners haling 'London United' and that was his message. The bombers hoped 'we would turn on each other like animals in a cage,' he said, 'and they failed.' Chief Rabbi Jonathan Sachs said, 'Grief is the language we speak today and let that grief unite us now.'

When the leader of the Muslim Council of Britain, Sir Iqbal Sacranie, took the podium, as Jonathan Freedland described the scene:

> the applause rang out before he had opened his mouth – the crowd's way of saying that it wanted no backlash against British Muslims, no blind lust for revenge.
>
> As the mayor put it, Londoners wanted to forge a better city from this tragedy. Not to 'worry about who to blame and who to hate'.
>
> (*Guardian*, 15 July 2005: 1)

New terrorisms

Richard Aldrich argues that, since 9/11, the world of secret intelligence has been focused on the 'new' terrorism but

> in retrospect, it turns out that the 'new' terrorism is not all that new. After 9/11 we were told that fundamentalists were not interested in bargaining and simply wanted to kill for the sake of killing. In reality, the timings of the bombings of Madrid and the recent attacks on London have been highly political.
>
> (*Independent on Sunday*, 10 July 2005: 28)

He recognises that pre-empting the so-called 'new' terror has been a US-led intelligence doctrine. As he explains: 'Its hallmark has been to focus on "states" of concern, on particular groups and on "getting" individuals. In fact important developments have been at a deeper level, involving networks, connections processes' (ibid.).

What is most troubling about the 'new' terrorism is its new context of being embedded within an accelerated globalisation that is working to make developed states more fragile. Because global trade has expanded unevenly, and because global communications have offered profound cultural provocations to some groups and new ways of spreading their messages, Aldrich argues globalisation is making terrorism easier to practice 'shifting the balance of advantage away from states in favour of terrorists'. Through the Internet, with 36 billion emails a day – and the number set to double every two years – people can seek out information and establish networks that have become increasingly difficult to interrupt.[3]

Young Muslim men estranged from their own families and communities can withdraw into their rooms as soon as they come home and they have access to a whole variety of Jihadist sites and networks. Within virtual space they can sustain different identities as they learn to identify with other spaces, feeling so displaced from their own. The fact that they are living in West Yorkshire becomes strangely irrelevant as they identify themselves with global Muslim networks. Local identities become *replaced* as people learn to think of themselves as Muslims who carry responsibilities for the sufferings of their brothers and sisters. Young men can be so used to living a 'double life' in their families that there is little problem in maintaining secret identities with others they might otherwise trust.

Politicians in the West often look towards intelligence-led approaches to break into these networks, and expect that their secret services will have access to relevant information that will allow these networks to be broken. As Aldrich explains:

> It allows for some escape from responsibility as all sorts of problems can often be attributed to 'intelligence failures'. The real intelligence failure here is a weak understanding of the nature of intelligence. Intelligence is quite good at finding out what has happened recently. It is not much good at predicting the future.'
>
> (Ibid.)

For Aldrich, the problem is not one of simply balancing security and freedom because we also have to deal with the pernicious side-effects of globalisation: 'The problem was balancing security, freedom and the globalising quest for luxury. In this complex three-way trade off, luxury was often the dominant factor' (ibid.).

Aldrich questions those who would still believe that it is acceptable to be in public space, or in cyberspace, and to remain faceless:

> In fact, throughout history, the hidden face, in a balaclava or a hood, has been intimidating. By contrast, human interaction based on honest, open and reliable identification has a superior and uplifting quality. Civil society is encouraged when people are known and can be held accountable for their actions.
>
> (Ibid.)

He wants to insist that misplaced anxieties about identification have been persistent and that 'ID cards will erode anonymity, but if they are set up correctly, should not make serious inroads into privacy'.

At the same time, he recognises: 'Curiously, ID cards, like passports are a rather old-fashioned concept. The technology might be futuristic, but the concept harks back to an old world of real borders and sovereign states.' But the globalised world we now inhabit, policed by neo-liberal internationalism, 'has meant projecting our values, sometimes through armed intervention.' We have had to make the world secure for globalisation that has meant securing resources like oil. But, as Aldrich realises, 'Such projections are a two way street. The corollary is that unpalatable groups will intervene in our own country and allow us to taste their values in return' (ibid.).

Lord Stevens, the former Metropolitan Police Commissioner, warned that the London bombers were unlikely to fit the caricature of al-Qaida fanatics from some backward village in Algeria or Afghanistan. They were more likely to be 'apparently ordinary British citizens, young men conservatively and cleanly dressed and probably with some higher education. Highly computer literate, they will have used the internet to research explosives, chemicals and electronics' (quoted in the *Guardian*, 13 July 2005: 23).

This observation resonated with a letter by the former editor of the *Sunday Telegraph*, Peregrine Worsthorne, that somehow helped to provide a historical context:

> Surely it is possible for a Muslim fundamentalist quite reasonable to see President Bush's aim of making the whole world safe for democratic capitalism as no less a mortal threat to his traditional way of life, or his traditional sacred values, as we saw the threats from Stalin and Hitler, or even from the Kaiser and Napoleon, as a mortal threat to our ways of life or sacred values. Once that effort of imagination is made, Muslim terrorism becomes understandable, not so much as a rational act to turn back the irresistible forces of modern capitalism, but rather as a form of madness which has many historical precedents – particularly in the cause of national self-determination – many of which posterity applauds.
>
> In any case, it may be relevant to remember that only quite recently western foreign policy envisaged thermonuclear destruction of the entire human race rather than risk the spread of communism. Having quite happily countenanced that MAD idea myself – better dead than red – I feel bound in conscience at least to give today's extremists the benefit of the doubt.
>
> (*Guardian*, letters, 12 July 2005: 23)

This is to question the idea that the 'new' terrorism has no rationality of its own, but is driven out of sheer hatred for Western democratic values and ways of life. As Bush framed the 'war on terror' after 9/11, it was because of their 'irrational' envy and hatred for the West that Islamist groups were targeting the West and trying to cause as much death and destruction as possible. But, as Jonathan Freedland has written:

> al-Qaida has a programme that predates and goes beyond Iraq. It seeks to end all western presence in those lands it deems Islamic....

When Tony Blair asks 'What was September 11 the reprisal for?' he should know the answer. It was for eight decades of US-led, western meddling in territory that al-Qaida believes should be Muslims' alone.

This is the ideology that defines al-Qaida and which explains why it was in business from 1993 and not just 2001 and after. Tellingly, those who monitor Islamism in Britain say the big surge in growth of extremist groups came not after 9/11 or Iraq, but in the mid-1990s – with Bosnia serving as the recruiting sergeant. In the same period Chechnya, Kosovo and Israel–Palestine all came into play – again pre-dating Iraq.

(*Guardian*, 20 July 2005: 21)

Although Blair has wanted to insist that the invasion of Iraq had nothing to do with the London bombings, it is clear from a *Guardian* ICM poll that 64 per cent of Britons disagreed, and they see the PM's decision on Iraq as bearing some responsibility for the London bombings. A Chatham House report also declared on Monday 18 July 2005 that the Iraq war had given a 'boost' to al-Qaida – though Jack Straw sought to drown its message through declaring on the same day 'The time for excuses for terrorism is over' (ibid.). But he can hardly deny that Britain's own intelligence services predicted just such a causal link, warning that the threat from al-Qaida would be 'heightened' by an invasion. There is also no doubt that the Iraq War has also served to anger and radicalise a generation of young Muslims across the globe.

But the government's insistence that there is no connection is bound to affect the ways it assesses the dangers that the country faces through the 'new' terrorism, and also the ways it chooses to deal with it. It might explain an external focus upon extremist imams who can somehow be held responsible so that their eventual exclusion from the UK can seem to return us to a space of relative safety. There is also a tendency to explain the 'brainwashing' of the bombers through the contacts they had in visiting madrasas in Pakistan. Of course, it is crucial to reveal global networks, but we also have understand the sufferings and injustices that also help to radicalise young Muslims in the first place.[4]

Fresh evidence emerged on Tuesday 19 July 2005 that the government had been privately warned by the intelligence services that the conflict in Iraq could provoke terrorist acts in Britain and compound anger among young British Muslims. Sections of the report by the Joint Terrorist Analysis Centre (JTAC) were published by the *New York Times*. A link between the government's foreign policy and disillusion among young Muslims – strenuously denied by ministers – was also made in a paper prepared for Blair by orders of the Home and Foreign Secretaries last year. The paper, 'Young Muslims and Extremism', which included input from the security services, said British foreign policy 'seems a particularly strong cause of disillusionment amongst Muslims, including young Muslims'. It referred to 'a perceived "double standard" in the foreign policy of western governments ... in particular Britain and the US'.

The report says 'The perception is that passive "oppression", as demonstrated by British foreign policy eg non-action on Kashmir and Chechnya has given way to "active oppression."' The 'war on terror', Iraq and Afghanistan were all seen by sections of British Muslims as being acts against Islam. 'This disillusionment many contribute to a sense of helplessness with regard to the situation of Muslims in the world, with a lack of any tangible "pressure valves", on order to vent frustration, anger or dissent,' said the paper. As I write this, on Thursday 21 July 2005, I have just returned from watching on TV another incident in Central London that seemed to involve young men with rucksacks detonating explosions, at Warren Street, Shepherd's Bush and the Oval as well as on a number 26 bus on Hackney Road.

The attacks seem to have been coordinated in time, in some way copying the attacks two weeks ago also on Thursday and showing the vulnerability of the public transport system in London to attack. With London still in a state of fear, with people returning to the tubes and buses, there will be considerable anger if the young men are caught. I fear for the community relations within the city that have already been severely tested. Again it is from calls from abroad that we were initially alerted, but thankfully I had already heard that my partner Anna, who was passing through Warren Street just an hour before the explosion, before her sister called from Sao Paulo, Brazil. She was safe with a friend in Covent Garden and was alerted to an incident through someone calling from the United States. It is as if the world is still nervous from the previous attacks and so many people are watching London with anxiety.

(Dis)connections

In a piece entitled 'It is an insult to the dead to deny the link with Iraq', Seumas Milne pointed out the 'wilful and dangerous refusal to face up to reality' so that anyone who 'questioned Tony Blair's echo of George Bush's fateful words on September 11 that this was an assault on freedom and our way of life has been treated as an apologist for terror'. He also recalls that we have been repeatedly told by authoritative sources that an attack on Britain was a certainty. 'The only surprise was that the attacks were so long coming' (*Guardian*, 14 July 2005: 24).

But Blair was insisting that there was no connection as he sought to lay blame on an 'evil ideology' that was a despicable perversion of Islam. George Galloway, who declared that Londoners had paid the price of a 'despicable act', for the government's failure to heed those warning, was accused by defence minister Adam Ingram of 'dipping his poisonous tongue in a pool of blood'. But many people agreed with the connection he was making with Iraq. As Milne recognised: 'Respect for the victims of such atrocities is supposed to preclude open discussion of their causes in the aftermath – but this is precisely when honest debate is most needed.' But as we moved into the second week, the government was increasingly being questioned. It was the government's stubborn refusal to acknowledge a connection that lost it considerable public support. By the time the anniversary of 7/7 came in 2006, it was clear that Blair had become relatively isolated and his premiership was deeply unpopular and estranged from civil society.

Milne believed that it has been government disinformation to insist that 'al-Qaida and its supporters have no demands that could possibly be met or negotiated over; that they are really motivated by a hatred of western freedoms and way of life; and that this Islamist ideology aims at global domination.' But we have to be careful if we acknowledge this possibility, not to *dismiss* an Islamist rejection of the freedoms of Western urban cultures, in relation to consumerism and sexualities. We can at the same time appreciate the rejection of moral relativisms and the focus upon individual moral choice within orthodox religious traditions that have a strong conviction in relation to behaviours and attitudes that are categorically judged as 'good' or 'evil'.

So it is not a simple alternative, as Milne seemed to suggest when he rejected BBC political reporter Andrew Marr's question of whether it was the 'very diversity, that melting aspect of London' that Islamist extremists found so offensive that they wanted to kill innocent civilians in London; instead, favouring Frank Gardner's insistence that 'What they find offensive are the policies of western governments and specifically the presence of western troops in Muslim lands, notably Iraq and Afghanistan' (ibid.). Whatever their objections to Western freedoms, this was not the reason for their actions. They want the withdrawal of Western troops from the Arab and Muslim world and an end of support for the Israeli occupation of Palestine. As even Osama bin Laden asked in his US election-timed video, if it was Western freedoms al-Qaida hated, 'Why do we not strike Sweden?'

The Labour MP Tony Wright has insisted that Blair's idea that the London bombings had nothing to do with Iraq was 'not only nonsense, but dangerous nonsense'. But Seamus Milne thinks that the policies of the US and UK were sufficiently distinct that Britain 'only became a target when Blair backed Bush's 'war on terror'. Afghanistan made a terror attack on Britain a likelihood; Iraq made it a certainty' (ibid.). But this is to ignore British involvement in Bosnia and the aftermath of the 1991 war against Iraq. Britain might have been able to steer a course that was independent of the US, and they might have insisted on framing their own 'war against terror' on different terms that sought the widespread causes of terror within the injustices perpetrated on the Muslim world, but London could still have been a target. Al-Qaida might make political calculations, but Britain has been implicated with US policies in Western strategies for a long time. It might be true that what the London bombers did 'was not "home grown", but driven by a worldwide anger at US-led domination and occupation of Muslim countries' (ibid.), but it remains significant that *they* were 'home grown' and this challenges the ways we understand ourselves in Britain.[5]

If Milne wanted to insist that Blair was also responsible, given the warnings by British intelligence of the risks in the run-up to the war, 'for knowingly putting his own people at risk in the service of a foreign power', he also needed to be careful not to minimise the part that Islamist religious doctrines played. He might have been right that 'Only a British commitment to end its role in the bloody occupation of Iraq and Afghanistan is likely' (ibid.) to extinguish the threat of another attack on London, but we still have to take religious ideologies seriously, in ways Blair does not do through labelling an 'evil ideology' that has nothing to do with Islam.

The questions we face are more complex and involve questioning a reductionist conception of ideology, often informed by an orthodox reading of Marx, that assumes it exists primarily as expressions of material inequalities and social injustices. al-Qaida's religious conservatism and dreams of restoring the medieval caliphate also have to be taken seriously as part of a rejection of what the West has to offer, even if they do not themselves give the chance to recruit young Muslims who feel identified with the suffering of their brothers and sisters in Palestine and Iraq. But they have to be taken seriously as *part of* the narrative, even if they challenge the secular rationalism that has shaped social and political theories in the West. This means that we need to develop social theories that are capable of appreciating both the significance of material interests, such as the part that oil plays in the conflict in Iraq, while at the same time recognising how beliefs and identifications can also inspire people towards action.[6]

As Steve Richards writes, 'Mr Blair's support for the war against Iraq was based largely on a pragmatic calculation about the value of an alliance with the world's only superpower' (*Independent*, 12 July 2005: 27). He insists on the question of how the war against Iraq has made Britain more secure, knowing that Bush and Blair are in no position to argue credibly that the conflict has improved security in the world. This puts the strategy of a 'war against terror' into question and Blair is bound to remain politically vulnerable in the face of the London bombings. But in the early days after the bombings, making any connection between the government's policy on Iraq and terror attacks in Britain at all, as Jackie Ashley realised, 'is apparently beyond the pale, in some strange way it is seen as disrespectful to those who died' (*Guardian*, 14 July 2005: 23). But she also realises:

> The 'war against terror' is unlike any previous war, and may not be winnable in traditional terms. As the Leeds connection shows, it is

genuinely a war without borders.... Far from 'draining the swamp', the Iraq war multiplied the territory available to Islamist extremists.

(Ibid.)

Of course, people understand the insurgents in different ways, and some on the left might insist that the insurgency in Iraq is resistance to allied occupation, more than anything to do with Islam.

But Jackie Ashley insists otherwise, for she argues:

Events in the Middle East have given new excuses to an extreme Islamist doctrine that is as evil as any variant of religious fascism can be. Yes, most Muslims are hostile to the bombers and the radicals, but there is a virulent anti-Semitism and anti-western rhetoric that has to be confronted and opposed.

(Ibid.)

In this way she also challenges Blair and the government line:

'Saying that the bombings have nothing to do with Islam is fatuous – as fatuous as saying that there is no connection between Christians and the anti-abortion militants in the US. It might be a perverted strain of Islam, or one variant of Christianity, but there's a connecting 'of'. This too needs to be honestly and openly debated in parliament, without the nervous thin syrup of evasion.

(Ibid.)

These issues are complex, as she begins to realise, but it does not help to fall into Blair's language of 'perversion' when talking about Islam; rather, we have to recognise diverse traditions, histories and cultures within diverse Islams. If the media is not to usurp the role of the Commons, then people have to realise that 'this is the very worst time for smothering political debate' (ibid.).[7]

(Re)thinking

Hanif Kureishi recognises that many people in the West no longer know what it is to be religious, and have not for a while. 'During the past 200 years sensible people in the west have contested our religions until they lack significant content and force.' He obviously includes himself in this description, and also when he says, 'To us "belief" is dangerous and we don't like to think we have much of it.' But this means

We also have little idea of what it is to burn with a sense of injustice and oppression, and what it is to give our lives for a cause, to be so desperate or earnest. We think of these acts as mad, random and criminal, rather than as part of a recognisable exchange of violences.

(*Guardian*, 19 July 2005: 22)

For Kureishi, this is also a matter of age, for

The burning sense of injustice that many young people feel as they enter the adult world of double standards and dishonesty shocks those of us who are more knowing and cynical. We find this commendable in young people but also embarrassing.

(Ibid.)

But it is also a matter of Western capitalism and the ways it can work to weaken moral and political ideals through the seduction of its own visions of maturity. As Kureishi reflects:

Consumer society has already traded its moral ideals for other satisfactions, and one of the things we wish to export, masquerading as 'freedom and democracy' is that very consumerism – what earlier was referred to as the luxuries of globalisation – though we keep silent about its consequences: addiction, alienation, fragmentation.

(Ibid.)

But he also appreciates how the myths of Iraq as a 'virtual' war have played on the unconscious of people in the West. He explains that 'virtual' wars are

conflicts in which one can kill others without either witnessing their deaths or having to take moral responsibility for them. The Iraq War, we were told, would be quick and few people would die. It is as though we believed that by pressing a button and eliminating others far away we would not experience any guilt or suffering – on our side.

(Ibid.)

This reflects more general processes within consumerist cultures because 'If we think of children being corrupted by video games – imitation violence making them immune to actual violence – this is something that has happened to our politicians'. They come to believe that we can murder real others in faraway places without the same thing happening to us or without any physical and moral suffering on our part. As we come to recognise this weakening and *deafness* to the sufferings of others, we have to learn to speak out and not be deceived by the lies of politicians who would always want to convince us that they are somehow acting in the nation's interest. Unless we are careful, as Kureishi appreciates, 'War debases our intelligence and derides what we have called "civilisation" and "culture" and "freedom".'

If it is true, as Kureishi says, 'that we have entered a spiral of violence, repression and despair that will take years to unravel, our only hope is moral honesty about what we have brought about' (ibid.: 21). We have to learn how to face the consequences of the support we have given to the 'war against terror' and the ways it has been fought in Afghanistan and Iraq. We have to accept the moral consequences of our own actions and also face the anger and violence that has been turned against those in the West that have supported these actions. But Kureishi also realises that

> religious groups have to purge themselves of their own intolerant and deeply authoritarian aspects.
>
> The body hatred and terror of sexuality that characterises most religions can lead people not only to cover their bodies in shame but to think of themselves as human bombs. This criticism on both sides is the only way to temper an inevitable legacy of bitterness, hatred and conflict.
>
> (Ibid.)[8]

John Berger has recognised a similar crisis in the West as he calls for people to also reflect upon the abuses of power and the sufferings they have often unwittingly produced, and have been deaf to for so long. He wants us to listen to the sufferings of those who were caught up in the London bombings for

> People underground are both sheltered and helpless.... To blow to pieces those going to work by public transport is to attack, in shameful stealth, the defenceless. The victims suffer more pain and for far, far longer than the suicide bomber. And such suffering gives them most surely the right to judge.
>
> (*Observer*, 17 July 2005: 26)

But Berger is aware that, before really listening to what the survivors have to say, as happened in New York after 9/11, 'the politicians rush in to speak in their name, while serving their own interests, which involve gross simplifications ... an attempt to justify themselves and their past, however disastrous the errors committed' (ibid.).[9]

Berger points out that the atrocities were planned to coincide with the G8 summit and that

> What happened at that meeting is not another story but another part of the same one.... Fanaticism comes from any form of chosen blindness accompanying the pursuit of a single dogma. The G8's dogma is that the making of profit has to be mankind's guiding principle before

which everything else from the tradition or aspiring future must be sacrificed as an illusion.... Those corporations consistently wage their own 'jihad' against any target that opposes the maximisation of their profit. The war in Iraq was conveniently removed from this year's G8 agenda ...

The so called war against terrorism is, in fact, a war between two fanaticisms. To bracket the two together seems outrageous. One is theocratic, the other positivist and secular.... One sets out to kill, the other plunders, leaves and lets die. One is strict, the other lax. One brooks no argument, the other 'communicates' and tries to 'spin' into every corner of the world....

(Ibid.)

The innocent victims that happened to be travelling in London on the Piccadilly line, the Circle line and the number 30 bus were 'struggling to survive and make sense of their lives, being inadvertently caught in the global cross-fire of these two fanaticisms'.

9   Fears, uncertainties and terrors

Fear

This chapter traces the disturbances that are produced in individual and communal lives when 'events' that people want to identify as exceptional and singular show themselves to be repeatable. Many people in London felt relieved after 7/7 knowing that an 'event' that was expected for so long after New York, Bali and Madrid had finally come to London and, however scary it had been, they had survived it and hopefully could return to some form of 'normal life'. But it was this expectation that was shattered in the shift of mood that took place as urban fears were intensified through the second wave of attempted bombings on the 21 July 2005, exactly two weeks later, again on a Thursday. It proved that others could imitate or copy once an 'event' had taken place.

The fear of terrorism that has been known in London with the IRA bombings had intensified with a realisation that suicide bombers were keen to murder civilians in great numbers as they took their own lives. People realised that life in London had in some crucial ways changed for good. This risks of everyday life in the global city had changed and this was to shape urban subjectivities. As the spirit of defiance began to fade in the wake of the second bombings, it was replaced by fear and uncertainties.[1]

Tim Dowling, on a front page for *Guardian 2* that consisted of a yellow page with the familiar blue and white tape across saying 'POLICE LINE DO NOT CROSS', written two weeks after the London bombings and a little time after the second attempted bombings, entitled his piece with an admission: 'OK, I admit it, I'm scared.' So many people in London had been feeling scared for sometime and talking to each other about ways of avoiding going on the Underground, that the admission seemed to say more about sustaining particular masculine identities in times of fear. He recalls: 'The spirit of the Blitz was invoked shortly after the bombings of Thursday July 7, and it seemed to resonate immediately.' He had been in Paris at the time, so he admits to having been 'merely inconvenienced' but could feel 'united by the idea that getting on with life sent the terrorists the right message'. He also recalls the hastily set-up website – www.werenotafraid.com – that 'became a clearing-house for various expressions of defiance, an almost direct response to the terrorist's online claim of responsibility, which asserted that 'Britain is now burning with fear'' (*Guardian G2*, 26 July 2005: 2).

What is striking is the ease with which the term 'terrorists' is being invoked, as if we clearly know what it means, and as if it did not need to be carefully explored since it could carry so many different kinds of meanings. A more careful response was evident in a letter in the *Guardian* on the same day from Canon Paul Oestreicher, who so often serves as a moral conscience in difficult times. He reminds us:

> Language betrays us. When the *Sun* talks of hunting terrorists, no surprise. When that has become the language of BBC reporting and even of the *Guardian*, it is time to stop and think. Language not only reflects a mood but creates it. To speak of hunting human beings, even the most despised, is to embrace the violence we rightly denounce. For our police to be both effective and human is a daunting task. Hunters they are not.
>
> (*Guardian*, 26 July 2005: 23)

In the week following 7/7, things did seem to be getting 'back to normal', with tourist numbers beginning to recover. Despite warnings from the security services, people wanted to believe that London had had its attack and so could join New York and Madrid as capital cities that had withstood the blows of al-Qaida so that it would be a good while before, as Dowling frames it, 'terrorists dared to test our vigilance again' (*Guardian G2*, 26 July 2005: 2). But it was not to be, for on midday that Thursday, exactly two weeks after the initial bombings – as Jonathan Freedland recalls:

> Initial word suggested a macabre rerun of that fateful day: four explosions, three trains and a bus, one blast for each point of the compass around the centre of London.
>
> The pattern looked identical, so Londoners repeated their own behaviour, as if weary veterans of this new form of urban warfare. They texted their friends and family; they picked up snippets of news from portable radios or the internet; they cut short their working day and left offices in mid-afternoon for a journey on foot they knew could take several hours.
>
> (*Guardian*, 22 July 2005: 3)

But if the ritual was a repeat, the mood was different. As Freedland reports, 'Much was made of the stoicism of Londoners on July 7, an unruffled calm exhibited even by those who narrowly escaped the attacks.' But it was no longer like that. Witnesses at the Oval station and elsewhere said that once they heard the sound of an explosion, or breathed in the acrid smell of smoke, passengers fell rapidly into a collective panic. They knew to fear the worst and their senses were attuned quite differently. They had not expected for there to be repeat bombings, but they also carried the fear that there might well be and that anyone who was on a tube or bus could be a target. Caitlin Jackson, 22, was at Leicester Square station as it was being evacuated, as the system was closed down after events at Warren Street, the Oval and Shepherd's Bush and the bus on Hackney Road: 'I never saw people move as fast as that in my life. Everybody was quiet, it was all silent. But they had that panicked look on their faces' (ibid.).

Freedland tries to make sense of the different responses: 'Perhaps on July 7 the sheer surprise of the attacks numbed Londoners' reactions. The memory of that day and the fear that they were about to experience an equally lethal rerun, seems to have had the opposite effect yesterday' (ibid.). Though at 7/7 they had not initially seen images of the destruction beneath ground, as time went on there were the release of images from mobile phones and first-hand accounts of the horrors witnessed. People had empathised with an acute sense that it could so easily have been them or at least people they knew well. Everyone had heard a story of what seemed like a 'near miss', so that people's senses had *absorbed* some of the terrors as well as the sense of loss that had been shared almost daily as families had to come to terms with the deaths of family and friends, and the details of people's lives were shared in the newspapers. Private grief became a part of public mourning as people felt it could so easily have been them. The numbers were comprehensible and the losses were not of a scale to overwhelm the senses. Rather, as the individual stories of loss and grief were shared in the following two weeks, people could feel a sense of kinship as they learned about the details of individual lives as they tragically found their way onto the Underground or the number 30 bus on 7/7.

Freedland recalls:

> once the panic subsided, it was not the stubborn resilience of London cliché that was revealed. Instead there was frustration, irritation and a glimpse of the one thing terrorists crave most: fear and a glum recognition that maybe life cannot go on a normal.
>
> (Ibid.)

'Personally, I'm feeling a lot of anxiety; I'm pissed off,' said Martina Leevan, 35, an officer with the Changing Faces charity. That morning she had asked herself whether it was really safe to travel on the Underground. She had decided not. Pointing at her orange trainers, she told me she had, for the first time, done the hour's walk from Bethnal Green instead. 'I'm wondering, is this my life now?'

(Ibid.)

She felt angry, not so much at the politicians or even the terrorists, but at 'the state of the world'.

Her colleague Michelle Bativala agreed. The revelation that one of the July 7 bombers had taught primary schoolchildren had shaken her badly. 'Before you were looking for someone fanatical,' she said. 'Now it could be anyone' (ibid.).

Fear was circulating as people in London were wondering whether it was safe to return to buses and tubes. It is as if the second attempted bombing had changed the situation, so that people could no longer *trust* what the future would bring. Suddenly the future had become uncertain in new ways. Suddenly it was not like New York or Madrid, a sudden event of horror that the city had gradually to accept as part of the narrative it told about itself. London was suddenly in a space all of its own and people did not know what to expect, nor could they look to other examples for guidance. It was difficult to know who could be trusted and even whether the information that was being passed on by the police was completely reliable. As Tim Dowling admitted:

> Since Thursday, carrying on as normal has become rather more diffi-cult. No one was injured in the attacks, but I know people in Shep-herds Bush who weren't allowed to go home for two days. In Kilburn, in Tulse Hill and Stockwell – parts of London previously enveloped in the safety of shaggy anonymity – residents found the anti-terrorists operation had arrived on their doorsteps. If most of us have thus far escaped tragedy, few Londoners remain untouched by fear.
>
> (*Guardian G2*, 26 July 2005: 2)

Tim Dowling admits, 'I can pretty well pinpoint the moment when my own spirit of defiance started to fade.' It was a Saturday morning and he was walking the dog in his local park, Little Wormwood Scrubs, only to find it had suddenly become the site of a massive police operation once the remains of a bomb was found. When he returned home, he was told he was not allowed to leave. The policeman said, 'clearly looking for a phrase to describe the seriousness of the situation without telling us any more than he needed to ... "It's got nails in." That was when my defiance evap-orated' (ibid.). As he says:

> I must admit I'm now afraid; afraid that another attack is imminent, afraid of the idea of 3,000 armed police in the streets, afraid that London will never quite be the same again, afraid that my children will find out how afraid I am (don't worry, they'll never read this far).
>
> (Ibid.)

I am not sure whether it would be such a bad thing if his children knew this because it might help them acknowledge their own fears. Allowing yourself to feel your own fear can help you become clearer about the risks you face, rather than somehow *denying* a fear that your children probably already know about, even if little has been said about it. Many parents instinctively wanted to protect their children from the fear trigged by these events; there were stories about how to talk to children about the events that were unfolding around them. With the development of a therapeutic culture that had acknowledged the failures of a traditional stoicism in the face of events such as the shootings of children in the school in Dunblane, Scotland, and the need for counselling and emotional support for both parents and children, there had been a shift over the past 20 years in how people felt they could face overwhelming events.[2]

Since the 1970s there has been a developing awareness of the significance of emotional literacy and the need for people to discover words that help them express what they are living through. Rather than regarding emotions as a sign of weakness, and so as a threat, particularly to male identities, there has been a realisation that it does no good to 'bottle your feelings up' because, as Freud taught, they have a way of returning as disturbances. People have learned, partly through counselling, the need to share what is going on with them emotionally and have recognised that it *takes time* to come to terms with traumatic events, both in their individual lives but also events in their collective lives. This shift was possibly most evident in the responses to the death of Princess Diana when people came to Kensington Palace in London to share their grief and to participate in rituals of public mourning. Again it was a moment where traditional journalistic accounts failed and people insisted on shaping their own narratives.[3]

Living pretty close to Stockwell tube station had its own special dangers for, as Dowling recalls:

> On Friday, the police shot an innocent Brazilian man in Stockwell station, and the potential for disaster expanded. It's not enough to spot terrorists on the tube, you must take active steps to avoid looking like one. Watching events unfold on television (interspersed with long, defiant stretches of cricket) I had the sense of things getting pretty unpleasantly close to home, and that was before someone left a nail bomb in the park where my children play. I know this hardly compares to the Blitz, in which 43,000 Londoners perished, but I still find the idea of exhibiting pluck in the circumstances oddly draining. I feel lucky, but I don't feel plucky.
>
> (Ibid.)

Threats

Whether we say that the young Brazilian, 27-year-old Jean Charles de Menezes, was shot dead or 'executed' by the police because they thought he was a suicide bomber as he entered the tube at Stockwell station, this was a tragic mistake that harmed the reputation of the police, with Sir Ian Blair initially saying publicly that the police had evidence connecting him to the attacks in London. This turned out to be false – there was no such evidence – and the police admitted that he was completely innocent, though in the days later there were confusing reports about his immigration status, as if this could have made any difference to his killing. A day before, he might have looked like anyone else in multicultural London, but on Friday morning everything was to change. When the police made their announcement, he was transformed into a 'potential terrorist' with evidence supposedly linking him to the bombings in London.

Somehow the police saw a threat – his Puffa jacket could have hidden a bomb, even though many people from abroad feel cold in the English weather. His jacket was deemed suspicious in the new climate of fear. As Gary Young reflects:

> In a world where every brown skin is little more than a 'clean-skin' … (a perpetrator with no history of previous terrorist involvement or affiliation) … waiting to happen, stop and search will inevitably become stop and shoot. The dominant mood that we are better safe than sorry is understandable. But after Friday's incident we are left with one man dead, nobody safe and everybody sorry. If there's one thing we have learnt over the past two years, it's that a pre-emptive strike with no evidence causes more problems than it solves.
>
> (*Guardian*, 25 July 2005: 17)

Somehow this young Brazilian who happened to walk out of the entrance of the block of flats that was shared by many flats, had been framed as a 'possible suicide bomber' by the police who followed him onto a bus that supposedly could have been a target for an attack, all the way to Stockwell station. It was as if his going into the space that had been marked as the starting point for three of the attempted bombings somehow 'proved' that he was a bomber. His big jacket worn in the middle of the summer and 'the way he looked' somehow all confirmed the picture so that when he ran, possibly in fright, from the police, it somehow became their task to shoot before questioning.

But neither of these details turned out to be firmly based. He was wearing a denim jacket, and did not jump over the barriers at Stockwell as the police initially alluded. In the landscape of fear created in the wake of the second round of attempted bombings, the media helped to circulate stories that, for many, seemed to explain, if not justify, the police actions. Now it seems, as Gary Younge surmises, 'Muslims now have to balance their fear of suicide bombers with the fear of a paramilitary-style execution at the hands of London's finest. That the victim was Brazilian will be of little comfort to Muslims' (ibid.). It extends the circle of those who might 'look Muslim' and so fear that they might themselves somehow become targets of the fear that grips the police as well as everyone else in London.

Younge recognises that

> For political and emotional reasons it has been necessary for some to dehumanise the bombers – to eviscerate them of all discernible purpose, cause and motivation. Stripped to their immoral minimal, they are simply 'evil monsters'. But this has its own dangers for in reality we discover from the images that they look like everyone else.
>
> (Ibid.)

This means, as Younge understands:

> If the security services are going to have any chance of infiltrating the bombers they must first humanise those involved. They need to find out what would motivate young men who apparently have so much to live for to die – and kill – in such a manner.
>
> (Ibid.)

But if the police have to dehumanise the 'terrorist', they will fear the potential terrorist and they will 'see them' potentially wherever they might, for whatever reason, suspect them to be. It was suggested that Mr De Menezes aroused suspicion because he was wearing a thick coat which could have concealed explosives and he had emerged from the block of flats, though not *the* flat, that the police were observing.

Others have insisted that his attire was not unusual, given he was from a hot climate, and it was unclear what kind of warning had been issued by the police officers. The police, it is thought, were not wearing uniforms, so he may have panicked, not knowing who they were. His mother told the *Guardian*, in floods of tears:

> I'm begging that the police be punished. It's not fair to kill an innocent worker.
>
> I told him to take care [in England] … but he laughed. 'It's a clean place, mum. The people are educated. There's no violence in England. No one goes around carrying guns. Not even the police.'
>
> (*Guardian*, 25 July 2005: 2)

He had been stopped by the police in the past, said his cousin, Alex Pereira, who said that this was a normal occurrence for young Brazilian men in London. He denied his cousin would have jumped over the barrier. 'Running, maybe. But not running from the police. Everyone runs for the underground. But he wouldn't jump. Why would he jump?' He questioned that De Menezes jumped the turnstile when ordered to halt by the police – and even though there were stories circulating in the media that this was confirmed by a number of people, it turned out that his cousin was right. The friend, who worked as an electrician with Mr Avila, said, 'I think that the police are inventing this thing about the thick jacket' (ibid.). Alex Pereira said, 'He was 100% good guy who never did anything wrong and had no reason to run. What the police have shown is that they are incapable and stupid' (*Guardian*, 25 July 2005: 1).

The Met refused to clarify what had happened but, as the *Guardian* understands, a separate armed unit was called to intercept him. As he entered the tube, officers 'were instructed to effect a "hard stop" – that is, arrest him. When he bolted on to the train, someone decided to shoot him'.

> The Met refused to say yesterday whether the final decision was taken by an officer at the tube station, or whether it was authorised by a 'gold commander' [senior officer] back at the control room, and, if so, at what point.
>
> (*Guardian*, 25 July 2005: 4)

The Metropolitan Police Commissioner later described Mr De Menezes' death as a tragedy and for the first time openly admitted to what is being termed a 'shoot to kill to protect' policy over potential suicide bombers, explaining the necessity of shooting them in the head rather than elsewhere in case the shot triggered any explosives strapped around the body. He admitted 'someone else could be shot' he told Sky News, adding, 'There is no point shooting at someone's chest because that is where the bomb is likely to be' (quoted in the *Guardian*, 25 July 2005: 4). But these explanations created their own fears in London, as there seemed to be so little information that the police were basing their judgements on: he had been at the wrong place and seemed to be wearing a heavy coat in the middle of summer and presumably 'looked suspicious'.

But questions remain. If he was seriously considered a potential suicide bomber, why was he allowed to leave the block of flats in the first place and allowed to board a bus? Why was he not stopped before he entered the station? As Aamer Anwar, a Glasgow-based human-rights lawyer, says:

> I understand the situation where if someone is carrying a bomb and looks as if he is about the detonate it, but this man was followed and chased. On what basis did they shoot to kill? There has to be public accountability.... To think what was going through that man's thoughts in his last moments being executed – five shots – it was an execution, and at the end of the day it is murder? What else could it be called? They shot an innocent man. It is not good enough to say 'we apologise, it's a tragedy'. Tomorrow it could be someone else's father, brother, sister that could be shot in similar circumstances.
>
> (*Guardian*, 25 July 2005: 5)

John Stalker, a former deputy chief constable of Greater Manchester, who headed an inquiry into shoot-to-kill allegations against the RUC in Northern Ireland, reminds us: 'A policeman in that situation is only as good as the information coming through his ear-piece' (ibid.).

The *Guardian* editorial, 'Death of an Innocent Man', also recognised that the unanswered questions are numerous:

> Was it a system failure or an individual at fault? It is usually the former. How good was the intelligence and the analysis that the officers carrying out the surveillance were receiving? ... Why was Mr De Menezes suspected, apart from an inappropriate winter coat, which could have been hiding explosive materials round his waist or chest? .. . On what grounds – and by whom – were the officers following Mr Menezes given the green light to proceed as though he was a terrorist? In precisely what form did the plain-clothes police officers identify themselves as police officers? Could they have been mistaken by Mr De Menezes for terrorists? ...
>
> (*Guardian*, 25 July 2005: 19)

So the question of who 'looks like' a terrorist becomes apparent in different contexts – and becomes threatening when they 'look like everyone else'.

But a day before the funeral was to be held in Brazil, Vivien Figueiredo, 22, a cousin who shared the flat with Jean Charles, revealed, after a meeting with the Metropolitan Police, that De Menezes was not wearing a heavy jacket that might have concealed a bomb. Nor did he jump the ticket barrier when challenged by armed plainclothes police. 'He used a travel card,' she said. 'He had no bulky jacket, he was wearing a jeans jacket. But even if he was wearing a bulky jacket that wouldn't be an excuse to kill him.' Another cousin, Patricia da Silva Armani, 21, said he was in Britain legally to work and study, giving him no reason to fear the police. 'An innocent man has been killed as though he was a terrorist,' she said (*Guardian*, 28 July 2005: 6).

But questions remain about how false stories were allowed to circulate and why they were not corrected by the police sooner. Scotland Yard initially claimed he wore a bulky jacket, that in some reports morphed into an overcoat, and said he had jumped the barrier when police identified themselves and ordered him to stop. On the same day, Sir Ian Blair said the shooting was 'directly linked' to the anti-terrorist operation. Of course it could be convenient to allow these stories to circulate for a while. When the pressure was on from family and friends, we learned about the question of his legal status, different stories emerging from different departments of state but enough for doubts to be raised. In a landscape of fear, it is difficult to discern the validity of what is being reported and urban myths circulate so much faster in the heated atmosphere. The police were slow to admit they had made a tragic mistake, and even though the family insisted that someone in the chain of command needs to be held responsible, there were to be no prosecutions of the officers directly involved or of others who might have carried overall responsibility. In the end, there were only to be charges on the basis of health and safety regulations and these were resisted by Scotland Yard.[4]

Birnberg Pierce, lawyers acting for the family, mounted a legal challenge against the decision not to charge individual officers involved in the shooting. A letter they sent to the Crown Prosecution Service say the prosecutors should have considered a charge of murder, 'or at the very least gross negligence manslaughter ... the choice of the health and safety charge falls foul of the reasoning'. They insist that 'Moreover the fundamental question of how the operation, which it was understood was intended to stop and detain Mr de Menezes, became one which resulted in him being stopped and killed has not been answered' (*Observer*, 1 October 2006: 7). In addition, they applied for a separate judicial review against the decision not to disclose the Independent Police Complaints Commission report into the shooting to the De Menezes family. The report catalogues a number of 'operational errors' that led to the mistaken shooting.

In a letter, the family's lawyer refers to the lack of witnesses among tube passengers to corroborate claims that officers shouted 'armed police' before they began shooting. The letter says that a jury might conclude that the officers 'did not honestly hold the belief that at the time they saw him (whatever they had been erroneously told earlier) he was a suicide bomber about to act'. It adds that the CPS was wrong to 'conclude that a jury would not be likely to reject self-defence on the basis that Mr de Menezes was forced back into his seat and restrained before he was shot – which again evidences a usurping of their function.' The Birnberg Pierce letter also says that no justification has been offered by CPS lawyers for the 'excessive force' used in the killing of Mr De Menezes. A spokesman for the family said, 'We are bringing these juridical reviews because we believe the IPCC and CPS have failed their responsibilities. The criminal justice system's response has been a complete failure' (ibid.).

Threatening 'normal lives'

After the July 7 attacks, a group calling itself the Secret Organisation of the al-Qaida Jihad in Europe posted a claim of responsibility on an Islamist website, declaring: 'The heroic mujahideen carried out a blessed attack in London, and now Britain is burning with fear and terror, from north to south, east to west.' The attempted bombings that followed at Warren Street, Shepherd's Bush, the Oval and the bus on Hackney Road followed the same pattern and seemed to have the same objective. Quite soon after, it was clear there was no loss of life, Tony Blair appealed on TV for people go about their 'normal lives' without being intimidated or looking for scapegoats. 'It is important that we respond by keeping to our normal lives and doing what we want to do because to do otherwise is in a sense to give them the very thing they are looking for,' he told reporters. He insisted that what these people want is 'to intimidate people and to scare them and to frighten them to stop them going about their normal business'. Again he denied that the attacks were a consequence of UK involvement in the occupation of Iraq, insisting 'What they want us to do is to turn round and say "Oh it's our fault". The people who are responsible for the terrorist attacks are the terrorists' (*Guardian*, 22 July 2005: 2).

Massoud Shadjareh of the Islamic Human Rights Commission responded to the second wave of bombings by saying, 'It is very unclear what has happened, but it is very worrying. It was bad enough what happened two weeks ago and we don't want any escalation' (ibid.). He reported that hostile incidents against Muslims had increased a great deal since the July 7 bombings: 'And that, of course, is only the number we are told about. This is not going to be helpful.' A spokesman for the Islamic Society of Britain said:

> We're all very shaken. This is not going to make anything easier for our community which has already been under an intense spotlight.
>   'We feel like [we are] on an ocean with no sign of the shore and we are going farther into the ocean. We don't know what to do. It's all too much.
>
> (*Guardian*, 22 July 2005: 2)

'Are we getting used to this?' asked Zekria Rahman, who runs the Pacific Net Café on Shepherd's Bush Green, 'I hope not.' Customers at his café were evacuated after the discovery of an explosive device at the Hammersmith and City line station at Shepherd's Bush. He told Duncan Campbell, reporting for the *Guardian*, 'If it happens again we will be looking at something very serious and if there are many more of these it will be very bad for London.' There had been no panic when police told people to leave the area, but then these people had not been caught underground. Trevor George, who works in IT at White City, was one of the few passengers walking through the station. 'We had this with the IRA and got accustomed to being more aware of things on the underground,' he said.

'What's happened now is a reminder, a wake-up call. I'm not relaxed about it but like all people I think the safest place is home. I'll still go to work' (*Guardian*, 22 July 2005: 5). It is as if *home* has been given a new significance as people see it as a refuge from a city that feels under attack. Often people are choosing to stay home whenever they can and are altering their lives accordingly.

Lisa McEvoy, 42, says, 'I won't go in the front carriage of a tube train', while Alan, an actor, reports:

> I'm getting buses not tubes when travelling alone, getting cabs if I'm in a group and regularly – almost too regularly – checking the news. And I'm feeling irrational anger with people who I feel aren't playing by the rules – playing music loudly out of car stereos, shouting in the streets and generally being a non-specific nuisance.
>
> (*Guardian G2*, 26 July 2005: 3)

Tom James recalls, 'My housemate got off a train at London Bridge and took a cab home last week because there was someone acting strangely in his carriage. He was furious with himself, but what can you do?' Pippa Leech, a social worker, reports, 'An Indian friend of mine – English, but Indian parentage – always carries a rucksack and won't use the tube now. He says it's been the first time in years he's felt really aware of his colour.'

But fears stretch beyond the Underground and the buses, as Jennifer Stone, 30, a stylist, admits, 'This morning, I found myself walking on the inside of the pavement rather than on the roadside edge, to put some distance between myself and the buses. How ridiculous is that?' Emily Smith, a teacher, 38, admits:

> I went shopping in yucky Brent Cross rather than Oxford Street today. I want my husband to leave in the morning so he's at work by 8.30, whereas before I'd want him to see the baby more in the morning as she's in bed when he gets home.
>
> (Ibid.)

Ben Farley, 28, a journalist, recognises how fears have spread into different areas of the city. He recalls:

> People even think that pie-and-mash shops are potential targets. I had lunch in one in Greenwich and a builder left his bag behind. People in the queue stopped talking and looked at it. The builder came back 20 seconds later looking red-faced. I heard people muttering, 'Well, you just don't know, do you?' and 'You can't be too careful.' And that's a pie-and-mash shop.
>
> (Ibid.)

At Warren Street, people talked about the fear and panic that followed the explosion on the Victoria line train, heading northbound towards Euston. Tammie Landau said:

> I was on the train and people came running through the carriage. Everyone was running really quickly. Someone said duck down. They

said something went off with a bang but I didn't hear it. We had to
smash through the train to get to the other end. By the time I was out I
was quite scared.

(Ibid.)

Ivan McCracken, a passenger on one train, told Sky News: 'Some were
falling, there was mass panic.' He had been told:

a man was carrying a rucksack and the rucksack suddenly exploded. It
was a minor explosion but enough to blow open the rucksack. The
man then made an exclamation as if something had gone wrong. At
that point everyone rushed from the carriage.

(Quoted in the *Guardian*, 22 July 2005: 5)

Jimmy Connor, 32, another passenger, left his bag on the train at Warren
Street as passengers struggled to leave the carriage: 'Everyone was just
waiting for the bomb to go off. People were trying to make their way to
the front of the train.... I thought I was going to die, everyone else
thought the same,' he added (ibid.).

Sofiane Mohellebi, a 35-year-old from Paris, who was also on the train,
said, 'People were trying to pull others down [in the carriage] to get out of
the way.' He said:

There was no way to get out, but everyone was trying, I just sat and
prayed and waited for it to happen. You don't know what it is like
until you are inside.

'I had been sitting down reading a book, but then there was a smell
coming from behind me. The smell was coming from another carriage.
There was no smoke, It smelt like rubber or wire [burning] then it got
worse.

(Ibid.)

He was so relieved when he got off the train that he started collecting
shoes that had been left behind. He is not sure why he did this, but it was
probably his way of dealing with the shock. He emerged from the Underground clutching three sandals abandoned in the panic. He had been
hoping to find the women who lost them. I recall seeing him on the TV as I
was watching events unfold from the safety of my home, just grateful that
I had not been caught up in the incident. The fact that it was happening
again, even though no people had died, was really shocking and it was difficult to take it in emotionally. You just felt so empathetic because you
realised that 'it could so easily have been you'.

Just as the people who placed bombs seemed to be 'like everyone else',
so did the passengers on the trains, but more so. People were trying to
explain the events that had been unfolding around them, transforming the

familiar into a landscape of fear. There was an abiding sense that there was *no* reason that they were caught up in the panic and you were not. It was a matter of luck, and the panic made visible what so many people in London were now feeling, even though it had been concealed in the reporting of 7/7. People suspected that all this talk of resilience referred to the rescuers and those who were watching, rather than those who had been directly caught up in the incidents. They were beginning to question the media's representations of events as they shaped their own narratives of fear and uncertainty. It was difficult to know *where* people could feel safe, and it could seem as if they were only safe within their own domestic spaces of home. As people made their way back home after the attacks, their sense of the fears awaiting them within public space transformed boundaries of safety.

As with the 7 July bombs, these would-be suicide bombers appeared happy to be identified. Forensic teams soon discovered documents in the rucksacks that gave vital clues to the individuals who planned the bombings. Police were also searching for possible connections with the 7/7 bombings. The government could try to insist on 'business as usual' because nobody had died and, with four live suspects on the run, the priority was the police investigation rather than the grief of a nation. But it also reflects, as the *Observer* reported, 'the grim knowledge that if such events are going to become regular occurrences, the world cannot stop every time – at least not without terrifying both Britons and potential overseas visitors alike' (*Observer*, 24 July 2005: 3).[5]

Amar Singh, editor of the *Eastern Eye* newspaper, said Muslim communities were on tenterhooks:

> There is genuine fear. At worst it is assault and abuse, at best it is strange looks and people looking away from you on the tube. After September 11 we looked at Americans and thought they were so ignorant. They didn't know the difference between a Muslim and a Sikh. I can't believe parts of Britain are just as bad. Just as xenophobic.
>
> (Ibid.: 7)

Aklis Ali, 39, who works at Best 1 convenience store in Brick Lane said:

> There has been a lot of police on the streets since 7 July. There is tension when my family goes out. When my wife wears a hijab people think she's a terrorist. We don't feel safe – you never know whether someone is going to attack you for being a Muslim.
>
> (*Observer*, 24 July 2005: 7)

He added: 'Just because of a few fanatics, you can't blame all Muslims. We all have the same feelings about 7 July. We're human beings' (ibid.).[6]

In Beeston, Leeds, after it became clear that three of the men responsible for the 7 July atrocities were from the area, the mood shifted from shock to disbelief. There were people talking of conspiracy theories and people saying, 'The moment a mother rang up about her son from West Yorkshire, they knew they had their fall-men.' After news of the further bombing attempts in London reached them, some of the young men Hussain and Tanweer hung around with relaxed more and one said: 'That should take the attention off Beeston.' By Friday, as news of the police shooting in the capital filtered through, the mood shifted again. 'London will be like Beirut, Belfast and Palestine now,' said one man. 'It will be part of life because Bush and Blair can't keep their noses out of other people's business.'

'Bush is the real terrorist,' muttered another (ibid.: 6).

10 The West, Islam and the politics of dialogue

The West

This chapter explores the relations between the West and Islam in the light of the London bombings and the questions that have been raised post-9/11 about the possibilities of dialogue between different traditions and civilisations. This is an issue that relates not only to Islam but to different religious traditions that have tended to be treated as forms of unreason within the secular terms of an Enlightenment rationalism. Classical forms of social theory have tended to reproduce a clear distinction between reason and faith that have made it difficult to illuminate the growing influence of religious beliefs and practices in contemporary societies. These issues have been intensified through the growth within the diverse Abrahamic faiths of Judaism, Christianity and Islam of influential fundamentalist and literalist traditions. Though there have been powerful movements towards increasingly secular societies in Europe, within the United States there has been a strengthening of fundamentalist Christianities that have gained significant influence in government circles.[1]

A YouGov poll, published on 23 July 2005 in the *Daily Telegraph*, reported that almost one in four British Muslims sympathise with the motives of suicide bombers. More than half say that, whether they sympathise or not, they understand why some people behave in the way they do. The research also showed that nearly one in three thinks that Western society is decadent and immoral and should be brought to an end. A total of 16 per cent of British Muslims told the survey that they do not feel loyal towards Britain and 6 per cent went as far as saying the London bombings were justified.

Findings like these produce complex reactions in young British Muslims like Fatima Dossa, 24, a pharmacy graduate from Eastcote, North-West London.

> There is no doubt that the double standards of Western foreign policy have an effect on Muslim youth. You can understand the motives of suicide bombers, but to kill people is different. It is not going to achieve anything.

If you go to university and see the youth – not just white British but Pakistani and Muslim youth – drinking and drug taking, you do feel where is society going? I'm sure the older white British society would agree society is decadent. But I wouldn't go so far as to say 'immoral'.

(*Observer*, 24 July 2005: 6)

Shahid Malik, Labour MP for Dewsbury, has also been struggling to come to terms with the fact that one of the 7 July suicide bombers, Mohammad Sidique Khan, was from Dewsbury, though he was born in Leeds and attended mosques there. As he tries to explain it to himself:

It is true that some young Muslims in my constituency have been angered, and frustrated by what they see as the double standards of the 'West' in relation to international Muslim areas of conflict: Palestine, Kashmir, Afghanistan, Iraq or Chechnya.

There is a feeling of alienation, often isolation; a feeling that somehow you don't belong; a feeling made much more acute by the fact that the party that came second in last year's local elections – ahead of Labour [the BNP] – says it wants an 'all-white Britain'. No wonder that young Muslims who travel to Pakistan come back with a sense of belonging and an inner peace that eludes them in their own country.

(*Observer*, 24 July 2005: 7)

Malik is also critical of his own behaviour towards extremist beliefs in the past, recognising 'The attacks of 7 July have shown us the danger that words can become deadly deeds'. He recalls, 'When I, and other British Muslims voiced condemnation of extremists in the past, we feared giving ammunition to far-right extremists. Equally, some feared stoking up tensions within the community.' He argues:

For British Muslims there is a sense of relief. We are no longer in denial. We will no longer pretend not to see or hear the fanatical few who stand outside our mosques, polluting young minds. The events of 7 July have changed that. The choices are stark yet clear – we either confront the enemy within, or are seen to condone.

(*Observer*, 24 July 2005: 7)

According to Jonathan Glover, the London bombings seem to be part of 'a cycle of violence in which we too are involved, a cycle of potential war between Islam and the west that threatens to spin out of control' (*Guardian*, 27 July 2005: 22). If we are not to make concessions that might encourage further violence, we have to understand that 'political violence is often a resentful backlash to a group's sense of being insulted or humiliated'. This tone shows itself in the al-Qaida rhetoric before 9/11: 'The people of Islam have suffered from aggression, iniquity and injustices.... Muslim's blood has become the cheapest in the eyes of the world.' The killings in Afghanistan fed Islamic resentment, as has the attack on Iraq where the West does not seem concerned to even account for the Iraq civilian deaths while they are careful to count their own losses.

This makes it imperative for the West to make efforts to break the cycle of violence and, for Glover, this 'requires a serious dialogue between the overlapping worlds of the west and Islam before irreversible mutual hatred sets in'. This would involve a *dialogue* between the different systems of belief on each side, as well as a consideration of different narratives of recent history. For Glover, within an analytical tradition, this partly involves a rationalist vision of the history of philosophy as a 'sustained investigation into the difference between good and bad reasons for holding beliefs'. If things go well, as he sees it, 'they hold their final beliefs more tentatively, aware of how precarious the foundations of any beliefs are. In religious and ideological conflicts, this sense of precariousness is the antidote of fanaticism.'[2]

According to Glover, 'Tackling the deep psychology of conflict involves persuading groups to listen to each other's stories and to look for the possibility of a narrative that does justice to the truths in both.' But what is needed is 'not a one-sided dialogue in which "we" undermine "their" fanaticism'. But there are questions to ask 'about settling political issues by murder or about settling moral issues by appeals to the supposed authority of texts claimed to be the word of God'. But Glover is also ready to acknowledge that there are also questions about 'our' morality: 'We allowed Falluja to be destroyed like Guernica. And there are questions about the supposed moral difference between bombs in the Underground and cluster-bombing civilians in an illegal war.' He recognises that in 'genuine dialogue both sides have positions at risk'. But his position is informed by a hope that 'The right kind of talk opens chinks that let in doubts. And in religion and politics doubts about beliefs save lives' (ibid.).[3]

Glover's moderated rationalism is in contrast with the kind of militant secularism that Polly Toynbee defends, that sees the second wave of London bombings as:

> a savage reminder of the unknown waves of demented killers lining up to murder in the name of God.
> Whatever was intended, the message was loud and clear: they can and will do this whenever they want and it does indeed spread very real terror.
>
> (*Guardian*, 22 July 2005: 25)

She sees this as an issue of religion, and so the need to curb and control its influence within public life. It should be maintained within an Enlighten-

ment tradition as a matter of individual belief within the private sphere
alone. She warns:

> In the growing fear and anger at what more may be to come, apolo-
> gists or explainers can expect short shrift. This is not about poverty,
> deprivation or cultural dislocation of second-generation immigrants.
> There is plenty of that and it is passive. Iraq is the immediate trigger,
> but this is about religious delusion.
>
> (Ibid.)

Religious beliefs of a fundamentalist character obviously play a vital
part, but it does not help to assume in advance that they are a 'delusion'
nor is it clear what connection they have with other factors that she
mentions, which might also be important in identifying individuals and
groups that might prove particularly susceptible to these beliefs. Toynbee
insists:

> all religious are prone to it, given the right circumstances. How could
> those who preach the absolute revealed truth of every word of a primi-
> tive book not be prone to insanity? There have been killer Christians
> and indeed the whole of Christendom has been at times bent on
> wiping out heathens. Jewish zealots in their settlements crazily claim
> legal rights to land from the Old Testament.
>
> (Ibid.)

The easy appeal to the 'primitive' and to 'insanity' when she talks about
religions somehow makes her less willing to consider 'the right circumstances' within particular social and historical contexts. She is also concerned with 'how far-right evangelicals have kidnapped US politics and
warped its secular, liberal founding traditions'. She warns us, 'Intense
belief, incantations, secrecy and all-male rituals breed perversions and
danger, abusing women and children and infecting young men with
frenzy, no matter what the nature of the faith.' Some of these warning are
well taken and we need to take seriously how religious fundamentalisms
have worked to reinforce patriarchal and homophobic power that
Western traditions have recently been forced to challenge within postmodern cultures.

As a defender of Enlightenment rationalism, and being somewhat deaf
to its critics, Toynbee insists:

> Enlightenment values are in peril not because these mad beliefs are
> really growing but because too many rational people seek to appease
> and understand unreason. Extreme superstition breeds extreme action.
> Those who believe they alone know the only way, truth and life will
> always feel justified in doing anything in its name.... If religions teach

that life after death is better then it is hardly surprising that some crazed followers will actually believe it.

(Ibid.)

The virulent intolerance of religion is not challenged strongly enough, because of 'an official intellectual conspiracy to pretend that religion is always or mainly beneficent. History suggests otherwise.' According to Toynbee, 'It is time now to get serious about religion – all religion – and draw a firm line between the real world and the world of dreams.' It has become vital to 'separate the state from all faiths and relegate all religion to the private – but well-regulated – sphere' (ibid.).

Toynbee's secular rationalism recognises that 'no one can police minds and no new draconian laws to silence thinkers and preachers will ever stop dangerous ideas'. This means that 'All the state can do is hold on to secular values. It can encourage the moderate but it must not appease religion.' But this means that the state should offer no support to faith schools and 'stop this madness and separate the state and its schools from all religion. It won't stop the bombings now but at least it would not encourage continued school segregation for generations to come' (ibid.).[4]

Karen Armstrong, who was herself a nun, offers a tone that is more open to dialogue between the religious and the secular. She says, 'Liberal-minded atheists can be just as strident as fundamentalists if their idea of faith is challenged in any way, even if they know next to nothing about religious history or theology.' She argues that we need 'to strike a balance between the kind of repression that I experienced in my convent and the intellectual idolatry that makes ephemeral and ill-founded opinion absolute.' It can be helpful to recall the repression, because it helps us recognise some of the dangers that Toynbee is all too conscious of within almost all religious traditions.

Karen Armstrong recalls in *The Spiral Staircase: a Memoir*, as a young nun in the 1960s she was

> not allowed to have any opinions. During our first week in the convent our mistress told us that many ideas and practices of the order would seem incomprehensible – even perverse at first – because we were spiritually immature and still tainted by secular values. As we progressed in the religious life we would find that these things gradually made sense. For now we should suspend our judgment.
>
> (Quoted in the *Guardian*, 27 July 2005: 21)

She recalls, 'I threw myself into this discipline because I was so eager to become wise and saintly.' She also recalls that, before the Second Vatican Council, 'nuns and priests were often trained systematically to distrust their own minds. Our views were of no value'.[5] This identifies an issue for religious education across diverse traditions, not only Christianity. It shows the strengths of an Enlightenment rationalism that learns, with Kant, the importance and difficulties of people learning to think for themselves as part of a process of becoming 'free and equal' moral agents.[6]

The trouble with the kind of training Armstrong received, as she now grasps:

> is that if you consistently deflect your mind from its bias towards truth you can damage it irrevocably. When potentially subversive ideas emerged I stamped on them so ruthlessly that after a while they ceased to come at all. After leaving the convent I studied at Oxford, only to find to my dismay that I was unable to think for myself. I marvelled at my fellow students, who could cry 'I think!' with such confidence during an argument.
>
> (Ibid.)

In this way she helps to identify a process of inner control that she had come to collude with herself, while having no language to appreciate the 'damage' that she was doing to herself. She has learned to recognise other issues that flow from living in a highly opinionated society where we are constantly bombarded with information, much of it superficial, from the mass media and Internet. She found this particularly in the US after 9/11, where she was often discussing Islam and fundamentalism, where she witnessed how people, as they 'struggled with their fear and confusion, they created dogmas that did not help them appraise the situation objectively'. She learned that if people have a right to their views, some ideas are more valuable than others.[7]

As Armstrong has come to understand it:

> Opinions change with each generation, but we like to cast our views in stone. It gives us a sense of security in a changing and frightening world. Secular dogmas are no different from religious doctrines. The Qur'an calls compulsory theology – zannah – self-indulgent guesswork about questions that are not verifiable, but which have split the faithful into warring sects.
>
> (Ibid.)

Armstrong has been learning from the example of Socrates when she says:

> The best way of countering the clashing dogmatisms of our time is to be suspicious of any idée fixe – including our own. Socrates made it his life's work to compel people to question their most fundamental assumptions. True knowledge was acquired only after an agonising struggle that involved your whole self.... When you realised the depths of your confusion your philosophical quest could begin.
>
> (Ibid.)

Islams

Two miles outside Islamabad, in a small village under wooded hills, is the shrine of Bari Imam, a local holy person who is a symbol of religious tolerance. On the portal to the tombs are engraved slogans for both Sunni and Shia Muslims. Outside, women light incense sticks and tie tinsel to a tree. Zaid Ahmed, 25, a shop worker from the city, has cycled to the shrine to ask for help with a family problem. This is a tradition of petition you can find in diverse religious traditions.

'The bombings in London are very bad,' he said. 'We believe in the brotherhood of man and that Islam does not allow the killing of innocents.' Men who stand beside him nod in agreement. But their rites would be considered anathema to more orthodox Muslims, even though the Barelvi represent Pakistan's silent majority. Jason Burke reports that there are hundreds of shrines like this throughout Pakistan but, as they are not political, few outside the country recognise their dominance.[8]

They too have known violence. Earlier this year the head cleric at the shrine was killed by drug dealers after he objected to them selling opium and heroin. Last May a suicide bomber killed 20 people at the shrine gates during a Shia festival. 'The Koran says that if you kill a single person you kill all humanity,' says Raja Jaffar, 75, the caretaker at the shrine. The sectarian groups behind the attack are thought to be linked to the second biggest strain in Islam, the Deobandis, named after the town in India where it was founded and close to the Taliban in neighbouring Afghanistan. 'They are everything the Barelvis are not,' said Ershad Mahmud, of Islamabad's Institute for Policy Studies. 'Their clerics are very active and very clever, and have successfully pursued a long-term strategy that has made them very fast growing' (*Observer*, 24 July 2005: 19). Many analysts agree, according to Burke, that 'a minority of Pakistan's 15,000 madrassas, almost all Deobandi, do preach a violent and prejudiced ideology' (ibid.).

Javed Ibrahim Parachar is a tribal leader, cleric and principal of three madrassas where 500 poor children are taught for free. It is one of the few ways poor parents can secure food and education for their children. He is a supporter of the Taliban, that 'were the best of all Muslims'. In his home in the town of Kohat he said:

> The bombing of the Bari Imam was a very good action. So was 9/11 and so were the London bombs. They are killing our wives, our children, our Muslim brothers. Is there any law for Falluja, Kabul, Chechnya, Palestine and Kashmir? It is all because of the Jews. They control the American and British governments through the economy.
>
> (Ibid.)

Parachar said the crackdown on madrassas 'will be unsuccessful. How can they control our minds and ideas?' he said.

The Deobandis are well entrenched in west Pakistan where an alliance of religious parties runs two provinces and is pushing through Taliban-style legislation. It has access to massive funding from sympathisers in the Arabian Gulf that allows the parties to build hundreds of new schools and mosques. Many are being built in Barelvi areas with the express intent of eradicating the more moderate strand. Speaking of Musharaf, who came to power in a bloodless coup in 1999, one professional in Lahore told Burke:

> He has got two faces. The West think he is a man they can do business with. But actually he has failed to push through any reforms that might counter the extremists. He needs their support so talks a lot but does nothing.
>
> (Ibid.)

Critics also say Musharaf has worked at eliminating groups connected to al-Qaida, but has spared the Kashmiri groups. 'Christians, Jews and Muslims all blame each other,' said Afnan Rauf, 42, a computer salesman. 'We should be honest and admit we are all to blame. It is a bad time. Pakistan is on edge. The whole world is on edge.'

The men who blew themselves up in the London bombings seem to have visited Pakistan a number of times, and there are investigations about the kind of support they could have received there and whether they themselves had been exposed to educational programmes in specific madrassas. But it is most likely that they had been radicalised in Britain. Like other recruits drawn to Islamic militancy, they are children of immigrants. According to Jason Burke:

> The history of Islamic militancy gives some useful clues as to why the dominance of immigrants might be so marked. In the developing world, mass international migration was preceded by mass internal migration from the countryside to the cities. Almost all the early wave of Islamic militants in the Sixties and Seventies had either left rural homes to move to the cities or come from families that had done so.
>
> (*Observer*, 24 July 2005: 8)

Syed Qutb, the pioneer of Egyptian Islamism, came from a poor family in a small village in Upper Egypt and moved to Cairo. The men who led the new wave of radicalism in Afghanistan in the early 1970s were almost all migrants to Kabul.[9]

A second generation of militants are likely to be people who have lived away from their homelands for some time, or the children of people who have done so. Khaled Sheikh Mohammed, the Pakistani architect of the 9/11 attacks, grew up in Kuwait. Mohammed Atta, the leader of the hijackers, had spent more than a decade in Germany before the 2001 attack. According to Burke, the targets are consequently less likely to be local and 'We are now in the throes of a radical militancy led by the second generation of activists and, unsurprisingly, their targets are international'. He argues:

> Just as migrants from rural environments felt confused in the crowded urban environment, so modern immigrants feel their own disorientation as they move around the globe. Stripped of sustaining cultural traditions, migrants are susceptible to the comforting certainties of fundamentalist ideologies.
>
> (Ibid.)

This allows Burke to conclude: 'This tells us that we are looking at a social phenomenon, not purely a religious one, and that, as immigration is not going to stop, we have to change the way we deal with it.'

Rather than view religious fundamentalist movements that have emerged in different religious traditions as regressions to a pre-modern past, and so as symptoms of irrationality, we need to rethink sociological traditions that make it difficult to appreciate how these are very much responses to a globalised postmodern world and the crisis of meaning. As Burke puts it: 'Above all, it tells us that contemporary Islamic militancy is not a dinosaur from the 15th or 7th century that has suddenly reared its ugly head, but is a function of our own modern, kinetic, globalised world' (ibid.).

Islamic (re)visions

The day the first bombs went off in London, Tariq Ramadan, a philosophy lecturer at the University of Geneva and president of the Swiss Muslim organisation, issued a press release condemning the outrage: 'The authors of such acts are criminals and we cannot accept or listen to their probable justification in the name of an ideology, a religion or a political cause' (the *Guardian*, 22 July 2005: 25). But the *Sun* warned against Ramadan being allowed into the UK, even though he had been invited to address young Muslims at a conference at London's Islamic Cultural Centre, sponsored by the Metropolitan Police. It warns that the 'soft-spoken professor' is 'more dangerous' than Hamza and Bakri because his 'moderate tones present a "reasonable" face of terror to impressionable young Muslims.' These claims were taken up by other media, even though he is a well-known reformist thinker who is despised by traditionalists for his progressive interpretation of Islamic sources.

As Naima Bouteldja, researcher for the Transnational Institute reports, 'Along with millions of non-Muslims in this country, he supported the right of Palestinians and Iraqis to resist occupation but has never supported suicide bombings' (*Guardian*, 22 July 2005: 25). She thinks the attacks on him probably have their source in France, where he wrote an article on the eve of the second European Social Forum in Paris in 2003, accusing a group of high-profile scholars of allowing their support for Israel to dictate their positions not just on the Iraq War and Palestine, but also on domestic policy issues relating to Islam and the problems of suburban French ghettos. He was quickly branded an anti-Semite and there was a press campaign against him that 'suggested that a terrorist blood-line passed directly to him from his grandfather, Hassan al-Banna, who founded the Muslim Brotherhood.' She argues that the attacks on Ramadan are not motivated by fear of religious extremism 'but by the cultural imperialism that grips France's republican white majority and the influence of Ramadan's challenge to it among France's 5 million Muslims, especially the youth.'

Ramadan takes on those traditionalists who equate Islam and Arab culture as synonymous. 'There is only one Islam,' he has stated, 'but it can be culturally African, Asian, European or American.' As Bouteldja explains, 'By asserting that "anything not explicitly forbidden by Islamic principles is permissible," Ramadan's interpretation of Islamic scriptures and western liberal democracy charts a clear path for European Muslims to live authentically Islamic lives and fully participate as European citizens' (ibid.). In an interview with Paul Vallely, after the London bombings, Ramadan explains that he wants to encourage young Muslims to think for themselves: 'Muslims now need, more than ever, to be self-critical' (*Independent*, 25 July 2005: 8). This means educating young Muslims in more than religious formalism. They must be taught that 'the capacity to promote social justice and the protection of the integrity of every individual, woman or man, rich or poor' is what determines authentic Islam.[10]

In a world in which Muslims and secularists in the West rarely listen or understand each other, Ramadan offers the possibility of a new kind of dialogue. It is deeply rooted in Islamic theology, but it is formed by a post-Enlightenment Western intellectual vision. The implicit message of the terrorists to Muslims, he said at the London conference, is, this is not an Islamic society, it is not your society. He responds, 'We have to say it is your society. Now more than ever it is imperative for Muslims to be active citizens and to be proactive' (ibid.). Similar arguments are often heard within Jewish communities where it can be said that it is not possible to 'live a fully Jewish life' in Britain, and that this is only possible in Israel. This is a vision that Jewish fundamentalists also appeal to, trying to convince young people that they cannot feel 'really at home' in Britain, and that it can never fully be their country because they will always be tolerated as a minority.[11]

But the force of these concerns shifts as the society has become more multicultural and where there is more public space for people to express their religious traditions and beliefs. London is a very different global multiculture city from the predominantly assimilationist city I grew up in the 1950s, in a refugee Jewish family where you felt strong pressure to be 'like everyone else' and so assimilate into a dominant and clearly defined culture. Religion was defined predominantly as a private matter to be practised within the confined space of home and synagogue. But the boundaries between public and private have mutated within a more culturally open and diverse urban space of routine everyday multiculture, where people can feel able to make certain claims upon public space for their own traditions and cultures, as long as they do not interfere or harm the rights of others. This is a shift that Ramadan recognises when he argues that young Muslims need to jettison the approach of their parents, which was to try to make themselves *invisible* to the rest of society.[12]

Ramadan recognises a need to develop a critical mind and knows:

> On the arts, literature, the way we eat, our sense of humour, the second generation feel close to the non-Muslims they went to school with. That's right. That's the Islamic way. The universality of Islam is shown by the way you can integrate into the local culture. Our young people need to be told: you can dress in European clothes – so long as you respect the principle of modesty. Democracy and pluralism aren't against your Islamic principles. Anything in Western culture that does not contradict the message of Islam can be accepted and integrated.
>
> (Ibid.)

To promote this, it is necessary to break what Ramadan calls 'this binary vision of reality – the Us and Them, the idea that everything Western is decadent and unIslamic.' But at the same time, this also encourages greater inter-religious dialogue:

> If you go back to the sources of our religions you find common values. It's important to read the scriptures of the other faiths and see how the others interpret these common values. It is high time for Muslims to say that anti-Semitism is not acceptable.
>
> (Ibid.)

At the same time, Ramadan has spoken out against traditional Islamic punishments such as cutting off hands for theft, stoning for adultery and using the religion to oppress women. He recognises that these penalties are Koranic. Some also occur specifically in the Bible where we can read about the stoning to death of women who have been adulterous and we can identify the very different treatment of women and men. But like Jewish orthodoxy, that insists on treating the Tenach as the revealed word of G-d and so has similar issues to deal with through diverse traditions of interpretation, Ramadan argues that the original social conditions under which they were set are nearly impossible to re-establish. The penalties, therefore, are 'almost never applicable'. He cites historical Islamic precedents for the suspension of such punishments.

Ramadan is clear that 'Islam is being used to degrade and subjugate women and men in certain Muslim societies'. He insists that the collusion of Muslims around the world in this 'literal and non-contextualised application of sharia law is a betrayal of the teachings of Islam'. Of course he is being challenged by traditionalists who call this Islam-lite and he knows 'The more literal will say I am Westernising'. But he defends himself by saying: 'I am not losing the universal principles. I'm just not confusing them with the culture of the countries that Muslims have traditionally come from' (ibid.). He understand the difficulty of the 'middle path' he is treading, 'I'm condemned from the Western point of view because I stand up for Muslim values. The West feels that the good Muslim is the less observant Muslim; that the practising Muslim is a potential terrorist.' As he explains the path:

> It is a path between text and context, which insists that in a changing world our interpretation of faith must also evolve, that there is no faithfulness without change. We need a deep faith, but a critical mind. Being British by culture and Muslim by religion is no contradiction. We need to get out of our intellectual ghettos and be freed from our narrow understanding. To do that is not easy. The easy way is to be an extremist.
>
> (Ibid.)[13]

Naima Bouteldja explains the impact that Ramadan has had in France:

> For third generation Muslims who are torn between the liberties and discriminations of French society and the traditionalist and spiritual stance of their parents, Ramadan's guidance has been a revelation. They have learnt that to become a genuine French citizen one does not have to renounce one's faith.
>
> But more fundamentally, he has challenged the dominant French assimilationist model, rooted across the political spectrum, that to be truly French, Muslims must abandon the right to their own identity. Ramadan follows in the footsteps of revolutionary thinkers such as Franz Fanon and Malcolm X in attacking notions of the west's superiority and its seemingly immutable values. He turns the paradigm on its head and establishes the universal values of Islam within the framework of western societies.
>
> (*Guardian*, 22 July 2005: 25)

But she also reminds us of the crucial importance of new forms of dialogue and the tragedy that follows if 'shutting down debate in Britain' means that 'scholars and clerics such as Ramadan, Qaradawi and even

Bakri cannot seriously be questioned in public debate by Muslims and non-Muslims on the vital issues of identity, citizenship and shared and contested values'. She recognises that this is an absolutely vital issue that concerns the possibilities of dialogue between Islam and the West and is 'about the very future of western Muslims and their fellow citizens living together in peace and mutual respect'.

11 Faith, martyrdom and suicide bombings

Faith

The phenomenon of suicide bombing has become a practice that has spread across the planet, to be deployed in very different kinds of conflicts from the Tamil Tigers in Sri Lanka to the almost daily attack on occupation forces in Iraq.[1] Social theories have generally been framed within the classical terms of a secular rationalism that has tended to assume that industrialisation would be accompanied by secularisation, though it was understood that this would generally be an uneven process around the world. But the return of religion as a major social force has challenged these deeply held assumptions that have so often guided social analysis of the contemporary world. Often this has meant that religious motivation has been interpreted as a regression to earlier, even medieval ways of thinking, largely dependent on faith. The idea that, with modernity, faith would be replaced by reason has needed to be challenged if we are to grasp that suicide bombings have become very much a feature of contemporary conflicts within a postmodern world.

Often we have little critical self-awareness of the frameworks through which we seek to make sense of contemporary realities. We might have questioned notions of historical progress intellectually while, at the same time, making assumptions that it is quite irrational in the contemporary world for people to contemplate taking their own lives as suicide bombers. But the initial shock and the disturbances it provokes in our taken-for-granted assumptions can be stilled as we witness how this practice spreads so quickly across geographical borders, partly because of the pervasive influence the global communications and the Internet. We might wish to think that it is an aberration that will disappear as people come to their senses. At the same time, we might recognise how traditions of classical philosophy and social theory seem to leave us bereft of terms in which to illuminate these contemporary realities.

It takes time to integrate these intellectual and emotional challenges and to discover narratives that seem helpful. There is often a temptation to rush to judgement, and it is only with time that we might appreciate the resonances of classical traditions while also recognising a need to *think differently* if we are to shape a public sociology that can help to negotiate the urban fears people have been forced to live with in a world of global terrors. With the dangers of global warming initiating processes that could soon move beyond a tipping point towards what could be a global natural catastrophe, brought about by the lack of care for the planet that has accompanied widespread industrialisation, there is a sense that threats are coming from different directions. These dangers can come together in particular landscapes of fear that people can seek to ward off as they attempt to focus upon their everyday lives, often hoping that their indifference will not be challenged. But sometimes it is through the mass media that connections are made, and families recognise they are implicated in ways that can shocking to them; for instance, when they have to face that a relative has been involved either as a victim of the bombings or even possibly as a suspect. The fears come home in threatening and uncertain ways.

The family of Muktar Said Ibrahim, who tried to set off a bomb on the number 26 bus in Hackney, were shocked when they saw his image on the national news. His family claimed that he had not lived with them since he was 18. They insisted:

> Muktar left this address in 1994. He is 27 years of age. He is not a close family member. He has not visited them for many months. The family in no way condone any acts of terrorism. This is a very difficult time for the family.
>
> (*Guardian*, 27 July 2005: 5)

A neighbour, however, said she had seen Said Ibrahim in the street as recently as two weeks ago. Sarah Scott, 23, said she had known him since she was 11. Last November, he had given her a pamphlet called *Understanding Islam*. Underlined was a passage from the Qu'ran saying: 'Anyone who says "there is no God (worthy of worship) except Allah" and dies holding to that (belief) will enter Paradise.'

She said he used to come to stay all the time, 'He wasn't allowed to smoke in the house so we used to smoke together. He was here about two weeks ago, I saw him walking past.' She recalls:

> The only deep conversation we had was about this book. He gave it to me before Christmas. We were having a fag and he asked me if I was Catholic because I have an Irish family. I said I didn't believe in anything and he said I should.
>
> He told me he was going to have all these virgins when he got to heaven if he praises Allah. He gave me this book and said it would change my views.
>
> (Ibid.)

Said Ibrahim had arrived in the UK from Eritrea, and was granted exceptional leave to remain as a dependent aged 14 in 1992. The son of Eritrean parents, Ibrahim moved to Saudi Arabia with his family before coming to Britain. He was granted a passport in September 2004. He had moved in with Yasin Hassan Omar, who had tried to blow up an Underground train at Warren Street. Omar had come to Britain at the age of 11 as a dependent of his elder sister and her husband who were seeking asylum in 1992 after living on the streets in Mogadishu. Jamal Mohammed, who played football with Omar, told the *Independent* that Omar had said he used to hang out with militia men in Mogadishu and was fascinated by their guns: 'He said he had lived on the streets during the day, getting what food he could' (*Time*, 8 August 2005: 22). In London, Omar moved through a series of foster homes and attended Aylward Secondary School in North London, where a schoolmate recalls, 'he was quiet and picked upon and didn't have friends' (ibid.). By the age of 18 he was declared a 'vulnerable young adult' and so was put into a one-bedroom apartment in Curtis House in Enfield, North London.

At a Turkish grocery a few roads from Curtis House, the owner's wife, Nursal, remembers once talking to Omar about a terrorist attack by al-Qaida, saying it was terrible, 'He said, "Why?" Those people [the victims] are killing Muslims.' His classmate recalls that 'he got religion three or four years ago and grew a beard. He changed. I think he was lonely' (ibid.). In contrast, Said was known as a bully at school and served time in five juvenile jails after being convicted in 1996 for gang robberies at knifepoint in the Welwyn Garden City and Stevenage areas of Hertfordshire. One of the jails, Feltham, was where shoe bomber Richard Reid had earlier turned to Islam. After leaving prison he is believed to have grown a beard, adopted Islamic dress and become devout.

At Curtis House, apparently, Omar and Said played football on Sundays with some East Africans, but mostly kept to themselves. Some neighbours said they held prayer meetings. Last month, Samantha Jones, whose son Conor, 11, used to play football with them, saw them take '40 or 50 cartons up in the lift. They said it was wallpaper stripper' (ibid.). 'At the time I thought it was a bit strange,' she said, 'I asked them, what have you got there? They said it was wall paper stripper, Now it's scary to think what could have been inside those containers' (*Guardian*, 27 July 2005: 5). The police now believe their apartment was the 'bomb factory' for the 21 July attacks. The police have said there does not seem to be any discernible operational link with jihadi networks in the Horn of Africa and so believe that the men had 'got jihad' in London. They seem to be taking seriously the idea of a self-starting cell that, despite earlier reports, seems to have little operational connections with the 7 July bombings in London.

Shane Brighton, of the Royal United Services Institute in London, says 'self-radicalisation' is a growing concern. 'If you already accept that there's a historic struggle between Muslims and the West and that the only resort is violence,' he says, 'you don't need to sit at the feet of an imam for months, You just need to watch the news to have your mind-set reconfirmed' (*Time*, 8 August 2005: 22). Those who have 'self-radicalised' can then turn to 'Google terror', using the Internet for information and support. But this also suggests that a focus upon the responsibility of radical imams for somehow 'corrupting' or 'polluting' the minds of the young can be misplaced. Standing near Curtis House in New Southgate, a friend of Said-Ibrahim's, who gave his name to Audrey Gillan as 'Kawser', said he had met him two years ago. 'At the time I wasn't a practising Muslim, but I became one about two months ago. He encouraged me to pray,' he said. 'As a Muslim I believe it's one of the most honourable ways to die, defending your beliefs... I hope the bombers go to paradise after giving up their lives as martyrs' (ibid.).

Vance Noor, 18, who lived in Arnos Grove and used to play football with them, said, 'They would always come every Sunday and always run round a lot. The tubby one [Ibrahim] was a mad tackler. He would give as good as he got.' Another resident of the Ladderswood Estate, who declined to be named, told Mark Honigsbaum, 'Omar was a very angry person. He was always talking about extreme things. They were very angry with westerners.' He said Omar, who he thought worshipped at the notorious Finsbury Park mosque, talked openly about waging jihad. 'I have seen one of their videos which showed fighters but they were very devious in the amount of information they would give you' (*Guardian*, 27 July 2005: 5).

Modernity and religion

Oliver McTernan, director of Forward Thinking and author of *Violence in God's Name* (Orbis Books, London) argues that 'The secularist mindset that has shaped western political thinking finds it difficult to understand that belief can form some people's political judgments and actions' (*Guardian*, 30 July 2005: 25). Within the terms of an Enlightenment vision of modernity there is institutionalised a radical split between reason and faith. This is why, according to McTernan, 'politicians prefer to attribute the atrocities to a political creed, a perverse ideology that has appropriated religious language and sentiments to further its own goals'. But if this has been the position adopted by Blair, echoing Bush after 9/11, it will help to shape their responses within their so-called 'war on terror'. But 'to see religion as no more than a passive agent waiting to be manipulated by political agitators is seriously to underestimate its destructive potential', as McTernan reminds us:

> The roots of faith-based terrorism lie in the religious intolerance and militancy embedded in the history and sacred texts of all the world's religions. Today's extremists can find sufficient selective texts which, if

interpreted in a literalist way, can be used to justify the atrocities they commit.'[2]

(Ibid.)

By acknowledging this, according to McTernan, 'we realise that there can be no top-down, military-style solution to the threat; an effective response requires engagement at every level'. He identifies 'the main root of the problem – the misinterpretation of their sacred texts by home-grown extremists.' But he recognises the difficulty of the task since many moderate believers, let alone extremists, oppose anything other than a strictly literalist acceptance of their sacred texts. 'This resistance is driven,' as McTernan explains, 'by the fear that any interpretation is open to error and damnation. The text is seen as God's truth; there is no room for compromise.' But this does mean that, for McTernan, 'We stand to gain more by encouraging religious leaders to engage rather than isolate extremists.' As he argues, 'The anger felt over what is happening in Iraq may well have determined the timing of the London atrocities, but it would be misleading to regard it as the reason behind the bombings.' But the implicit opposition that appeals to a language of 'reason' hardly seems helpful, especially when it leads McTernan to the idea that 'The real reason, according to my Muslim friends, lies in what they describe in an institutionalised hatred of the west that has prevailed unchallenged within certain sections of their faith community for a century or more' (*Guardian*, 30 July 2005: 25).

Derrida's deconstructive reading of Kant's *Religion Within the Limits of Reason Alone* shows that Kant's attempt to provide religion with a rational justification ends up with the paradoxical consequence of having reason founded on religion, and more specifically, Christianity. This helps to explain how a modernity that often presents itself as a secular project of a reason radically separated from faith is implicitly framed within the terms of a secularised Christianity. Derrida recognises that Kant implicitly identified in Christianity the archetype of the only moral religion when Kant expresses, in an axiomatic form:

It is not essential and hence not necessary for everyone to know what God does or has done for his salvation but it is essential to now *what man himself must* do in order to become worthy of his assistance.

(Cited in Derrida, 'Faith and Knowledge', 2002: 49)[3]

As Derrida recognises, this entails that pure morality and Christianity are indistinguishable: if this is true, the whole apparatus of Kantian moral theory, including the 'unconditional universality of the categorical imperative', is evangelical. In 'Faith and Knowledge: The Two Sources of "Religion" at the Limits of Reason Alone' (in *Acts of Religion*, Gil Anidjar (ed.), Routledge, 2002), Derrida recognises: 'The moral law inscribes itself at the bottom of our hearts like the memory of the Passion. When it addresses us, it either speaks the idiom of the Christian – or is silent' (2002: 50). Kant's efforts to moralise religion has pushed him, according to Derrida, to the paradoxical result of having transformed morality into a religious endeavour. The concept of tolerance is an example of this Kantian double bind since it presents itself as being religiously neutral, and yet it is framed within the terms of a dominant Christian tradition.[4]

This is an insight that Derrida recalls in his dialogue with Giovanna Borradori, in *Philosophy in a Time of Terror* (Chicago University Press, 2003):

> The word 'tolerance' is first of all marked by a religious war between Christians, or between Christians and non-Christians. Tolerance is a *Christian* virtue, or for that matter, a *Catholic* virtue. The Christian must tolerate the non-Christian, but even more so, the Catholic must let the Protestant be.
>
> (2003: 127)

When Borradori comments that he seems to understand tolerance as a form of charity, Derrida responds:

> Indeed, tolerance is first of all a form of charity. A Christian charity, therefore, even if Jews and Muslims might seem to appropriate this language as well. Tolerance is always on the side of the 'reason of the strongest', where 'might is right'; it is a supplementary mark of sovereignty, which says of the other from its elevated position, I am letting you be, you are not insufferable, I am leaving you a place in my home, but do not forget that this is my home...
>
> (Ibid.)

Of course, as religious others learn that they are required to be grateful for this tolerance, there is part of them that remains silently resentful, for there is a recognition that they are being offered something other than what is being presented to them. It is as if they are being offered something closer to hospitality when this is not being offered. Borradori brings this out in her question: 'Would you agree with the claim that tolerance is a condition of hospitality?' This allows Derrida to say clearly:

> No. Tolerance is actually the opposite of hospitality. Or at least its limit. If I think I am being hospitable because I am tolerant, it is because I wish to limit my welcome, to retain power and maintain control over the limits of my 'home', my sovereignty...
>
> (Ibid.: 128)

As Derrida goes on to explain:

But tolerance remains a scrutinised hospitality, always under surveillance, parsimonious and protective of its sovereignty ... We offer hospitality only on the condition that the other follow our rules, our way of life, even our language, our culture, our political system, and so on.

(2003: 128)[5]

Listening and reading

Karen Armstrong reminds us 'Hitherto the scriptures had always been transmitted orally, in a ritual context that, like a theatrical production, put them in a special frame of mind.' Part of the problem now is that we read our scriptures rather than listen to them. Protestant fundamentalists, for example, claim they read the Bible in the same ways as the early Christians, but, as Armstrong insists, 'their belief that it is literally true in every detail is a recent innovation, formulated for the first time in the late 19th century'. She continues:

> Before the modern period, Jews, Christians and Muslims all relished highly allegorical interpretations of scripture. The word of God was infinite and could not be tied down to a single interpretation. Preoccupation with literal truth is a product of the scientific revolution, when reason achieved such spectacular results that mythology was no longer regarded as a valid path to knowledge.
>
> (*Guardian*, 11 August 2005: 25)[6]

Armstrong recognises that we distort our scriptures if we read them in an exclusively literal sense. At the same time, she is aware that within modernity many people still assume that if the scriptures are not historically and scientifically correct, they cannot be true at all. But this is not how scripture was originally conceived. All the verses of the Qur'an, for example, are called 'parables' (*ayat*); its images of paradise, hell and the last judgement are also *ayat*, 'pointers to transcendental realities that we can only glimpse through signs and symbols'. She warns us:

> The last thing anyone should attempt is to read the Qur'an straight through from cover to cover, because it was designed to be recited aloud. Indeed the word *qur'an* means 'recitation'. Much of the meaning is derived from sound patterns that link one passage with another, so that Muslims who hear extracts chanted aloud thousands of times in the course of a lifetime acquire a tacit understanding that one teaching is always qualified and supplemented by other texts, and cannot be seen in isolation. The words that they hear again and again are not 'holy war', but 'kindness', 'courtesy', 'peace', 'justice' and 'compassion.'
>
> (Ibid.)[7]

Through the modern invention of printing, and with the development of widespread literacy enabling people to read for themselves, they have been able to read selectively, focusing on isolated texts that they can read out of a larger context and ignoring others that might question their predilections. So Christian fundamentalists often concentrate on the aggressive *Book of Revelations* while paying little attention to the Sermon on the Mount, while Muslim fundamentalists rely on the more belligerent passages of the Qur'an while overlooking the oft-repeated instructions to leave vengeance to God and make peace with the enemy. The Qur'an insists that its teaching must be understood 'in full' (20.114), which questions those who have interpreted jihad reductively as 'holy war' and so given it a centrality that it never had before. This has helped redefine Islam for many non-Muslims.

The notion of martyrdom that has been significant in diverse Abrahamic traditions was important in Shia Islam, but much less so within a dominant Sunni tradition where it would acquire significance in the Palestinian struggle against occupation. On one side they were considered as 'suicide bombers', but for the Palestinian resistance these young people who sacrificed their lives for the cause were claimed as martyrs and their families celebrated. It was in Gaza, mainly through Hamas, that 'suicide bombing' came to be used as an instrument of war turned against civilian populations. Young men learned that, by becoming suicide bombers, they could claim an honoured place within the community, and their families would be honoured. Supposedly there was no higher duty than to die as a martyr for the cause. Death was not to be feared as the end of life, but was somehow to be welcomed. There was a belief that those who died as martyrs had not really died at all but would somehow go on living.[8]

This is a notion that Christianity can recall in its own vision of martyrdom, even though it might want to insist that it values life while Islam somehow values death. This is a misleading contrast, since central to Christianity has been the notion of sacrifice, whereby Jesus supposedly 'gave his life' so that others could be 'saved'. Derrida talks about Christianity as a religion that understands itself in terms of the death of God. The idea that life in this world is to be a sacrifice for an eternal life in the next is not an idea that is foreign to Christianity but, rather, one that has been central to its theology, and so provides an opportunity to understand martyrdoms in Islam. Possibly, through this recognition, people can prepare the ground to appreciate the ways that martyrdom has featured within different Abrahamic religious traditions. But we also need to recognise how martyrdom can appeal to particular masculinities that are often reasserted against the threats of autonomy and independence offered to women by feminisms. It can affirm a traditional gender order that otherwise can feel threatened as young men can often take the lead in enforcing gender ideals.

Suicide bombings

Jonathan Freedland, writing in the *Guardian*, recognises the difficulty facing the mayor, Ken Livingstone: 'He cannot easily shut out someone like Qaradawi, a respected Muslim cleric who condemns the London bombings. He needs his advocacy to win the war against the terrorists.' But, he argues:

> More deeply, Livingstone and friends need to break their equation of radical Islamism with Islam – for that has been their working assumption, reflected in two ways. First, by proceeding as if the chief way to reach British Muslims is through Islamist voices like Qaradawi; second, by denouncing anyone who attacks such extreme Islamism as Islamophobic. In fact one can oppose hardline Islamism without opposing Islam. The two are not the same, and we smear British Muslims if we say they are.
>
> (*Guardian*, 27 July 2005: 21)

But it is not clear that these distinctions can so easily be made, any more than you can separate Judaism from some of its fundamentalist forms that present themselves as 'authentic' expressions. We need to be much more specific in identifying strains in diverse religious traditions that can foster violence and lead to a disregard for human rights. We need to follow these through the lives and narratives of young men as they make transitions from secular to religious masculinities, sometimes through their experience of juvenile jails that have aided their conversions towards a jihadist Islam.

Yasmin Alibhai-Brown has recognised 'British Muslims feel too that the present delicate situation is being exploited by the pro-Israeli lobby'. This feeling was intensified through the war in Lebanon between Israel and Hizbullah in the summer of 2006. She has noted that, since the failed bombings of 21 July 2005, the mood among Muslims is altering. The killing of an innocent Brazilian, she argues, has made Muslim parents intensely fearful, much more than the bombs. She writes:

> Interviewers regularly push Muslim spokespeople into an admittance that Palestinian suicide bombs are an exact equivalent of the London blasts. The suffering is the same but the two situations cannot be compared. Israel wants to cleanse itself of any culpability. To kill innocent Jewish people in clubs and at bus stops is indeed horrific but so is the shooting of young Palestinian boys and other citizens by Israeli soldiers.
>
> (*Independent*, 25 July 2005: 31)

On *Channel 4 News* in the UK, Livingstone was asked about his public embrace of Sheikh Yusuf al-Qaradawi, who had praised suicide bombers in Jerusalem and Tel-Aviv while condemning them in London. Livingstone

explained that al-Qaradawi wanted to say that the context was different so
that the strategy and ethics of suicide bombing depend upon context for
their legitimation. Livingstone added: 'while Israel had fighter jets and
tanks, the Palestinians "only have their bodies" and not other way to
"fight back".' Livingstone's own position is to condemn all suicide bombings, and he was at pains to stress that Qaradawi is against them anywhere
outside the Palestine–Israel conflict. As Freedland writes:

> This was meant to be comforting but for some reason I did not feel
> comforted. For one thing it is illogical. The arguments that Qaradawi
> applies to Israel–Palestine could just as easily be applied by al Qaida
> agents and their sympathisers.... Those men from Leeds had no jet
> planes or tanks. They too 'only had their bodies'.... Unless, of course,
> Israel is a uniquely special case. That is a hard argument to make.
>
> (*Guardian*, 27 July 2005: 21)

Freedland asks:

> in a world full of brutalities and mass slaughter, by what logic is Israel
> reviled as the uniquely heinous culprit, the one state whose civilians
> are fair game?
>   Qaradawi's argument is that there is no such thing as an Israeli
> civilian. Israeli women can be called into national service; Israeli chil-
> dren will grow up to be soldiers. The sheikh has ruled that even the
> unborn Israeli child in the womb is a legitimate target for death
> because one day he will wear a uniform.
>   This ceases to be a political stance; this becomes the demonisation
> of a people. Only one nation on the planet has no civilians; only one
> nation must recognise its children can legitimately be torn apart by
> nail bombs on buses. Not the Russians for what they have done in
> Chechnya, nor the Arab Sudanese in Darfur, nor the Americans and
> the British in Iraq, but the Israelis.
>
> (Ibid.)

We can appreciate Freedland's arguments while, at the same time,
acknowledging with Alibhai-Brown that the present delicate situation in
the wake of the London bombings is being used by some pro-Israeli
lobbies to identify the use of suicide bombers as 'terrorism' in ways that
delegitimate Palestinian struggles against an illegal occupation. She insists
that we also remember that the actions of the Irgun movement in 1946
'were as merciless as the Palestinian terrorists today. Both were and are
fighting for the same cause, a homeland. The Irgun attacked King David
Hotel leaving 91 dead.' At the same time, she argues:

> Muslims, rightly, have been asked to wake up and act to redeem their
> faith and rescue the young faithful from the temptations of glory

offered by murderous Islamicist warriors. But our young will not look our way if they see a duff deal, if Western governments avoid any blame for the state we are in. Their interventions in the world have made it easier for terrorism to flourish.

(*Independent*, 25 July 2005: 31)

Martyrdom

Sensitive issues around martyrdom that have become vital in understanding the nature of ethnic and political conflict in the world cannot be displaced through identifying them as 'religious', and so as concerning motivations that cannot be understood within rationalist terms. We have to recognise the limits of an interpretative tradition that insists that people are free to assign whatever meanings they want to give to their experience. At the same time, orthodox Marxist accounts that insist upon the influence of class interests also have to be questioned as we listen to what young men have to say about their involvements as they reflect upon their histories and experiences. This calls for a *capacity to listen* to what is being communicated as we engage critically with the terms in which these discourses are framed. But, at the same time, they can point to the limits of a discursive analysis that often fails to appreciate tensions between the political and psychic pressures people live with in spaces of conflict, and the discourses available to them within the broader culture to make sense of decisions they make for themselves.

As a teenager, Khaled al-Berry belonged to a radical Egyptian Islamist group. His experience resonates with some of the research into the lives of the young men from Beeston who carried out the London bombings. As he explains:

I wasn't attracted to their brand of religion; I was attracted to them as people. I was 14 and the first time I knew one of them, we were playing football and he was a very decent person who took care of people around him. If I was absent for some time, he would ask about me. We built up a relationship as human beings.

... I felt a sense of protection and power. From the outside you would think there was brainwashing in the sense that some people are giving you a lecture about what you should do. But it's not. It's like a new group of friends who approach you to play football. Then you start talking about religion.

At that time you already like them and want to be one of them because you like their courage and sense of donation.

(*Observer*, 24 July 2005: 8)

According to initial findings into the London bombings, there is no evidence of any al-Qaida 'mastermind' or senior organiser. As the *Independent* reported:

The disclosure that the July 7 team were working in isolation – and were radicalised by Mohammed Sidique Khan, the oldest man – has caused concern among anti-terrorist officers.... Anti terrorist officers are worried by the evidence that previously unknown 'clean skin' terror cells are forming in Britain with little or no help from abroad.

(*Independent*, 18 August 2005: 1)

The 21 July bomb incidents are thought to have been 'copycats', targeting tube trains and buses. 'The key point is that the events are not connected,' said one counter-terrorist source.

It appears they were self-contained, rather than being organised by some kind of mastermind.

'It is concerning that none were on the intelligence radar.... They only have to be lucky once – and they have been. At some point there will be another suicide or bombing group.

(Ibid.: 2)

A police source said:

All the talk about 'Mr Big' and al-Qa'ida masterminds looks like something from a film script at the moment. Of course, things could change if new intelligence comes through, but it looks increasingly as if these people were largely working on their own. It is not something we expected.

(Ibid.: 2)

Senior Police sources in West Yorkshire also suggest that gyms and boxing clubs in Leeds – rather than mosques – were the key to the development of the young men into bombers. Already an accomplished youth worker, Khan appears to have brought both Hussain and Tanweer to a gym established in the basement of the Hardy Street mosque, also in Beeston. Later he was forced to move to another gym at the former Hamara youth centre in Lodge Lane, where he was noted for not allowing adults in while the boys were training.

As Khaled al-Berry says of his own experience in Egypt:

We started to go to the mosque more frequently and learning the basics of religion. This was in 1986 and Egyptian society was not religious. We created a new way of looking at life. It was not just how to play, it was asking questions like, what is the meaning of being religious? What is the meaning of Islam? It stated that this life is very short and real life is after death.

So when I believed in this I didn't question myself further. They taught us that Islam means you can't argue about texts because the text is what God said. We applied this to different aspects of religion: fasting, praying, all kinds of things.

At a later stage, you have to think of other aspects which require you to sacrifice more. This depended on changing the regimes which didn't apply the word of God. We learnt that we couldn't do this except by using violence because God doesn't change our lives. We are tools of God, so we have to do it ourselves. If we didn't do it, nobody would.

(*Observer*, 24 July 2005: 8)

As he goes on to explain:

You don't know exactly how they choose such people for operations, but we were told that they choose people who showed a very high degree of obedience. This word is used in Islam's terminology in a different way. It means obedience to God, because they think they are the carriers of God's words, rather than being submissive.

At one stage I thought I would love to be chosen. I spent a great deal of time thinking: 'What if they ask me?' The idea of suicide bombing was not obvious but the idea of martyrdom was prominent. I would have liked to do something I thought mattered – sacrificing yourself to establish heaven on Earth. For me the real question was: 'Am I able to sacrifice more or not?' It wasn't: 'Am I going to do a wrong thing or right thing?' I knew I was right. For me at the time, the Koran said so. When Islamist people become suicide bombers they believe that God is ordering them to do it. They are not lying to themselves. They are not bad people. Your life is completely being lived for its sake until a point when you can't really differentiate between yourself and your ideology. If they destroy this ideology, they destroy you.

(Ibid.)

Khaled al-Berry wrote up his story as *Life is More Beautiful than Paradise* and, as he explained to David Smith, it was only when he moved from Assiut to Cairo and began to mix with other people at the university that he started meeting other people and questioning some of his own views. He came to be occupied with other ideas and concerns so that now he cannot imagine how he ever believed in those ideas, but he did. Former CIA agent Robert Baer, who was stationed in the Middle East during the first suicide bomb attack on a Western target, the April 1983 Beirut American Embassy bombing, determined to understand the phenomenon of suicide bombing that had killed 63 people, including many close colleagues. He talks rhetorically about 'a new plague on the streets of London, the pathological virus of the cult of suicide bombing'. He insists:

The first think we have to do is understand the nature of our enemy. We are continually looking for the one foreign, turbaned, mastermind who we secretly hope will be responsible for everything. Kill him and our nightmare is over.

(*Observer*, 7 August 2005: 25)

But he warns – and the evidence seems to bear it out:

You are fighting an enemy within. An enemy that can spring up like a virus from nowhere without reference to any far-flung leader or foreign terrorist organisation. And all they need to get into the killing business is a list of instructions on how to make explosives from the internet and their own willingness to die.

(Ibid.)

As the 21 July attempted bombings showed, they do not always succeed, but we need to think carefully about whether this language of 'enemy' is helpful, and whether it is not itself a consequence of Bush's misleading language of a 'war against terror'.[9]

As Jacques Derrida warns in 'Autoimmunity: Real and Symbolic Suicides', his dialogue with Giovanna Borradori:

we would also have to recognise, *against* Schmitt, that the violence that has now been unleashed is not the result of 'war' (the expression 'war on terrorism' thus being one of the most confused and we must analyse this confusion and the interests such an abuse of rhetoric actually serve). Bush speaks of 'war', but he is in fact incapable of identifying the enemy against whom he declares that he has declared war.... As for states that 'harbor' terrorist networks, it is difficult to identify them as such. The United States and Europe, London and Berlin, are also sanctuaries, places of training or formation and information for all the 'terrorists' of the world. No geography, no 'territorial' determination, is thus pertinent any longer for locating the seat of these new technologies of transmission or aggression.

(2003: 101)

Baer, in his Channel 4 TV programme entitled *The Cult of the Suicide Bomber*, explores how, as he calls it:

the cult of suicide bombing has grown more virulent. Today in Iraq there are more suicide bombings in a month than in a decade of conflict in Israel.... It swirls across the Islamic world as an expression of rage against the West for the invasion of Iraq, support for Israel, and for Western dominance of the world economy.

Amid the rage is the glorification of martyrdom. In a Gaza mosque

I saw 'official certificates of martyrdom' being handed out like graduation diplomas to the families of suicide bombers.

(Quoted in the *Observer*, 7 August 2005: 25)

As I watched these scenes in his film, you could see the pride that parents were expected to feel, and he interviews a father who talks proudly about the exploits of his son that has elevated the honour of the family within the larger community. His son has died a martyr's death and he has become well known through his death. Martyrdom becomes a way of *giving status* to a life that could otherwise lack meaning. His son had become a hero for other young people to emulate as they learned about the sacrifice he was making for the cause of Palestine. It was not uncommon for young people with hardly any religious training to want to die as a *shahid* because of the political climate created in Gaza through the years of occupation. Even if you have not come from an observant family, religious instruction in school can contribute to a decision to volunteer for an organisation such as Islamic Jihad. Suicide bombing had become a way that people could earn honour within their communities. It was a way they had learned to inflict fear and terror into the lives of their Israeli enemies. When his mother was asked about her concern for the innocent civilians, she says that there are no civilians in Israel.

Baer recognises that 'Stopping suicide terrorism will not be easy', but he also says:

> The worst possible mistake the British authorities could make is the one they are making right now; targeting and stopping and searching young Muslim-looking males catching trains or tubes. It is stupid and counterproductive.
>
> Such blanket searches are supposed to intimidate the bombers. But how can you intimidate someone who wants to die? In the end all you are likely to do is spread resentment among young British Muslim males and play into the hands of the bombers and the cult.
>
> (Ibid.)

This is a danger that Yasmin Alibhai-Brown also recognises from her own personal experience. As she states:

> My son – tall, dark, uppity – walks and takes the tubes and buses because he can't drive. What if plainclothes officers go for him and he resists? I have been talking to my Asian friends and we share the same anxieties. All of us understand and do accept (though it is incredibly hard) that our boys will be stopped more and questioned and sometimes treated harshly because of the identity of the bombers. But we don't accept that our men must now expect to be shot too, just because policemen suspect them of no good.
>
> (*Independent*, 25 July 2005: 31)

She recalls years ago, as a journalist in Stoke Newington police station, where an alarming number of black men were being beaten up in custody, 'I got some of the officers to admit that black men terrified them and the fear led them to over-react. It is highly likely the same syndrome is appearing today with Asian terror suspects' (ibid.).

Baer argues that, to stop suicide bombers, you have to intercept them in the planning stage. He argues, 'You cannot rely on telephone taps but only on old-fashioned spies and informers.' But he recognises that 'The only real solution lies within Islam itself. It is only when the vast majority of law-abiding Muslim societies reject the cultural virus of suicide bombing and cease to glorify it that this plague will burn itself out' (*Observer*, 7 August 2005: 25). But this is to turn the problem back into the Muslim community, rather than to appreciate the ways this has developed as a *response* to young men and women growing up in Britain, and the appeal that these Islamist ideas can have for people who feel uprooted and displaced. To engage creatively with the challenges that terrorism presents us with, we have to learn how to listen to what these young men and women are saying about their lives. We have to understand the appeal of jihadist ideas as they speak into particular lives, rather than to assume that young people are docile bodies whose minds have been 'twisted' by radical clerics who have their own political agendas.

Jason Burke has consistently argued that current Islamic militancy has its origins 'not in the Middle Ages or in violence inherited in a major faith, but in real problems in the real world – so real solutions are possible'. This means recognising that 'al-Qaida' is an ideology that has spread across borders and virtual spaces, not an organisation. He writes, 'Merely saying that the bombers are mad, when there is no evidence that militants are mentally ill or backward, and when contemporary radical Islam clearly has its roots in the conditions of the modern world, does not help' (*Observer*, 7 August 2005: 15).

Burke also insists:

> The 7 July bombers were not 'brainwashed' by anyone. Radical Islam provided them with an explanation of what was happening in the world and suggested actions that made sense to them. So we need a broad range of measure to ensure that such ideologies are less likely to convince in the future.
>
> (Ibid.)

He also acknowledges, 'Some causes of terrorism do exist within the UK. They include identity issues and poor economic performance of many British Muslim communities as much as the activities of radical rabble-rousers from overseas.' But Burk also acknowledges, 'But the real causes are international – and can be dealt with through real policies. Militants often cite Chechnya, Kashmir and Palestine as examples of western oppression of Muslims.' He recognises that 'Merely making an obvious effort to solve problems in a fair-minded way would be extremely helpful in restoring the goodwill many in the Islamic world once felt towards Britain' (ibid.).

By also developing major programmes to develop civil society, including literacy, human rights and micro-credit, with a particular emphasis on involving women, 'can help us to show that our way of life does not mean "neo-imperialism" or "moral corruption" but is about tolerance, justice and empowerment of the weak'. He acknowledges, though, that 'None of these measures will end the threat of terrorism, but central to our efforts must remain a simple fact: violent Islam militancy is not inevitable.' At the same time, we should be worried, alongside Alibhai-Brown, that the swell of Muslim support is receding after the second wave of attacks 'because the people charged with keeping us safe within the rule of law are themselves succumbing to hysteria, unlawful acts, scapegoating and double talk'. She warns that 'British Muslims are again being made to feel that they are not entitled to the same rights and respect given to others'. As she says, 'You don't want this resentment growing just when the country needs to come together in trust and cooperation to face the next attack, which will surely come soon' (*Independent*, 25 July 2005: 31). As Jason Burke fears: 'Another major bombing in the UK could damage community relations beyond repair' (*Observer*, 7 August 2005: 15).

12 Religion, 'race' and multicultures

Disenfranchised

Exploring the break between the generations within migrant communities involves understanding how a politics of belonging needs to be *refigured* for each generation, and that the solutions an older generation of migrants discovered for themselves often do not work for their children's generation.[1] Often the second generation, many born and educated in Britain, had not grown up with the same feelings for place that their parents often carried with them; and often they do not feel a similar connection to the countries where their parents came from. With global media, a younger generation who have been brought up by parents schooled in Britain sometimes regain a connection with language that their parents had lost. In the Bangladeshi community in East London, for example, there are young children with a more intense relationship with the language and culture of their grandparents than their parents who had been eager to learn English and so become 'like everyone else'. The possibility of watching programmes on satellite TV in different languages has sometimes encouraged a fluency that their older siblings lack. So we need to be aware of how new media technologies create opportunities for particular generations that allow them to forge complex identities of belonging of their own.[2]

Global communications have allowed for connections across space, and so with cultural familiarities that can help to shape the complex cultural identities of belonging of younger generations. They can also bring home terrible tragedies, as for example with the earthquake in Pakistan in the summer of 2005, where people can feel strong affiliations with their families who have been caught up with these losses. This helps to sustain lines of sympathy and identification that cross the traditional boundaries of the nation state and so the frameworks of identity and belonging that have traditionally shaped classical forms of social theory. People often inherit *complex loyalties* that can be sustained through the global media as they are refigured for each generation.

But it also means that people can feel identifications with the sufferings of their fellow co-religionists that can make them angry and dissatisfied with the actions of their own governments. To grasp how these sympathies can be mobilised politically involves tracing flows of identification across the boundaries of nation states. If these diasporic identification have existed before, they seem to have gained a new *intensity* within a globalised postmodern world that often allows more regular contacts to be maintained. Within multicultural societies, there is also more recognition of complex loyalties and identifications that might formerly have been muted as they were deemed to potentially threaten traditional conceptions of citizenship and primary loyalties towards the nation state. As cultures of assimilation came to be challenged, there were different accommodations with multicultures reached in different countries about how identity and difference were to be reconciled.[3]

Questions about the history and shaping of British traditions of multiculturalism became central concerns in the wake of the London bombings as people sought to navigate the new landscapes of fear they found themselves inhabiting. People looked to the experiences of different countries, and social theorists were concerned to illuminate the diverse traditions and national experiments in multicultures through which people with different backgrounds and cultures could learn to live in peace next to each other.

There were fears expressed about the indifference that often seemed to accompany British experiences of multiculturalism that could often mean diverse communities were living in isolation with little contact with other communities around them. Often this seemed to mean that social inequalities went unchallenged and people could be left feeling isolated and alone, as if there was no real care and concern for their fates.

Abdul-Rehman Malik, contributing editor for *Q-News, the Muslim Magazine*, recognises that most young Muslims in Leeds, Oldham or other northern towns have never heard of the 'moderate' Muslim leaders that the Prime Minister asked to speak in their name after the London bombings. He recalls that, after an hour-long session, 'they emerged to announce the creation of a task force charged with tacking the "evil ideology" of militant Islam, combating social exclusion and encouraging political engagement'. He argues:

> Few have been able to put forward a vision of British Islam that is convincing to the most marginalized, disadvantaged and prone to militancy. It's not a matter of whether they deserve a voice at the table, but whether they are trusted by the Muslims they claim to speak for.
>
> (*Observer*, 24 July 2005: 29)

Malik reminds us that it is foolish to speak of a 'Muslim community', as if it were undifferentiated and homogeneous. The government needs to rethink assumptions it makes about 'faith communities', as if they exist with leaderships that can speak in their name. For instance, the Jewish community is much more divided and fragmented than its official leadership in the board of deputies would want to acknowledge. They like the idea of speaking with a united voice to government, partly because it assures them a certain status in their own eyes and helps to sustain a myth of homogenised community that is no longer reflected in the realities of the present. But, for the government, this was often the model they followed when they looked to create a representative body that could somehow 'speak for' Muslims in Britain.[4]

An *Observer* investigation into the Muslim Council of Britain (MCB), which presents itself as the mainstream organisation best able to represent the diversity of views, shows that its secretary-general, Sir Iqbal Sacranie, and its media spokesman, Inayat Bunglawala, have both expressed admiration for Maulana Maududi, founder of the radical Jamaat-I-Islami party, which campaigns for an Islamic state in Pakistan by non-violent means. But presumably similar connections can be found in other religious organisations that seek to position themselves as 'mainstream', for instance connections with settler organisations on the West Bank within some Jewish leaderships. Within bodies that claim to be representative, there are always difficult judgements to be made about the extent and quality of representation and *who* they are really speaking for.

Salman Rushdie warned in an article 'the right time for an Islamic reformation' in *The Times* (7 August 2005) p. 307 that Sacranie had been a prominent critic during the *Satanic Verses* affair, so that he should not be viewed as a moderate. In 1989, Sacranie said 'death was perhaps too easy' for the writer. Rushdie also criticised Sacranie for boycotting January's Holocaust Memorial Day ceremony. 'If Sir Iqbal Sacranie is the best Mr Blair can offer in the way of a good Muslim, we have a problem,' said Rushdie. The origins of the Muslim Council of Britain can be traced back to the storm created around the publication of Rushdie's *Satanic Verses* in 1988. Opposition to the book in Britain united people committed to a traditionalist view of Islam as well as bringing together different generations.[5]

But the MCB some argue also threatened to bring issues around gender to the fore since Maulana Maududi, founder of Jamaat-I-Islami, was claimed as a fierce opponent of feminism who believed that women should be kept in purdah and so secluded. Although the MCB's leadership distances itself from these teachings, it has been criticised for having no women prominently involved in the organisation. But similar issues around feminism have proved divisive within other orthodox faith traditions, including Jewish communities, where there is also a view that would see feminism as a secular 'Westernised' movement that needs to be resisted. It can be deemed to be a threat to traditional Judaism as much as for traditional Islam. I draw attention to these resonances across different religious traditions to show there are complex divisions within these traditions as well as between them, and that faith dialogues need to be carefully framed if issues are not to be often tacitly framed through dominant secularised Christian frameworks.

The strain of Islamic ideology favoured by the MCB leadership and many of its affiliate organisations is inspired by Maulana Maududi, a thinker respected across the Islamic world. His writings call for a global Islamic revival and the establishment of a Caliphate. He was deeply critical of notions of nationalism as well as feminism, and called on Muslims to purge themselves of these Western influences. As he explains in *Jihad in Islam*:

> The objective of Islamic 'jihad' is to eliminate the rule of an un-Islamic system and establish an Islamic system of state rule. Islam does not intend to confine this revolution to a single state or a few countries; the aim of Islam is to bring about a universal revolution.
>
> (*Observer*, 14 August 2005: 9)

According to Abdul-Rehman Malik, 'Maududi divided humanity into true believers or those in a state of ignorance. Many of the affiliates of the Muslim Council of Britain are inspired by Maududi's ideology' (ibid.). The ways in which 'humanity' comes to be perceived as divided between 'true believers' and those 'in a state of ignorance' is an issue for other religious traditions that are founded on a unique revelation. Sometimes it is harder *within* religious traditions to acknowledge the dignity of difference.

Abdul-Rehman Malik points out that, in towns like Oldham, there are parallel communities – for example, Pakistani and Bangladeshi, divided along ethnic and sectarian lines. There are divisions of caste and class, as well as breaks between the generations that often inhabit quite different worlds and find it almost impossible to communicate with each other. Young people get so used to not telling their parents anything about their lives and living a *double life* inside the home, where they might feel obliged to show respect, and the very different lives they live with their friends on the street. They are used to living with their own secrets so that it should not be surprising that, for example, those close to the young men in Beeston, who were responsible for the 7 July bombings in London, had no idea of what they had been planning. This can be difficult for a liberal middle-class to understand since, within Protestant cultures, emphasis is placed upon continuities between thoughts, speech and behaviours. In other traditions, these are often separated realms and people can often live more split and compartmentalised lives. For people who have grown up within dictatorships, this can also be easier to grasp since they are familiar with an experience of having to learn to distrust and keep their own counsel out of fear that others might act as informers for the state.[6]

As Rehman points out:

> Mosques have little actual authority in the lives of ordinary Muslims and the edicts of imams can be ignored or followed as Muslims wish. With most mosques not accessible to women and with more young

people, like the bombers, seeking guidance outside them, British mosques are caught in a crisis of relevance.

(Observer, 24 July 2005: 29)

He says:

> It is the street-level voluntary and community sector organisations that represent the British Islam's hidden civil society, working to meet the needs of neighbourhoods struggling with violence, drug abuse and teenage pregnancy. These are the front lines of the fight against militancy and desperation.

(Ibid.)

This is an experience shared in the Channel 4 TV drama *Yasmin*, first screened January 2005 and repeated soon after 7/7 on 11 August 2005, which shows the experience of a young woman moving between different worlds. She does her duty to her family through accepting a marriage with a relative, but insists that she will have little to do with her husband from Pakistan who speaks no English and comes from a very different cultural background to her own experience in Britain. She keeps this relationship to herself as she strikes up a friendship with a colleague, an English man from the same West Yorkshire town. They work together in social services, collecting people with learning difficulties to take them to school. She moves between different worlds, stopping her car on the moors to change her clothes. But she is challenged by the events of 9/11 and the responses of those she works with, who seem to expect some kind of apology from her 'because she is a Muslim'. She finds this difficult to handle, as events in the world somehow *transform* the ways she is seen by the people she works with. She used to think she was accepted as 'one of the gang' only to feel that she is on her own when it comes to the aftermath of 9/11.

The drama follows her brother, who is angered when his father does not seem to take offence when the police raid their house and he is held up at gunpoint. He is shown living his own double life, where he is ready to chant at the mosque for his father, while at the same time living a life dealing drugs. There is a moment when the police offer him a bribe if he will tell on others in the community, but he refuses. He is a gradually drawn into a circle of young men who teach him what it means to be a 'good Muslim' and how his brothers and sisters are suffering in other lands and it is up to him to do something about it. He decides to leave his family and go to Pakistan where he will train for a mission. The drama presented some of the conflicts familiar to the young men of Beeston who carried out the London bombings, and it was shown again a month after the attacks.

I watched it again and realised that, with the impact of the events of 7/7, I was watching differently, and that there was so much I had missed the first time around. Somehow, 7/7 had helped to create a different landscape of fear, in which different threats and uncertainties seemed to make urban life precarious in new ways. There was a sense of *displacement* the young men felt, unable to identify with their parent's generation and seemingly less able to find their way, as Yasmin does, between the two worlds, because of the absence of work for many of them. It is often difficult for them to feel that their lives have meaning and that they are not 'losers'. Through militant Islam, they seem to find a different kind of place and identity for themselves. It seems to promise a way of giving their lives meaning, but it also sets them apart within groups they had learned to identify with as they were growing up in these northern towns. Certainties and a sense of responsibility for the sufferings of other Muslims were being offered that seemed to provide less precarious masculinities that helped them feel better about themselves.

Abdul-Rehran Malik argues:

> Muslims who think that the recent attacks have nothing to do with Islam are simply in denial. Since the 1960s a literalist, puritanical form of Islam has been gaining ground in Britain. Well funded and promoted in slickly produced manuals of 'correct' doctrine and 'authentic' practice, this aberrant theology saw to remove the celebration of difference and flexibility of law that lies at the heart of Islam's classical past. Gone were the interpretative ambiguities, replaced by certainties of right and wrong, good Muslim and bad.
>
> (Ibid.)

He argues that this form of Islam has become increasingly mainstream and popular under the watch of Muslim organisations. Spurred by strident religious tracts, some have conceived the Ummah, the global Muslim community, not as a spiritual brotherhood but as a political one in opposition to an immoral, imperialist and decadent West. 'Such literalism', Malik says, 'allowed for a hatred of "the other" that was hitherto unknown in Muslim civilisation' (ibid.).

Feminisms

Nick Cohen was sitting in on a conference, 'Women and Entrepreneurial London', at the London Muslim Centre, a bright, modern building in the East End. Modern Bengali women were discussing ways of creating new businesses. He recalls:

> The practical advice stopped stone dead when assistants wheeled in a wide-screen television so that an imam from a local mosque could describe what careers were open to Muslim women. Very few it turned out.

He informed the audience that they had no need for feminism. God had given roles to men and women and the woman's divinely ordained task was to look after her husband, produce children and then look after them. This didn't leave much time for entrepreneurial dynamism, and just about the only firm he could imagine them having the spare time to manage would be an internet business ...

(*Observer*, 14 August 2005: 27)

Cohen surmises:

Had the Archbishop of Canterbury told women members of the CBI that they must look after Dad and the kids, there would have been hell to pay, not least for the assumption that the women were Christians and should take instructions from him.

(Ibid.)

But nobody seemed to see anything amiss in the East End, as Cohen explains, 'For the purposes of official classifications, they weren't British or British Asians or English or working class or Londoners or Bengalis or women. They were Muslims and their religious leaders must have a large say in how they lived.'

He recalls:

Anti-racism used to mean treating people equally. Differences in skin colour or religious faith counted for little when set against the universal claims of common humanity. No cliché was more pleasing to the liberal mind than the assertion we were all the same under the skin. To say that feminism was fine for whites but not for browns would have been an outrageous assertion of racist values. Now there are different rules for different religions. In the name of the noble virtues of tolerance and broad-mindedness, liberal people have segregated with the enthusiasm of an apartheid police chief and left common humanity out in the cold.

(Ibid.)

Though this is somewhat rhetorical, Cohen identifies a paradox within liberal political theory that finds it difficult to engage with cultural and religious traditions. How do we respect different traditions if we feel they are oppressive to women who remain as second-class citizens unable to work outside of the home? Is this to impose unwelcome Western values?[7]

Reflecting back on feminism in Britain in the 1970s, and its difficulties dealing both theoretically and politically with immigrant communities, Fay Weldon recalls:

We knew they tended to be sexist, but we looked the other way. Since Asian communities were small – an estimated 400,000 Muslims, 300,000 Hindus and 200,000 Sikhs in 1975 – we assumed that as they assimilated, the standards of the wider community would take over; equal rights, opportunities, wages and sexual self-determination for women would become theirs. We natives had to acquire them first, mind you.

(*Sunday Times*, 14 August 2005: 15)

She recalls that

the West Indians were well established and assimilated: indeed, women earned and were in more regular employment than their menfolk. Proper wages for women meant power and dignity. Before the passing of the Sex Discrimination Act of 1975, a woman could not take out a mortgage in her own name.

(Ibid.)

Weldon recalls the

shock/horror when black feminists broke away from the Wages for Housework Campaign to found their own group and while liberal women were confronted with what men were beginning to experience – what it felt like to be disliked and despised for something historical and no fault of their own. So our patronising attitudes became evident to us. This to some extent explains our reluctance to batter our way into other cultures and put them to rights. But most of all it was because we did not want to be labelled 'racist'.

Sure Muslim communities were 'sexist', but our interference could be seen as 'racist' and that was far, far worse an epithet. Social workers and crusading feminists kept away and the police, too. There were language problems and it was all too difficult.

(Ibid.)[8]

Nick Cohen recalls:

Until the 1980s, people talked about 'blacks'. This was an incredibly broad term which covered not only Afro-Caribbeans (who had large differences of their own), but anyone from the Indian subcontinent or, at the broadest, anyone with a dark skin.

(*Observer*, 14 August 2005: 27)

He recognises that the use of 'blacks' or later 'blacks and Asians' made sense because, whatever differences of class, status and wealth, people 'had a common interest in fighting colour prejudice'. As Herman Ousely, a former chairman of the Commission for Racial Equality, recalls in a *Guardian* conversation with Paul Gilroy:

> There was a time when race relations in Britain could be symbolised by the very simple reference to there being No Black in the Union Jack! White people had the power, control, resources and empire. Black people were seen as exotic immigrants doing low-grade jobs and disfiguring the landscape, the labour and housing markets. Over the decades different groups of people have had to assert themselves to get their grievances heard, sometimes engaging in uprisings.
>
> (*Guardian*, 30 July 2005: 22)[9]

A new generation of young British Muslims educated in British schools, less concerned than their parents with religion, was emerging by the mid-1980s. According to Weldon:

> The Koran might emphasise male supremacy, but it had become evident that in terms of earning power, the freedom to choose sexual partners outside marriage, the use of contraception and so on, women were equal enough. The old men looked on aghast.
>
> (*Sunday Times*, 14 August 2005: 15)

This was a freedom that Yasmin was assuming, even though she recognised she had to behave differently when she was at home. She insisted on getting her own red VW Golf, a car with sex appeal, against the advice of her English boyfriend who advised a safer choice. She had the freedom to move outside the community when she wanted and shape her own relationship with Islam, though she had been obliged to agree to an arranged marriage she had not wanted, to sustain the honour of the family. She insisted on a divorce and so with being able to live her own life as she moved back closer to Islam. Through making visible the often-ignored conflicts within a Muslim community, as experienced by Yasmin, others may feel affirmed in their own struggles.

According to Fay Weldon, it was the impact of the fatwa on Rushdie that united the faithful in Britain. There were book-burnings, riots and deaths:

> The Prophet had been insulted and worse, his wives. Muslim youth was back in the fold. The girls covered up again. The atheist Rushdie, born into a Muslim household, was an apostate. Apostates must be killed. Muslim ranks closed.
>
> The feminists had lost their opportunity. Married women in Islam are again discouraged from earning: it is for their husbands to provide. Contraception has been politicised as a western plot to reduce Islamic

numbers.... Girls and boys are educated separately. Dress must mark them out from the host community.

(Ibid.)

Weldon warns, 'Multiculturalism ends up as ghettoisation, the exploitation of cheap labour and the subjugation of women. Even the kindness of local authorities in putting up street signs in Arabic backfires – why learn English if there's no need?' But somehow she remains hopeful that

they, too, look at the advertisements, want ringtones, iPods. The bastions of male supremacy will fall as standards of living rise and women's income is increasingly needed in the home. With wages comes freedom, power and dignity. Consumerism may yet save us. Or not. One source of fanaticism is rejection of the false solutions that consumerism offers ...

(Ibid.)

'Race' and faith

Herman Ouseley argues that the uprisings and disturbances in Bradford, Burnley and Oldham in 2001 highlighted the gulf between poor white and deprived Muslim communities and 'This forced a redefinition of the race-equality project, and faith, belief and religious identity are now regarded as issues warranting explicit consideration' (the *Guardian*, 30 July 2005: 22). But Gilroy responds that he 'does not agree that Muslim assertiveness is a primary source of our new circumstances, or that the "race-equality project" should be redefined in terms of faith'. But recognising a new significance of issues of faith does not have to mean, as Gilroy seems to suggest, 'redefining in terms of faith', though he is right that 'Britain's official race-equality strategies will not suddenly start to work better if we can just redescribe cultural minorities more accurately'. This seemed to be a suggestion made by Hazel Blears for the Home Office. She hopes that redescribing people as 'British Muslims' will help. But these redefinitions are often the result of complex and painful personal and political struggles as people come to experience their histories and present lives in different terms, rather than something to be legislated by government.

Gilroy recognises that

A few young people from all backgrounds will respond to the siren call of political Islam because it offers them a strongly ethical response to the erotic dazzle of consumer culture, from which they feel excluded. Fundamentalism's oversimple solutions harness the disenchantment that grows with marginalisation. What healthier, secular alternatives can we offer them?

(Ibid.)

But why do they necessarily have to be secular, and what kind of assumptions about religion as a form of irrationality is Gilroy tacitly making? Earlier in his exchange with Ouseley, he argues, 'We need to know what varieties of injury promote the absurd belief among young British people that an austere, political Islam can be a viable vehicle for their hopes for an improved world.' But again, he seems to assume that religious beliefs are somehow 'absurd', as if there is a clear standard of rationality against which they are being evaluated. This makes it difficult for Gilroy to acknowledge the significance that Islam has come to have in the lives of many when he calls them 'young British people', and the difficulties that secular traditions of social theory have in grasping the nature of a religious appeal.[10]

Gilroy is more helpful when he explores how 'Blair's belligerent revival of empire and the occupation of "Muslim lands" are obvious potential causes, but another hatred seems to have festered in Beeston and other dead zones of England's post-industrial economy.' He is closer also when he refers to 'the problems that derive from unacknowledged colonial crimes' and the need for political leaders to acknowledge these historical injustices as a possible way of increasing their moral authority and political credibility. As he explains, 'they might also gain support from excluded people who might otherwise dismiss all this chat about diversity. The national solidarity you aspire to can only be built on trust, and an acknowledgement of the damage done by racism' (ibid.).

This is a helpful way of reframing what Hazel Blears calls for, 'If you want a society that is really welded together, there are certain things that unite us because we are British.' But there are also dangers in somehow holding the 'Muslim community', however we understand its complexity, to be somehow responsible for the atrocities, and so with a special duty to inform the police. As Gilroy recognises, 'It is only racism that holds all British Muslims responsible for the wrongs perpetrated in the name of their faith by a tiny minority' (ibid.). This was an unfairness that Yasmin felt in the drama when, after 9/11, her colleagues at work seemed to see her differently and somehow demand some kind of apology, as if she had something to do with it because she came from a Muslim background. Suddenly she felt isolated and alone. She felt angry at the ways they were responding to her.

But Gilroy is much less helpful when he says, somewhat generally, 'Transposing these large cultural, political and economic problems into the language of faith and religion is a counterproductive oversimplification, recycling the "clash of civilisations" idea.' It is misleading to think that Ouseley's attempts to rethink the race-equality project to take into consideration 'faith, belief and religious identity' are a matter of translation into a language of faith and religion, and that it is necessarily 'a counterproductive oversimplification'. Rather, it is a matter of *taking seriously* the transformations in the ways some young Muslims have come to think and experience changes in their lives.[11]

In this context, it is important to draw distinctions between different forms of religious and spiritual belief, rather than to automatically assume within the terms of an Enlightenment rationalism that religion is a form of unreason and superstition. Rather, we need to critically challenge the appeals of fundamentalisms within diverse religious traditions, while at the same time *refusing* to identify religion as an organised hierarchy of belief with spiritualities that can also often enjoy their own traditions and draw upon a diversity of sources. This allows us to question the dominance of consumerism within the West and the spiritual emptiness that it can often produce in people's lives through developing a rich enough narrative of material and spiritual needs.

An awareness of the conversations that have happened across the boundaries of religious traditions and ways they have learned from each other across time also helps us to question homogenised notions of religious cultures and traditions. It also helps us towards terms that allow us to engage with what some have identified as a 'spiritual crisis' in the West and diverse responses to it, rather than to feel we are obliged to defend all forms of consumerist culture.[12] This also allows us to engage more directly with the critiques of consumerism and celebrity cultures from more radical positions without having to defend traditions that need to question their own sexism, racisms and homophobias.

Racisms

Hussein Osman, one of the men alleged to have participated in London's failed bombing on 21 July 2005, told Italian investigators that they prepared for the attack by watching 'films on the war in Iraq', *La Republica* reported, 'Especially those where women and children were being killed and exterminated by British and American soldiers ... of widows, mothers and daughters that cry' (quoted in the *Guardian*, 13 August 2005: 20). Naomi Klein says, 'It has become an article of faith that Britain was vulnerable to terror because of its politically correct anti-racism.' Yet, she suggests, 'another possible motive for the acts of terror against the UK: rage at perceived extreme racism.' For, she suggests:

> what else can we call the belief – so prevalent that we barely notice it – that American and European lives are worth more than the lives of Arabs and Muslims, so much so that their deaths in Iraq are not even counted?
>
> (*Guardian*, 13 August 2005: 20)

Klein goes on, 'It's not the first time that this kind of raw inequality has bred extremism', recalling that Sayyid Qutb, the Egyptian writer viewed as a vital intellectual architect of radical political Islam, shaped his views while studying in the United States. Not only was he shocked by Colorado's licentious women, but also by what he later described as America's 'evil and fanatic racial discrimination'. Arriving in the United States in 1948, the year of the creation of the state of Israel, he witnessed an American blindness to the plight of thousands of Palestinians made permanent refugees. As Klein frames it, 'For Qutb, it wasn't politics it was an assault on his identity: clearly Americans believed that Arab lives were worth far less than those of European Jews' (ibid.).

Klein (*Guardian*, 13 August 2005: 20) reports Yvonne Hadad, a professor of history at Georgetown University, as saying that this experience 'left Qutb with a bitterness he was never able to shake'. When he returned to Egypt, he joined the Muslim Brotherhood, but was arrested, severely tortured and convicted of anti-government conspiracy in a show trial. Qutb's political theory was profoundly shaped through his experience of torture for, not only did he conclude that his torturers were subhuman infidels, he stretched that categorisation to include the entire state that ordered this brutality, including the Muslim civilians who passively lent their support to Nasser's regime. This helped to shape a tradition within radical Islam that tended to see 'others' who were not of the true faith as 'infidels'.[13]

As Klein understands it, 'Qutb's vast category of subhumans allowed his disciples to justify the killing of "infidels" – now practically everyone – as long as it was done in the name of Islam.' Again we have to be careful to explore this category of the 'subhuman' and the ways it differs from a tradition within European modernity tracing a line between colonialism and Hazum, that could also treat those who were deemed '(un)civilised', or as lacking reason, to be 'subhuman'. We have to investigate the particular ways 'infidel' comes to be invoked in radical Islamist movements. If suicide bombers, for instance, can think that they are somehow doing 'God's work' when they are concerned to accomplish the tasks they have been given, then possibly it can sometimes be argued they do not fully recognise as they should the pain they are causing civilians.

Barbara Jones tells of a meeting organised by Hassan Batt, raised in Manchester and the leader of the now-defunct Al-Mahajiroun in Pakistan, with a young Britain who called himself Dr Hakani, who had been educated in Church of England schools in Luton and, according to Jones, 'was now committed to waging a Holy War on the country that nurtured and educated him' (*Mail on Sunday*, 17 July 2005: 9). Hakani said he was the son of respectable Bangladeshi immigrants. After studying at Manchester University, he became sickened by the frivolity of his fellow students. He said, 'Unlike America, we do not want to harm civilians. We will be hitting public buildings, government and military targets and leading politicians like Tony Blair. All of us who have fought with Al Qaeda would welcome martyrdom.' According to Jones, Hakani said he suffered racism as he grew up, developing a disgust for people he described as 'infidels' at university. 'Their idea of living was to get drunk and let women behave little better than prostitutes. I looked in the mirror and didn't want to call myself British any more,' he explained.

He was later befriended by extremist Muslims at the London hospital where he was working. He said:

> There were all Al Qaeda. They inspired me to fight back for all our people who have suffered. They had been busy recruiting in Britain at universities and hospitals.
>
> They were clever, drinking with non-activist Muslims in pubs and appearing to join in the lifestyle, but at the same time subtly indoctrinating.
>
> (Ibid.)

The word 'indoctrinating' seems surprising. Hakani quite his job and came to Pakistan to train in Bin Laden's camps. 'By the time we arrived we were already willing to died for Allah,' he said. Hakani said he and other Britons were in Kabul with Al Qaida when the Americans invaded Afghanistan in 2001.

> We thought, yes, this is our chance to fight them face to face. We lost the battle for Afghanistan and we were driven out, but we did not lose the war. We will take it to them again and again. There are many millions of us.
>
> (Ibid.)

Barbara Jones reported Hakani as saying in their meeting in January 2002, 'It's true I had a privileged background and trained as doctor in England but today things have gone full circle for me. Even my parents believe in what I am doing.' He also said:

> Islam is my land but it is occupied, treacherously, by so-called Christians. Spain is one of those countries we will target. We will use all our power to have that land back in our hands. That is what we are training young people for, that is the motive we teach them. There is a bigger goal than just attacking America or Britain. The goal is to regain our land.
>
> Young British Muslims come to us and we give them physical and psychic training to get their minds ready for the work ahead. I've kept in close touch with British mosques. ... I am proud to say I have helped form many cells back in Britain. ... The mullahs are our universal soldiers, fighting against the Western way of life. We don't want to alienate the British public. They are all potential Muslims who could one day be on our side and react against the derelict way of life they see around them.
>
> (Ibid.)

Naomi Klein recognises that 'so-called Islamist terrorism was "home-grown" in the west long before the July 7 attacks – from its inception it was the quintessentially modern progeny of Colorado's casual racism and Cairo's concentration camps' (*Guardian*, 13 August 2005: 20). She thinks it is vital to know the histories of these movements because

> the twin-sparks that ignited Qutb's world-changing rage are currently being doused with gasoline: Arab and Muslim bodies are being debased in torture chambers around the world and their deaths are being discounted in simultaneous colonial wars, at the same time that graphic digital evidence of these losses and humiliations is available to anyone with a computer. And once again, this lethal cocktail of racism and torture is burning through the veins of angry young men.
>
> (Ibid.)

It is young men within the tradition who carry a particular burden of responsibility to protect others against suffering. So if we think about the pressures on young Islamic masculinities, often unable to find dignified employment for themselves and often berated by their patriarchal fathers, they need to find their own ways of proving themselves. They need to know that their lives count for something, even if it is through the sacrifice of their lives to 'do something' to prevent the sufferings of women and children, the focus of the videos that feed the imagination and rage of young men like Hussein Osman.

According to Klein, 'Qutb's history carries an urgent message for today: its not tolerance for multiculturalism that fuels terrorism; its tolerance for barbarism committed in our name.' She fears

> into this explosive environment has stepped Tony Blair, determined to pass off two of the main causes of terror as its cure. He intends to deport more people to countries where they will likely face torture. And he will keep fighting wars in which soldiers don't even know the names [in Iraq] of the towns they are levelling. (To cite just one recent example, an August 5 Knight Ridder report quotes a marine sergeant pumping up his squad by telling them, 'these will be the good old days, when you brought ... death and destruction to – what the fuck is this place called?' Someone piped in helpfully, 'Haqlaniyah.')
>
> (Ibid.)

Meanwhile there is also evidence of the 'evil and fanatical racial discrimination' that Qutb denounced. There have been widespread racist abuse and attacks aimed at the Muslim community since 7/7. Scotland Yard says hate crimes are up 600 per cent from this time last year. In March 2005, before the bombings, a *Guardian* poll reported, 'One in five of Britain's ethnic-minority voters say that they are considering leaving

Britain because of racial intolerance.' Often multiculturalism, particularly outside London, seems to work to, according to Klein, 'keeps ethnic minorities tucked away in state-funded peripheral ghettos while the centres of public life remain largely unaffected by seismic shifts in the national ethnic makeup.' But we have to be wary of Klein's generalisations, which fail to appreciate significant differences in relation to the multiculturalisms practised in different European states.

At the same time, she helpfully calls for 'deeply multi-ethnic societies, rather than shallow multicultural ones' in which 'the diversity now ghettoised on the margins of western societies – geographically and psychologically – were truly allowed to migrate to the centres'. She thinks this 'might infuse public life in the west with a powerful new humanism' – what I frame as a critical multiculturalism. She also believes that a society 'that truly lived its values of equality and human rights ... would rob terrorists of what has always been their greatest recruitment tool: our racism' (ibid.). Tahir Butt of the Muslim Safety Form (MSF) said there was a sharp rise in Islamophobic crimes the day after the first London bombings. The rate decreased a few days later, then increased again after the suspects were revealed to be British-born Muslims.

Butt said there were serious concerns about the backlash and, while he praised police for their efforts to protect Muslims, he raised questions about how prepared they were for the level of reprisal attacks. 'There are bigots out there who are reading some media reports and deciding to take their law into their own hands,' he said.

> The message from everyone is zero tolerance, but we need action. We need to hear about people being arrested for these attacks on Muslims who are threefold victims. They are targets of terrorists, targets of the islamophobic backlash and they will be targets of anti-terror legislation.
>
> (*Observer*, 24 July 2005: 7)

A sense of how a critical multiculturalism has helped to transform race relations, at least in London, is given by Zoe Smith in the *Observer*. She says:

> Growing up in London my circle of friends resembles a Beneton ad. Inter-racial dating was never an issue for us. When people have asked me what it's like to date 'outside my race' it always struck me as a glaring non-issue.
>
> (*Observer*, 14 August 2005)

She says, 'In an age when inter-racial couples are regularly seen on television soap operas and appear in ads selling everything from sofas to cereals I had forgotten that mixed relationships could even be a subject of debate in Britain.' This is partly why she was so shocked to see the headlines in the first week of August 2005 reporting the death of Anthony Walker, a

teenage boy in Huyton, Liverpool, who was axed to death by racists just because he chose to date a girl from a different race. It forced Smith to ask an uncomfortable question, given how she saw things for herself in London, 'How far have we progressed from the days of slavery if a black man can still be lynched simply for being seen in the company of a white woman?'

Smith insists, however, 'we no longer live in the dark ages of the Fifties and Sixties when lack of familiarity with different cultures and races and ignorance about the lives and backgrounds of newly arrived immigrants bred contempt.' As she says:

> Young adults of my generation (I was born in 1980) who have been brought up in metropolitan areas have been mingling with people from a rainbow of backgrounds since nursery school. By the time we were of university age, integrating with people from different ethnicities should have become second nature.
>
> (Ibid.)

But

> That is not to say that London is a Utopia. There are certain parts of East London that I would never step foot in (there's no point in asking for trouble in areas which have a history of racial violence) and I avoid trips to the south London suburb of Brixton with my boyfriend as much as possible. I can't help feeling pissed off when, as happens all too often, black men mutter comments including the word 'Bounty' (meaning a black person who is white on the inside) as I saunter down Coldharbour Lane with my guy.
>
> (Ibid.)

In the wake of the London bombings and the racial tensions awakened by the events in Huyton it is important 'that people do not withdraw into their communities.' She is convinced from her own experiences that 'Living segregated lives cannot lead Britain to unity. Embracing our country's diversity offers the securest defence against racists, fundamentalists and bigots.' She reflects, in her optimism, a routine everyday multiculture in the ways that urban Britain has changed irreversibly since the Empire Windrush docked in Tilbury in 1948.

Few of those early immigrants intended to stay in the country for long, so there was probably little internal conflict about their sense of cultural identity, though they had to deal with the everyday reality of racism in London. More than 50 years on, Akin Ojumu writes:

> it is clear that people like me, the child of African immigrants, have a kind of dual identity. On one hand we are British born and bred; on

the other, our African heritage is the deeper part of ourselves. So what happens when you grow up removed from it?

(Observer Review, 14 August 2005: 16)

Ojumu made his first visit to Nigeria in his twenties. He recalls:

> I spent the first few days feeling like a fraud, until I began to realise that my experience was commonplace and accepted by Nigerians, although I was conscious of how I had neglected my African side as a teenager, keener instead to forge a sense of myself as a black Briton.

(Ibid.)

The sense of not quite knowing where you belong is also the starting point of Ekow Eshun's *Black Gold of the Sun* (London, Hamish Hamilton 2005) that Ojumu reviews. Although Eshun spent time in Ghana and Britain as a child, he feels caught between two cultures and, as Ojumu says, 'goes home to try and sort it out'. He contrasts his London adolescence with the experience of returning to Ghana, ending with the disastrous discovery that one of his ancestors was a slave trader. He gives a sense of what it is like to be a young person of African descent who is unquestionably British. As Ojumu remarks:

> The experience of being black and British is different from the way it was for their parent's generation. Many of the old certainties that come from a strong sense of belonging to a motherland are gone, but the question of how to be both British and from somewhere else is more relevant than ever.

(Ibid.)

13 Civilisations, terrorisms and hospitalities

Terror(s)

As a traumatic event that seemed to come out of the blue, even if at some level it had been expected ever since 9/11, the London bombings had the effect of stopping many people in their tracks. Those who were directly involved, or those who had lived through anxious and uncertain times, not knowing whether those close to them had survived, or those who just felt fortunate to have escaped a fate that could have easily included them in some way, know that it is an event they will never forget. It was an event that helps to define the psychic map of a generation, and defines a landscape of fear they have lived with. Years later, people know that they will recall where they had been on that fateful day, just as previous generations recall the moment they heard about the death of President Kennedy in Dallas or of Princess Diana in Paris. These events help to define the times a generation has lived through, and they show that time is not linear but is constantly *disrupted* by events that people know they will have to 'come to terms with' in their own ways. It can provoke memories and associations that people can be surprised by and link present to past in new ways.

Had it not been for the bomb on the Piccadilly line in London on 7/7 and its awful consequences, Ian Jack, editor of *Granta*, might never have remembered where he saw *The Battle of Algiers* in a cinema about a hundred yards from King's Cross. As he explains, 'Then, after July 7, I became slightly obsessed with a particular memory of the film, rented it on DVD, watched it twice, and recalled how much it had troubled me in 1971 or 1972 or whenever it was' (*Guardian Review*, 30 July 2005: 6). Pontecorvo's film tells the story of the Algerian insurrection against the French in the late 1950s. As a politically committed film-maker, he seems to have taken for granted that his audience's sympathy would instinctively side with the rebellious Algerians, the Muslims of the casbah. As Jack points out, 'The historical injustice of their situation is never spelled out. Instead, Pontecorvo focuses narrowly on the conflict, trying to deepen our understanding of the barbarous behaviour on both sides, bombs from the Algerians and torture from the French' (ibid.).[1]

Jack realises:

> As I looked at it again, what struck me was its prescience; how it
> described a world now familiar to all of us, when at the time of its
> appearance in 1965 it described only a particular Algerian world that
> had recently been left behind.

(Ibid.)

The most terrible moments, as Jack recalls, are when three women leave
the casbah to plant their bombs. Each woman goes her own way with a
bomb in her basket – to a fair, a milk bar and the offices of Air France.
They slide the bombs under their stools and chairs they sit on, pushing
them back with their heels. The French are entirely innocent of their fate,
ordinary people doing ordinary things. Pontecorvo splices the scenes of
their unbearable unknowingness with shots of a clock as its hands move
towards 5.45. The women leave, the bombs explode. The camera captures
the shock and incomprehension of the bloodied survivors as they stumble
from the wreckage. Jack recalls a conversation with a friend on the way to
the tube when he said something like, 'Terrorism is an awful thing'. 'My
friend wasn't so shocked. What he saw in the film was the difficult route to
victory in a liberation struggle.'

Jack's friend points out that the French had air-bombed Algerian vil-
lages. A leader of the FLN makes the same point in the film when he is verbally challenged by a French journalist for deploying bombs in baskets to
kill innocent civilians: 'Give us your bombers [your aircraft] and you can
have our baskets.' Jacks admits that he could see himself as a European in
the café, his son eating an ice-cream, but less easily could he see himself as
a Berber villager cowering under the sound of French jets. He worries, 'My
problem may have been – may still be – a want of empathic imagination.'
But at some level he cannot deny that there is 'some truth trickling down
from Sartre's statement' in the introduction to Fanon's *The Wretched of
the Earth*, where he wrote: 'It is the moment of the boomerang' (1956: 6).[2]

Jacques Derrida, who had himself grown up in Algeria before moving
to Paris, says in *Philosophy in a Time of Terror*:

> let's not forget the trouble we would have in deciding between
> 'national' and 'international' terrorism in the case of Algeria, North-
> ern Ireland, Corsica, Israel or Palestine. No one can deny there was
> state terrorism during the French repression of Algeria from 1954 to
> 1962. The terrorism carried out by the Algerian rebellion was long
> considered a domestic phenomenon insofar as Algeria was supposed
> to be an integral part of French national territory, and the French ter-
> rorism of the time (carried out by the state) was a presented as a police
> operation for internal security. It was only in the 1990s, decades later,
> that the French Parliament retrospectively conferred the status of 'war'

(and thus the status of an *international* confrontation) upon this conflict so as to be able to pay the pensions of the 'veterans' who claimed
them. What did this law reveal? That it was necessary, and that we
were able, to change all the names previously used to qualify what had
earlier been so modestly called, in Algeria, precisely the 'events' (the
inability, once again, of popular public opinion to name the 'thing'
adequately). Armed repression, an internal police operation, and state
terrorism thus all of a sudden became a 'war'.

(2003: 104)[3]

Derrida questions the idea that can be drawn from Carl Schmitt, the
German legal scholar, that a war can only be declared between nation
states, whereas terrorism is a conflict between forces other than a nation
state.[4] As Derrida says:

It will no doubt be said that not every experience of terror is necessarily the effect of some terrorism. To be sure, but the political history of
the word 'terrorism' is derived in large part from a reference to the
Reign of Terror during the French Revolution, a terror that was
carried out in the name of the state and that in fact presupposed a
legal monopoly on violence.

(Ibid.: 103)

But when we are thinking about 9/11 and its aftermaths, we have to
realise we are, according to Derrida, dealing with a terror where 'No geography, no "territorial" determination, is thus pertinent any longer for
locating the seat of these new technologies of transmission or aggression'
(ibid.: 102). As Derrida recognises, 9/11 calls for a philosophical response,
'a response that calls into question, at their most fundamental level, the
most deep-seated conceptual presuppositions in philosophical discourse'.
As he goes on to explain, 'The relationship between earth, *terra*, territory,
and terror has changed, and it is necessary to know that this is because of
knowledge, that is, because of technoscience. It is technoscience that blurs
the distinction between war and terrorism' (ibid.: 101).

Derrida recognises what was potentially scary about 9/11 was that,
however terrible and unthinkable it might have been before it happened,
there was little sense that something worse could *not* happen in the future.
This meant that things could not 'return to normal' and people could not
feel 'it's all over, it won't happen again, there will never again be anything
as awful than that'. At least this could have meant that mourning could
have been possible in a relatively short period of time. But Derrida reminds
us:

But this is not at all what happened. There is a traumatisation with no
possible work of mourning when the evil comes from the possibility to

come of the worst, from the repetition to come – though worse. Traumatisation is produced by the *future*, by the *to come*, by the threat of
the worst *to come*, rather than by an aggression that is 'over and one
with'.

(Ibid.: 97)

Derrida is thinking about the future threat that is already and unconsciously *felt* in the present of a chemical or bacteriological attack – he
recalls in the weeks immediately following September 11, it was thought
that this was actually taking place – but especially the threat of a nuclear
attack.[5]

Derrida recognises that the attempt to name the event as '9/11' is itself
an attempt to fix the event in ways that can somehow name 'September
11' – 'and in so doing to neutralise the traumatism and come to terms with
it through a 'work of mourning' (ibid.: 93). But it is because we cannot
know of the threats that we face in the future that we are haunted by an
unconscious fear of absolute terror

> because of the anonymous invisibility of the enemy, because of the
> undetermined origin of the terror, because we cannot put a face on
> such terror (individual or state).... all these efforts to attenuate or
> neutralise the effect of the traumatism (to deny, repress, or forget it, to
> get over it) are but so many desperate attempts.
>
> (Ibid.)

This means that societies that might be the object of terrorist attacks live
in precarious and uncertain times where people learn to live with an
unspeakable dread of what they could imagine happening. This produces
an anxious cultural imaginary that social theories need to be able to
engage with as they help to define these new landscapes of fear that have
become strangely inescapable.

Civilisations

When Derrida was asked about what role he sees religion playing in the
context of 9/11, he responded by saying:

> We have been speaking of a strange 'war' without war. It often takes
> the form, at least on the surface, of a confrontation between two groups
> with a strong religious identification.... a confrontation between two
> political theologies, both, strangely enough, issuing out of the same
> stock or common soil of what I would call an 'Abrahamic' revelation.
>
> (Ibid.)

But this reinforces Derrida's insistence that

Those called 'terrorists' are not, in this context, 'others', absolute others who we, as 'Westerners,' can no longer understand. We must not forget that they were often recruited, trained, and even armed, and for a long time, in various Western ways by a Western world that itself, in course of its ancient as well as very recent history, invented the word, the techniques, and the 'politics' of 'terrorism'.

(Ibid.: 115)[6]

At the same time, Derrida recognises that it 'said over and over: "We are not fighting Islam; the three monotheistic religions have always taught tolerance." We know, of course, that this is largely inaccurate, but little matter, it's certainly better than the contrary' (ibid.: 127). He clarifies this remark, saying:

Though I clearly prefer shows of tolerance to intolerance, I nonetheless still have certain reservations about the word 'tolerance' and the discourse it organises. It is a discourse with religious roots; it is most often used on the side of those with power, always as a kind of condescending concession ...

(Ibid.)

When Barradori then tries to clarify by saying, 'You seem to understand tolerance as a form of charity ...', Derrida then responds:

Indeed, tolerance is first of all a form of charity. A Christian charity, therefore, even if Jews and Muslims might seem to appropriate this language as well. Tolerance is always on the side of the 'reason of the strongest,' where 'might is right'.

(Ibid.)

So, for Derrida:

tolerance remains a scrutinised hospitality, always under surveillance, parsimonious and protective of its sovereignty.... We offer hospitality only on the condition that the other follow our rules, our way of life, even our language, our culture, our political system, and so on. This is a hospitality as it is commonly understood and practised, a hospitality that gives rise, with certain conditions, to regulated practices, laws and conventions on a national and international scale – indeed, as Kant says in a famous text, a 'cosmopolitical' scale.

(Ibid.: 128)[7]

Religion, in Derrida's reading, is an ancient Roman creation subsequently appropriated by Christianity. In light of the complex etymology, Derrida insists that both sacredness and indebtedness are intrinsic to the

Western religious experience. Eventually, as Borradori explains, with the expansion of Christianity, religion becomes progressively more focused on indebtedness and obligation, and moved further from any sense of sacredness over and beyond any exchange. In Derrida's opinion, this focus injects juridical issues into religion, binding religion to the sphere of law. This is also clear in Kant's writings, which look to law as the way of clarifying his understanding of morality as a secularised Christian ethics.[8]

For Derrida, the deconstruction of Latin and Christian limits of religion, wrongly taken to be a neutral descriptive term, may open the gates of a new, and more properly 'religious', sensibility. He tends to think that religion in the Abrahamic definition tends to resist true openness towards the other, but he may have questioned this with more familiarity with Jewish and Islamic sources. But this is what he means when he writes that 'A Christian – but also a Jew or a Muslim – would be someone who would harbor doubts about this limit; about the *existence* of this limit or about its reducibility to any other limit' ('Faith and Knowledge', p. 53).

Deconstructing the familiar sense of religion and responsibility has a political urgency because of what Derrida describes as the unhappy marriage between religion and digital technology. This is an alliance full of tensions and contradictions. As Borradori explains Derrida's position:

> All the constitutive components of religion – the respect for the sacredness of the harvest, a sense of obligation to God, and the promise of absolute truthfulness – speak of religion's profound wariness of displacement, fragmentation, and disembodiment, which are instead the conditions of existence of digital technology. While the global information network and its technological underpinnings represent the forces of abstraction and dissociation, religion remains anchored in the need for inscription and embodiment. If information circulates in the language of bits, religion propagates itself in human idioms.... Religion, writes Derrida, which is inextricably linked to the body and to linguistic inscription, feels dominated, suffocated, expropriated by the global information system. This feeling of expropriation and self-estrangement explains the primitive modality of the new wars fought in its name.
>
> (2003: 157)

Though the oppositions here are left somewhat abstract and generalised, they help to identify a significant terrain of investigation. He suggests that the body itself takes revenge on its own expropriation and this will be shown globally in images of beheadings.

Kant's efforts to moralise religion have pushed him, according to Derrida, to the paradoxical result of having transformed morality into a religious endeavour. Kant's attempt to provide religion with a rational justification has ended up with the paradoxical result of having reason founded on religion, and more specifically, Christianity. This confirms what I have argued in *Unreasonable Men: Masculinity and Social Theory*, about the ways that modernity was shaped through Kant as the project of a dominant secularised Christianity.[9] The concept of tolerance is an example of this Kantian double bind: it presents itself as being religiously neutral, and yet it is shaped through a Christian vision. As Derrida says, 'Tolerance is a *Christian* virtue, or for that matter a *Catholic* virtue' (2003: 161). This contrasts tolerance with the kind of hospitality that Derrida calls 'pure and unconditional':

> hospitality *itself*, opens or is in advance open to someone who is neither expected nor invited, to whomever arrives an absolutely foreign *visitor*, as a new *arrival*, nonidentifiable and unforeseeable, in short, wholly other. I would call this a hospitality of *visitation* rather than *invitation*.
>
> (Ibid.: 129)

But there is a different vision of Abraham's hospitality that is offered by Jonathan Sacks in *The Dignity of Difference* that helps question ways Derrida locates the Abrahamic root in the meaning of forgiveness to the possibility of expiation.[10] For punishment to be calculable, it needs to be finite, immanent, and temporally delimited. According to Derrida's vision of Abraham, forgiveness apparently applies only to what is reparable. In this way we can connect it to his discussion of the limits of hospitality understood as conditional. But, at the same time, Derrida is fundamentally opposed to what fundamentalist Islam represents as a threat to the aspirations of a cosmopolitan international law.

As he explains, in tones that seem to resonate with Habermas more easily than with the radical critique of modernity we can associate with French deconstruction:

> If we are to put any faith in the perfectibility of public space and of the world juridico-political sense, of the 'world' itself, then there is, it seems to me, *nothing good* to be hoped for from that quarter. What is being proposed, at least implicitly, is that all capitalist and modern technoscientific forces be put in the service of an interpretation, itself dogmatic, of the Islamic revelation of the One. Nothing of what has been so laboriously secularised in the forms of the 'political,' of 'democracy,' of 'international law' ... seems to have any place whatsoever in the discourse of 'bin Laden'.
>
> (Ibid.: 113)

Derrida makes clear that what is unacceptable in the 'bin Laden effect' is

> not only the cruelty, the disregard for human life, the disrespect for law, for women, the use of what is worst in technocapitalist modernity

for the purposes of religious fanaticism. No – it is, above all, the fact that such actions and such discourse *open onto no future and, in my view, have no future.*

(Ibid.)

But this means we also have to be very careful in the ways we relate to Islam as a civilisation, for it would be quite wrong to argue, along with Huntington, that if the politics of the future would no longer be ideological in the twentieth-century sense, there would still be profound differences and antagonisms between the West and the rest that would be 'civilisational'. Not every conflict needed to be between nation states, economic systems or political philosophies. Nor would they be internal wars between contending parties in the West. In *The Clash of Civilisations and the Remaking of the World Order* (Simon and Schuster, New York, 1996), Huntington argued that the more international conflict became global, the more it would become civilisational, a clash between codes of meaning, religion, culture and behaviour. Much of the rethinking about the contours of the post-Cold War world has recapitulated Tocqueville's discovery in *Democracy in America* (Fontana, London, 1968) about the surprising tenacity of religion in the United States. 'Eighteen-century philosophers,' he wrote, 'had a very simple explanation for the gradual weakening of beliefs. Religious zeal, they said, was bound to die down as enlightenment and freedom spread. It is tiresome that the facts do not fit this theory at all' (1968: 364).

Derrida warns us

not to consider everything that has to do with Islam or with the Arab Muslim 'world' as a 'world', or at least as one homogeneous whole. And wanting to take all these divisions, differences, and differends into account does not necessarily constitute an act of war; nor does trying to do everything possible to ensure that in this Arab Muslim 'world', which is a not a *world* and not a world that is *one*, certain currents do not take over, namely, those that lead to fanaticism, to an obscurantism armed to the teeth with modern technoscience, to the violation of every juridico-political principle, to the cruel disregard for human rights and democracy, to a nonrespect for life. We must help what is called Islam and what is called 'Arab' to free themselves from such violent dogmatism. We must help those who are fighting heroically in this direction *on the inside*, whether we are talking about politics in the narrow sense of the term or else about an interpretation of the Koran.

(2003: 113)

This means, for Derrida:

We must (il faut) more than ever stand on the side of human rights. *We need (il faut) human rights.* We are in need of them and they are in need, for there is always a lack, a shortfall, a falling short, an insufficiency; human rights are never sufficient. Which alone suffices to remind us that they are not natural. They have a history – one that is recent, complex and unfinished.... To take this historicity and this perfectibility into account in an affirmative way we must never prohibit the most radical questioning possible of all the concepts at work here.... For justice does not end with law. Nor even with duties (*devoirs*), which, in a still wholly paradoxical way, 'must', 'should' go beyond obligation and debt.

(Ibid.: 132–3)

So, while critical of certain aspects of a human rights discourse that can present themselves too quickly in universalist terms, Derrida appreciates the significance that human rights discourses have come to play in challenging unjust and oppressive rule in different countries across the world.

Security

Four weeks after 7/7, London streets seemed half empty as fear of a bomb attack gripped Britain. As Gaby Hinsliff and Martin Bright reported for the *Observer*:

For those of the small group assembled in Tony Blair's study that July morning who did not know him well, it was something of an eye-opener.

Banging the table with a frustrated fist, as the Home Secretary and his two startled opposition counterparts looked on, the Prime Minister was demanding to know 'why the fuck' it was so impossible to rewrite human rights legislation to allow decisive actions against a terrorist threat.

'He just kept saying, 'Why can't we do this?' and looking at his officials for answers,' says one source from the meeting. 'And they were just shrugging their shoulders.

(*Observer*, 7 August 2005: 13)

Blair was convinced that the world had changed in the wake of 9/11, and now 7/7, and this meant developing new laws to cope with these threats.

By 5 August 2005, the Prime Minister decisively got his way, sweeping aside not just the caveats of his officials – plus those of his own wife, who warned in July of that year that it was easy to respond to terrorism in a way that 'cheapens our right to call ourselves a civilised nation' – but also the reservations of his Home Secretary, Charles Clarke. As the *Observer* reported:

> Hijacking at the last minute what had been planned as a much lower-key announcement by the Home Office minister Hazel Blears, Blair last Friday unveiled a package that profoundly changed the terms of the domestic war against terror. Not only would foreign-born preachers of hate now be deported as Clarke had already suggested, but Britain would, if necessary, rewrite the Human Rights Act to do it – a personal victory for Blair.
>
> (Ibid.)

Blair had been consumed by frustration, and by a sense that – particularly since the second bombing – the world had changed, and his government was not keeping pace:

> 'It is very dangerous if you get into a position where it looks as if the Government is behind public concerns,' says a senior Downing Street source. 'People do not want to hear, 'We are thinking about it and we will get back to you in three months.'
>
> (Ibid.: 14)

The Home Office had been caught out because it had been suggesting that it would take much of August to ponder the perfect package. But Blair was not waiting for anyone, and the measures that he announced – from closing mosques suspected of extremism to house arrests for British nationals under suspicion – shattered the uneasy cross-party consensus formed after the 7 July bombings. It was the first time that opposition MPs – told by Clarke they would be consulted every step of the way – had heard much of it.

Blair had been demanding of officials why, if France operates under the same human rights considerations, they appear able to go further. 'In France there is a long tradition of political exile, but on condition that people who accept asylum do not use French territory to propagate hate campaigns,' says Dennis McShane, the former minister for Europe who had argued for Britain to take a stronger line, 'I am pleased that Britain is now coming into line' (ibid.). As the *Observer* reported, 'But the negotiations have exposed growing differences between the cautious civil servant's son Clarke, and his hyper vigilant master' (ibid.). Downing Street thought the mood in the country had shifted and they could get any legislative changes through parliament. 'Why go public on something that is so capable of whipping up anger and dissent when you have don't even have a concrete proposal?' said a Liberal Democrat official. Hence Charles Kennedy, the then-leader of the Liberal Democrats, argued that the crackdown on extremism risked alienating the very young men about whom there was most concern.

Jeffrey Jowell QC, Professor of Public Law at UCL, argued:

> One explanation for the Prime Minister's readiness to chip away at the Human Rights Act probably lies in his frustration at senior judges' objections to some of the government's earlier anti-terror acts. Last year, the Law Lords declared incompatible with the European Convention the statute that permitted the detention without trial of foreign terror suspects at Belmarsh Prison.
>
> (*Observer*, 7 August 2005: 15)

Jowell recognises the 'need for governments to reassure the public that they are "doing something" about terrorism', but he also recognises with Derrida that 'the reality is that no society, liberal or oppressive, is immune from increasingly inventive forms of assault from those who live and happily die for terror'.

The future cannot be guaranteed against, and this was what was so scary about the second attempted bombings in London, which shattered the idea that people could breathe easily because London had somehow survived and it would be somewhere else next time. The recognition that this could be part of an ongoing campaign, meaning *life had changed* and could no longer be expected to 'return to normal', was frightening. This is an urban fear that helped to shape a new landscape that Blair wanted to think he could somehow contain with his measures. But Jowell argues:

> Accepting that unfortunate fact is by no means an argument for inaction. It is, however, an argument against the temptation to unravel the rights-based model of democracy introduced by Blair just a few years ago, and which should be recorded as one of his most impressive legacies.
>
> (Ibid.)

Charles Clarke, Home Secretary at the time of the attacks, had said that it is absolutely foolish to assume there will not be a third terrorist attack in London. This is a fear that people will have to get used to living with. Within cities, people were going to have to realise that fear had become part of everyday life as they had to learn to live with new landscapes of fear. It is also why Blair felt he needed to be seen to be doing something and why he told journalists on 5 August 2005 that 'the rules of the game are changing'. It was then that he announced 12 'security measures' including deportation, extending the use of control orders and refusing asylum automatically to 'anyone who has participated in terrorism or has anything to do with it anywhere'. However, as Richard Norton Taylor, the *Guardian*'s security affairs editor, notes:

There is no evidence that any of these measures would have caught the 'home-grown' July 7 bombers or the alleged July 21 bombers. It is not the lack of anti-terrorist legislation or gaps in the criminal law; it is the lack of intelligence. Clarke appears to recognise that, as do the security and intelligence agencies. Blair, apparently, does not.

There is a real danger that Blair's 12-point outburst will be counter-productive, alienating the very people that the government – and not least these agencies – need on their side.

(*Guardian*, 19 August 2005: 25)

Internal Whitehall correspondence leaked early in 2005 shows that, in 2004, senior ministerial advisers had identified some of the critical issues. In April 2004, Sir Andrew Turnbull, the Cabinet Secretary, wrote a letter marked 'restricted policy' to the top official at the Home Office, Sir John Grieve. 'Are we listening enough to the Muslim communities (here and abroad) and understanding what we hear (even where we do not agree with it)?' he asked. 'Are we communicating the right messages to the right parts of the Muslim community effectively?'

Sir Andrew did not shy away from addressing the government's foreign policy. 'Should our stance (eg on the Middle East peace process or Kashmir) be influenced more by these concerns?' he asked. 'How do we communicate our foreign policy to the Muslim community? Where are they getting their information and opinion from?'

As Norton-Taylor reports:

Sir John wrote back to the cabinet secretary a month later. It was a long letter identifying the problems, including issues of identity, the threat of terrorism, and how to overcome disaffection, of which 'extemism' was a symptom. He also referred to 'anger' – a word he emphasised – among many young British Muslims borne out of a perception of double standards in British foreign policy, where democracy is preached but oppression of the Ummah (one nation of believers) is practised or tolerated.

Sir John described a 'perceived western bias in Israel's favour over the Israel/Palestine conflict' as a 'key long-term grievance of the international Muslim community which probably influences British Muslims.' That perception, he added, seems to have become more acute since the 9/11 attacks.

'The perception is,' wrote the permanent secretary at the Home Office, 'that passive "oppression", as demonstrated in British foreign policy, eg, non-action on Kashmir and Chechnya, has given way to "active oppression" – the "war on terror" in Iraq and Afghanistan are all seen by a section of the British Muslims as having been acts against Islam.'

(Ibid.)

This correspondence shows, as Norton-Taylor recognises, that at least some of the Whitehall mandarins are working on 'more fertile ground than Blair's rhetoric about a "war on terror" that the most draconian of laws and the most authoritarian of ministers could not win'. Sir John referred to the lack of any tangible 'pressure valve' to vent frustration or dissent – leading to a desire for what he called a simple 'Islamic' solution to the perceived oppression. Rather than engaging with the justice of the claims, and so the sources of anger that are recognised, the correspondence reveals the ways political protest is imagined as a tangible 'pressure valve'. It shows the ways the political establishments in Britain work to maintain their positions. But it also sustains a prevailing vision of religion as essentially 'irrational' within the terms of an Enlightenment rationalist tradition that sets the framework of political discourse. But if this makes it difficult to appreciate the appeals of radical Islam to disaffected young men, it shows the needs for new forms of social theory that can think beyond these traditional rationalist frameworks as they learn to listen to the narratives these young men are producing.

Hospitalities

My parents found hospitality in Britain, away from the growing Nazi domination of Europe in the late 1930s. They were lucky to find refuge and they had the necessary connections. As children who learned to be proud of having been born in England, we did not really think of our parents as 'refugees', though we did recognise them as 'foreign'. We knew that they had come from *somewhere else* but these were not countries that they considered they could ever return to. As children growing up in the 1950s, we did not live with parents who dreamed of returning to their 'homelands'. We knew that we wanted to belong and we were anxious around whether we could assimilate into the dominant culture while, at the same time, maintaining connections with inherited Jewish traditions.[11]

Britain in the 1950s did not claim an aspiration towards being a multi-cultural country. There was a dominant culture and if you wanted to belong you needed to assimilate into it. We recognised, as children with 'foreign parents', that if we wanted to be 'accepted' then we would have to do our best to 'become' English. This was something we wanted to achieve, knowing that it was what our parents expected of us, even if they could not hope for it for themselves. 'Being English' was a way of achieving a degree of safety and security in the shadows of the Holocaust that was to remain largely ignored until the 1980s. We very much wanted to belong and many of us readily accepted the historical narratives we learned at school as our own. We knew about Alfred burning the cakes and about the Crusades and Nelson at Trafalgar. We rarely allowed ourselves to imagine that, as Jews, our ancestors, like Muslim populations, had been the victims of murder and abuse during the Crusades.

Some of these fears and silences continued but were refigured in the multicultural Britain that was being imagined through the different immigrations that followed in the 1950s and 1960s, and were gradually to shape London as a global city. Generations of children of Afro-Caribbeans and Asian migrants from the sub-continent were to be born in Britain and find their own ways of creating their identities as 'Black British' and 'British Asians'.[12] Hospitality was being offered on wider terms and people no longer felt the same pressure to assimilate into the dominant culture. There were more spaces for belonging within an everyday multiculture and the boundaries between public and private spaces were being redefined so that, for example, people no longer felt that religion was a matter of private concern to be practised exclusively within family and sacred spaces. But fears and anxieties remained. As Sarfraz Manzoor recalls:

> For a child of immigrants, the most hurtful insult that could be hurled was the one which challenged the right to call this country home. The challenge usually took the form of three words: 'Go back home.' These words stung because they implied that the immigrant did not truly belong in Britain; he had lucked out to be living here but home, the insult suggested, was somewhere else.
>
> (*Observer*, 21 August 2005: 25)

Manzoor recalls that the taunt haunted his family and that, in the week Margaret Thatcher was elected, his father warned the rest of the family 'to be ready to be packed and ready to return to Pakistan; the fear of repatriation hung heavy over my childhood. It was a fear clouded with confusion because I only knew Britain to be home.' As far as he was concerned, 'Pakistan, the motherland, was somewhere described by parents in stories, frozen in time and place in the instant it was left.' For most children, going to Pakistan and going on holiday was the same thing. When he went there for the first time, 20 years ago, he remembers:

> I imagined and perhaps feared that the trip would ignite some deep realisation that it was truly where I belonged. It only confirmed that home was some 5,000 miles to the west.
> Pakistan was where I was from, but it was not what I was about. There was a reason why my parents had left. They came here because they wanted this country to be their new home.
>
> (Ibid.)

Manzoor recognises that global communications and travel have interrupted the traditional arc of the immigrant story, where the second generation often integrates into the mainstream and the old country retreats to a place of myth and memory. With contemporary young British Muslims, 'Thanks to intercontinentally arranged marriages, cheap flights and telephone calls, it is easier than ever to keep in touch with Lahore and Karachi.' People often learn to live between these different spaces as children who can afford it send their elderly parents to Pakistan to protect them from the British winter, and parents often send their children in the summer holidays to know something of where their family came from.[13]

Whether it is because of the ease of contact or because of their experiences of racism and exclusion, young people can feel more identified with Pakistan and their identities as Muslims than they do with Britain. As Hasan Butt, a 25-year-old British Pakistani from Manchester who helped to recruit radical Islamic young men to fight in Afghanistan, says in August 2005's *Prospect* magazine: 'I feel absolutely nothing for this country. ... I have no problem with the British people ... but if someone attacks them, I have no problem with that either.' Like others of his generation, he does not identify with 'being British' in any way, but thinks of the passport as giving him certain rights of abode that carry few obligations to his fellow citizens.

As Manzoor explains:

> For those individuals who exploit the rights that come with being British but deny that there are any responsibilities, I have no problem suggesting that they relocate to somewhere they find less offensive. ...
> It is one thing to disagree on British foreign policy or even to support Pakistan in a cricket match, quite another to feel complete indifference or contempt.
>
> (*Observer*, 21 August 2005: 25)

Manzoor recognises:

> The question of the motives of the bombers and those who support them has focussed mostly on religion and politics but for me, the most important question is: why did these people and other young Muslims not feel that this country is their home?
>
> (Ibid.)

For an answer, he suggests, 'we are too reticent in this country to celebrate what is good about it ... [and] we are reluctant to champion what makes Britain special, the sorts of things that attract immigrants.'

But, at the same time, Manzoor admits that he does not know what Blair meant when he said that, when people come to this country, they must 'play by our rules and our way of life'. He asks, in relation to a judge who recently referred to people who, thanks to binge drinking, were 'simply savages, angry, blind and brutal ... they are so ill-educated or made crude by inadequately civilising influences in their homes', whether this was also part of 'our way of life?' In this way, he questions the terms of hospitality, recognising how an assimilationist idea no longer convinces and that the

> idea that there is a singular way of life which all immigrants need to sign up to assumes that Britishness is something frozen and fixed, whereas it is and always has been a work in progress, a continuing historical narrative in which we all play our part. Fifty years ago, 'our way of life' would not have included Bengali restaurants, Pakistani doctors and Indian shop owners; each have contributed and changed Britain.
>
> (Ibid.)

He fears that when people speak about 'our way of life', they play into the hands of those who would like to use the tragedy of the London bombings not simply to reconsider the terms of multiculturalism and the forms of hospitality it fosters, but to retreat to an outdated notion of 'Britishness' that carries implications of 'whiteness' and echoes of empire.[14]

Manzoor speaks for many diverse immigrant groups when he says:

> the recent attacks on multiculturalism have made me feel uncomfortable, not because I do not agree that Muslims need to make more efforts to integrate but because the criticisms feel like coded attacks on the idea of Britishness being a diverse and multicultural story.
>
> (Ibid.)

But, at the same time, he does not think it helpful to ban such groups as Hizb ut-Tahrir. Instead, the government should be encouraging young Muslims to feel that they are not under threat or being surveilled as if they cannot really belong. Rather, 'the government ought to encourage and remind them, that this country is our home: we are not tenants' (ibid.). This is to affirm what have proved themselves as sources of dignity and self respect within traditional multiculturalism as they are imagined differently within a vision of integration, not as a form of assimilation, but as a revitalised critical multiculturalism that recognises the complexity of diverse and transnational British identities.

14 Multicultures, belongings and ethics

Racisms/multiculturalisms

The events of 7/7 were responsible for initiating a wide debate into the nature and future of British multiculturalism which had, for many, been proved wanting by the fact that the young men responsible for the London bombings had been born in Britain and educated in British schools. There was a widespread sense that the events of 7/7 would mark a *turning point* in the nature of British race relations and that there needed to be a wide public discussion about the history of British multiculturalism and how it had come to take the institutional forms it had. For a time at least, it looked as if traditions of multiculturalism were somehow to be blamed for the events of 7/7 because the bombers themselves had been killed in the Underground and on the bus at Tavistock Square. Since they could not be brought to trial, and so brought to justice and made to pay, it seemed as if the target for displaced fear and anger was to be multiculturalism itself.[1]

But if we are to recognise 7/7 as a turning point in some way, we need to carefully reflect upon the experiences of diverse multiculturalisms in Britain as well as to contrast with the historical and political experiences of other countries as we shape a new vision of critical multiculturalism. We should not assume that a notion of 'integration' will somehow solve the plurality of questions raised. It might well be that we need to encourage more convivial relationships across different communities, and we need to resist the notion, as Amatya Sen has argued, of defining individuals with complex identities, loyalties and affiliations through a singular and homogenised notion of ethnic or cultural identity.[2] We need to ask questions about whose voice is being listened to and whether, for example, gender and sexual hierarchies are not being consolidated and oppression of women, gay men, lesbians, bisexuals and transgender people being reproduced. We need to confront complex questions about the politics of identity and belonging so that we develop viable transnational and cosmopolitan narratives within renewed traditions of social and political theory that can help to illuminate the contemporary realities we face within postmodern societies.

One of the ugly consequences of the London tube bombings, said Max

Hastings in the *Sunday Telegraph*, is the harm done to race relations. Knowing that there are British Muslims who so hate this country that they will massacre its inhabitants has made many white Britons 'instinctively look askance at young Muslims' (quoted in *The Week*, 6 August 2005: 18). A letter writer to th*e Spectator* related how, on a journey from Liverpool to London, the writer and his fellow passengers had noted a young Asian with a backpack standing on the platform the train was drawing into. There was an 'uneasy silence' as the youngster made to board the carriage; and then a large passenger in a tracksuit stood up.

> He shoved a hand into the Asian's chest saying 'Not on this train, mate; off yer pop', and dumped the young man on his behind on the platform. The man in the tracksuit then resumed his seat, and those in the carriage broke into loud applause.
>
> (Ibid.)

Enoch Powell's ghost is 'holding up his spectral arms in grim victory', said Yasmin Alibhai-Brown in the *Independent* (quoted in ibid.: 13). Muslims as a group are being demonised and commentators across the political spectrum are arguing about the need to reassert a sense of British identity, as if by forcing Muslims to sing 'God Save the Queen' in Urdu can somehow make the bombers vanish. Whatever terrorist outrages lie in store for the United States, said Charles Krauthammer in the *Washington Post*, we can at least take comfort that our enemies 'overwhelmingly reside overseas'. He thinks that the numbers of young Muslims who express some sympathy for the bombers in London attests 'to a massive failure of assimilation' and are 'inconceivable in the United States'. He says that teeming suburbs of disaffected immigrants simply do not exist here and that the UK is paying the price for its failure to integrate immigrants, and for 'a suicidal civic openness that permits imams to openly preach jihad in Britain' (*The Week*, 6 August 2005: 13).

But William Pfaff has reminded people to be much more circumspect in their judgements, as 'It is unclear whether al-Qaeda remains a group with a disciplined structure and the organisational capacity for international action'. Pfaff argues that the most significant think about Islamic terrorism today

> is that it is a politicosocial phenomenon among apparently self-motivated individuals and small groups. There are volunteers in a loose international movement of religious revival and radicalisation that offers alienated young Muslims an explanation for the unsettling forces at work in their lives and a mission.
>
> (*Observer*, 21 August 2005: 24)

According to Alibhai-Brown, those who think the solution lies in a return to a traditional sense of British identity don't realise that 'the reason so many young Muslims and black men feel and behave like outsiders in the UK is that they have been made to feel like outsiders since they were children'. That does not make them bombers or criminals, 'but it does make integration impossibly difficult' (*The Week*, 6 August 2005: 18).

Pfaff argues that 'The argument that terrorism is an organised global menace continues to be put forward in Washington, although with fading conviction'. He thinks it remains essential for Bush and Blair to be able 'to say that staying the course in Iraq can disable or end the terrorism practised by young Muslims in Europe and elsewhere. The argument ignores or implicitly denies the cultural and social sources of Islamic extremism in the West.' Even so, Pfaff recognises:

> Few today would seriously deny that the war in Iraq generates terrorist sympathisers among members of Western Europe's Muslim communities, as the Palestinian intifadas did. The war clearly provides a continuing obstacle to the integration of these communities into the larger society, in Britain as elsewhere.
>
> (*Observer*, 21 August 2005: 24)

He also argues, mistakenly and somewhat too generally, that 'a half century of a well-intentioned but catastrophically mistaken policy of multiculturalism, indifferent or even hostile to social and cultural integration, has produced in Britain and much of Europe a technologically educated but culturally and morally unassimilated immigration demi-intelligentsia' (ibid.).

Henry Porter argues that the liberal impulse to explain the Muslim aversion to Western society as a 'defence mechanism against racism and prejudice' is deeply mistaken. He thinks that, at least in Notting Hill where he lives, traditionally a multicultural area, one gets the sense that Muslims have voluntarily segregated themselves: 'A proud disdain for Western society seems to have overwhelmed any meaningful desire for assimilation.' If you doubt that, consider the YouGov poll for the *Daily Telegraph* in which 24 per cent of Muslims said that, while not condoning the bomb attacks, 'they had some sympathy with the feelings and motives for those who carried them out', and 31 per cent agreed with the statement: 'Western society is violent and immoral and Muslims should seek to bring it to an end but only by non-violent means' (ibid.: 18).

Aatish Taseer, in *Prospect* (January/February 2006), argued somewhat differently that we need to reconsider inherited notions of 'Britishness', saying that, for young British Pakistanis in a place like Beeston, they feel that being British is the most nominal part of their identity. Why would it be otherwise, he challenges, when 'Britons themselves were having a hard time believing in Britishness'? When the bombers were growing up, the very idea that Britishness was a good thing worth imposing on minorities was seen as 'offensive'. What no one seemed to realise, explains Taseer, was that if you denigrate your own culture 'you face the risk of your new arrivals looking for one elsewhere'. Unless we can recognise and value what is positive in British identities, it is difficult to teach others to do so. But this shifts the terms of discussion, since there has been discussion, partly provoked by the Parekh report for the Runneymede Trust which brought together quite different views about *how* 'Britishness' should be culturally reimagined within a multicultural society. Some people argued that 'Britishness' is too tied to histories of empire and, unless we engage critically with how these histories still help to shape the present, it will be difficult to bring different communities with such diverse histories into meaningful dialogue.[3]

Within post-imperial Britain, there have been too many uneasy silences that have blocked Britain from coming to terms with its diverse histories of slavery, empire and colonial rule while, at the same time, creating visions for the present. This is a view that has been argued at different times by Stuart Hall and Paul Gilroy, but it is a view that also needs to come to terms with the revival of Islamic religious beliefs.[4] In their different ways, they both recognise the importance of coming to terms with histories of empire, but within a taken-for-granted tradition of secular rationalism. Coming to terms with empire is also a task for contemporary social and political theories that have tended to think within the terms of the nation state, where questions of 'race' and ethnicity tend to be framed as issues of migration and *cultural integration* of 'minorities' as citizens into the nation state. The tendency to think 'race' in relation to class has also made it difficult to think 'race' in ways that can come to terms with anti-Semitism and the centrality of the Holocaust to modernity.[5] It is striking how long this silence around the Holocaust was sustained in theories of race and ethnicity, and now that this has changed and these have become central concerns, partly because of the re-emergence of Islamaphobia and anti-Semitism in Europe, we need also to rethink the intellectual frameworks that allowed these silences to continue for so long.

In the response to the Parekh report, Labour politicians like Jack Straw argued that, even though there were the historical associations with empire within contemporary Britain, notions of 'Britishness' had been redefined. He believed that there were many young people with Afro-Caribbean or Asian backgrounds who might be wary of identifying themselves as 'English', carrying with it resonances of 'whiteness', but would more easily think about themselves as 'Black British' or 'British Asian'. As athletes competing in international competitions have re-appropriated the Union Flag, so that they feel easy wrapping it around themselves as they take a lap of honour, so we need to trace the *different* designations that are culturally given to symbols that in different times and spaces carried strong identifications with empire. But this is still very much at odds with the way Gordon Brown, on a trip to Mozambique, told journalists they should stop apologising for colonialism. The truth is, according to Richard

Drayton, 'that Britain has never even faced up to the dark side of its imperial history, let alone begun to apologise' (*Guardian*, 30 August 2005: 18).

Robert Beckford, in his Channel 4 programme *The Empire Pays Back* asked why Britain as the principle slaving nation of the modern world had made no apology for African slavery, as it had done for the Irish potato famine? Why was there no substantial public monument of national contrition equivalent to Berlin's Holocaust museum? Richard Drayton, author of *The Caribbean and the Making of the Modern World*, insists:

> African slavery and colonialism are not ancient or foreign history; the world they made are around us in Britain. It is not merely in economic terms that Africa underpins a modern experience of (white) British privilege. Had Africa's signature not been visible on the body of the Brazilian Jean Charles de Menezes, would he have been gunned down on a tube at Stockwell? The slight kink of the hair, his pale beige skin, broadcast something misread by police as foreign danger ...
>
> This universe of risk, part of the black experience, is the afterlife of slavery. The reverse of the medal is what W.E.B. DuBois called the 'wage of whiteness', the world of safety, trustworthiness, welcome that those with white skins take for granted.[6]
>
> (*Guardian*, 20 August 2005: 18)

Islam/Black masculinities

Robert Beckford shares a story of how he held a meeting with a refugee from the Democratic Republic of the Congo at the end of the summer term at the University of Birmingham. A well-educated academic, he had escaped the civil war in his country. In the middle of their conversation about the state of Africa, he reminded Beckford that there were 'many well-educated white males engaged in acts of terror in his country'. As Beckford explains:

> He was not referring to suicide bombers but to middle-class corporate executives who fund warlords and lowranking politicians in exchange for access to diamonds and other precious minerals. Their act of terror was to be part of the ethnic cleansing, rape, child abduction and murder conducted by the renegades they financed.
>
> (*Guardian*, 16 August 2005: 18)

As Richard Drayton reminds us:

> the fragility of contemporary Africa is a direct consequence of two centuries of slaving, followed by another of colonial despotism. Nor was 'decolonisation' all it seemed: both Britain and France attempted to corrupt the whole project of political sovereignty.... The real

appetite of the west for democracy in Africa is less than it seemed. We talk about the Congo tragedy without mentioning that it was a British statesman, Alec Douglas-Home, who agreed with the US president in 1960 that Patrice Lumumba, its elected leader, needed to 'fall into a river of crocodiles.'

(*Guardian*, 30 August 2005: 18)

According to Beckford, black men converting to Islam should be placed within the religious context of their communities, where religion still matters. He argues that 'Many black men, including Reid and Lindsay, were impressed by Islam's African-centred preaching and positive association with blackness'. Malcolm X had himself made the journey from Christianity to Islam in search of black redemption.[7] Beckford remembers, 'My artist friend says mainstream Islam provides him with a social awareness and commitment to justice that is mostly ignored in black churches' (*Guardian*, 16 August 2005: 18). The daily regime of Islam also provides many people with the tools for personal discipline and an interest in intellectual thought. Like some of the evangelical Protestant churches, it provides a clear moral agenda and so can provide support for giving up substance misuse and taking on familial responsibilities. The Caribbean educator Edward Wilmot Blyden argued as early as 1888 that Islam was more respectful of black culture and easier to translate into Caribbean culture than Christianity. At the same time, Beckford argues there will always be a few captivated by an extremist version of Islam that exploits the continued disaffection and marginalisation of working-class black youth. After all, as Beckford explains, 'with as little potential for social mobility as their migrant grandparents, it is difficult to sell them the New Labour dream of living in a meritocratic "stakeholder" society' (ibid.).

Issues of race and religion emerge with a different tone in an 'open letter' written to Ken Livingstone, mayor of London, from some young Islamic militants. Though it is difficult to establish the exact provenance of this letter, its contents remain revealing as a narrative. The letter gives expression to some young Muslim voices, saying:

We are the new generation, the children of Muslims who have suffered at the hands of our left-wing socialist values. Most of our parents were imported into Britain to work in industries British workers no longer cared for, and when those industries collapsed they were abandoned to poverty and hopelessness in cold inner-city ghettos, made to feel unwanted and unwelcome.

You and your political allies in London socialist boroughs first classified us as a race. The result was that thousands of Muslim children were given over to black Christian foster parents instead of white Muslims because your left-wing anti-religious ideology failed to understand that we are a religion, not a race.

As a lapsed Christian, you simply do not understand what we stand for religiously. You delude yourself into thinking that because you throw us a few sops and buy our votes by being anti-Israel you can continue to insult our religious values through your support for homosexuals, women's equality and pornography and other abominations in the eyes of Allah, May He Be Praised. You yourself stand for everything we despise in a post-Christian, godless, secular world deprived of spiritual values and rooted in Marxist materialism.

The open letter refuses a distinction between state and religion, and insists on the sovereignty of religious values when it declares its 'ultimate goal of evicting Western influence from Dar El Islam':

We want to purge the West of its loose morality and replace its ineffective failed religions with the only true, dynamic growing monotheism in the world today. This is our mission. We will employ the means we deem fit to achieve it.

They also say defiantly:

You think you can court the older generation of Muslim leaders and invite them to talk and ask them to help you remove the so called 'terrorists' from London, but they are old ineffective men who were cowed into submission and were grateful for whatever handouts the White Empire condescendingly granted them or careerists with their own agendas.

Though I was unclear about the source of the document, it remains revealing and seems to establish the terms for a generational conflict of masculinities. The younger generation are claiming their own masculinities, saying, 'We no longer want handouts. We want our rights. Our rights are to be governed by Muslim values and Muslim laws, not yours.' This discourse invokes a discourse of rights to claim a sharp demarcation between the West and Islam. Again, they take themselves to be learning how to use the system for their own ends, saying:

You have taught us how to use the Law, the European Court of Human Rights and the freedoms you so cherish, to fight for our own ways of dressing, eating and education. We have begun to get you to change your laws to ensure you respect our religion. In due course we will fight for the right to be governed by Shaaria, not secular, religionless law.

This refers to the case of the right to wear the longer version of the Hajib that was won in the European Court for Human Rights against a school with a Muslim head teacher that had an agreed dress code which, far from banning the hajib, allowed for what would be accepted as religiously appropriate dress.

Addressing the Mayor directly, they say:

> You have pretended you want a free and open society and that was why you allowed so many political refugees to come and live in London. This is why even we called you the Major of Londonistan. You thought that what some others called hate-filled sermons should be tolerated in the name of free speech. And now all of a sudden you have changed your mind. Why? Are you worried about the Olympics?
>
> Now it becomes clear that the only freedoms you want are yours, not ours. You want to limit the right of Muslims to honestly declare who their real enemies are and who the ultimate jihad must either win over or exterminate.

Tolerance of religious differences as part of a multicultural country is to be questioned by these young Muslims, for there is a singular religious truth that has to win out against its enemies. The notion of a singular religious truth has been historically part of Christianities that assumed there was no salvation outside of the Church. As the open letter declares:

> Tolerance is the tool of the weak. In Islam we have seen that, historically, weakness leads to defeat and retreat. Only strength wins and conquers. You have heard Omar Bakri, a resident of London for twenty years, this week declare that he does not condemn the bombs in London. Now let me assure you, he is revered by many young Muslims in Britain, not merely a minority as you think. You think that suicide bombing is a product of political injustice. That is why you keep on blaming Israel, something we are very grateful for but incidental to our mission. The fact is that Africans suffer far more injustices and oppression but only Muslim Africans resort to suicide bombings. That is because we understand, if you do not, that this is a religious issue. This is a tool in our jihad. But, of course, as you are deaf to religion so you cannot hear this! No Sir, you Christian or secular British would never become suicide bombers. You are not passionate enough in your devotion to religion.

Reading this 'open letter' can help us to grasp some of the diverse sources that can feed this particular form of Islamic militancy, and also how Anjem Choudray, follower of Omar Bakri, can so confidently declare on television that British citizenship implies no allegiance to the law and that a British passport is 'just a travel document'. Nationality simply becomes a flag of convenience as people come to define themselves exclusively in relation to their religious identities as 'Muslims'. They happen to be living in the UK, but they could just as well be living anywhere else. It is not so much that religion has provided their primary identity and no longer exists as 'private' within the terms of an Enlightenment modernity, but for some young people *no* other national identity comes to have any significance for them. Since many people inherit complex identities that make themselves felt in different ways, it often takes time for people to explore these different hybrid aspects of self-identity. They can feel torn between different loyalties and, at different times in their lives, different identities can assume an importance for them. They have identities that move across national boundaries and they can feel pulled in different directions as they shape complex belongings within a critical multiculturalism.

Western culture

With the de-centring of Western culture, and the challenges of postmodernity, the superiority that the West so long assumed in relation to its colonised others has been questioned. Classical forms of social and political theory tended to assume that the future has been realised within Western modernities and that, with time, 'others' would follow a similar path as they made a transition from nature to culture, from tradition to modernity. Modernity was an aspiration that was supposedly universally shared, but it was a condition that only the West had fully achieved or could take for granted. It was because the West could alone take its reason and rationality for granted that its supremacy was guaranteed and the legitimation of its colonial dominations secured. As Simone Weil appreciated, the working-class sailor who arrived in Polynesia could assume an automatic superiority to the indigenous peoples because he was the bearer of scientific knowledge that they lacked, even though he was hardly schooled himself.[8]

But the authority of the West has been challenged, and the ways in which it has traditionally come to understand itself in terms of its philosophy and social theories, that have often assumed an evolutionary vision of progress, are being interrogated. Walter Benjamin has proved vital in questioning the ideals of progress that were integral to Western conceptions of modernity. He says:

> In every era the attempt must be made anew to wrest tradition away from conformism that is about to overpower it. The Messiah comes not only as the redeemer, he comes as the subduer of Antichrist. Only that historian will have the gift of fanning the spark of hope in the past who is firmly convinced that even the dead will not be safe from the enemy if he wins. And this enemy has not ceased to be victorious.[9]

If we recall Schopenhauer saying 'How man deals with man is seen, for example in Negro slavery, the ultimate object of which is sugar and coffee', we know that the self-questioning of the West will take careful self-scrutiny and an awareness that the past can only be set to rest if it has been *fully* acknowledged, both intellectually and emotionally. We know the efforts that feminisms and queer theories had to make for the West to recognise how its visions of the 'human' had been framed in relation to a dominant white, European, heterosexual masculinity. Of course people will be positioned differently in relation to these histories and will have different ancestral connections to it. We learn within a liberal moral culture to say too easily that we have to 'put the past behind us', as if this can be managed as a matter of will alone. This is part of the weakness of a Kantian inheritance that taught a liberal moral culture which stated that history and culture are forms of unfreedom and determination that people need to put aside if they are to live independent and autonomous lives. But it has been this *disavowal* of history and culture that has framed its own forms of cultural and historical blindness as it has shaped traditions of philosophy and social theory.[10]

They despise our decadence, said Minnett Marrin in the *Sunday Times*, and can you really blame them?

> One of the things that strikes me more, not less, forcibly as time has passed is the contempt that Muslim extremists feel for us. They despise us for our decadence, and I feel more and more forced to accept the painful truth that they have a point ... without proper discipline from parents, children can never learn to develop self-discipline. And it is on self-discipline and self-restraint that a civilised society rests.
>
> (Quoted in *The Week*, 6 August 2005: 18)

Sharing a prevalent conservative response against multiculturalism, she also argues that, for all our celebrated freedom and wealth, 'we have somehow created a society characterised by growing disorder, uncertainty and loss'. We have lost faith in our institutions and traditions; our schools, 'where illiteracy is beyond belief and disruptive behaviour normal', are a shambles and parents (myself included) seem unwilling to control their children, as if discipline itself were a dirty word.

Similar conservative sentiments were expressed by Bel Mooney in the *Mail on Sunday*, who asked how we can expect young Muslims to be enamoured of Western 'freedom' when freedom so often seems synonymous with 'aggressive materialism' based on the principle of securing your own pleasure. According to Mooney, we have created a dumbed-down culture, contemptuous of the values of self-restraint and self-sacrifice, disrespectful of authority and drenched in images of sex and violence in the mass media – one which demeans our shared humanity (*The Week*, 6 August 2005: 18). Why would Muslims want to embrace it?

Mike Hume in *The Times* expresses similar sentiments, saying Britain is 'a degenerate place full of violent drunks, child abused and pregnant teenagers, whose people believed in nothing except football and getting fat in front of the television'. He also thinks we are a self-flagellating nation intent on denying there is anything good about living here. 'The reason so many immigrants to this country have learnt to hate it is that we ourselves have invited them to do so' (ibid.).

Andrew Sullivan recalls significantly that you heard the same arguments 30 years ago in the United States. Nobody believed that things could or would improve. As he recalls, 'Many conservatives assumed that the 1970s had all but ended civilised life, and that only a minor miracle could rescue the family from terminal decline as a social institution. Crime would merely spiral upwards; ditto illegitimacy and divorce' (*Sunday Times*, 14 August 2005, News Review: 1). He argues, 'These days, even in the terrifying wake of 9/11, New York City boasts record low crime rates, a solid economy, rising educational standards, less racial tension and lower and lower levels of illegitimacy and domestic violence.'

Sullivan acknowledges, 'The revival baffled the pessimists. The social collapse of the "decadent" West had been hailed regularly for years – and the era after the sexual revolution seemed like the final twist downward.' He recognises:

> The boom in abortion, illegitimacy and divorce in the late 1960s to the mid-1980s undoubtedly hurt a generation of offspring. Even today it is hard for many Americans in my generation to see pictures of their parents rolling about in the mud at Woodstock without a twinge of embarrassment and a wave of bafflement.
>
> A loss of a sense of what matters – or worse, a deeply misplaced sense of what counts as real – can indeed lead to divorce, depression, reality television and abortion clinics. When religious faith declines, so too can the inhibitions on behaviour that, though personally pleasing, can be socially destructive.... When families disintegrate, and fathers become distant or non-existent, teens can become delinquents.
>
> (Ibid.)

But if America is any guide, Sullivan recognises that we've learned in the past few decades that these truths are a little more complicated than they might appear. We have learned to appreciate the more equal treatment of women and gays and racial minorities that was pioneered in the 1960s and 1970s. Societies, it appears, are not inherently self-destructive, and open societies, because they disseminate information more efficiently, can help people to *learn* from the mistakes of the past, as well as their own misjudgements. Religion or traditional values do not account for the changes. The US 'Bible Belt' witnessed no greater progress than secular areas. For example, crack cocaine, which is ferociously addictive, was clearly destroying lives, neighbourhoods and families as it took hold in the late 1980s and early 1990s. Now it's a fraction of its former power. Informal social pressures gradually forced it out. Faced with the results of the epidemic – brain-damaged children, imprisoned husbands, wrecked lives, murdered teens – inner-city blacks moved away from and essentially stigmatised the drug.

Among the middle classes, the children of the Sixties generation inevitably mounted their own backlash as they learned from the mistakes of their parents. They decided that they would want to bring their children up differently and, though grateful for the gender and sexual equality fought for by feminisms and gay liberation, they were concerned to find their own ways into the world, even if it meant making their own mistakes. As Sullivan recognises:

> The greater economic and social power of women forced a whole generation of men to become far more involved as fathers than their own dads had ever been....And the divorce rates for college educated couples also dropped steadily as the reality of our own parents' sometimes damaged lives sank in.
>
> (Ibid.: 2)

As Sullivan helpfully admits:

> We learnt in other words, from the 1960s, and the lesson was not that sex was somehow evil or that pleasure was to be avoided or that we had to return to the inhibitions and repressions of the 1950s. It was that the social gains of the 1960s could be tempered by the chastening reminders of their excesses. We could be freer but with a more attuned and finessed sense of the need for more responsibility as well. This was not a lesson given to citizens by a bossy government. It was a lesson absorbed person by person, one generation at a time.
>
> Think for example, of the gay rights movement in America – perhaps the most tangible social revolution of the last 20 years of conservative ascendancy ... a formerly ostracised community defined by counter-cultural radicalism went on to claim not simply sexual freedom but also the responsibilities of military service and civil marriage. What happened – backlash and all – was a civilising synthesis of the 1960s and the 1990s.
>
> (Ibid.)

This was a learning across generations, but it is not a learning that often seems to happen. But it is a learning that takes *time* and *attention* and an awareness that we do not have to repeat the mistakes of earlier generations. But this is also a learning that social theories can learn from, because often they assume an individualism that leaves little space for social learning. Of course there can also be losses as a younger generation can forsake some of the hard-won learnings of a previous generation whose experience made possible an awareness, for instance, of how the 'personal is political'.

Sexual politics

Cherry Potter, a freelance writer and psychotherapist writing in *The Times* 18 August 2005, recognises that when it comes to sex both genders are involved, and that when it comes to extreme forms of aggression and violence, sublimated sexual fear and repression are all-too-often at the root of the problem. In Muslim societies, so-called 'honour killings' are not uncommon, and the authorities often either turn a blind eye or impose short prison sentences. Men can be obliged to display their masculine dominance by murdering their sisters if they are suspected of losing their virginity before marriage, or killing their wives if suspected of adultery. Potter writes:

> Fundamentalists demand that women be veiled and segregated at every level of society, starting at puberty. Public displays of affection between husbands and wives are forbidden. Wife-beating is so prevalent, many see it as a normal part of marriage. In bed any sexual position where the woman is on top is *haram* or sinful. It is difficult to imagine how either gender can enjoy intimacy in such a climate.

In multicultural visions that talk about the need to respect different cultural and religious traditions, we often find ourselves implicitly legitimating forms of homophobic and sexual oppression. This was a danger that Susan Okin warned against when she asked *Is Multiculturalism Bad For Women?*[11] Often, religious traditions come together in their insistence that feminism and gay liberation are facets of a 'western culture' that need to be resisted, as if the issues they raise can have no place within their religious traditions. But it is *the terms* of discussion between religious traditions and modernities that need to be reconsidered. What do young men do and how are their masculinities shaped within fundamentalist traditions that have defined sexuality as 'animal' and so as a threat to their status as spiritual beings? How do young men learn to deal with 'their unacceptable sexual fantasies fuelled by the strict regime and the temptations of the mysterious hidden feminine world?' As Potter understands, 'Too often they project their self-disgust on to their object of desire, whom they blame for causing them to have "impure" thoughts'. In this way, 'the supposedly sexually licentious West becomes, and remains, "the Great Satan", purveyor of all evil that must be destroyed'.

The connections between sexual repression, extreme violence and a male obsession with war and death are recognisable in the West. Potter gives the example of Christian Reconstructionists in America, a fundamentalist sect that also advocates the death penalty for adultery, homosexuality and 'unchastity before marriage' (but for women only). She recalls how studies of the psychology of fascism show how

> the Nazi cult of obeying, adoring and fearing the Fuhrer is rooted in the patriarchal family obeying, adoring and fearing the father. The Nazis, like modern Islamic and Christian fundamentalists, were also obsessed with virgins and women as submissive housewives and perfect mothers. Their extreme masculinity values, above all else, male bonding and sacrificing their lives for the fatherland's high ideals of racial or religious purity, with the promise of glorious martyrdom.
>
> (Ibid.)

Of course, we need to be careful about these historical identifications and warn against misreadings that might seem to impugn complex and multifaceted religious traditions. But, at the same time, it can be helpful to recognise certain resonances where, for example, with fundamentalist traditions the symbolic world is often *split* between those they hopelessly idealise as pure and good, and those they denigrate as evil and out to destroy them. Potter argues that Western and Islamic feminists often find it difficult to evaluate the importance of sexual freedom to visions of human dignity, justice and self-worth as they can be caught up within the terms of a multiculturalism that argues 'we must respect the diversity of beliefs and traditions even if these include human rights abuses of women in Muslim countries'. She argues that attitudes towards gender and sexuality are *not* just feminist issues and that 'where women are seen as equal, men also benefit – they are more tolerant, more able to enjoy intimacy and less aggressive towards women and each other'.[12]

But this means a readiness to question the terms of critical multiculturalism so that we can also engage with the emotional complexities of gendered and sexed relationships while recognising how issues of justice and human worth are being worked through. Often there can be disturbing blends of sexual and romantic love tied up with relations of power and subordination. While recognising the principles at stake, we can recognise that it is not simply a matter, as Potter suggests, of assuming 'that the sexual freedoms enjoyed by Western women should be a gold standard of how to live in the modern world'. We can respect the choices that women want to make for themselves, while keeping open options that traditional cultures might foreclose – say, for women to be equally educated and an insistence that legal courts grant the statements of women equal value with those of men. This has become an issue with the new constitution in Iraq where women's groups have protested that an Islamic state would restrict the rights to education and work that women had taken for granted for years.

Ethics

Jonathan Sacks, in *The Dignity of Difference*, argues:

> The central insight of monotheism – that if God is the parent of
> humanity, then we are all members of a single extended family – had
> become more real in its implications than ever before. The Enlighten-
> ment gave us the concept of universal rights, but this remains a 'thin'
> morality, stronger in abstract ideas than in its grip on the moral imagi-
> nation. Far more powerful is the biblical idea that those in need are
> our brothers and sisters and that poverty is something we feel in our
> bones.
>
> (2002: 112)

Sacks recognises that something stronger than toleration is needed within a
globalised world that involves the decentralisation of power combined
with maximum vulnerability, such that individual acts of terror can desta-
bilise large parts of the world. He argues that 'Until the great faiths not
merely tolerate but find possible value in the diversity of the human condition, we will have wars, and their costs in human lives will continue to
rise' (ibid.: 200).

In articulating one possible form of an idea that could be equal to
the challenge of our time, Sacks presents an idea of the dignity of difference:

> It is that the one God, creator of diversity, commands us to honour his
> creation by respecting diversity. God, the parent of mankind, loves us
> as a parent loves – each child for what he or she uniquely is. The idea
> that one God entails one faith, one truth, one covenant, is countered
> by the story of Babel.
>
> (Ibid.: 200)

The patriarchal terms of Sacks' language also make us wonder whether
gender and sexualities are to be given an equal dignity of difference, or
whether his orthodox Judaism somehow blocks the dignity that can be
afforded to different traditions, orthodox, reform and progressive,
within Judaism itself. But he challenges religious traditions when he
argues:

> the idea that we fulfil God's will be waging war against the infidel, or
> converting the heathen, so that all humanity shares the same faith is
> an idea that ... owes much to the concept of empire and little to the
> heritage of Abraham, which Jews, Christians and Muslims claim as
> their own.
>
> (Ibid.: 201)

Sacks, helpfully argues, 'fundamentalism, like imperialism, is the attempt to impose a single truth on a plural world. It is the Tower of Babel of our time.' He also recognises:

> It was not until the Abrahamic faith came into contact with Greek and Roman imperialism that it developed into an aspiration to conquer or convert the world, as we must abandon it if we are to save ourselves from mutual destruction.
>
> (Ibid.: 201)

He goes on to say:

> our most fundamental questions remain Who am I? And To which narrative do I belong? The great hope of the liberal imagination, that politics could be superseded by economics, replacing public good with private choice, was bound to fail because economics as such offers no answer to the big questions of 'Who' and 'Why.'
>
> (Ibid.: 41)

At the same time, Sacks learns from Isaiah Berlin that the one belief that has proved most dangerous to humankind is:

> the belief that those who do not share my faith – or my race or my ideology – do not share my humanity. At best they are second-class citizens. At worst they forfeit the sanctity of life itself. They are the unsaved, the unbelievers, the infidel, the unredeemed; they stand outside the circle of salvation. If faith is what makes us human, then those who do not share my faith are less than fully human.
>
> (Ibid.: 46)

It was the *ease* with which modernity adopted a secularised form of the notion that others could be 'less than human' that proved so historically dangerous and ended in preparing the ground both for colonial genocides and the Holocaust.

Sacks points out that, since the Second World War, not only has the dominance of the market within globalisation had a corrosive effect on the social landscape, but neighbourhoods in many Western cities have become even more economically segregated. Public spaces have been replaced by shopping malls and entertainment complexes, open only to those with the ability to pay. Trust as an element of social solidarity breaks down as there is less mixing across social differences. But the market, as Sacks recognises, has 'also eroded our moral vocabulary, arguably our most important resource in thinking about the future.' He quotes MacIntyre's *After Virtue* as saying: 'We possess indeed simulacra of morality, we continue to use many of the key expressions. But we have – very largely, if not entirely – lost our comprehension, both theoretical and practical, of moral-ity' (1981: 2). But, at the same time, Sacks sustains a somewhat limited Kantian vision of morality when he says, 'It is difficult to talk about the common good when we lose the ability to speak about duty, obligation and restraint, and find ourselves only with desires clamouring for satisfac-tion' (2002: 32).

Sacks helpfully recognises that not just Western philosophy, as White-head thought, but Western religion has also been haunted by Plato's ghost: 'The result is inevitable and tragic. If all truth – religious as well as scient-ific – is the same for everyone at all times, then if I am right, you are wrong' (ibid.: 20).

> It is the idea that, as we search for truth or ultimate reality we progress from the particular to the universal. Particularities are imper-fections, the source of error, parochialism and prejudice. Truth, by contrast, is abstract, timeless, universal, the same everywhere for everyone.
>
> (Ibid.: 19)

If we are inclined to see resurgent tribalism as the great danger of our fragmenting world, it is not the only danger. For Sacks, 'The paradox is that the very thing we take to be the antithesis of tribalism – universalism – can also be deeply threatening, and may be equally inadequate as an account of the human situation'. A global culture tends to

> see as the basis of our humanity the fact that we are ultimately the same. We are vulnerable. We are embodied creatures. We feel hunger, thirst, fear, pain. We reason, hope, dream, aspire. These things are all true and important. But we are also different. Each landscape, lan-guage, culture, community is unique. Our very dignity as persons is rooted in the fact that one of us ... is replaceable, substitutable, a mere instance of a type. That is what makes us persons, not merely organ-isms or machines. If our commonalities are all that ultimately mat-tered, then our differences are distractions to be overcome.
>
> (Ibid.: 20)

For Plato particularity – the world of the senses and the passions – is the source of conflict, prejudice, error and war. Universality is the realm of truth, harmony and peace. Progress is supposedly marked through a move from the parochial to the cosmopolitan, the local to the global reflecting a journey from particular attachments to universal reason. By reversing the normal order, and charting instead a journey from the universal to the particular, the Bible, according to Sacks, represents the great anti-Platonic narrative in Western civilisation. The Bible argues that the universalism is the first, not the last, phase in the growth of the moral imagination.

Babel, the first global project, is the turning point in the Biblical narrative. From then on, God will not attempt a universal order until the end of days. According to Sacks, whatever Christianity and Islam took from Judaism, it was not its 'particularist monotheism':

> It believes in one God but not in one religion, one culture, one truth. The God of Abraham is the God of all mankind, but the faith of Abraham is not the faith of all mankind. There is no equivalent in Judaism to the doctrine extra ecclesiam non est salus, 'outside the Church there is no salvation.' On the contrary, Judaism's ancient sages maintained that 'the pious of the nations have a share in the world to come'.
>
> (Ibid.: 53)

But Sacks was challenged by other Jewish orthodox authorities when he wanted to argue:

> God is universal, religions are particular. Religion is the translation of God into a particular language and thus into the life of a group, a nation, a community of faith. In the course of history, God has spoken to mankind in many languages: through Judaism to Jews, Christianity to Christians, Islam to Muslims.
>
> (Ibid.: 55)

This is a vision that can work to minimise the historical and bloody struggles between different religions. But, for Sacks, it at least means:

> God is God of all humanity, but no single faith is or should be the faith of all humanity. Only such a narrative would lead us to see the presence of God in people of other faiths. Only such a worldview would reconcile the particularity of cultures with the universality of the human condition.
>
> (Ibid.)

Sacks argues, at least in the first edition, that 'This means that religious truth is not universal'. But this does not mean they are relative, for there is a difference, all-too-often ignored according to Sacks, between absoluteness and universality. He makes this clear through an example of the absolute obligation I have to my child, which is not a universal one. As he explains, 'Indeed it is precisely this non-universality, this particularity, that constitutes parenthood – the ability to feel a bond with *this* child, not to all children indiscriminately' (ibid.: 55). This is what makes love, love: not a generalised affection for persons of such-and-such a type, but a particular attachment to this person in his or her uniqueness. According to Sacks, 'This ability to form an absolute bond of loyalty and obligation to someone in particular as opposed to persons-in-general goes to the very core of what we mean by being human' (ibid. 55). What Judaism has taught humanity is a complex truth that 'We are particular *and* universal, the same *and* different, human beings as such, *but also* members of this family, that community, this history, that heritage' (ibid.: 56).

This gives Biblical ethics a different character from philosophical ethics that, true to its Platonic origins, focuses upon what we have in common. For example, reason – radically separated from nature within Kantian ethics – characterises the rational moral self. As I argued in *Kant, Respect and Injustice* (1986), this leaves us with a thin and attenuated conception of self, divorced from constitutive attachments to family, friends, community and history. Though Sacks recognises this, he does not question the identification of morality with duty and obligation, and the discounting of emotions, feelings and desires within Kantian ethics. There are other sources within Jewish traditions that could have allowed for this challenge, but this would take him beyond his particular vision of orthodoxy.

Even though he challenges what gives philosophical ethics its 'thin' or context-free character, he does *not* recognise the force of feminist critiques of the distinction between reason and emotion, so allowing him to remain, in vital respects, within a patriarchal tradition. Although he recognises the moral universal of the dignity of the human person, this does not allow for the dignity of sexual expression or gender equality that remain aspects of a threatening modernity. He tends to sustain a position that, unfortunately, cannot appreciate that feminism could be a strain within a Jewish tradition, as it can be with Islam and Christianity, rather than an external Western tradition that is maintaining an externalised challenge in its visions of gender and sexual equalities. This shows the limits of Sack's orthodoxy, and its unwillingness to recognise sources of gender and sexed oppressions. This is a particularly distressing limit after so many homosexuals, Jews amongst them, died along with other Jews in Nazi extermination camps.

The universality of moral concern is not something we learn by being universal but by being particular. As Sacks knows:

> Because we know what it is to be a parent, loving our children, not children in general, we understand what it is for someone else, some-where else, to be a parent, loving his or her children, not ours. There is no road to human solidarity that does not begin with moral particu-larity – by coming to know what it means to be a child, a parent, a neighbour, a friend. We learn to love humanity by loving specific human beings. There is no short-cut.
>
> (Ibid.: 58)

In *Thick and Thin* (University of Notre Dame Press, Notre Dame, 1994), Michael Walzer expresses a similar insight, that 'thick' or context-laden moralities are more fundamental than 'thin' or universal ones:

Societies are necessarily particular because they have members and
memories, members with memories not only of their own but also of
their common life. Humanity, by contrast, has members but no
memory, and so it has no history and no culture, no customary practices, no familiar life-ways, no festivals, no shared understanding of
social goods. It is human to have such things, but there is no singular
human way of having them.

(1994: 8)[13]

The singularity of Biblical ethics is probably shown most clearly in its
treatment of the problem of the stranger, the one who is not like us. As
rabbis noted, the Hebrew Bible in one verse commands, 'You shall love
your neighbour as yourself', but in no fewer than 36 places commands us
to 'love the stranger'. In Exodus it says, 'You shall not oppress a stranger,
for you know the heart of the stranger – you yourself were strangers in the
land of Egypt' (23:9). It suggests that only those who can remember for
themselves what it is to be slaves understand at the core of their being why
it is wrong to enslave others. Sacks believes the Hebrew Bible's single
greatest and most counterintuitive contribution to ethics is the idea that
'We encounter God in the face of the stranger'.

As he says, 'God creates difference; therefore it is in one-who-is-differ-
ent that we meet God' (2002: 59). He remembers that Abraham encounters God when he invites three strangers into his tent. This is a lesson that
people can learn from, whatever their religious or secular traditions. As we
think about the different places our families have travelled from and the
different histories of trauma, loss and displacement they have carried into
the present, we can develop a *moral imagination* that appreciates the sufferings of others who have been forced into exile to find better lives for
themselves.

Globalisation threatens to eliminate diversity in the name of its own
vision of a single socio-political order, and Islamist groups have fought
back in the name of their own singular truth. Benjamin Barber, in his 1992
essay 'Jihad versus McWorld' (*Atlantic Monthly*, New York, March 1992),
already recognised that the forces that were linking the world into a single
interconnected network, driven by technology and mass communications,
were producing their own counter-reaction in the form of 'a threatened
Lebanonization of national states in which culture is pitted against culture,
people against people, tribe against tribe'. 'The planet', he concluded, 'is
falling precipitately apart and coming together at the very same moment.'[14]

Through these movements of capital and peoples across national
boundaries, sometimes as refugees seeking a safe haven from war or as
economic migrants from economies devastated through globalisation, difference has now become part of the texture of everyday life. This can be an
enriching experience or a threatening one. As Barber pointed out, there are
centripetal and centrifugal forces at work – on the one hand McWorld, a

largely American culture conveyed by multinational corporations, branded goods, mass media and the Internet; and on the other hand resurgent movements that in different ways reject Western 'decadence' and want to reclaim spaces for themselves.

If we are to live in close proximity to difference, as in a global age we do, we will need more than a code of rights, more even than mere tolerance. Too often, universal rights work to suggest that, as Sacks frames it:

> the particularities of culture are mere accretions to our essential and indivisible humanity, instead of being the very substance of how most people learn what it is to be human. In particular, it understates the difficulty and necessity of making space for strangers – the very thing that has been the source of racism and exclusion ...
>
> (2002: 62)

Sacks has drawn inspiration from Isaiah Berlin who, from a diverse range of sources within social and political theory, seemed to develop insights that, Sacks argues, could have been available to him from traditions of Biblical ethics. In some notes Berlin wrote in 1981 for a friend who was preparing to give a lecture, he writes words that have an added relevance in the wake of 9/11 and the bombings in Bali, Madrid and London:

> It is a terrible and dangerous arrogance to believe that you alone are right: have a magical eye which sees *the* truth: and that others cannot be right if they disagree. This makes one certain that there is *one* goal and only one and for one's nation or church or whole of humanity, and that it is worth any amount of suffering.... But no Kingdom of Love sprang from it – or could ... '
>
> (Berlin, *Liberty*, Oxford University Press, Oxford, 2002: 345)[15]

15 Conclusions

Citizenship, multiculturalisms and complex belongings

(Re)memberings

The aftershock of traumatic events, both in individual lives and in the lives of the community, take time to register and to shape personal and theoretical responses. Often it takes time for those who have been most immediately involved to emotionally acknowledge *what* they have lived through, and allow the resonances to take shape within personal and cultural narratives. Often there are unresolved tensions between what individuals might remember for themselves and the attempts of the larger community to gather these memories into a collective representation. Within these in-between liminal spaces – that Victor Turner recognises can sometimes 'be described as a futile chaos – there is 'not by any means a random assemblage but a striving after new forms and structure, a gestation process'. In this way he acknowledges the need for a creative pause, as Nietzsche understands it, to give time for memories to find their shape and for people to 'make sense' of the disruptions they have lived through. As Turner puts it, 'The cosmology has always been destabilized, and society has always had to make efforts, through both social dramas and esthetic dramas, to restabilize and actually *produce* cosmos' (1985: 300–1).[1]

Turner describes the aftershocks of traumatic events as a marginal period that is 'malleable', one of 'ambiguity and paradox, a confusion of all customary categories', where individuals exist in a suspended state, symbolically 'neither living nor dead', yet 'both living and dead'. Often for these processes of change to take place, people have to question inherited cultural assumptions that teach them to 'put the past behind them' so that they can focus upon the future. But, as Freud recognised, these cultural assumptions can make it more difficult for people to come to terms with the traumatic events they have lived through and, unless they are encouraged to *face* these experiences, the somatic shocks they have registered at different levels of embodied experience can produce their own forms of sickness.[2] As Turner recognises:

> Liminality may perhaps be regarded as the Nay to all positive structural assertions, but as in some sense the source of them all, and ... as

a realm of pure possibility whence novel configurations of ideas and relations may arise.

(1967: 93–111)

Change is initiated through symbolic actions that lie 'at the heart of the liminal' (ibid.).[3] Turner appreciates that it is often through particular forms of theatre that cultures come together to institutionalise a collective remembering; these forms can also have the power to silence personal memories that might offer alternative meanings.

The families and friends of the victims of the July 7 London bombings came together on Tuesday 1 November 2005 for a memorial service at St Paul's Cathedral in the heart of London. It had all the trappings of a state occasion, with the Queen and Tony Blair, the Prime Minister, joining members of the emergency services. The different stations at which the bombs had gone off were being recalled as if they were sites of battles within a war, though little was made of those who were dying as civilians and soldiers in the Iraq war. The human losses that we were witnessing on the streets of Baghdad and other cities through suicide bombings were supposedly to be remembered on another occasion. At the heart of the ceremony was an act of remembrance: the lighting of four candles – one for each of the blast sites at Aldgate, King's Cross, Edgware Road and Tavistock Square. The visible signs of the bombs' terrible effects were clear to see, in the injured on crutches or in wheelchairs.

Although the Bishop of London, the Right Reverend Richard Chartres, led representatives of the major faiths in a declaration of unity in the face of terrorism, their voices were otherwise not to be heard. This remained firmly a Christian occasion, even though many people who lost their lives and had been caught up in the bombings belonged to other faiths, or none. It was for the Archbishop of Canterbury, Dr Rowan Williams, to speak for all, saying:

> To those who proclaim by their actions that it doesn't matter who suffers, who dies, we say in our mourning, No. There are no generalities for us, no anonymous and interchangeable people. We live by loving what's special, unique in each person. Everyone matters.
>
> (*Daily Mirror*, 2 November 2005: 9)

But it was difficult to not also remember that this was exactly the complaint of so many about the failure of the United States and UK forces in Iraq to even properly *count* the civilian deaths in a conflict that millions of people had marched in cities around the world to stop. For so many in Britain and around the world, it was an illegal war that had undermined the authority of the international law and the United Nations. Though British soldiers fighting in the war were remembered, the controversies were not.

Some 700 relatives joined 500 of the injured at the moving service which was also shown on a giant screen in Trafalgar Square. Many people simply felt they needed to return for a time of remembering, even if they could not get into St Paul's. London recalled the terrible moments of the bombings and, for a moment at least, refused to return to normal life, recognising that, for so many, urban life could not be the same. Urban fears could not be put aside and global terrorism had shown the destruction it could cause. Many of the mourners had ventured into London for the first time since the bombings. Janet and Graham Foulkes had not been on the Underground since son David, 22, from Oldham, died, but took the tube to the service. Mrs Foulkes, 55, said, 'It was spontaneous. I just felt it was the right thing to do.' David's girlfriend, Stephanie Reid, said, 'I had never been on the underground before. It was a big step' (*Daily Mirror*, 2 November 2005: 9).

Garri Holness, 37, of Streatham, South London, who had lost a leg in the bombing, said, 'It was a very emotional day for me trying to put to rest what has happened over the last four months.' Philip Duckworth, 36, of St Albans, Hertfordshire, who had lost an eye, said, 'It was important for us to feel like we've been recognised.' His wife Heather, 32, said, 'I was very aware of how I could have been sitting with the bereaved families. You realise that you are one of the lucky ones' (ibid.). Mari Fatiya-Williams, whose son Anthony had died and who had shared her lamentation a few days later at Tavistock Square, felt more critical. She said, 'It was a Government Service. I was just another number. Some of the prayers were moving but they could have done a bit more to include the families.' Brian Carrol, a close friend of victim Ciarin Cassidy, 22, of Finsbury Park, said, 'It didn't reflect Ciaran at all. They could have read out a list of names at least' (ibid.).

After the ceremony, the Queen met some of the bereaved families. She was presented with a posy of flowers by seven-year-old Ruby Gray, whose dad Richard, 41, from Ipswich, was killed at Aldgate. Her mother Louise was with her, but her 11-year-old brother Adam refused to go because he blames Tony Blair for making London a terrorist target because of the Iraq war. A number of papers, including the *Daily Mirror*, noted his absence, which remained a comment that could not easily be ignored. The pain that so many of the survivors have been forced to live with every day since the attack is so easy to forget as the city 'returns to normal'. This is why it is important to listen to individual voices as they share their experiences. Richard Kirkland was on the Piccadilly line train that left King's Cross and never made it to Russell Square. He shares his memories and what it has been like since:

> Squeezed in tight against the door that connected to the carriage where the bomb exploded, I'm haunted by the momentary wander along the platform that stopped me from getting on the first carriage where so many passengers were killed.
>
> Anybody who was on the train has been scarred.
>
> (Ibid.)

As Richard Kirkland recalls:

> For nearly forty minutes we were in the dark, crammed so tightly that
> we could not move, suffocated by the fumes and dust.
>   It was a nameless fear and a place I have returned to in my night-
> mares many times since.
>   The words of the 23rd Psalm came back to me: 'Though I walk
> through the shadow of the valley of death I will fear no evil'.
>   Except down there I think we probably did fear evil.
>   And since the day of the bomb I know I have been a real pain to all
> my family and friends.
>   On one given day I can be confused, miserable, hyperactive, self-
> indulgent, forgetful, scared, tearful and angry. But I also know that I
> was lucky.
>
>   (Ibid.)

Asking himself vital questions, he wonders:

> How do you recover from something so shattering? I have begun to
> realise that it is probably wisest to accept that in many ways you
> don't.
>   'But there are things that you can do to make you feel better and
> which allow you to help others.
>   After weeks of feeling isolated and lost, I was found the group
> King's Cross United and their friendship and bravery has been an
> inspiration.
>   I think today was the day to remember the beauty of the lives taken
> and celebrate the courage of both the bereaved and the survivors.
>   Recovery is a long way off but I'm sure it begins with moments like
> this.
>
>   (Ibid.)

A family that was marked in a different way by the London bombings
was the family of the young Brazilian, Jean Charles de Menezes, who was
shot as he boarded a Northern line train at Stockwell Underground
station. Details of a second inquiry by the Independent Police Complaints
Commission were announced on 28 November 2005, which will focus on
allegations that Sir Ian Blair, the Chief Commissioner, and the Metropolitan Police lied to the family and misled the public immediately after his
death. The family were particularly upset at suggestions that De Menezes
ran from the police, and an official Met statement on the day of the shooting alleged the dead man's 'clothing and behaviour' were suspicious
(*Evening Standard*, 28 November 2005: 1). This inquiry will be separate
from the current investigation into the shooting on 22 July.
    Even though it had emerged that Mr De Menezes did not run from

police and was not wearing bulky clothing, as had earlier been claimed, the family was to remain disappointed with the official inquiries. The family had also complained about comments allegedly made by Sir Ian Blair when he linked the killing to anti-terrorist operations. He said he understood the man who was shot had fled when challenged by police. The Commissioner, who has insisted he did not know the wrong man had been shot until the next morning, also faced criticism for initially refusing the IPCC access to the scene. In the middle of November 2005, Sir Ian Blair warned that the UK, in particular London, remained a major target, saying, 'The sky is dark' (Evening Standard 28 November 2005: 6). It seemed as if nobody was really going to be held responsible for this death and, for many, it remained an injustice that would continue to haunt the future.

Reflections

The bombs that detonated in London placed Islam at the centre of national debate. They also challenged traditional forms of social theory that tended to accept that religion, framed within the terms of an Enlightenment rationalism had to be separated from politics and was a matter for the private sphere of individual belief. But religion had returned to the public sphere and demanded a shift in intellectual culture that could allow for dialogues not simply framed as 'inter-faith', but able to move across the boundaries of the secular and the spiritual. I felt a need to bring different voices into dialogue with each other and hopefully to shape more adequate social thoughts and learn lessons that crossed these boundaries. I wanted to shape a vision of critical multiculturalism that could also engage critically with faith traditions.

This has meant reconsidering a postmodern displacement of the taken-for-granted assumptions of a dominant white Eurocentric vision that had been implicitly set within the terms of a secularised Christian tradition. Modernity set the terms towards which 'others' were obliged to aspire. Within this framework both Judaism and Islam were framed as 'other' with Judaism explicitly framed as a religious traditions that had been explicitly *superceeded* by Christianity and so unable to speak into the present. If social theories needed to be revisioned to allow for a plurality of different voices they also needed to be able to engage critically with the ethical and spiritual resources of religious traditions that have been silenced within traditional discourses. As feminisms had taught social theory to name its patriarchal and masculinist assumptions, so we also needed to recognise how the project of modernity, as Weber acknowledged, had been largely framed within the terms of a secularised Protestant Christian tradition that has and the ways it has worked to frame traditions of social and political theory.[4] Through Simmel, Benjamin, Scholem and Kafka we have at least begun to hear voices of Jewish traditions. This is yet to happen to Islamic, Hindu and Chinese traditions amongst others that have often been disavowed as 'pre-modern' and so in their own ways rendered unable to speak into a globalised present.

The influential Muslim scholar Tariq Ramadan, addressing the second annual Guardian Muslim Youth Forum, held five months after the bombings, said young Muslims must stop complaining, be clear about the source of their problems and get themselves organised into 'critical citizens'. Unlike the riots in France, the bombs in Britain were 'a religious problem, so you should deal with that', he told them. Madeleine Bunting reported on the meeting for the *Guardian*, wrote that Ramadan's move to the UK could be important:

> Steeped in a French republican tradition of strong citizenship, he is remarkably challenging to his Muslim audiences. Who else can talk about the passivity and victim mentality of the Muslim community, as he did in the forum last week, and still get spontaneous applause?
>
> (*Guardian*, 21 November 2005: 27)

But then, it is a question of who he is talking to, in an audience of mainly university-educated Muslims, and what they are prepared to hear.[5]

According to Bunting, the mood of the forum shifted in unexpected ways. There was less anger than before the bombings from the 60-plus participants:

> but what had replaced it was, perhaps, even more worrying – a pervasive sense of frustration. Much of it targeted at the government, but some is also directed at the Muslim community – why can't it make itself heard? Why can't it address its problems of poverty and underachievement? And the persistent questions about representation: who claims to speak for 'the community' and why?
>
> (Ibid.)

According to Bunting:

> The problem is that the frustration – and its close relative, defensiveness – threaten to drown out all other discussions. It leaves little room these days for the outrage and horror one might still have expected in comments on the atrocities of 7/7. ... The impulse to apportion blame very simply on Iraq and Blair has overwhelmed the soul searching widely apparent back in July; yes, Iraq was a major factor, but there were others. Some things, however repetitive, still need to be said; namely, that the July attacks were a terrible misuse of Islam, There were, as the Islamic scholar Tariq Ramadan told the forum participants, not just 'un-Islamic, they were anti-Islamic'.
>
> (Ibid.)

But, presumably, the discussion has also moved on, and if Bunting is right that 'The widely held perception is of a community under siege', this is to be expected. The government's current proposals to regulate 'places of worship' – aimed at mosques – is an unprecedented intrusion of the state that will only work to increase Muslim alienation. Though Ramadan warned 'It is easier to be against something than for something', what Bunting was forced to acknowledge was how the media, including the *Guardian*, had misread *how* profound the disillusionment was when hundreds of thousands came onto the street in 2003, the first major mobilisation of the Muslim community into mainstream politics, and it seemed to have no impact whatsoever. Blair went ahead with his plans to attack Iraq, and it seemed as if the deal with Bush had already been made and that, for months, it has been an issue of how he could get the British people onside. He knew what was best, but it would take time to persuade others, which was why we heard so much about WMDs – weapons of mass destruction – that was supposed to frighten people into compliance. This made it difficult for different communities to trust the government's intentions. It was not simply an issue of Blair's declining authority within his own party, but a widespread sense that the democratic process had been betrayed.

As Bunting recognises:

> That disillusionment is fed by specific Muslim dilemmas; for starters, in a democracy the political priorities of a minority, however passionately held, will never make much headway. The welfare of Chechnya and Kashmir, even Palestine, is never going to be the guiding principle of British foreign policy.
>
> (Ibid.)

But this helps to explain the appeal to young Muslims of groups like Hizb ut-Tahir, who think they cannot get their views heard in British politics so that, like their non-Muslim peers, they often feel there is no point in voting or engaging with mainstream politics since it makes no difference to what happens. They advocate an Islamic caliphate and a sense of transnational obligation to the Muslim ummah. They encourage young Muslims to feel that they are 'Muslim first'.

For instance, Sultanah Parvin, a member of Hizb ut-Tahir, which says voting is a sin, says she is politically active in different ways:

> Voting is not going to have all the solutions my parents' generation believed it would have. There's a third way to get our voices heard and reach out to a wider society. I've been active in what I would classify as political work at grassroots level, talking about drugs, talking about crime, talking about projects which we can get the youth to be involved in rather than acts of violence.
>
> (*Guardian*, 21 November 2005: 9)

At the same time, she insisted this was not a recipe for segregation or the isolation of the Muslim community. Hizb ut-Tahrir sought dialogue and debate with non-Muslims. 'Our position of political activism is not insular. It's not just talking to the Muslim community' (ibid.).

According to Bunting:

> These particular Muslim predicaments are underscored by a problem endemic in British political culture – a weak tradition of citizenship. In place of a powerful concept of citizen's rights and responsibilities, we are still subjects of a hereditary monarchy. We use nationalism not citizenship to generate a sense of belonging and entitlement; that disables an immigrant minority.
>
> (*Guardian*, 21 November 2005: 27)

This is a vital insight that helps to illuminate particular predicaments of belonging and ways they have been framed in Britain – in a move from an assimilationist culture in the 1950s and 1960s, where it was a matter of 'others' learning to 'become like everyone else' if they wanted to be able to belong, towards a more multicultural politics that allowed more spaces for difference(s).[6]

But if you cannot easily participate in contemporary ways of living and behaving, you can be left feeling stranded and isolated. Language is not a problem for a younger generation that have been schooled here, but can be for older generations as it can for new migrations from Eastern Europe. There are other factors that can make integration difficult, for example, as alcohol consumption has soared in the last two decades, Muslims have been left to negotiate its centrality in British social life, at work, school or university, or in neighbourhoods, with great difficulty. 'From 16 onwards, alcohol is a significant factor in integration,' said Kamran Maskin, 'I couldn't go to discos. Muslims end up clumping together.' 'At work, when they choose to go to the pub, you're being excluded,' said Khadija El Shayyal at the forum. As Bunting recognises, 'Alcohol is probably now one of the most effective and unquestioned forms of exclusion practised in the UK, affecting every kind of social network' (ibid.).

But if Muslim communities are interrogating themselves and reflecting upon relationships with broader British society, the forum showed there is also anger that their own reflections were not matched by a spirit of self-criticism in government or an acceptance that its policies in Iraq and Afghanistan helped extremism to take root. They have not listened enough when it comes to Blair's framing of anti-terrorist laws, and many young Muslims feel dissatisfied with *how* politicians are talking and listening to them. Sometimes it seems to be a matter of listening for what they already want to hear. Many were sceptical about the government's professed desire to 'reach out' to them. 'These politicians are out of touch. People are saying take me to your leaders – it's a colonial thing,' said Shahedah

Vawda, founder if Islamic peace movement Just Peace. 'The government hasn't a clue what's going on on the ground.' 'The government doesn't talk to young people,' said Andleen Razzaqm, a teacher. 'At a community consultation meeting I went to, there were only three youths. The government only talks to older Muslims' (*Guardian*, 21 November 2005: 9).

Citizenships

Dissatisfied with the dialogue offered by the government, most delegates at the forum felt their own community had failed to communicate its successes and debate its failings. Ramadan said that 'intra-community dialogue' and self-confidence were still lacking. Rather than embrace victimhood, Muslims must criticise themselves and engage with criticising their government. 'The easiest way to be in politics is to be against something,' he said. 'It's very easy to be against the war. It's very difficult to be for the future of the society. Self-criticism is part of what we need today. A true citizenship is a critical citizenship' (ibid.). This means, for instance, that if Muslims want British-trained imams, they'll have to pay for them instead of donating to international solidarity campaigns. You can best help the oppressed around the world by being a good citizen here, Ramadan commented. But for many young people concerned with the fate of Muslim suffering at the hands of Western powers, this might be difficult to hear.

At the forum, there was a broader view about extremism and alienation, which many agreed were the result of social and economic deprivation specific to British Muslims that pre-dated the war in Iraq and the 'war on terror' after 9/11. The most likely victims of race attacks in Britain are Pakistanis and Bangladeshis, who are the dominant ethnic groups among Muslims. This was even before the bombs sparked a significant rise in Islamophobia. This is compounded by economic deprivation, with Bangladeshis having the highest rate of unemployment, reaching just over 25 per cent for men under 25.

As Gary Younge has argued:

> These people are not segregated; they are alienated. If they need to be integrated into anything as a matter of urgency, it is the workplace and the educational system. A decent job and a decent income is still the best path out of the crudest forms of racism and fundamentalism. Polls and studies show a link between wealth and the propensity to integrate.
> (*Guardian*, 19 September 2005: 23)

He reminds us:

> The reason black people could not get out of New Orleans was not because they were separate but because they were unequal – the

wealthier ones left. Equality of opportunity is the driving force behind integration, not the other way round, but their relationship is subtle and symbiotic, not crude and causal.

(Ibid.)

He goes on to explain:

Britain has a great many qualities where race is concerned. But the image so eagerly touted after the bombings, of an oasis of tolerant diversity that has been exploited by Islamic fundamentalists who hail from a community determined to voluntarily segregate, simply does not square with the facts. If fair play is a core British value racism is no less so.

(Ibid.)

Racism can also be deadly, so it is rightly feared and we need to engage with the ways racism bears down differentially in different areas, classes and communities if we are to develop a viable vision of a critical multiculturalism. Anthony Walker, a devout Christian and would-be lawyer standing at the bus stop with his white girlfriend, looked as integrated as you could be, but that did not stop him being killed by a single axe blow to the head, following a torrent of racist abuse. Younge recalls 'that it seems to make no difference how segregated their lives are, white people rarely ever seem to live in ghettos'. He also remembers that the four young men who created bloody havoc on 7/7 led neither deprived nor segregated lives. Mohammed Sidique Khan was a graduate who helped children of all religions with learning difficulties.

Younge writes: 'The cause of integration has become so fetishised since the July bombings that it has been elevated to the level of an intrinsic moral value – not a means to an end but an end in itself' (ibid.). It has been made a central theme in the government's task force to tackle Muslim extremism. He also recalls the speech made in Manchester by Trevor Phillips, the head of the Commission for Racial Equality, that warned the country against 'sleep-walking' into a 'New-Orleans-style' quagmire of 'fully-fledged ghettoes'.[7] As far as Younge is concerned:

This is fine as far as it goes. The trouble is, unless integration is coupled with the equally vigorous pursuit of equality and anti-racism, it does not go very far. Rwanda had plenty of inter-ethnic marriages before the genocide; Jews were more integrated into German society than any other European nation before the Holocaust. Common sense suggests that the more contact you have with different races, religions and ethnicities, the less potential there is for stereotyping and dehumanising those different from yourself. But even that small achievement depends on the quality and power dynamics of the contact.

(Ibid.)

This means that it can be important to learn about the social relations of gradual exclusion – say, of Jews in Nazi Germany – and ways they were marginalised from cultural life and the dangers this presents for democratic civil society. We need to be careful, for example, that the kind of discussions Jack Straw initiated around women's choices concerning the hijab in September 2006 do not unwittingly work to further isolate the Muslim community, even if their explicit intention is to make moves towards 'integration' and 'social cohesion'. It shows the potential dangers often implicit in these rhetorics, and the need to listen carefully to what women have to say for themselves when they say they feel more protected and that, for some young women, it has been refigured as a space of freedom from patriarchal gaze and authority. Some young women are asking that they be allowed to pray in mosques as they supposedly did in the time of the Prophet, rather than being isolated in their homes. Some women have set up their own spaces in which they can pray together as part of a community. The demands for greater gender and sexual equality that flow from ideas of equal respect, when young women feel they should be shown the same respect and freedoms as their brothers, has been a challenge to the patriarchal forms of Abrahamic religious traditions. As young women educated in Britain feel a greater sense of *entitlement*, so they question traditional religious forms of subordination and seek new forms in which they can express their religious and spiritual lives.

We also have to be aware of the power dynamics at work when a government minister asks a young women to remove her niqab, and the difficulty she might feel in refusing. Straw said he felt the wearing of a veil also made better community relations 'more difficult', while at the same time confessing, 'My concerns could be misplaced but I think there is an issue here.' The discussion that he provoked, which continued for several weeks, showed that he had touched a raw nerve. His stance sparked anger among many Muslims, especially among the 30,000 in his Blackburn constituency where people seemed to feel his remarks were disrespectful and could only cause anger and division. Muhammed Umar, chairman of the Ramadhan Foundation, said:

> Jack Straw should be ashamed. He should be aware that it is laid down in the teachings of the Koran that it is God's will that women should dress modestly and not expose their face to anyone but their husband. Without a veil she feels naked.
>
> To expect one of his constituents to remove her veil before speaking to him is disgraceful.
>
> (*Daily Express*, 6 October 2006: 9)

But if women are to be able to voice their own experiences and make decisions for themselves, we also have to realise that relatively few women choose to wear the niqab and that there are movements in different directions with some young women choosing not to wear the hijab and feeling clearer in their religious identity because of this. Modesty can be interpreted in different ways. But there is also a disrespectful tone and a certain arrogance of power that is revealed in how Straw presented his decision. As Straw explains how, almost a year previous to his statement, a 'pleasant lady' with a broad Lancashire accent turned up at his weekly surgery wearing a burkha and told him: 'It's really nice to meet you face-to-face.' He said that he thought, but did not say out loud: 'The chance would be a fine thing.'

Mr Straw explained:

> The lady was wearing the full veil. Her eyes were uncovered but the rest of her face was in cloth.
>
> Her husband, a professional man, was with her. She did most of the talking. We parted amicably.
>
> All this was about a year ago and the encounter got me thinking. In part, this was because of the apparent incongruity between the signals which indicate common bonds – the entirely English accent, the couples' education (wholly in the UK) – and the fact of the veil.
>
> Above all it was because I felt uncomfortable about talking to someone face-to-face who I could not see. So I decided that I wouldn't just sit there the next time a lady turned up to see me in a full veil, and I haven't.
>
> (Ibid.)

The fact that he 'felt uncomfortable' did not open up a discussion in which he shared his feelings but, rather, 'I decided that I wouldn't just sit there' – and he has the power to raise it as a broader issue.

Writing in his local newspaper during the sensitive month of Ramadan, Mr Straw added:

> Now, I always ensure that a female member of my staff is with me. I explain that this is a country built on freedoms. I defend absolutely the right of any women to wear a headscarf. As for the full veil, wearing it breaks no laws.
>
> However, I can't recall a single occasion when the lady concerned had refused to lift her veil and most I ask seem relieved I have done so.
>
> (Quoted in *Daily Express*, 6 October 2005: 9)

How he knows that they 'seem relieved' we are not told, but it does convey a sense that he is somehow helping them in a situation where they might have otherwise felt constrained and that the full veil has to be sign of women's oppression. But it is also that Straw raised these issues at a time when the Muslim community felt under attack from so many different directions, having just been told by the Home Secretary John Reid in a meeting in East London that they should look for signs of radicalism in their children and look out for fanatics who were 'looking to groom and brainwash your children for suicide bombing'. At the Labour Party conference, Reid insisted that Britain 'would not be bullied by Muslim fanatics' and he would not tolerate 'no-go' neighbourhoods. It was as if the whole community had been put under suspicion, especially following the arrests in August 2006 in relation to the suspected attempts to blow up aeroplanes over the Atlantic in an event that would have matched the destructions of 9/11.

But it was also the ways Straw's comments were reported in the tabloid press that showed how easily his words could be used. For example, in the *Express* there was a headline, 'Fury as Straw asks women: Please take off your veil', as if he is being reasonable but is being met with a furious and thereby 'irrational' response. Next to the story is an image of a women wearing a niqab with the words underneath, 'HIDDEN: Veils worn by women like this in Mr Straw's constituency yesterday make him feel "uncomfortable"'. Then underneath the story is a question that is being raised for readers to respond to, shifting the terms of debate by asking, 'Should Muslim women be forced to remove their veils?'

Straw's remarks that women who wear the niqab make relations between communities more difficult was endorsed by the Chancellor, Gordon Brown, and by novelist Salman Rushdie, who was widely reported as saying that the Muslim veil 'sucks'. Tessa Jowell, the Culture Secretary, said that veils were a symbol of women's subjugation and that women who covered their faces were failing to take a 'full place in society.' Ms Jowell told BBC Radio Five Live, 'We fought for generations for the equality of women, for women to take their equal place in society' and 'Women who are heavily veiled, whose identity is obscured to the world apart from their husband, cannot take their full place in society' (*London Lite*, 16 October 2006: 6). Her intervention came as ministers backed the sacking of a teaching assistant who refused to remove her veil in the classroom.

Communities Secretary Ruth Kelly seemed to signal a shift in government attitudes when, at the launch of the Commission on Integration and Cohesion, she questioned whether multiculturalism was not encouraging segregation. Rather than reflect carefully about the shortcomings of certain multiculturalisms and ways they had been institutionalised and practised, there seemed to be an attempt to *blame* multiculturalism and argue that it should somehow be 'replaced' by something called 'integration'. She seemed to pile on the pressure when she later also called on local communities to do more to tackle extremism. At a summit of police chiefs and local authorities, she said: 'The world has changed since 11 September and 7/7. The government has to change and respond to that and we appeal to local authorities to do the same.' Ms Kelly wants police and local councils to counter more aggressively the militant propaganda fed to young Muslims via websites and radical clerics. The Department of Education was reported as wanting lecturers to monitor 'Asian-looking' and Muslim students they suspect of involvement in extremism. But Muhammad Abdul Bari, head of the Muslim Council of Britain, said in a letter to Ms Kelly that the 'drip feed' of comments from the Government had 'stigmatised' the entire Muslim community (ibid.).

Yasmin Alibhai-Brown, who has long been vehemently opposed to the politics of Jack Straw, for his backing of the war in Iraq and for domestic laws that curtail civil liberties, finds herself 'in the unusual position of agreeing with Straw's every word'. She recognises that 'Feminists have denounced Straw's approach as unacceptably proscriptive, and reactionary Muslims say it is Islamophobic', but, she argues:

> it is time to speak out against this objectionable garment and face down the obscurantists who endlessly bait and intimidate the state by making demands that violate its fundamental principles. That they have brainwashed young women, born free, to seek self-subjugation breaks my heart.
>
> (*Time*, 16 October 2006: 64)

She argues, 'the most important reason for opposing the veil is one of principle. So long as it ensures genuinely equal standards for all, a liberal nation has no obligation to extend its liberalism to condone the most illiberal practices.'

Alibhai-Brown consistently argues that overtly religious symbols are divisive and that the French government was right in 2004 to ban the hijab because schools and colleges should be places of social integration. She argues, 'Protests against the injunction soon died down and many Muslim French girls were happily released from a heritage that has no place in the modern world. Belgium, Denmark and Singapore have taken similar steps' (ibid.). She recognises that Britain has been 'both more relaxed about cultural differences and over-anxious about challenging unacceptable practices'. She insists that the 'robe is a physical manifestation of the pernicious idea of women as carriers of original sin' and that 'Few Britons have realised that the hijab – now more widespread than ever – is, for Islamicist puritans, the first step on a path leading to the burqa, where even the eyes are gauzed over' (ibid.). Though we might not want to follow the French republican example, and instead acknowledge that women should have the right to wear the hijab if it feels appropriate to them, we need to be aware of pressures exerted by gender relations of power and the iconic significance that the status of women has assumed in the discourses between the West and Islam.

For some women, wearing the hijab may have been adopted as a sign of their independence from patriarchy, but we might be wary when the niqab is adopted because of the ways it makes face-to-face communication more difficult. We might go along with Alibhai-Brown when she says, 'The niqab rejects human commonalities', while questioning the confidence with which she says, 'The women who wear it want to observe fellow citizens, but remain unseen, as if they were CCTV cameras'. But she is clearly right to warn us that the Taliban is using violence to force Afghan women into the burqa and that, in Iran, educated women who fail some sort of veil test are being imprisoned by their oppressors. She also warns:

> Exiles who fled such practices to seek refuge in Europe now find the evil is following them. As a female lawyer from Saudi Arabia once said to me: 'The Koran does not ask us to bury ourselves. We must be modest. These fools who are taking niqab will one day suffocate like I did, but they will not be allowed to leave the coffin.'
>
> (Ibid.)

These are complex issues, but it is important within democratic societies to sustain the centrality of free speech, *even if* it means causing offence to religious communities who might sincerely hold notions of male superiority to women and ideas that homosexuality is an evil practice. These are beliefs that are often shared between Abrahamic religious traditions, and they have had to find their own ways of compromising with women's human rights and the rights of gays, lesbians and bisexuals. Some traditions have insisted that these social movements are 'Western' and so external to their own religious traditions but, as women within different religious traditions have insisted, it is often patriarchal cultural traditions that have worked to silence women and deprive them of rights, say, to worship in the mosque or the synagogue that they had in earlier times.[8]

Jack Straw thought carefully before making his remarks, but he might have been surprised by the impact they had. The remarks caused particular surprise within the Muslim community because Straw is credited by many with a genuine interest in and understanding of Islam that few ministers share. As Shahid Malik, MP for Dewsbury, makes clear, 'I don't think any malice was intended. No home secretary in recent times has done more on issues of race and equality – from the Stephen Lawrence inquiry to Muslim chaplains in hospitals and prisons' (*Guardian*, 6 October 2006). But what helped to produce a sense of crisis over the government's attitudes towards multiculturalism was that Straw's remarks came at the end of a week in which problems seemed to coalesce. Anger over a Muslim police officer who asked to be excused guard duties at the Israeli embassy combined with tensions in Windsor, where plans to build a mosque sparked three nights of violent clashes, giving British Muslims a frustrating sense of once again being made scapegoats. Days after Straw's intervention, police in Liverpool said a man had snatched a veil off a Muslim woman as she waited at a bus stop. Khalid Mahmood, Labour MP for Birmingham Perry Barr, had already said, 'I think Jack is at risk of providing succour to people holding anti-Muslim prejudices' (*Guardian*, 6 October 2006).

But, possibly, the concerns also reflected a sense that the government's perspective on relations with Muslim and other ethnic minority communities appeared to have shifted significantly since the London bombings. Its immediate reaction to 7/7 was to reach out to community representatives to discuss how the problems of extremism might be tackled. But, according to Dr Drabu of the Muslim Council of Britain, attempts at rapprochement with the Muslim community were a 'charade'. 'They had these working groups, but when it came out that they would like an inquiry, that was totally ignored. When they said it was all to do with foreign policy, that was ignored' (*Guardian*, 7 October 2006: 4). Madeleine Bunting also recognises how many Muslims have become profoundly cynical about government responses since 7/7. She recalls how, in August 2006:

> Muslim MPs and peers have been roundly ticked off by a succession of government ministers as if they were imperial vassals who should know their place. Yet they were simply stating the obvious – that British foreign policy is incubating (we can argue whether it's the root cause another time) Muslim extremism.
>
> (*Guardian*, 16 August 2006: 25)

Bunting recalls:

> The ministerial tours, the meetings with selected Muslims – most of whom are as baffled by Islamic extremism as ministers – were the responses to last summer's London bombings. The danger is that as the government's 'community cohesion' policy flounders, there is no shortage of media commentators ... [who argue] ... the government can't talk to extremists because they endorse violence and/or are nutty and irrational, and can't talk to 'moderates' (warning: the word is on the point of becoming a term of abuse in the Muslim community) because they're not representative.
>
> (Ibid.)

She discerns that there 'is a profound confusion in government policy as to what to do about British-grown Islamist terrorism, apart from large amounts of surveillance and frequent use of detention. Beyond that, the hearts-and-minds strategy is running on empty' (ibid.). She recognises that 'Muslim brotherhood' is a global phenomenon that has taken many different guises in different places, and that many of those 'in this country influenced by this strand of anti-colonial political Islamism have subsequently developed their thinking in entirely different directions' (ibid.). This means that the government has to work with the Muslim Council of Britain, to which 40 per cent of British mosques are affiliated, as well as to the new Sufi Muslim Council of Britain. She recognises that the government has 'an urgent task ahead to assuage anxiety as the possibility looms of a second-class status for Muslims in this country – profiled, suspected, searched, endlessly quizzed and found wanting' (ibid.).

Similar fears are expressed by Shahid Malik, MP for Dewsbury, who said of Straw's speech:

> It's not so much what he has said as the climate in which he has said it, in which Muslims – and non-Muslims – are getting tired of Muslim stories. The veil isn't the problem; the problem is that people are frightened of it – they've never spoken to someone with a veil. This cannot and must not be about blaming one group, but about saying we have all got to take collective responsibility.
>
> (*Guardian*, 7 October 2006: 4)

Rachel Ashhead, 20, a Business Studies student at Manchester Metropolitan University, agrees when she says:

> It's their choice to wear the veil and they've an absolute right.... I've no problem with it all when I meet one – there are loads of them at uni. A more important issue is the way these things are discussed in the news, how they get simplified and people set against each other.
>
> (Ibid.)

Asma Mirza, 29, a housewife in Blackburn, explains:

> I certainly don't agree with Jack Straw because my religion demands that I wear this. I have taken the full veil for 16 years now and I am much more comfortable wearing it. It is a matter of modesty as well as religion. I hope that it will not put other people off. Once they talk to me and get to know me, I think that problem disappears.
>
> (Ibid.)

As a young woman in full veil adds:

> OK, it's religion first but modesty comes into it a lot for me. I started using the full veil eight months ago and it's done so much for my self-respect. It's comfortable, I feel protected and I happily eat out at McDonald's in it. I've developed this special way of getting the food up behind the material.
>
> (Ibid.)

Though the veil has been a lightning rod issue since Turkey banned headscarves as a rejection of Ottoman conservatism, it can be helpful to trace how the status and dress of women have become critical markers in the West's relationship to Islam. Even though the West has only very recently – since the 1970s – conceded demands being made by the women's movement and begun to come to terms with its homophobic traditions, issues around gender and sexuality remain critical in affirming Western modernity and 'superiority' in relation to Islam – while at the same time being heavily contested, particularly through the strength of Christian fundamentalisms in the United States. The 2004 ban on 'conspicuous' religious symbols in French state schools was seen as a means of shielding the secular state from the perceived threat of Islamic fundamentalism.[9]

Ghulan Choudhari of Radio Ramadan Blackburn said that only a small minority of women in Blackburn wore the full veil, but numbers were growing. He said, 'It's partly down to the increased interest in our religion, especially among young people.' This is connected to the much better-organised Islamic teaching locally. As one mother, wearing a headscarf and shalwar kameez but not a full veil, explains:

> When our mums and dads came here it was all work, work, work for them, no time to study and no mosques. Now we have lessons in English, Urdu and Arabic and women are learning what their religion really asks them to do.
>
> (Ibid.: 5)

According to Phil Riley, Straw's constituency party secretary:

> The big worry here is that Blackburn is becoming a divided town. Either you stand by and watch that process, doing nothing, or you engage people in a debate about it. Jack's started a conversation.... I know he's worried about the number of Blackburn-born girls who are taking it up. As he says, in the context of cultural cohesion it's something which just doesn't help.
>
> (Ibid.)

Although Muslim opinion on the street was not unsympathetic to Straw, hardly anyone put other communities' feelings before the religious right – or *duty* in the eyes of a sizeable minority – to wear the full veil. But as a self-employed electrician explained, the roots of social division were much older than veil wearing:

> It's all to do with the way we were treated in the 70s – I was regularly chased along here when I was a kid by white lads. Other communities just did not want to know about us – funny that they're all so interested now in things like veils. I was a soldier in the British army for 11 years and I can tell you very clearly now I couldn't get anywhere because I wasn't white but brown.
>
> (Ibid.)

Multiculturalism(s)

Gary Younge recognises:

> the value of integration is contingent, on whom you are asking to integrate, what you are asking them to integrate into and on what basis you are asking them to do so. The framework of the current debate is flawed on all three fronts. It treats integration as a one-way street – not a subtle process of cultural negotiation but full-scale assimilation of a religious group that is regarded, by many liberals and conservatives, as backward and reactionary. It is hardly surprising that many Muslims would not want to sign up to that.
>
> (*Guardian*, 19 September 2005: 23)

I think these dangers are important to recognise since remains tempting to think of integration as an end in itself and to welcome any moves in that direction. There are different kinds of segregation some of which are forced because of poor housing and unemployment and others which are freely chosen because people want to be close to sites of prayer. The dangers of segregation was a theme also explored in David Edgar's play *Playing with Fire*, that reached similar conclusions to Phillips (see above, page 232) – namely, that Britain is increasingly in danger of being divided into segregated districts that will look like American ghettos, unless government policies intervene.[10] But Danny Dorling in the *Observer* (25 September 2005) argued that Phillips got it wrong and that, if Britain has ghettos, it is not in our neighbourhoods as they are in the US, but above the fifth floor of our tower blocks which are almost entirely populated by non-whites.

But, as Will Hutton writes, 'nearly all Phillips's big points still stand and the trends are ominous. There are still signs of polarisation reflected in schooling and friendship networks.' It is these trends that need to be taken seriously and they can be exacerbated through faith schools. According to Hutton:

> Phillips's speech was intellectually brave, but he does not go as far as Edgar. He castigates Sikhs for not recognising the importance of free speech in their protests against a play, Africans for traumatising children in ritual exorcisms for witches and whites for fleeing schools with Asian kids. But he is silent about Muslim sexism and the problems posed by Muslim dress codes. He is brave to argue that multiculturalism has too readily stressed respect for differences and not what Britain needs to hold in common; and he is right to insist that the better response is aggressive integration around the principles of equality of opportunity, participation and interaction.
>
> (*Observer*, 25 September 2005: 28)

I would argue that there is still a danger of setting up false polarities and that we can imagine a critical multiculturalism that seeks ways in which people can integrate into a vision of Britishness that has found the courage to *face* the indignities and oppressions of its colonial pasts of empire.

Following a liberalism that is often uneasy with both group identifications and ceding public spaces for religious traditions that, within an Enlightenment rationalism, are framed as private matters of individual belief, Hutton recognises with Phillips that integration '"doesn't just happen" – it has to be willed, and it has to be willed by all sides. Muslim fundamentalists don't want equality of opportunity, participation and interaction if it implies treating their women as equals' (ibid.). Young women within changing Muslim communities are making decisions for themselves and would properly resent the idea of being figured as 'their women' to be negotiated about, rather than listened to. We need to appreciate the *processes* of change and the realities of everyday multiculture that have become a reality in many urban areas, particularly for younger generations. Part of the resistance to identity politics is because it threatens to enclose and fix people into pre-given identities and so limit spaces of possibility and becoming that are often shaped through music and media cultures.

According to Hutton:

> Britishness is an elastic and tolerant enough concept to accommodate every cultural and faith group as long as there is some buy in to a minimum set of values, including male and female equality. We have to be clear; it is outrageous that two-thirds of Muslim women are economically inactive and discriminated against, so that poverty reinforces race as a source of disadvantage. But, equally, the wearing of full length jihabs makes their integration much more difficult, and like Ataturk in Turkey and today's French government, we should object, and insist our objection hold in public spaces such as schools and hospitals. The Koran does not require this garb; it is male sexism that does.
>
> (Ibid.)

But Hutton tends to think of 'Britishness' in terms of values of tolerance, freedom and fair play in ways that disavow the ways in which migrant populations from the new Commonwealth are marked by *different* histories of empire and colonial subordination. They have suffered from a different experiences of 'Britishness' that should *not* be forgotten.

Of course the French government did not allow the wearing of the smaller hijabs either when it came to schools. The idea within a French republican tradition was that public space was a shared secular space that people could only claim access to as individuals citizens who were prepared to concede that religion was a private matter of individual religious belief alone. But the tone of Hutton's 'The Koran does not require this garb; it is male sexism that does' feels strident and unhelpful, especially if we realise how resistant men have been in the West to consider issues around men and masculinities as part of their aspirations towards greater gender equality. We need to be careful about the judgements we make.

Hutton acknowledges that Phillips's approach 'involving tough concessions on fair housing, school and university access by the white majority community and no less tough concessions by the ethnic minorities over cultural behaviours they currently regard as non-negotiable, is surely the only way forward.' But again there is something unhelpful in this generalised talk about 'ethnic minorities' and about *the terms* in which these negotiations take place if they concern issues regarded as 'non-negotiable'. Issues around gender and sexuality are contested within diverse religious traditions as they are still within a dominant Anglican tradition within Britain. This makes it vital to concede that there will be diverse and conflicting interests within religious and ethnic cultures. A traditional multicultural discourse too often overlooks these tensions in its vision of discrete homogenised communities who could somehow be relied upon to discipline and regulate their own. It is *this* vision of multiculturalism that has long been questioned within research traditions that have learned to be suspicious of easy notions of 'community' that are often invoked to sustain prevailing relations of traditional power and dominance.

Often it is unhelpful to counterpose integration with multiculturalism and the task for a *critical multiculturalism* is to the think the complex interrelations between them so that we allow a vision that is sustained by equal dignity and human rights. As Lee Jaspers recognises, 'Culturally distinct communities can be hugely positive and beneficial. We have many examples of people choosing to live in an area where they are able to worship, shop and bring up their children within the context of their culture.' But appreciating this does *not* mean, as Phillips and Hutton have argued, that multiculturalism elevates difference and therefore enhances segregation. We have to be careful in assessing the argument that multiculturalism intensifies segregation. But I think we also have to be careful in evaluating Jaspers' claim that 'In the real world, this onslaught translates into an approach that says: "Assimilate, accept the majority's norms – because if you don't, your failure to integrate, not racism, is the problem".' It all depends upon who is doing the translation, and it would be too quick to assume, as Jaspers seems to, either that issues that have been brought up around integration have to mean a return to the assimilation we know from the 1950s *or* necessarily involves a shift away from concerns with racism and racial inequality to 'blaming black and Asian communities for the problems they face' (*Guardian*, 12 October 2005: 32).

Jaspers is strong in his defence of anti-racism, but we need to be careful to identify the range of issues that have emerged in discussions around integration and the attacks on multiculturalism. Jaspers helpfully reminds us that Phillips

> Asked whether the word multiculturalism should be killed off, he replied: 'Yes, let's do that. Multiculturalism suggests separateness.' Confronted by the *Spectator*'s Rod Liddle and asked if Islam was an issue for the CRE – in particular if it was 'merely a matter of culture' rather than race – Phillips's response spoke volumes. 'Well privately I would go quite a long way down the route you're taking. It is not primarily an issue of race.' Hence the emphasis on segregation rather than racism.
>
> (Ibid.)

But, if anything, this reveals the difficulties of thinking relations between 'race' and religion in contemporary societies where so many people inherit complex transnational identifications. If we are to take Islamophobia and anti-Semitism seriously we need to rethink the secular terms that have shaped theories of race and ethnicities.

But the truth, as Jaspers appreciates it, is

> that vile anti-Muslim prejudice, using the religion of a community to attempt to sideline and blame it for many of society's ills, is the cutting edge of racism in British society. Those who consider themselves to be anti-racists need to wake up to this fact.
>
> (Ibid.)

As Jaspers makes clear, as far as he is concerned, in his role as the Mayor of London's director of policing and equalities:

> Any CRE chair who does not know if councils should print documents in more than one language, or whether 'coloured' is an appropriate term, or whether holy days should be respected wherever possible, should seriously consider whether he is in the right job.
>
> (Ibid.)

Of course difficult *judgements* have to be made and we have to evaluate carefully what has led people to these different positions. But while we might be wary of generalised claims we need to recognise how traditional notions of multiculturalism in one country needs to be reimagined if we are to take seriously the transnational connections so many people inherit as well as the complex belongings so many seek to honour.

Belonging(s)

Within different European countries there are issues about how second-generation Muslims define themselves. It can be helpful to recall these different European situations so that we recognise how different national traditions still have an important and continuing influence in ways that cannot easily be wished away by those who aspire towards a transational cosmopolitanism. Many young people say they do not feel connected to their parents' heritage, possibly only having visited the countries where their parents migrated from a few times in their lives, but nor do they feel a sense of belonging in the country of their birth. Often their sense of belonging is made more difficult for the second generation by the narratives of return parents constantly invoke. I recall talking to a Nigerian student who was educated in South East London about the impact of her parents constantly talked about their future lives in Lagos. It was as if they were living between spaces in a way that seemed to make their lives provisional. The parents might be have been able to handle this but it created difficulties for their children, adding to their precarious sense of belonging.

That some young men in France are forced to live on the dole only enhances their sense of estrangement. The attitude of Riad, a 32-year-old French citizen who has been unemployed since 2002, is all-too-common. Sitting in a café in the Lyon suburb of Venissieux, he says, 'They say we are French, and we would like to believe that as well. But do we look like normal French people to you?' His friend Karim, 27, insists they are discriminated against because of their long beards. 'Who will give us a job when we look like this? We have to fend for ourselves and find a way' (*Time*, 31 October 2005: 30). Integration is still very much a work in progress and, with the debris of the riots still smouldering, Prime Minister Dominique de Villepin acknowledged, 'France is wounded. It cannot recognise itself in its streets. The effectiveness of our model of integration is in question' (ibid.).[11]

The French ideal of equality, rights and citizenship has failed people from dreary banlieues like Clichy-sous-Bois, working-class migrant areas that ring Paris. The state is officially blind to colour and religion, recognising only individuals as citizens of the French state with rights. Successive French governments have refused the models of multiculturalism developed in other states and have insisted on a French Republican tradition that means they have refused to acknowledge or even compile data on racial or ethnic origins. There is a single unified French identity that recognises no combined identities of, for instance, Algerian French or French Malian.

Discrimination is illegal, but banlieu residents routinely report they are turned away once a potential employer spots an Arabic name or undesirable postal code. Research by Jean-Francois Amadieu showed that CVs from white male applicants with French names elicited five times more job offers than those that could have come from North Africans. 'There's a massive gap between what we say and what we do,' says Amadieu (*Time*, 21 November 2005: 30).

Traore, 26, grew up as one of 15 children of a Malian street cleaner in a project like Clichy-sous-Bois. He lives with his girlfriend in a one-room apartment a block away from his parents' flat. He works as a mediator, hired by the local council. It is his task to break up arguments before they turn violent. 'They're talking about deporting immigrants!' shouts Paul, who moved to Clichy-sous-Bois from Congo when he was two. 'We aren't immigrants! We're French!' The other man bellows back, 'They're not going to deport immigrants!' Agitated and upset, Paul gives the other guy a shove. And that's when Gouneidi Traore steps in, urging them to head on home. This is what he has done most night of the riots. He deplores the violence that has rocked France, but he knows first-hand the anger and resentment that fuelled it:

> If someone has a record with the police, he's finished. They won't get a job. I tell them, 'Look, I've been through misery and I'm a bit integrated. I have my own apartment.' To them, I'm a success story.
>
> (*Time*, 21 November 2005: 30)

Assigned to public housing projects, immigrants, their children and grandchildren found themselves captives of places like Clichy-sous-Bois, segregated from white society and marginalised from economic and political life. There were very few who made it through the French educational system and they were absent from the political and cultural elites. They were out of sight and largely out of mind, as far as the establishment was concerned. Second- and third-generation French grew more disillusioned, more resentful and alienated. The young men behind the riots that marked France in November 2005 'are rioting not because they hate the Republic,' says Dounia Bouzar, an anthropologist who has works in the banlieu, 'but because they want to be included in it' (ibid.).

The lack of connection is experienced differently within diverse European societies, depending on different national and cultural traditions. Zaheer Khan, a 30-year-old British Muslim who grew up in Kent, thinks his experience was fairly common for his generation. He was drawn into radical Islam while in college in the mid-1990s, he says. The Wahhabi and Salafist recruiters

> would tell you that things like taking out car insurance is against Islamic principles, or voting – this is *haram*, forbidden. Slowly the disengagement [from British society] was there. You didn't say, 'Let's explore what it means to be living in Britain.' This didn't come up.
>
> (*Time*, 31 October 2005: 36)

Although he has rejected radical Islam, he is still devout, but he thinks the feelings he had then are widely shared among second-generation Muslims across European countries. When young Muslim men from different countries meet, they will often *recognise* each other as 'brothers', even if they come from different backgrounds. After 9/11, in different European countries it is reported that people no longer see young people as Turkish, Pakistani, Bangladeshi, or Moroccan but just see them as Muslims. They do not make the distinctions they used to.

Young Muslims in different European countries can feel that they are being watched with suspicion as an enemy, or at least a potential enemy. There are different European traditions but, in countries such as Germany and Holland, where migrants were welcomed as 'guests' who would eventually return and not as citizens, it can also be difficult for the second generation who grow up there to hear narratives of return, but then witness their parents doing very little about it. They can live in a state of uncertainty, unsure of *where* they can belong themselves, even if they have been born in the country. They might feel, for instance, that if both their parents were born in Morocco, even if they themselves were born in Holland and have grown up with certain aspects of Dutch culture, they are Moroccan. But even if they recognise themselves as Muslims, they are very aware of differences of nationality and culture that non-Muslims might no longer recognise. At the same time, young Muslims in France, for instance, can feel that it is difficult to feel they have roots *anywhere* because, when they are in Tunisia, for instance, they are considered foreigners, while when they are in France, they are considered foreigners.

Many of the young men who go on to become identified with radical Islam have little knowledge of Arabic or religion so they go on the Internet and read all these sites. Many young Muslims raised in secular households and communities are often too unfamiliar with Islamic doctrines to question radical interpretations they read. Rather, they can be drawn to these interpretations that seem to make sense of the isolation and sense of rejection they feel. Many, in particular *young* Muslims, suffer disproportionately from Europe's high unemployment and slow-growth economies. On the whole, Muslims in Europe are far more likely to be unemployed than non-Muslims. In Britain, 63 per cent of all children of Pakistani and Bangladeshi origin, ethnic groups that together account for some 60 per cent of British Muslims, are categorised as poor when the national average is 28 per cent. Often they suffer racial discrimination and economic hardship, but the anger and disaffection shared by many young Muslims has coalesced around the war in Iraq. Many young Muslims feel that the loss of civilian life in Iraq somehow proves that the US and Britain are bent on eradicating Islam, and that the only proper response is to fight back.

In neighbourhoods of North and East London, Sajid Sharif, a 37-year-old civil engineer who goes by the name of Abu Uzair, used to hand out leaflets for the now-dissolved al-Muhajiroun group, founded by Omar Bakri Muhammad, one of the first clerics to lose his right to live in Britain after the London bombings. Since 7/7, Sharif has adopted a lower profile. He has stopped recruiting on the streets and now leads a radical group from his home. Sharif is bearded and wears a traditional white gown. His

Pakistani parents are secular Muslims and still speak very little English. In his youth he smoked and went to night-clubs. It was not until he was a university student in London that he embraced Islam. 'Since I have come to Islam, I have a lot of tranquillity,' he says. Now he tries to steer people away from drugs, drink, crime and smoking. His supporters refused to vote in elections because they only recognise Sharia, not secular, law. While he does not support terrorism, he says the July 7 bombings were retaliation for Britain's support of the wars in Afghanistan and Iraq. 'The majority of Muslims in the UK are frustrated but cannot speak,' he says. 'They will not condone the London bombings, but inside they believe that Britain had it coming' (*Time*, 31 October 2005: 36).

But many young Muslims feel that the bombings have made a difficult situation so much worse for them. At a youth and job-seeking centre in the depressed Belgian industrial town of Mechlin, between Brussels and Antwerp, Yassin el-Abdi, 24, an accountant who has been unemployed for three years, recently scanned job listings on a computer and complained bitterly about the extremists in Europe who, in his view, are making a bad situation for Muslims even worse. 'These people who are planting the bombs are wrecking things for us,' says el-Abdi. But the reality, says el-Abdi's friend, Said Bouazza, who runs the centre, is that joblessness among Muslims can only add to jihadist ranks. 'It is like a ticking time bomb. There are people who fight back by opening their own store. Or they plant bombs' (ibid.: 38).

Newer migrants into Europe often have less patience for second-generation radical Islamists. Moroccan Farid Itaiben, 30, who has lived outside Madrid for ten years, came to Europe to find a job and a more comfortable life. 'If we had work at home, believe me, we'd get out of Europe,' he says. 'We're not here to spread the Word, we're here simply to make a living.' His brother Mohammed was among those killed by the train blasts in Madrid on 11 March 2004. 'Those people,' he says, 'weren't Muslims who did this thing. How can they call themselves Muslims?' (ibid.).

Many young Muslims feel secure in their beliefs that Islam forbids violence and the bombing of innocent people. Many would agree with the young Muslim who says 'Our hearts are bleeding for the [July 7] victims' only to criticise in the next breath the US and Britain for ignoring the ways in which their policies may be adding to young Muslims' feelings of alienation. So many young Muslims hold both these views and we have to appreciate that, for them, there is nothing contradictory. As a result, many young people feel frustrated and feel that their voices are *not being heard*. If they are to create their own sense of belonging, then we need to rethink conceptions of citizenship, identity and belonging, so that a second generation can feel a sense of entitlement and connection. There are present dangers that the anti-terror legislation being passed into law in different European countries could work to further isolate a community of young people who feel that, for too long, they have not been listened to.

Democratic liberties

Journalists like Henry Porter have been significant public voices in insisting that, even in a time of terror, liberties must be preserved and we must resist those who would reduce personal liberties if we are to 'consider the qualities that liberal democracy must retain in order to survive' (the *Observer*, 12 October 2006: 25). At the same time, he recognises:

> in response to 9/11 the planning and execution of the war in Iraq, though flying under the colours of a campaign of liberation, were not rational. The perfervid romantic mission of the neoconservative camp, with its vision of highly mobile armies bringing democracy and civilisation in less time that it takes to make a Hollywood film, was not rational.
>
> (Ibid.)

That madness has been exposed in the 2006 mid-term elections in the US, which saw the downfall of Donald Rumsfeld, the Defense Secretary, who had pushed so hard for the war in Iraq.[12]

Porter recognises that the temptation to 'become irrational' in the fight against home-grown terrorism in Britain is equally dangerous. As he says:

> It is easy for politicians and their friends in the tabloid press to scream for ID cards and every possible form of mass surveillance without having to account for the effectiveness of such measures in the fight against terrorism. It is easy for the same people to avert their eyes to the internment and torture that have taken place since 9/11 and to mumble that the greater good is probably being served somehow. They are guilty of careless, impatient utopianism which is not so distant from the neoconservative position – one more push, one more law, one more restriction and we're in the promised land of total order.
>
> (Ibid.)

Rather, if liberal society is not to be undermined through attacks on vital civil liberties, then people have to define more clearly the *values* that sustain democratic politics if they are to survive what the head of MI5, Eliza Manningham Buller (in a speech to a conference in Queen Mary College, London, in early October 2006) identified as a long war that could last a generation. 'It is,' she said, 'a sustained campaign, not a series of isolated incidents. It aims to wear down our will to resist' (quoted in the *Observer*, 12 November 2005: 25).

However we understand these threats, and whether we accept that she was simply placing critical information in the public domain, Porter firmly believes that 'the gradual reduction of everyone's liberties is an irrational, if not a cynical, response to the threat we face'. But there is something illiberal in the tone Porter adopts when he argues:

> If the perpetrators of these outrages are Muslim ... and the members of the 200-odd cells that MI5 are investigating are Muslim, it is not good enough for Muslims to fall back on bristling victimhood. To the rest of us, it simply seems nonsensical that a community which is the source of such menace, and which has offered support to it, can at the same time claim persecution.
>
> (*Observer*, 12 October 2006: 25)

But this is to offer a homogenised vision of the 'Muslim community' that comes close to being demonised as 'the source of such menace', which works to estrange the vast majority of Muslims who do not need to be reminded of their commitment to ideals of peace, law and order or to be told 'this is not a religious matter; it is about law and order in a secular society' (ibid.). Possibly, Porter should also be more careful about his language than he seems to be when he talks of 'Islamist fascism – I use that word without worry' as a threat to liberal democracy, since a reference to 'fascism' comes too easily and suggests historical references that need to be carefully handled.

Hanif Kureishi readily acknowledges 'Our avowed and necessary enemy – since the attack on the World Trade Centre – is Islam in its radical version, which is increasing in strength, particularly since the failed invasion of Iraq'. Though he recognises that, since 9/11, there has been much talk about a 'clash of civilisations', as if Islam and liberalism are only ever opposed to each other, with one or other of them being defeated in the end, he questions whether they are as alien to one another as we might think. Rather, he identifies a 'mutual fascination' between 'these seemingly opposed philosophies – one of certainty, fixity and moral absolutes based on the unshakeable authority of one book, while the other is one of postmodern scepticism, doubt and flux'. He also insists there is far more 'mixing or "multiculturalism" than we would like to admit', pointing out, for instance, 'All over the Muslim world people are compelled not only by consumerism and materialism but by the idea of a free and fulfilling education for their children' (*Guardian*, 30 September 2006: 30).

But, Kureishi argues, 'Muslims are far more aware than we are of our self-deceit, of the "spiritual" price we pay for our freedom. They can see that the beautiful ideas we are peddling – democracy, free speech, individualism – bring considerable negatives with them' (ibid.). As a way of developing this insight, he says, 'If the body of the suicide bomber has become a symbol of the Islamist's defiance, determination and an almost inexplicable commitment to religious ideals, the way we in the west characterise our bodies is equally telling'. As he points out, 'Our media and our lives are full of stories of obesity and anorexia.... We either consume too much or too little. We can never get it right; we feel out of control. There is self-harm and addiction everywhere.' He continues:

> Our notions of 'east' and 'west' are screens onto which we can project our fantasies. If we can say the east envies the west while wanting to distance itself from it – 'they' refuse to integrate; why don't they want to be like us if they want to live here? – we can say that the self-disgust of the west conveys a profound confusion about the ways we view ourselves now.
>
> (Ibid.)

We might also say that the narratives we have inherited within social and political theories somehow fail to illuminate the realities we face.

According to Kureishi:

> From this point of view the Muslim is telling us what we already feel about ourselves but cannot yet own up to. The more alien this seems, the closer to home it is likely to be. Radical British Muslims wishing to attack and destroy something they belong to, crudely and violently represent something which comes from within rather than from without. If the east has too many values, which are over-constraining, the west, according to this view, has too few.
>
> (Ibid.)

He thinks that our contemporary visual culture and our writers often work to reveal a moral emptiness in which

> they are saying we have sold our souls for the freedom to shop and screw as and when we wish. Furthermore, don't we claim to enlightened, liberal and democratic while unleashing a whirlwind of disaster and death on the Muslim world, day after day?
>
> (Ibid.)

Then there is the realisation that 'We live in a country of more or less total surveillance, but it is an indifferent or hostile gaze which indicates that our extreme individualism has isolated us from one another' (Ibid.).

Kureishi touches an important chord when he says:

> If we have little idea of who we want to be or where we are going, for some of us this is an agreeable state of entertaining disorientation. But this confusion fails to give us the conviction we require to assert ourselves, to really think about what it is the Thatcherite world failed to deliver, thus leaving a space which Islam can occupy.
>
> (Ibid.)

He recognises that the world we inhabit in contemporary Britain was partly brought about by what Thatcher's party considered in the 1980s to be freedom. Her neo-liberal notions of deregulation, the liberal market and consumerism have been much extended under Tony Blair and his government, even if some of their worst effects have also been ameliorated. But if New Labour was also invested in a discourse of values, its visions of respect, self-worth and community were often tied to a punitive vision of the state that was to be used against 'anti-social behaviour'. But its guiding vision was *unable* to inspire a dialogue across differences and a vision of democracy that could sustain notions of 'good' authority.

Of course I am drawing upon both social theory and philosophy in framing an authority to bring these different voices into relation with each other. I felt a need to listen to voices not traditionally heard within social and political theory out of a sense that the events of 7/7 brought into sharp relief in London questions that had been raised globally by 9/11 and the 'war on terror'. I felt that we needed to ask different questions as we acknowledged ignorance of Islamic traditions that had been marginalized as 'religious' and so outside the framework of an Enlightenment rationalism that shaped traditions of social theory that had emerged from modernity.

Aware of the difficulties I had had in valuing what could be learnt from Jewish traditions that had also been silenced in their time and the need to come to terms with a refugee experience of my own within a family who were convinced that there were no places they could return too after the Holocaust, I felt I might have something particular to bring to these discussions. My parents had an lifelong sense of gratitude to Britain for providing refuge in a time of need and as the second generation I often found this difficult because at another level they were marked out as different by their accents and experienced themselves as 'bloody foreigners'. I had grown up with an experience of the limits of liberal tolerance and had learnt to appreciate the freedoms and self-expressions offered in the renegotiation of distinctions between private and public spaces by the moves towards a more global and multicultural Britain. At some level I suppose I feel that if Britain could face the scars of is imperial and colonial past, as it was beginning to do, somewhat hesitantly in relation to the bicentenary of the ending of the slave trade a critical multiculturalism could help renew and revitalise democratic politics. The ending of slavery was to take another 30 years so it takes time for an imperial culture to face its traumatic legacies of empire.

This is part of a politics of recognition that can validate rather than shame the transational connections that migrant families have. Rather than learn to be silent about histories they can be shared. Kitty Hart, a survivor of Auschwitz recalls *In Return to Auschwitz* (London: Sidewick and Jackson, 1981) how she was warned to maintain silence about what she had lived through when she came to Britain. She was told that nobody would want to know. I would hope that she would have a different reception now, though the fate of many asylum seekers and refugees makes me wonder. It takes courage for a country to face its own histories especially when it means questioning dominant narratives of the past. We are positioned differently in relation to these histories and we should not pretend otherwise, even if we have been schooled to treat these histories as our own. But this made it all the more shocking for me to have been handed a leaflet recently telling of a gathering outside the Deptford Town hall that now belongs to Goldsmiths.

On 4 June 2007 a group of people wearing yokes and chains stopped outside the Town Hall, as the leaflet said:

> to make reparations for the acts of the seamen carved in stone on the front of the building, The statues are of three figures with disreputable histories: Sir Francis Drake was a pioneer of the slave trade making at least three royally sponsored trips to West Africa to kidnap Africans and sell them into slavery.
>
> Robert Blake was Cromwell's chief admiral and fought the Dutch to secure the trade triangle between the Caribbean, West Africa and England.
>
> Lord Horatio Nelson was a fierce advocate of the trade, He wrote from the Victory on the eve of Trafalgar that as long as he would speak and fight he would resist 'the damnable doctrines of Wilbeforce and his hypocritical allies.'

This raises issues to do with reparation and apology but also about the histories that we teach to present and future generations. Why did I never learn these things in my history lessons? Why does it seem so shocking to have lived so long in this kind of ignorance? How could these events have been forgotten so easily and so lost their place in the historical narratives we learnt. Of course it can be said that histories are constantly being renegotiated and that we cannot judge the past with the standards of the present. But if we are to avoid a moral relativism we have to duly honour these complex histories of Empire and the different ways people are positioned in relation to them. We cannot remake the past but we *can* acknowledge the grievances that people carry in relation to it.

Of course people carry different historical inheritances and they help shape complex senses of belonging. But if we are to question an Enlightenment rationalism that teaches us to 'put history behind us' so we can focus upon relationships within the present we need to recognise, after Nuremberg, the need to acknowledge *publicly* historical losses and grievances, even if only to lay them to rest and allow people to 'move on' in their lives. In this way we can help create a critical multiculturalism in which different communities and individuals can feel more at peace with themselves and more able to commit themselves to democratic values and social justice in the present. Hitler was convinced that 'nobody would remember what happened to the Armenians' and this was partly what made the Holocaust

possible. They are still waiting for a public acknowledgement of their sufferings. Of course there are different kinds of grievances and we need to
use judgement in evaluating them if we are to refuse claims of the BNP to
its own version of identity as a cultural politics of whiteness. As England
has moved to new terms of settlement with Northern Ireland, Scotland and
Wales so we need to recognise how complex histories make themselves
present.

Too often we assume that living in a globalised world means forgetting
about historical and cultural differences so that we 'live in the present' and
create future hopes out of whatever cosmopolitan opportunities are available in the present. But I am wary of the easy dismissal of *historical* awareness that has so often characterised postmodern theory. It fosters a kind of
sustained forgetting of the past while the ghosts of the past, as Freud
taught, can only be lifted if they are emotionally acknowledged and
named. Rather than laying histories aside it is important to give them due
acknowledgement within a critical multiculturalism that can show the
equal value and worth of individual lives within a framework of social
justice.

We have learnt that people will be held accountable in international law
for 'crimes against humanity' as part of a transformation of global ethics
and that nation states will no longer be free to attack their own citizens. In
this way the rights of minorities might be protected in law but the insecuri-
ties of a world in which conflicts both within and between states fosters
mass migration which is bound to intensify because of global warming
means so many asylum seekers and refugees confront harsh and impover-
ished realities. There is nothing new in these mobilities, as histories of the
slave trade remind us, but hopefully we have a renewed commitment to
global justice that awakens us to the global emergencies we face.

As the planet stands on the edge of a global crisis due to global
warming, there is a pressing need to raise deeper questions of value about
the forms of life that have developed with industrialisation and globalised
capitalisms. Through engaging with the impact of particular events like
9/11 and 7/7, we hopefully find ourselves in a creative pause in which we
can re-examine taken-for-granted values and face pressing issues about
how people with diverse backgrounds *can* learn to live together in
communities of equal respect. This involves learning how to listen to the
voices of others who have long been marginalised and silenced within the
traditional discourses of the nation state.

A sense of shared vulnerability and the precariousness of lives in the
face of terror can hopefully foster a sense of shared humanity across differences. But if we are not to surrender to cultures of fear we need to renew a
commitment to democratic politics and refuse the demonisation of others
and unnecessary limitations to civil liberties that frame the very claims to
'civilisation' that are under attack. If people are to feel recognised as equal
citizens they have to be offered hospitality that goes beyond the traditional

tolerance of the liberal state. If Britishness is to be redefined then it has to show honesty and courage in coming to terms with its own complex histories that have been marked by both colonial domination and cultures of freedom, tolerance and democracy. But this is to go beyond the idea of multiculturalism in one country to recognise the transational loyalties that have been created within a globalised world and the complex histories and belongings they help create. But if nations are to be re-imagined and we are to listen to voices that cross boundaries and frame complex and uncertain belongings, we also need to create new forms of social and political theory that can help define values that can bring people together while allowing people to celebrate their own differences.

Notes

Preface and acknowledgements

1 Wittgenstein's remark is quoted in Richard Wall, *Wittgenstein in Ireland* (London: Reaktion Books, 2000).
2 For some helpful discussions that can help us recall the days around the death of Princess Diana, see for instance, Roger Silverstone, *Why Study The Media?* (London, Sage, 1999), pp. 68–77; Jane Haynes and Ann Shearer (eds), *When a Princess Dies: Reflections from Jungian Analysts* (London: Harvest Books, 1998); Elin Diamond (ed.), *Performance and Cultural Politics* (London: Routledge, 1996).
3 I was reminded about the significance of Nietzsche's thinking on the need for a creative pause to help people to learn well from traumatic events when reading the PhD submitted by Carole Kew (*Creative Impulses – Creative Pauses: Nietzsche and the Expressive Dance of Mary Wigman*, Goldsmiths College, University of London, 2006). This work has provided the source for a number of the quotations I have used, although I am using them to quite a different purpose. The viva with Dee Reynolds was a stimulating event that was itself a rich experience of dialogue across disciplinary differences.
4 For reflections upon these events in northern towns in May 2001 see, for instance, D. Ritchie, 'Oldham Independent Review: One Oldham One Future', *Oldham Independent Review*, 2001; C. Alexander, 'Imagining the Asian Gang: Ethnicity, Masculinity and Youth after the Riots', *Critical Social Policy: a Journal of Theory and Practice in Social Welfare* 24(4) 2004: 526–549; T. Clarke, 'Burnley Task Force Report', 2001; and for the official report, T. Cantle, 'Community Cohesion: a Report of the Independent Review Team', London: Home Office, 2002.
5 In *Shadows Of The Shoah: Jewish Identity and Belonging* (Oxford: Berg, 2000), I explored the time it took for me to begin to come to terms with the Shoah – the Holocaust – that had such a catastrophic effect on both sides of my family's history. With a strong push to assimilate into a dominant British culture, it was easy to feel that it was a relatively small price to pay to disavow your own traumatic histories. We learned to put these histories behind us in our anxieties to belong. It takes time to develop a different relationship to personal and cultural memories and histories and it was a journey with my partner to Poland, where my father's family had come from, that also stimulated reflections about my own uncertain belongings.
6 Judith Butler shares her responses to 9/11 in *Precarious Life: the Powers of Mourning and Violence* (London and New York: Verso, 2004), p. xii.

1 Introduction: traumatic events, precarious lives and social theory

1 For some helpful discussions around how a globalised world was forced to rethink the terms in which it had presented itself in the face of 9/11 and 7/7, see, for instance, Zygmunt Bauman, *Liquid Love* (Cambridge: Polity Press, 2005); Ulrich Beck, *World Risk Society* (Cambridge: Polity Press, 1999); 'The Terrorist Threat: World Risk Society Revisited', *Theory, Culture and Society* 19(4) 2002: 39–55; 'The Cosmopolitan Society and its Enemies', *Theory, Culture and Society* 19(1–2) 2002: 17–44; and 'The Truth of Others: a Cosmopolitan Approach', *Common Knowledge* 10(3) 2004: 430–449.

2 For some helpful engagements with postmodern theory and its impact in challenging classical forms of social theory, see, for instance, Zygmunt Bauman, *Intimations of Postmodernity* (London: Routledge, 1992); *Postmodern Ethics* (Cambridge: Polity Press, 1993); and his later rethinkings in *Liquid Modernity* (Cambridge: Polity Press, 2000); Linda Nicholson (ed.), *Feminism/Postmodernism* (New York and London: Routledge, 1990); L. Nicholson *et al.*, *Feminist Contentions* (New York: Routledge, 1995).

3 Max Weber's *The Protestant Ethic and the Spirit of Capitalism* (London: Allen and Unwin, 1930) is still a vital and illuminating text to grasp the shaping of the work ethic within contemporary capitalisms, even though we have to rethink its terms within a culture that would readily celebrate pleasure and sexuality. We also need to be aware of how capitalisms have been shaped differently in traditionally Catholic cultures so helping us grasp, for instance, differences in work cultures between the north and south of Europe. For some interesting reflections on Weber in the light of the new capitalism, see Richard Sennett, *The New Capitalism* (New Haven: Yale University Press, 2005).

4 For discussions about the relationship of feminisms to post-structuralism, see, for instance, Rosi Braidotti, *Patterns of Dissonance* (Cambridge: Polity Press, 1991); Judith Butler, *Gender Trouble: Feminism and the Subversion of Identity* (New York: Routledge, 1990); and *The Psychic Life of Power: Theories in Subjection* (Stanford: Stanford University Press, 1997); A. Scott and J. Butler (eds), *Feminists Theorize The Political* (New York: Routledge, 1992); Linda Nicholson, *Feminism/Postmodernism* (New York: Routledge, 1990). For a discussion that brings different strands of feminist theory into dialogue with each other, see Seyla Benhabib and Drucilla Cornell (eds), *Feminism as Critique: on the Politics of Gender* (Minneapolis: University of Minnesota Press, 1987) and Linda J. Nicholson (ed.) *Feminist Contentions: a Philosophical Exchange* (New York: Routledge 1995).

5 C. Wright Mills, *Sociological Imagination* (New York: Oxford University Press, 1959 has remained a vital text that has been able to speak across different generations. It has clearly helped to shape Zygmunt Bauman's more recent introduction to social theory and sociology, *Thinking Sociologically* (Cambridge: Polity Press, 1990). If this is a vision that needs to reworked in relation to questions of sex, gender, 'race' and ethnicities, its potential openness to the significance of psycho-social discourses shows its richness.

6 The relationship of an Enlightenment modernity to a dominant white European masculinity and its influences in shaping different traditions of social theory is a central theme in Victor Jeleniewski Seidler, *Unreasonable Men: Masculinity and Social Theory* (London: Routledge, 1994).

7 See, for instance, Richard Sennett's recent work, for example *Respect: the Formation of Character in an Age of Inequality* (London: Penguin Books, 2004), in which he is seeking to bring together different kinds of voices within the text. He shows the importance of listening to others in ways that can often be narrowed if you are seeking, in positivist terms, to test a pre-given

hypothesis. An awareness of how people you interview are often trying to anticipate what you expect from them is a theme that goes back to his early work interviewing in South Boston in the late 1960s with Jonathan Cobb, in *The Hidden Injuries of Class* (New York: Vintage Books, 1971). Here they found people often did their best to conceal racist views that would not have been deemed acceptable by the interviewers.

8 Some of these reflections were stimulated by a meeting between the postgraduate group NYLON with the Young Foundation that took place on the theme of 'public sociology' on Friday 3 November 2006, which was initiated through an exchange of views between Geoff Mulgan and Richard Sennett. The discussion that followed touched on the significance of developing new research methodologies that were aware of the complexities of social life while open to the need for making social innovations.

9 For some helpful discussion that explores the growth and development of Islamophobia, see, for instance, Bhikhu Parekh (ed.), *Law, Blasphemy and the Multi-Faith Society* (London: Commission for Racial Equality, 1990); S. Poulter, *Ethnicity, Law and Human Rights: the English Experience* (Oxford: Clarendon Press, 1998); P. Werbner and T. Modood (eds), *Debating Cultural Hybridity: Multicultural Identities and the Politics of Anti-Racism* (London: Zed Books, 1997); and A. An-Na'im (ed.), *Human Rights in Cross-Cultural Perspectives: a Quest for Consensus* (Philadelphia: University of Pennsylvania Press, 1992).

10 For some discussions about the wearing of the hijab and the different views taken about it within diverse Islamic cultures, see, for instance, Leila Ahmed, *Women and Gender in Islam* (New Haven: Yale University Press, 1992); Margot Badran, *Feminists, Islam and Nation: Gender and the Making of Modern Egypt* (Princeton: Princeton University Press, 1995); Chilla Bulbeck, *Re-Orienting Western Feminisms: Women's Diversity in the Post-Colonial World* (Cambridge: Cambridge University Press, 1993); Camilia Fawzi El-Sohl and Judy Mabro, *Muslim Women's Choices: Religious Belief and Social Reality* (Providence: Berg, 1995); Barbara Freyer Stowasser, *Women in the Qur'an: Traditions and Interpretations* (Oxford: Oxford University Press, 1994); Carolyn Moxley Rouse, *Engaged Surrender: African American Women and Islam* (Berkeley: University of California Press, 2004); Fatima Mernissi, *Beyond The Veil: Male–Female Dynamics in Modern Muslim Society* (Bloomington: Indiana University Press, 1987); Chandra Talpade Mohanty, Ann Russo and Torres Lourdes (eds), *Third World Women and the Politics of Feminism* (Bloomington: Indiana University Press, 1991).

11 Ulrich Beck's discussion of global politics after 9/11, and the cosmopolitan vision that he wants to help shape, is in *Cosmopolitan Vision* (Cambridge: Polity, 2006), p. 99.

12 Paul Gilroy's discussion that questions the possibilities of a renewed Britishness that has not been prepared to face the dark histories of its violent and brutal histories of Empire is explored in *After Empire: Melancholia or Convivial Culture?* (London: Routledge, 2004).

13 See the discussion of politics in relation to religion and the ways this is invoked separate Islam as a religious from Jihadist traditions of radical Islamism in Ulrich Beck, *Cosmopolitan Vision* (Cambridge: Polity, 2006), p. 113.

14 For some interesting reflections upon secularism and its relationships with religious faith, see Abdullahi Ahmed An-Naim, 'The Interdependence of religion, secularism, and human rights: Prospects for Islamic Societies', *Common Knowledge*, Spring 2005, p. 71.

15 Frisch is quoted by Zygmunt Bauman in *Alone Again* (London: Demos, 2002), p. xii.

16 Some interesting reflections on feeling the pain of others are developed by

Susan Sontag, *Regarding the Pain of Others* (London: Hamish Hamilton, 2003) where she recognises, talking of 9/11 in New York, 'Something becomes real – to those who are elsewhere, following it as "news" by being photographed. But a catastrophe that is experienced will often seem eerily like its representation' (2003: 19). See also John Berger, *All Our Faces, My Heart, Brief As Photo* (New York: Vintage International, 1991); and Judith Butler, *Precarious Life: the Powers of Mourning and Violence* (London: Verso, 2004).

17 For some discussion that helps to place the Goethe who wrote *East–West Divan* (London: Anonymous Press, 1994) in historical and cultural context, see, for instance, Stuart Atkins, *Essays on Goethe* (London: Camden House, 1996).

2 Urban fears and terrors of 7/7

1 For an interesting discussion on the impact of global media on the reshaping of experience in postmodern cultures, see, for instance, Roger Silverstone, *Why Study Media?* (London: Sage, 2004). Rather than focusing simply upon the impact of events on audiences, he explores issues of displacement, memory and forgetting in the ways media help to shape contemporary subjectivities.

2 For an interesting historically informed narrative of the place of these critical events in the moral history of the twentieth century, see, for instance, Jonathan Glover, *Humanity* (New Haven: Yale University Press, 2001)

3 For a striking discussion of the impact of global warming upon the social lives of people in the West, and the need for change, see George Monbiot, *Heat: How to Stop the Planet Burning* (London: Allen Lane, 2006).

4 An interesting discussion of the fragmentation of precarious lives in postmodern cultures, see, for instance, Zygmunt Bauman, *Life in Fragments: Essays in Postmodern Morality* (Cambridge: Polity, 1995) and his more recent *Liquid Modernity* (Cambridge: Polity, 2000) and *The Individualist Society* (Cambridge: Polity, 2000).

5 For a helpful discussion of Ulrich Beck's ideas on the place of risk in contemporary societies, see *World Risk Society* (Cambridge: Polity, 1999). For reflections upon the changes wrought by risks intentionally created in the wake of 9/11 and the 'war on terror'. see Ulrich Beck's revisions suggested in 'The Terrorist Threat: World Risk Society Revisited', *Theory, Culture and Society* 19(4) 2002: 39–55.

6 The relationship between masculinity and self-control within the terms of an Enlightenment rationalism have been explored in Victor Jeleniewski Seidler, *Rediscovering Masculinity: Reason, Language and Sexuality* (London: Routledge, 1989). The implications for the framing of dominant traditions of social theory were explored in my *Unreasonable Men: Masculinity and Social Theory* (London: Routledge, 1994).

7 For an illuminating discussion of the Blitz and the resilience of the population of London, see Angus Calder, *The People's War* (London: Pimlico, 1992).

8 For an illuminating collection of George Orwell's essays, see, for instance, *The Collected Essays, Journalism and Letters: Volumes 1, 2 and 3*, Sonia Orwell and Ian Angus (eds) (London: Penguin Books, 1970). For some helpful biographies that help to place Orwell's life in historical and cultural perspective, see, for instance, Raymond Williams, *Orwell* (London: Fontana Books, 1971). Michael Shelden, *George Orwell* (London: William Heineman, 1991) and Gordon Bowker, inside *George Orwell*: Biography (London: Palgrave Macmillan, 2003).

9 John Gray has explored his understanding of the relationship of Al-Qaida to modernity in (Black Mass: apocalyptic religion and the death of Utopia (London: Allen Lane, 2007). See also Milan Rai, *7/7: the London Bombings, Islam and the Iraq War* (London: Pluto Press, 2006).

3 Urban dreams, fears and realities

1 For some helpful discussion about the shaping of the 'war on terror' by President Bush in the wake of 9/11, see, for instance, Walter Laquer, *No End To War: Terrorism in the Twenty-First Century* (New York and London: Continuum, 2004). See also, Wole Soyinka's Reith Lectures 2004 collected as *Climate of Fear* (London: Profile Books, 2004); J. Baudrillard, *The Spirit of Terrorism* (London: Verso, 2002); and *The Intelligence of Evil. Or, the Lucidity Pact* (Oxford: Berg, 2005); Benjamin Barber, *Fear's Empire: War, Terrorism and Democracy* (New York: W.W. Norton and Company Inc., 2003); S. Zizek, *Welcome to the Desert of the Real* (London: Verso, 2002); and *Iraq: the Borrowed Kettle* (London: Verso, 2004)

2 For some interesting discussions about the contemporary nature of Islamist terror, see, for instance, Martha Crenshaw (ed.), *Terrorism in Context* (University Park: Pennsylvania State University Press, 1995); Gilles Kepel, *Jihad* (Cambridge, MA, 2002); Jessica Stern, *The Ultimate Terrorists* (Cambridge, MA, 1999); and her more recent, post-9/11 *Terror in the Name of God: Why Religious Militants Kill* (New York: HarperCollins, 2003); Olivier Roy, *The Failure of Political Islam* (Cambridge, MA, 1994); Ahmed Rashid, *Jihad: the Rise of Militant Islam in Central Asia* (New Haven: Yale University Press, 2002); Bernard Lewis, *What Went Wrong? Western Impact and Middle East Response* (Oxford and New York: Oxford University Press, 2002); and John Esposito, *Unholy War: Terror in the Name of Islam* (New York: Oxford University Press, 2002).

3 For some reflections upon the history of London, see, for instance, Roy Porter, *London: a Social History* (London: Hamish Hamilton Ltd, 1994); P. Ackroyd, *London: the Biography* (London: Vintage, 2001); G. Steadman Jones, *Outcast London: a Study of Relations Between Classes in Victorian Society* (London: Penguin Books Ltd, 1976); Judith Walkowitz, *The City of Dreadful Delight: Narratives of Sexual Danger in Late Victorian London* (London: Virago, 1992); and Ian Sinclair, *Lights Out of The Territory* (London: Granta, 1997).

4 For some reflections on London as a globalised multicultural city, see, for example, Patrick Wright writing on inner-city Dalston, *A Journey Through Ruins: the Last Days of London* (London: Radius, 1992); Paul Gilroy, *There Ain't No Black in The Union Jack: the Cultural Politics of Race and Nation* (London: Hutchinson, 1987); Paul Gilroy, *After Empire: Melancholia or Convivial Culture?* (London: Routledge, 2004); G. Bridge and S. Watson, *A Companion to the City* (Oxford: Blackwell, 2002); Phil Cohen (ed.), *New Ethnicities, Old Racisms* (London: Zed Books, 1999); C. Knowles and P. Sweetman, *Picturing the Social Landscape* (London: Routledge, 2004); Nirmal Puwar, *Space Invaders: Race, Gender and Bodies Out of Place* (Oxford: Berg, 2004); Michael Keith, *After Cosmopolitanism* (London: Routledge, 2006); Doreen Massey, *Space, Place and Gender* (Cambridge: Polity, 1994); Paul Gilroy, *Between Camps: Nations, Cultures and the Allure of Race* (London: Allan Lane, 2000); and Hanif Kureishi's writings on suburbia in *The Buddha of Suburbia* (London: Faber and Faber, 1991).

5 For some interesting reflections upon the impact of new telephone technologies on the reshaping of personal and social relationships and people's senses of connection over space, see, for instance, J. Baudrillard, *Symbolic Exchange and Death* (trans. I. Grant, London: Sage, 1993); and *Selected Writings*, M. Poster (ed.) (Cambridge: Polity, 1988); Patricia Clough, *Autoaffection: Unconscious Thought in the Age of Teletechnology* (Minneapolis: Minnesota University Press, 2000); Ulf Hannerz, *Exploring The City: Inquiries Towards an Urban Anthropology* (New York: Columbia University Press, 1980); Graham MacPhee, *The Architecture of the Visible: Technology and Urban Visual Culture* (London:

Continuum, 2002); and Mark Poster, *The Mode of Information* (Cambridge: Polity Press, 1990).

6 Explorations of the impact of the Internet on the changing character of social relations within virtual space are offered by John Wood (ed.), *The Virtual Embodied: Presence, Practice, Technology* (London: Routledge, 1998); Paul Rabinow, *Anthropos Today: Reflections on Modern Equipment (In-formation)* (Princeton: Princeton University Press, 2003); G. Bender and T. Druckrey, *Culture On The Brink: Ideologies of Technology* (Seattle: Bay Press, 1994); G. Robertson *et al.*, *Futurenatural* (London: Routledge, 1996); and J. Brook and I. Boal, *Resisting the Virtual Life: the Culture and Politics of Informations* (San Francisco: City Lights Books, 1995).

7 For some reflections upon the way in which particular images can become iconic, see, for instance, Roland Barthes, *Mythologies* (London: Grenada Books, 1973); and his later *Camera Lucida Reflection on Photography* (London: Penguin Books, 1993); Elizabeth Grosz, *Architecture from the Outside: Essays on Virtual and Real Space* (Boston: MIT Press, 2001); Susan Buck-Morss, *The Dialectics of Seeing: Walter Benjamin and the Arcades Project* (Boston: MIT Press, 1989); G. Gilloch, *Myth and Metropolis: Walter Benjamin and the City* (Cambridge: Polity, 1996); and Susan Sontag, *On Photography* (London: Penguin Books); and her more recent *Regarding The Pain of Others* (London: Hamish Hamilton, 2003).

4 Missing, loss, fear and terror

1 For some interesting reflections upon the significance of narrative and the need to relate through personal voices to understand larger social and political transformations, see, for instance, Richard Sennett, *Respect: the Formation of Character in an Age of Inequality* (London: Penguin Books, 2004). This shows the significance of moral concerns in illuminating social relationships that were already present, though in a different way, in his earlier study with Jonathan Cobb, *The Hidden Injuries of Class* (New York: Vintage Books, 1970). A related sensibility can also be found in the work of Lillian Rubin, for example in *Intimate Strangers* (London: Fontana Books, 1983) and *Worlds of Pain: Life in the Working-class Family* (New York: Basic Books, 1976). This is a turn that can also be associated with feminisms and their appreciation of the relations between the personal and the political, even though this was often difficult to sustain with the turn towards post-structuralist feminisms that had different strengths in relation to the fragmentation of identities in postmodern cultures.

2 For some helpful reflections upon the changing nature of urban multiculture in relation to London, see, for example, Paul Gilroy, *After Empire: Melancholia or Convivial Culture?* (London: Routledge, 2004); Michael Keith, *After the Cosmopolitan* (London: Routledge, 2005). For some illuminating historical work on the changing character of the urban experience, see Richard Sennett, *The Fall of Public Man* (Cambridge: Cambridge University Press, 1977); *The Conscience of The Eye* (London: Faber, 1990); and his more recent *Flesh and Stone* (London: Penguin, 1994). See also discussion of the urban in M. Berman, *All That is Solid Melts into Air* (London: Verso, 1982); Ian Chambers, *Border Dialogue* (London: Comedia/Routledge, 1990); M. de Certeau, *The Practice of Everyday Life* (Berkeley: University of California Press, 1984); David Bell and Gill Valentine (eds), *Mapping Desire: Geographies of Sexualities* (London: Routledge, 1995); and Nancy Duncan (ed.), *Bodyspace: Destabilising Geographies of Gender and Space* (London: Routledge, 1996).

3 For some helpful reflections upon the historical sources of Weber's notion of *verstehen*, see, for instance, Anthony Giddens, *Capitalism and Modern Social*

Theory (Cambridge: Cambridge University Press, 1971); and *New Rules of Sociological Method* (London: Heinemann, 1976); H.H. Gerth and C.W. Mills (eds), *From Max Weber: Essays in Sociology* (London: Routledge, 1946); and R.W. Bologh, *Love Or Greatness: Max Weber and Masculine Thinking* (London: Unwin Hyman, 1990); and Victor Jeleniewski Seidler, *Unreasonable Men: Masculinity and Social Theory* (London: Routledge, 1994).

4 Reflections upon migrations from Bangladesh into East London and the experience of different generations are provided in Mohammad Ali Asghar, *Bangladeshi Community Organisations in East London* (London: Bangla Heritage Ltd, 1996); John Eade, *The Politics of Community: the Bangladeshi Community in East London* (Aldershot: Avebury, 1989); J. Rex and S. Tomlinson, *Colonial Immigrants in a British City* (London: Routledge, 1979); David Widgery, *Some Lives! A G.P.'s East End* (London: Sinclair Stevenson, 1992); Barnor Hess (ed.), *Unsettled Multiculturalisms: Diasporas, Entanglements, Transruptions* (London: Zed Books, 2000); Jane Jacobs, *Edge of Empire: Postcolonialism and the City* (London and New York: Routledge, 1996); Dolores Hayden, *The Power of Place: Urban Landscapes as Public History* (Cambridge, MA: MIT Press, 1995); C. McEwan and A. Blunt (eds), *Postcolonial Geographies* (London: Continuum, 2002); James Duncan and David Ley (eds), *Place/Culture/Representation* (London: Routledge, 1993); S. Westwood and J. Williams (eds), *Imagining Cities* (London: Routledge, 1997); D. Massey, *Space, Place and Gender* (Cambridge: Polity, 1994); Michael Keith, *After the Cosmopolitan* (London: Routledge, 2005).

5 For some reflections that bring together different views within Muslim communities to the events of 9/11 and questions of terrorism, see, for instance, *The Quest For Sanity: Reflections on September 11 and the Aftermath* (London: Muslim Council of Britain, 2002). This is an interesting collection that brings together a variety of different voices. For a brief introduction to Islam, see, for instance, Tahir Ben Jelloud, *Islam Explained* (New York: The New Press, 2002); Abdel Haleem, *Understanding The Qur'an – Themes and Styles* (London and New York: I.B. Taurus, 2001); and Fazlur Rahman, *Major Themes of the Qur'an* (Chicago: Kazi Publications, 1994).

6 For some helpful discussions on the nature of British multiculturalism, see, for instance, Bhikhu Parekh, *Rethinking Multiculturalism: Cultural Diversity and Political Theory* (Basingstoke: Palgrave, 2000); Les Back, *New Ethnicities and Urban Culture* (London: UCL Press, 1996); Les Back and Vron Ware, *Out of Whiteness: Color, Politics and Culture* (Chicago: University of Chicago Press, 2001); Stuart Hall, in D. Morley and K.-H. Chen, *Critical Dialogues in Cultural Studies* (London: Routledge, 1996); D.T. Goldberg, *Racist Culture: Philosophy and the Politics of Meaning* (Oxford: Basil Blackwell, 1993); T. Modood, *Not Easy Being British: Colour, Culture and Citizenship* (Stoke-on-Trent: Trentham Books, 1992); and T. Modood and P. Werner (eds), *The Politics of Multiculturalism in the New Europe: Racism, Identity and Community* (London: Zed Books, 1997).

7 In *Shadows of The Shoah: Jewish Identity and Belonging* (Oxford: Berg, 2000), I explore an experience of growing up in London in the 1950s within a culture of assimilation in which there was considerable pressure to become 'like everyone else'. Through drawing comparisons with earlier periods of migration, we can explore different possibilities of assimilation and multiculturalism as part of re-imagining the nature of Britishness for the twenty-first century.

8 For reflections upon migrations into Britain in the post-war period, see, for instance, Paul Gilroy, *There Ain't No Black in the Union Jack* (London: Unwin Hyman, 1987); Catherine Hall, *Civilising Subjects: Metropole and Colony in*

the English Imagination 1830–1867 (Cambridge: Polity Press, 2002); Les Back, *New Ethnicities and Urban Culture* (London: UCL Press, 1996); and Roger Hewitt, *White Talk Black Talk: Inter-racial Friendships and Communication Among Adolescents* (Cambridge: Cambridge University Press, 1986); J. Rex, *Ethnic Minorities in the Modern Nation State* (London: Macmillan, 1996).

9 For some reflections on the early migration of Afro-Caribbean communities to London, see, for instance, Paul Gilroy, *There Ain't No Black in the Union Jack* (London: Hutchinson, 1987); Robert Miles, *Racism* (New York and London: Routledge, 1989); T. Phillips and M. Phillips, *Windrush* (London: Harper-Collins, 1999); S. Hall and M. Sealy, *Different: a Historical Context, Contemporary Photographers and Black Identity* (London: Phaidon Press, 2001); R. Ramdin, *Reimagining Britain* (London: Pluto Press, 1999); E. Soja, *Thirdspace* (Oxford: Blackwell, 1996); S. Pile and M. Keith (eds), *Place and Politics of Identity* (London: Routledge, 1993); and *Geographies of Resistance* (London: Routledge, 1997); B. Schwartz, *The Expansion of England: Race, Ethnicity and Cultural History* (London: Routledge, 1996).

10 For a sense of the political movements that developed in the East End of London, see, for instance, W.J. Fishman, *East London Jewish Radicals* (Gerald Duckworth & Co Ltd: London, 1975) and *The Streets of East London* (London: Duckworth, 1979); Chaim Bermant, *A Point of Arrival: a Study of London's East End* (London: Eyre Methuen, 1975); Noreen Branson, *Popularism 1919–1925* (London: Lawrence and Wishart, 1979). For a more contemporary discussion, see, for instance, J. Rex, *Race, Colonialism and the City* (London: Routledge, 1973); Thomas J. Sugrue, *The Origins of Urban Crisis: Race and Inequality and Postwar Detroit* (Princeton: Princeton University Press, 1996); Michael Keith, *After the Cosmopolitan* (London: Routledge, 2005).

5 Fears, traumas and insecurities

1 For some helpful historical discussion about the ways social life is shaped through fear, see Joanna Bourke, *Fear: a Cultural History* (London: Virago, 2005). She recognises that poverty was 'the hell that Englishmen fear most', as the essayist Thomas Carlyle put it, and how this fear seared the emotional lives of Britons and Americans in the nineteenth and early twentieth centuries. Increased state provision of welfare did not eradicate the fear of poverty, but merely diluted its intensity.

2 A helpful exploration of the impact of Walkman technologies on the ways young men and women organise their journeys through urban spaces is provided by Michael Bull, *Sounding Out the City* (Oxford: Berg, 2000). See also L. Back and M. Bull (eds), *The Auditory Culture Reader* (Oxford: Berg, 2003).

3 Some interesting explorations of the changing character of London as a global city are offered in Peter Ackroyd, *London: the Biography* (London: Chatto and Windus, 2000); Steve and Nigel Thrift (eds), *City A–Z* (London: Routledge, 2000); Ian Sinclair, *London Orbital* (London: Granta Books, 2002); Michael Keith, *After the Cosmopolitan* (London: Routledge, 2005); S. Westwood and J. Williams (eds), *Imagining Cities* (London: Routledge, 1997); Richard Sennett, *The Conscience of the Eye: the Design and Social Life of Cities* (London: Faber, 1990); Roger Silverstone (ed.), *Visions of Suburbia* (London: Routledge, 1997); and B. Schwartz, *The Expansion of England: Race, Ethnicity and Cultural History* (London: Routledge, 1996).

4 For discussions of how second-generation immigrants from the Sub-Continent and South Asia have been redefining themselves against their parent's identification with their countries of origin through asserting the primacy of their Muslim

identities, see, for instance, Tariq Madood, *Multicultural Politics: Racism, Ethnicity in Muslims in Britain* (Edinburgh, Edinburgh University Press, 2005); Hurnavum Amdari, *The Infidel Within: The History of Muslims in Britain*, (London: C. Hurst & Co, 2004; Mohammad Ali Ashgar, *Bangladeshi Community Organisations in East London* (London: Bangla Heritage, 1996); M. Keith and S. Pile (eds), *Place and the Politics of Identity* (London: Routledge, 1993); R. Visramn, *Ayahs, Lascars and Princes* (London: Pluto Press, 1986); L. Back, *New Ethnicities and Urban Culture: Racism and Multiculture in Young Lives* (London: UCL Press, 1996); Abdullah Hussein, *Émigré Journeys* (London: Serpent's Tail, 2000); and R. Ramdin, *Reimagining Britain* (London: Pluto Press, 1999).

5 For more of a sense of Ian Sinclair's writings on London, see, for instance, *London Orbital* (London: Granta Books, 2002).

6 For some helpful discussion on the rise of Islamophobia in Britain post 9/11, see, for instance, the diverse discussions gathered in *The Quest For Sanity: Reflections on September 11 and the Aftermath* (London: Muslim Council of Britain, 2002). See also *Islamophobia: a Challenge for Us All* (London: Runnymede Trust, 1997); A. Hussein, *Western Conflict With Islam: Survey of the Anti-Islamic Tradition* (Leicester: Volcano Books, 1990); C. Allen and J. Nielsen, *Summary Report on Islamophobia in the EU after 11 September 2001* (Vienna: European Monitoring Centre on Racism and Xenophobia, 2002); and G. Nonneman *et al.*, *Muslim Communities in the New Europe* (Reading: Ithaca Press, 1996).

7 The ways in which 'common sense' is historically framed through different layers that carry their own histories is a theme central to Gramsci's writings in the *Prison Notebooks*, especially the later sections that deal with the relationships between philosophy and sociology. This is a theme that I have explored in *Recovering the Self: Morality and Social Theory* (London: Routledge, 1994). Gramsci offers us a different understanding of relationships between power and knowledge to that offered by Foucault, though because Gramsci tended to be interpreted within post-structuralist terms, it is harder to recognise. It is also possible to argue that Foucault was reaching for something closer to these insights in his later writings, exploring relationships between ethics and subjectivities. See the way Foucault attempts to explain the development of his own writings in his essay, 'Technologies of the Self', published in *Technologies of the Self*, Martin *et al.* (eds) (Amherst: University of Massachussetts Press, 1998).

8 For a critical engagement with the aspect of Weber's work that tends to foster the idea that people are free to assign meanings to their own experience, see my discussion in *Unreasonable Men: Masculinity and Social Theory* (London: Routledge, 1994).

9 For some helpful discussion on the changing character of 'Britishness' and how this bears upon issues of citizenship, see Bhiku Parekh, *Rethinking Multiculturalism: Cultural Diversity and Political Theory* (Basingstoke: Palgrave, 2000); C. Harris 'Beyond Multiculturalism? Difference, Recognition and Social Justice', in *Patterns of Prejudice* (London: 2003), pp. 28–45; Barnor Hesse (ed.), *Unsettled Multiculturalisms: Diasporas, Entanglements, Transruptions* (London: Zed Books, 2002); B. Schwart, *The Expansion of England: Race, Ethnicity and Cultural History* (London: Routledge, 1996); Monque Deveaux, *Cultural Pluralism and Dilemmas of Justice* (Ithaca: Cornell University Press, 2000); Paul Gilroy, *There Ain't No Black in the Union Jack* (London: Hutchinson: 1987); *Between Camps: Race, Identity and Nationalism at the End of the Color Line* (London: Viking, 2000); and *After Empire: Melancholia or Convivial Culture?* (London: Routledge, 2005); and Tariq Modood, *Multicultural Politics: Racism, Ethnicity and Muslims in Britain* (Edinburgh: Edinburgh University Press, 2005); and *Multiculturalism* (Cambridge: Polity, 2007).

6 Young masculinities, Islam and terror

1 For some discussion of the secularisation thesis that has been framed differently within different disciplines, see, for instance, Alasdair MacIntyre, *After Virtue* (London: University of Notre Dame Press, 1984). See also his earlier discussion in *Secularisation and Moral Change* (Oxford University Press, 1967). See also Keith Thomas, *Religion and the Decline of Magic* (London: Weidenfeld and Nicolson, 1971); A. Macfarlane, *The Culture of Capitalism* (Oxford: Blackwell, 1987); Peter Winch, *The Idea of Social Science*, 2nd edn (London: Routledge, 1990); Ernest Gellner, *Postmodernism, Reason and Religion* (London: Routledge, 1992); D. Bell, *The Cultural Contradictions of Capitalism* (London: Heinemann, 1979); C. Campbell, *The Romantic Ethic and the Spirit of Modern Consumerism* (Oxford: Blackwell, 1987); and R.W. Fevre, *The Demoralisation of Western Culture: Social Theory and the Dilemmas of Modern Living* (London and New York: Continuum, 2000).

2 This relationship to time is an assumption within Durkheim, *The Division Labour in Society* (New York: The Free Press, 1964) and it also provides a framework for his *The Rules of Sociological Method* (New York: The Free Press, 1950). For work that helps to place Durkheim in historical and intellectual context, see Steven Lukes, *Emile Durkheim: His Life and Work* (London: Allen and Unwin, 1983; more recently (Penguin Books, 1992).

3 For some helpful discussion on the impact of the Iranian Revolution, see, for instance, F. Kazemi, *Poverty and Revolution in Iran* (New York: New York University Press, 1980); N. Keddie, *Roots of Revolution* (New Haven: Yale University Press, 1981); and N. Keddie (ed.), *Religion and Politics in Iran: Shi'ism from Quietism to Revolution* (New Haven: Yale University Press, 1983); F. Halliday, *Iran: Dictatorship and Development* (Harmondsworth: Penguin, 1979); M. Fischer, *Iran: from Religious Dispute to Revolution* (Cambridge, MA: Harvard University Press, 1980); and Ali Mirsepassi, *Intellectual Discourse and the Politics of Modernization: Negotiating Modernity in Iran* (Cambridge: Cambridge University Press, 2000). It is striking that Mirsepassi argues against the simple idea that the Iranian Revolution was a clash between modernity and tradition, and for recognising that it was an attempt to accommodate modernity with a sense of authentic Islamic identity, culture and historical experience.

4 For a sense of the historical sources for the ways the United States has learned to understand itself as bringing good things like freedom and democracy to the rest of the world, see, for instance, R. Bellah, *Beyond Belief: Essays on Religion in a Post-Traditional World* (Berkeley: University of Los Angeles Press, 1991); Tzvetan Todorov, *The Conquest of America: the Question of the Other* (New York: Harper, 1984). For some discussion of responses to the question framed through 9/11, of why other countries seem to hate the United States so much, see, for instance, Noam Chomsky, *Imperial Ambitions* (London: Penguin Books, 2006) *Conversations with Noam Chomsky of the post 9/11 World and Power and Terror post 9/11 Talks and Interviews* (New York: Seven Stories Press, 2003).

5 Simone Weil, in *The Need for Roots* (London: Routledge, 1988), shows how the separation of the humanities from the sciences that was part of a tradition of European Humanism worked to prepare the ground that identified power and moral greatness, so making Hitler's identification with Roman power comprehensible within the Western tradition, rather than as an irrational break with it. Weil was concerned to show how Hitlerism cannot be well understood in relation to traditions of German nationalism, but had to be grasped within the terms of Western modernity. For some discussion of Weil's position, see Lawrence Blum and Victor Jeleniewski Seidler, *A Truer Liberty: Simone Weil and Marxism* (London and New York: Routledge, 1991). For a helpful context

to Weil's writings, see D. McLellan, *Simone Weil: a Radical Pessimist* (Basingstoke: Macmillan, 8888).

6 For a sense of the intellectual crisis that followed in the wake of the First World War, see, for instance, Andreas Huyssen, *Present Pasts: Urban Palimpsests and the Politics of Memory* (Princeton: Princeton University Press, 2001); Paul Gilroy, *Black Atlantic* (Cambridge: Harvard University Press, 1998); David Frisby, *Fragments of Modernity* (Cambridge: Polity, 1985); and *Cityscapes of Modernity* (Oxford: Blackwell, 2001); and Michael Lowy, *Redemption and Utopia: Jewish Libertarian Thought in Central Europe* (London: Athlone, 1992).

7 For their different challenges to an Enlightenment vision of modernity, see, for example, for Adorno, Gillian Rose, *The Melancholy Science: an Introduction to the Thought of Theodor W. Adorno* (London: Macmillan, 1981); for Wittgenstein, Ray Monk, *Ludwig Wittgenstein* (London: Vintage Books, 1991); and, for Weil, Lawrence Blum and Victor Jeleniewski Seidler, *A Truer Liberty: Simone Weil and Marxism* (New York and London: Routledge, 1991).

8 For some useful debates across the boundaries of religious traditions, see, for instance, Karen Armstrong, *A History of God* (New York: Vintage, 1999); Mehdi Abedi, *Debating Muslims: Cultural Dialogues in Postmodernity and Tradition* (Madison: University of Wisconsin Press, 1990); Leila Ahmed, *Women and Gender in Islam* (New Haven: Yale University Press, 1992); Yvonne Yazbeck Haddad, *Contemporary Islam and the Challenge of History* (Albany: State University of New York, 1982); bell hooks, *Sisters of The Yam: Black Women and Self-Recovery* (Boston: South End Press, 1993); Julia Kristeva, *Powers of Horror: an Essay on Abjection* (New York: Columbia University Press, 1983); Carolyn Moxley Rouse, *Engaged Surrender: African American Women and Islam* (Berkeley: University of California Press, 2004).

9 For some discussion about changes that have taken place in Muslim communities post 9/11, see, for example, *UK Report Sept. 11–Dec. 31st 2001*, EU Monitoring Centre on Xenophobia and Racism, May 2002.

10 For some discussion of generational conflicts within diverse Muslim communities, see, for instance, R. Ramdin, *Reimagining Britain* (London: Pluto Press, 1999); N. Merriman, *The Peopling of London* (London: Museum of London, 1994); Chandra Talpade Mohanty, Ann Russo and Lourdes Torres (eds), *Women and the Politics of Feminism* (Bloomington: Indiana University Press, 1991); Max Farrar, *The Struggle for 'Community' in a British Multi-Ethnic Inner City Area: Paradise in the Making* (New York and Lampeter: Edwin Mellen Press, 2002).

7 Young men, Islamic cultures and belonging(s)

1 For some helpful reflections upon the nature of second-generation migrant experiences and histories, see, for instance, in relation to South Asia and the Sub-Continent, R. Ramdin *Reimagining Britain* (London: Pluto Press, 1999); Nirmal Puwar, *Space invaders: Race, Gender and Bodies Out of Place* (Oxford: Berg, 2004); S. Sharma, J. Hutnyk and A. Sharma, *Disorienting Rhythms: the Politics of New Asian Dance Music* (London: Zed, 1996); N. Yuval-Davis, *Gender and Nation* (London: Sage, 1997); Ian Chambers, *Migrancy, Culture, Identity* (London: Routledge, 1994); and R. Chow, *Writing Diaspora* (Bloomington: Indiana University Press, 1999).

2 For some discussion about the significance of culture in the ways young men shape their masculinities and relationships with their friends and themselves, see, for instance, Victor Jeleniewski Seidler, *Young Men and Masculinities: Global Cultures and Intimate Lives* (London: Zed Books, 2006). For discus-

sions that focus directly upon the diversity of Muslim masculinities, see, for instance, Lahoucine Ouzgane (ed.), *Islamic Masculinities* (London: Zed Books, 2006). For a more general discussion about changing young men's lives, see Bob Pease and Keith Pringle (eds), *A Man's World? Changing Men's Practices in a Globalised World* (London: Zed Books, 2004).

3 For some helpful historical research into the development of Muslim communities in Britain, see, for instance, J. Rex and S. Tomlinson, *Colonial Immigrants in a British City* (London: Routledge, 1979); L. Gordon, *Bengal: the Nationalist Movement 1876–1940* (New York: Columbia University Press, 1974); D. Hiro, *Black British, White British* (London: Monthly Review Press, 1973); E.J.B. Rose, *Colour and Citizenship* (Oxford: Oxford University Press, 1969); R. Visram, *Ayahs, Lascars and Princes: Indians in Britain 1700–1947* (London: Pluto Press, 1992); P. Lewis, *Islamic Britain: Religion, Politics and Identity Among British Muslims* (London: I.B. Taurus, 1994); M. Rustin (ed.), *Rising East* (London: Lawrence and Wishart, 1996); M. Keith, *Race, Riots and Policing: Lore and Disorder in a Multi-Racist Society* (London: UCL Press, 1993); A. Blunt and G. Rose (eds), *Writing Women and Space: Colonial and Postcolonial Geographies* (New York: Guilford Press, 1994); and Mohammad Ali Ashgar, *Bangladeshi Community Organisations in East London* (London: Bangla Heritage, 1996).

4 For some discussion about conversion to Islam within the West, particularly in the last decade, see, for instance, A. al-Azmeh, *Islams and Modernities* (London: Verso, 1993); S. Zubaida, *Islam: the People and the State* (London: I.B. Taurus, 1993); B. Turner, *Orientalism, Postmodernism and Globalism* (London: Routledge, 1994); Carolyn Moxley Rouse, *Engaged Surrender: African American Women and Islam* (Berkeley: University of California Press, 2004); Leila Ahmed, *Women and Gender in Islam* (New Haven: Yale University Press, 1992); Margot Badran, *Feminists, Islam and Nation: Gender and the Making of Modern Egypt* (Princeton: Princeton University Press, 1995); John Esposito, *Islam: the Straight Path* (New York: Oxford University Press, 1998); Clifford Geertz, *Islam Observed: Religious Developments in Morocco and Indonesia* (New Haven: Yale University Press, 1968); Fatima Mernissi, *Beyond The Veil: Male–Female Dynamics in Modern Muslim Society* (Bloomington: Indiana University Press, 1987).

5 Discussion about the historical struggles over the control of Kashmir, and the ways this has been a continuing source of tension between India and Pakistan, are given in Karan Singh, *Heir Apparent* (Oxford: Oxford University Press, 1982); Sumantra Bose, *The Challenge in Kashmir* (Cambridge: Harvard University Press, 1984); Victoria Schofield, *Kashmir in Conflict* (London: Taurus, 2000); Sumit Ganguly, *The Crisis in Kashmir* (Cambridge: Cambridge University Press, 1997). For more general discussions in relation to developments in Hindu nationalism, see, for instance, Chetan Bhatt, *Hindu Nationalism* (Oxford: Oxford University Press, 2001); Sobhag Mathur, *Hindu Revivalism and the Indian National Movement* (Jodhpur: Kusumanjali Prakasham, 1996); and A. Varshey, *Ethnic Conflict and Civic Life: Hindus and Muslims in India* (New Haven: Yale University Press, 1996).

6 The fear of weakness as a threat to male identities is a theme that is shaped differently within different cultural traditions. It can reach a particular intensity within migrant communities where there is often a need experienced by young men to struggle against the 'feminisation' of ethnic masculinities used by the dominant masculine culture. This was used in relation to Asian young men and the racist violence of 'Paki-bashing'. For some helpful discussion, see Paul Gilroy, *There Ain't No Black in the Union Jack: the Cultural Politics of Race*

and Nation (London: Hutchinson, 1987); Les Back, *New Ethnicities and Urban Cultures* (London: UCL Press, 1997); Michael Keith and Steve Pile (eds), *Place and the Politics of Identity* (London: Routledge, 1993); Doreen Massey, *Space, Place and Gender* (Cambridge: Polity, 1994); Nancy Duncan (ed.), *Bodyspace: Destabilising Geographies of Gender and Sexuality* (London: Routledge, 1996); and Victor Jeleniewski Seidler, *Young Men and Masculinities: Global Cultures and Intimate Lives* (London: Zed, 2006).

7   For some interesting discussion of issues of masculinity, race, sexuality and schooling, see, for instance, M. Mac an Ghail, *The Making of Men: Masculinities, Sexualities and Schooling* (Buckingham: Open University Press,); M.A. Messner, *Power at Play: Sports and the Problem of Masculinity* (Boston: Beacon Press, 1992); A. Nayak and M. Kehily, 'Playing it Straight: Masculinities, Homophobias and Schooling', *Journal of Gender Studies* 5(2) 1996: 211–230; Ken Plummer, *Telling Sexual Stories: Power, Change and Social Worlds* (London: Routledge, 1981); Victor Jeleniewski Seidler, *Rediscovering Masculinity: Reason, Language and Sexuality* (London: Routledge, 1989); L. Steinberg, D. Epstein and R. Johnson (eds), *Border Patrols: Policing the Boundaries of Heterosexualities* (London: Cassell, 1997).

8   For discussions about the experience of different racial and ethnic groups of boys, and questions of achievement in education, see, for instance, D. Epstein, J. Elwood, V. Hey, J. Maw (eds), *Failing Boys? Issues in Gender and Achievement* (Buckingham: Open University Press, 1998); and Pat Mahoney, *School For Boys? Co-Education Reassessed* (London: Hutchinson, 1985); S. Frosh, A. Phoenix and R. Pattman, *Young Masculinities* (Basingstoke: Palgrave, 2002).

9   For some helpful discussions around questions of 'Britishness', particularly as it relates to questions of Islam and Muslim communities, see, for instance, T. Modood, *Not Easy Being British: Colour, Culture and Citizenship* (Stoke-on-Trent: Trentham Books, 1992); P. Lewis, *Islamic Britain: Religion, Politics and Identity Among British Muslims* (London: I.B. Taurus, 1994); Bhikhu Parekh, *Rethinking Multiculturalism: Cultural Diversity and Political Theory* (Basingstoke: Palgrave, 2000); R.K. Fullinwider (ed.), *Public Education in a Multicultural Society: Policy, Theory, Critique* (Cambridge: Cambridge University Press, 1996); R. Baubock, A. Heller and A. Zolberg (eds), *The Challenge of Diversity: Integration and Pluralism in Societies of Immigration* (Aldershot: Avebury, 1996).

10 For some interesting discussions about the politics of contemporary belongings within the post-national state, see, for instance, Nira Yuval-Davis (ed.), *Women, Citizenship and Difference* (London: Zed Books, 1999); and *The Situated Politics of Belonging* (London: Sage, 2006); Iris Marion Young, *Justice and the Politics of Difference* (Princeton: Princeton University Press, 1990); Victor Jeleniewski Seidler, *Shadows of The Shoah: Jewish Identity and Belonging* (Oxford: Berg, 2000); C. Willet, *Theorizing Multiculturalism: a Guide to the Current Debate* (Oxford: Basil Blackwell, 1998); Christine Boyer, *The City of Collective Memory: its Historical Imagery and Architectural Entertainments* (Cambridge, MA: MIT Press, 1995); Barnor Hess (ed.), *Unsettled Multiculturalisms: Diasporas, Entanglements, Transcriptions* (London: Zed Books, 2003); A. Gutman (ed.), *Multiculturalism* (Princeton: Princeton University Press, 1994); M. Keith, *After the Cosmopolitan* (London: Routledge, 2005); A. Quayson and D.T. Goldberg, *Relocating Postcolonialism* (Oxford: Blackwell, 2002); A. Mbembe, *On The Postcolony* (Berkeley: University of California Press, 2005).

11 For some discussion of the changing place of religion as a source of identity within postmodern societies in the West, see, for instance, B. Anderson, *Imagined Communities* (London: Verso, 1995); Bryan Turner, *Weber and Islam*

(London: Sage, 1998); Paul Heelas, *Religion, Modernity and Postmodernity* (Oxford: Blackwell, 1998); A. al-Azmeh, *Islams and Modernities* (London: Verso, 1993); and H. Moghissi, *Feminism and Islamic Fundamentalism* (London: Zed, 1999).

12 An interesting study that draws upon interviews with a number of religious militants, and attempts to explore their complex and diverse motivations, is Jessica Stern, *Terror in the Name of God: Why Religious Militants Kill* (New York: ECCO, HarperCollins, 2003); Kerry Noble, *Tabernacle of Hate: Why They Bombed Oklahoma City* (Prescott: Voyageur Publishing, 1998); Walter Reich (ed.), *Origins of Terrorism: Psychologies, Ideologies, Theologies, States of Mind* (Cambridge: Cambridge University Press, 1990); and Chetan Bhatt, *Liberation and Purity: Race, New Religious Movements and the Ethics of Post-modernity* (London: UCL Press, 1996).

8 Global terror, Islam and citizenships

1 For some discussion on the origins of Hizb ul Tahrir, see Suha Taji-Farouki, *A Fundamental Quest: Hizb al Tahrir and the Search for the Islamic Caliphate* (London: Grey Seal Books, 1996). See also, P. Lewis, *Islamic Britain: Religion, Politics and Identity Among British Muslims* (London: I.B. Taurus, 1994); B. Sayyid, *A Fundamentalist Fear: Eurocentrism and the Emergence of Islam* (London: Zed, 1997); W. Montgomery Watt, *Islamic Fundamentalism and Modernity* (London: Routledge, 1998).

2 For discussion around the ethics of suicide bombing as a form of political violence, see, for instance, Ted Honderich, *Violence in Equality*, 1980 (Harmondsworth: Penguin Books, 1980); and Mark Juergensmayer, *Terror in the Mind of God: the Global Rise of Religious Violence* (Berkeley: University of California Press, 2000); Rudolph Peters, *Jihad in Classical and Modern Islam* (Princeton: Markus Wiener Publishers, 1996); Amir Taheri, *Holy Terror: Inside the World of Islamic Terrorism* (Bethesda: Adler and Adler, 1987). As Jessica Stern recognises in *Terror in The Name of God*:

> 'Martyrdom operations' have become part of the popular culture in Gaza and the West Bank. For example, on the streets of Gaza, children play a game called *shuhada*, which includes a mock funeral for a suicide bomber. Teenage rock groups praise martyrs in their songs.
>
> (2003: 53)

3 For some reflections on the rise of global networks and their place in shaping forms of globalisation, see, for instance, Manuel Castells, *The Rise of the Network Society* (Cambridge, MA: Blackwells, 1996); Ulrich Beck, *What Is Globalization?* (Cambridge: Polity Press, 2001); Martin Shaw, *Civil Society and the Media in Global Crisis* (London: Continuum International Publishing Group, 1996); Z. Bauman, *Globalization* (Cambridge: Polity Press, 1998); David Held, *Democracy and the Global Order* (Cambridge: Polity, 1995); R. Robertson, *Globalization: Social Theory and Global Culture* (London: Sage, 1992); David Held and Anthony McGrew, *Globalization/Anti-Globalization* (Cambridge: Polity Press, 2002); David Harvey, *The Condition of Postmodernity* (Oxford: Blackwell, 1989).

4 For some background to the development of Islamist currents within Pakistan, and links between different groups, see, for instance, Rohan Gunaratna, *Inside Al Qaeda: Global Network of Terror* (New York: Columbia University Press, 2002); S. Akbar Zaidi, *Issues in Pakistan's Economy* (Karachi: Oxford University Press, 2000); Peter L. Bergen, *Holy War, Inc: Inside the Secret World of*

Osama bin Laden (New York: Free Press, 2001); J.B. Das Gupta, *Islamic Fundamentalism and India* (Gurgaon, Hayanda: Hope India Publications, 2002); and Chetan Bhatt, *Liberation and Purity: Race, New Religious Movements and the Ethics of Postmodernity* (London: UCL Press, 2002).

5 For discussion about the relationship of 7/7 to the war in Iraq, see Milan Rai, *7/7: the London Bombings, Islam and the War in Iraq* (London: Pluto Press, 2006); F. Halliday, *Two Hours That Shook The World* (London: Saqi, 2002).

6 I have tried to explore both the strengths of Marx's analysis of capitalism at the same time as questioning ways this inheritance has been framed as a form of economism through traditions of orthodox Marxism in *Recovering the Self: Morality and Social Theory* (London: Routledge, 1994). It was partly Simone Weil's recognition of the materiality of beliefs that both fostered her break with orthodox Marxism and, at the same time, developing her own vital insights into relationships between power, philosophy and social theory. This development in her work is explored in Lawrence Blum and Victor Jeleniewski Seidler, *A Truer Liberty: Simone Weil and Marxism* (New York and London: Routledge, 1991).

7 For some useful discussions that help with identifying different traditions within Islam, see, for instance, M. Ruthven, *Islam: a Very Short Introduction* (Oxford: Oxford University Press, 2000); A. Salvatore, *Islam and the Political Discourse of Modernity* (Reading: Ithaca Press, 1999); Akbar Ahmed, *Islam Today: a Short Introduction to the Muslim World* (New York: I.B. Taurus, 1999); and Leila Ahmed, *Women and Gender in Islam: Historical roots of a modern debate* (New Haven: Yale University Press, 1992).

8 For some helpful discussions about the nature of the body and sexuality within different religious traditions, see, for instance, Peter Brown, *The Body and Society: Men, Women and Sexual Renunciation in Early Christianity* (London: Faber 1988); James Brundage, *Law, Sex and Christian Society in Medieval Europe* (Chicago: Chicago University Press, 1987); Elaine Pagels, *Adam, Eve and the Serpent* (London: Allan Lane, 1988); Marina Warner, *Alone of All Her Sex: Myth and the Cult of the Virgin Mary* (London: Palladin, 1976); Daniel Boyarin, *Paul: a Radical Jew* (Berkeley: University of California Press, 1994); David Bial, *Eros and the Jews* (New York: Basic Books, 1992); Howard Eilbeerg Schwartz (ed.), *People of the Body: Jews and Judaism from an Embodied Perspective* (Albany: New York University Press, 1992); Amina Wadud-Muhsin, *Qur'an and Women: Rereadings of the Sacred Texts from a Woman's Perspective* (New York: Oxford University Press, 1999); and Leila Ahmed, *Women and Gender in Islam* (New Haven: Yale University Press, 1992).

9 John Berger appreciates the importance of taking time to listen to the survivors themselves, and so recognise the authority of their own voices. This is too-easily forgotten within traditional sociological accounts that seek far too quickly for generalisations out of a false conviction that the personal is 'merely subjective' or 'anecdotal'. This tends to reproduce assumptions within a rationalist modernity that undermines people's own experience and voices at the same time as it seems to value them within a democratic rhetoric. Berger has been a significant voice pointing to different possibilities for social research ever since his early inspiring work, *A Fortunate Man* (Harmondsworth: Penguin Books, 1966) and his work on migrants in *A Seventh Man* (Harmondsworth: Penguin Books, 1970). Others, like Richard Sennett, have also consistently appreciated the significance of narrative and learning how to listen as necessary parts of the training of social researchers. See, for instance, *Respect: the Formation of Character in an Age of Inequality* (London: Penguin, 2004).

9 Fears, uncertainties and terrors

1 Some reflections on life in global cities and on rethinking the nature of the urban in the context of globalisation are given in Martin Albrow, *The Global Age* (Cambridge: Cambridge University Press, 1996); D. Held *et al.*, *Global Transformations* (Cambridge: Polity, 1995); S. Toulmin, *Cosmopolis: the Hidden Journey of Modernity* (New York: Polity, 1990); M. Featherstone (ed.), *Global Culture: Nationalism, Globalization and Modernity* (London: Sage, 1990); and M. Featherstone, S. Lash and R. Roberston (eds), *Global Modernities* (London: Sage, 1995); Saskia Sassen, *Globalisation and its Discontents* (Chicago: University of Chicago Press, 1998); and Will Hutton and Anthony Giddens (eds), *Global Capitalism* (New York: The New Press, 2000); D. Frisby, *Cityscapes of Modernity* (Oxford: Blackwell, 2001); P. Chearh and B. Robbins (eds), *Cosmopolitics: Thinking and Feeling the Nation* (Minneapolis: University of Minnesota Press, 1998); Barnor Hesse (ed.), *Unsettled Multiculturalisms: Diasporas, Entanglements, Transruptions* (London: Zed Books, 2003).

2 For some reflections on the changes towards emotional life and a recognition of a shift towards a therapeutic culture, see, for instance, Robert Bellah, R. Madsen, W. Sullivan, A. Swidler and S. Tipton, *Habits of The Heart: Individualism and Commitment in American Life* (Berkeley: University of California Press, 1985); and their later *The Good Society* (New York: Alfred A. Knopf, 1991). See also S. Mestrovic, *Postemotional Society* (London: Sage, 1997); G. Himmelfarb, *The De-Moralization of Society: From Victorian Values to Modern Values* (New York: Alfred A. Knopf, 1995); and Arlie Hochschild, *The Managed Heart: Commercialisation of Human Feeling* (Berkeley: University of California Press, 1983); and her *The Second Shift: Working Parents and the Revolution at Home* (New York: Avon Books, 1989); and C. Lasch, *The Culture of Narcissism: American Life in an Age of Diminishing Expectations* (New York: W.W. Norton, 1979).

3 For some reflections upon the impact of the death of Princess Diana and the changes in moral culture it seemed to reflect, see, for instance, Jane Haynes and Ann Shearer, *When A Princess Dies: Reflections from Jungian Analysts* (London: Harvest Books, 1998).

4 For some reports into the events surrounding the shooting of Charles de Menezes, see, for instance, *Report of the Official Account of the Bombings in London on 7 July 2005* (London: The Stationery Office, 11 May 2006); *Intelligence and Security Committee Report on the London Terrorist Attacks in July 2005* (London: Houses of Parliament, May 2006).

5 For some interesting discussion on the different ways that fear changes the ways people feel and behave towards others, see Joanna Bourke, *Fear: A Cultural History* (London: Virago Press, 2005); Joseba Zulaika and William A. Douglas, *Terror and Taboo: The Follies, Fables, and Faces of Terrorism* (New York: Routledge, 1996).

6 For discussion of responses in the different Asian communities in Britain to the events of 9/11 and 7/7, see, for instance, Milan Rai, *7/7: the London Bombings, Islam and the Iraq War* (London: Pluto Press, 2006); and Tariq Modood, *Multicultural Politics: Racism, Ethnicity and Muslims in Britain* (Edinburgh: Edinburgh University Press, 2005).

10 The West, Islam and the politics of dialogue

1 For some helpful discussions about the growth of fundamentalisms within different Abrahamic traditions, see Karen Armstrong, *The Battle For God: Fundamentalism in Judaism, Christainity and Islam* (London: Harper Collins,

2000); P. Beyer, *Religion and Globalisation* (London: Sage, 1994); C. Bhatt, *Liberation and Purity: Race, New Religious Movements and the Ethics of Postmodernity* (London: UCL Press, 1996); Steve Bruce, *Fundamentalism* (Cambridge: Polity, 2000); John Esposito, *Islamic Threat: Myth or Reality?* (Oxford: Oxford University Press, 1992); and *Unholy War: Terror in the Name Of Islam* (New York: Oxford University Press Inc, 2003); H. Moghissi, *Feminism and Islamic Fundamentalism* (London: Zed, 1999); Bassam Tibi, *The Challenge of Fundamentalism* (Berkeley: University of California Press, 1998); T. Modood and P. Werbner (eds), *The Politics of Multiculturalism in the New Europe: Racism, Identity and Community* (London: Zed, 1997).

2 For some discussions of tolerance as an antidote to fanaticism, see, for instance, David Heyd (ed.), *Tolerance: an elusive virtue* (Princeton: Princeton University Press, 1996); M. Walzer, *On Toleration* (New Haven: Yale University Press, 1997); J. Raz, *Ethics in the Public Domain: Essays in the Morality of Law and Politics* (Oxford: Clarendon Press, 1996); A. Phillips, *Democracy and Difference* (Philadelphia: Pennsylvania University Press, 1993); Susan Mendus, *Toleration and the Limits of Liberalism* (Atlantic Highlands: Humanities Press, 1989); W. Kymlicka, *Multicultural Citizenship: a Liberal Theory of Minority Rights* (Oxford: Clarendon Press, 1995); W.A. Galston, *Liberal Purposes: Goods, Virtues, and Diversity in the Liberal State* (Cambridge: Cambridge University Press, 1991); and W. Connolly, *Identity/Difference: Democratic Negotiation of Political Paradox* (Ithaca: Cornell University Press, 1991).

3 Issues about the possibilities of dialogue are explored in D. Archard (ed.), *Philosophy and Pluralism* (Cambridge: Cambridge University Press, 1996); R. Bellamy, *Liberalism and Pluralism: Towards a Politics of Compromise* (London: Routledge, 1999); S. Benhabib (ed.), *Democracy and Difference: Contesting the Boundaries of the Political* (Princeton: Princeton University Press, 1996); J. Carens, *Culture, Citizenship and Community* (Oxford: Oxford University Press, 2000); F. Dallmayr, *Alternative Visions: Paths in the Global Village* (Lanham: Rowan and Littlefield, 1998); S. Hampshire, *Morality and Conflict* (Oxford: Basil Blackwell, 1983); and F.M. Barnard, *Herder on Social and Political Culture* (Cambridge: Cambridge University Press, 1969).

4 For some discussion around the relationship of education and religion, and issues around faith schooling, see, for instance, I. Shapiro and C. Hacker-Cordon (eds), *Democracy's Edges* (Cambridge: Cambridge University Press, 1994); A. Grillo, *Pluralism and the Politics of Difference: State, Culture and Ethnicity in Comparative Perspective* (Oxford: Clarendon Press, 1998); A. Guttman and D. Thompson, *Democracy and Disagreement* (London: The Belknap Press, 1997); T. Modood (ed.), *Church, State and Religious Minorities* (London: Polity Studies Institute, 1997); and R.K. Fullinwider (ed.), *Public Education in a Multicultural Society* (Cambridge: Cambridge University Press, 1996).

5 For a sense of the development of Karen Armstrong's thinking, see her autobiography, *Spiral Staircase* (London: Harper Collins, 2005).

6 For an exploration of issues of respect, freedom and equality in Kant's ethical writings, see, for instance, Victor Jeleniewski Seidler, *Kant, Respect and Injustice: the Limits of Liberal Moral Theory* (London: Routledge, 1986); and M. Sandel, *Liberalism and Limits of Justice* (Cambridge: Cambridge University Press, 1982); and Joseph Raz, *The Morality of Freedom* (Oxford: Oxford University Press, 1986).

7 For a sense of Karen Armstrong's work on Islam and fundamentalisms within diverse Abrahamic traditions, see, for instance, *Islam: a Short History* (London: Weidenfeld and Nicholson, 2001); *Muhammad* (London: Harper Collins, 2007) and *Battle For God* (London: Harper Collins, 2000).

8 For a sense of Jason Burke's writings on Pakistan and Afghanistan, see, for instance, *Al-Qaeda: The True Story of Radical Islam* (London: Penguin Books, 2004) and *On the Road to Randahar: Travels Through Conflict in the Islamic World* (London: Penguin Books, 2007).

9 For some discussion on the history and political struggles within Afghanistan, see, for instance, Peter L. Bergen, *Holy War Inc.* (New York: Phoenix, Orion Publishing Group, 2001); and, for a guide to the years of Taliban rule in Afghanistan, see Ahmed Rashid, *Taliban* (London: I.B. Taurus, 2002).

10 For some helpful discussions that explore the complex relationships between diverse traditions of Islam and modernity, see, for instance, Akbar Ahmed, *Islam Today: a Short Introduction to the Muslim World* (London: I.B. Taurus, 1998); Leila Ahmed, *Women and Gender in Islam* (New Haven: Yale University Press, 1992); A. al-Azmeh, *Islams and Modernities* (London: Verso, 1993); S. Zubaida, *Islam: the People and the State* (London: I.B. Taurus, 1993); B. Lewis, *Islam and the West* (Oxford: Oxford University Press, 1993); A. An-Na'im (ed.), *Human Right in Cross-Cultural Perspective: a Quest for Consensus* (Philadelphia: University of Pennsylvania Press, 1992); B. Barber, *Jihad vs McWorld* (New York: Time Books, 1995); and A. Salvatore, *Islam and the Political Discourse of Modernity* (Reading: Ithaca Press, 1999).

11 For some discussions around the growth and development of Jewish fundamentalist movements in the West, see, for instance, Ehud Sprinzak, *Brother Against Brother* (New York: Simon & Schuster, 1999); Eliezer Don-Yehiha, 'The Book and the Sword', in Martin E. Marty and R. Scott Appleby (eds), *Accounting For Fundamentalisms* (Chicago: University of Chicago Press, 1994). Meir Kahane, the leader of the Jewish Defence League, sought to operate as a terrorist group and the same time operate as a political party in Israel. Founded in Brooklyn in 1968, Meir Kahane moved to Israel in 1971. He wrote a number of books including *Never Again* (Los Angeles: NATL Book Network, 1972) and *Israel: Revolution or Referendum* (New York: Barricade Books, 1991).

12 I have explored the experience of growing up in post-war London within a refugee Jewish family that sought refuge in Britain in the late 1930s – escaping Hitler's power in continental Europe and considering the pressures of assimilation – in *Shadows of The Shoah: Jewish Identity and Belonging* (Oxford: Berg, 2000). This was also a study showing how traumatic historical events like the Holocaust can remain largely unspoken but influence the shaping of second-generation lives into the future. This is also well shown in Ann Karpf, *The War After* (London: Vintage, 1998).

13 For a sense of the reconciliation that scholars like Ramadan seem to be seeking between Islam and the freedoms and liberties offered within Western liberal democratic societies, see, for instance, A. al-Azmeh, *Islams and Modernities* (London: Verso, 1993); S. Zubaida, *Islam: the People and the State* (London: I.B. Taurus, 1993); A. Salvatore, *Islam and the Political Discourses of Modernity* (Reading: Ithaca Press, 1999).

11 Faith, martyrdom and suicide bombings

1 For some helpful discussions on the emergence of suicide bombing as a technique deployed in different conflicts, see, for instance, Walter Laqueur, *No End To War: Terrorism in the Twenty-First Century* (New York and London: Continuum, 2004), pp. 71–97; Jay Baird, *To Die For Germany* (Bloomington: Indiana University Press, 1990); R. Hoole *et al.*, *The Broken Palmyra* (California: Claremont, 1990); Eberhard Searuky, *Im Namen Allahs* (Berlin, 2001); Maurice Pinguet, *Voluntary Death in Japan* (Cambridge: Cambridge University Press,

1993); John Kelsay and James Turner Johnson (eds), *Just War and Jihad* (Westport: Greenwood Press, 1991); Suzanne Goldenberg, 'A Mission to Murder', the *Guardian*, 11 and 12 June 2002.

2 For reflections on relationships between the West and radical Islam in the wake of the shock of 9/11, see, for instance, Craig Calhoun *et al.*, *Understanding September 11* (New York: New York University Press, 2000). For a collection of views coming from universities in the South trying to enlighten their American colleagues, see, Eric Hershberg, *The World Responds to September 11* (New York: W.W. Morton, 2002); see also Edward W. Said, *Orientalism* (New York: Vintage Books 1978); and *Covering Islam* (New York: Vintage Books, 1997); John L. Esposito (ed.), *Voices of Resurgent Islam* (New York: Oxford University Press, 1983); J.G. Jansen, *The Dual Nature of Islamic Fundamentalism* (Ithaca: Cornell University Press, 1997).

3 For some diverse reflections upon the discussions initiated by Kant's *Religion Within the Limits of Reason Alone*, trans. T.M. Greene and H.H. Hudson (New York: Harper Torchbooks, 1960), particularly around issues of radical evil, see, for instance, Richard J. Bernstein, *Radical Evil: a Philosophical Interrogation* (Cambridge: Polity, 2002); Jacques Derrida, 'Faith and Knowledge: the Two Sources of "Religion" at the Limits of Reason Alone' (in French, 1996; in English 1998), in *Acts of Religion*, ed. Gil Anidjar (New York and London: Routledge, 2002); Jean Amery, *At the Mind's Limit: Contemplations by a Survivor on Auschwitz and its Realities* (Bloomington: Indiana University Press, 1980); and Susan Neiman, *Evil in Modern Thought: an Alternative History of Philosophy* (Princeton: Princeton University Press, 2004).

4 For discussions of diverse traditions of tolerance, see, for example, David Heyd (ed.), *Toleration: an Elusive Virtue* (Princeton: Princeton University Press, 1996); Will Kymlicka, *Liberalism, Community and Culture* (Oxford: Clarendon Press, 1989); and *Multicultural Citizenship: a Liberal Theory of Minority Rights* (Oxford: Oxford University Press, 1995); Lawrence Blum, 'I'm Not a Racist But ...': *the Moral Quandary of Race* (Ithaca: Cornell University Press, 2003); Susan Mendus (ed.), *Justifying Toleration: Conceptual and Historical Perspectives* (Cambridge: Cambridge University Press, 1988); Joseph Raz, *Ethics in the Public Domain: Essays in the Morality of Law and Politics* (Oxford: Clarendon Press, 1994); Iris Marion Young, *Justice and the Politics of Difference* (Princeton: Princeton University Press, 1990); and *Intersecting Voices: Dilemmas of Gender, Political Philosophy and Policy* (Princeton: Princeton University Press, 1997).

5 For a sense of how Derrida develops his notion of hospitality, see his 'notes' for sessions of his lectures on this theme gathered as 'Hospitality', in *Jacques Derrida: Acts of Religion*, edited with an introduction by Gil Anidjar (New York and London: Routledge, 2002). Derrida's *Of Hospitality* includes two earlier sessions of his seminar on hospitality. Anidjar points out:

> The threat of hospitality – here explicitly linked to forgiveness and friendship, to humor and transcendence – can be found in Derrida's work since at least *Writing and Difference*, most notably, though not exclusively in his readings of Levinas. It has emerged in more explicit fashion in *Politics of Friendship, Adieu To Emanual Levinas*, and recently in *of Hospitality*.
>
> (2002: 356)

6 For a fuller exploration of Karen Armstrong's work on fundamentalisms within different Abrahamic traditions, see *The Battle For God* (London: Harper Collins, 2000).

7 For some helpful accounts of Islam that help us to explore values of peace, justice and compassion, see, for instance, Abdullah Yusuf Ali, *The Holy Qur'an*

(Ware: Wordsworth Classics, 2000); Martin Lings, *Muhammed: – His Life Based on the Earliest Sources* (Cambridge: Islamic Texts Society, 1983); Muhammad Abdel Haleem, *Understanding the Qur'an: Themes and Styles* (London and New York: I.B. Taurus, 2002); Fazlur Rahman, *Major Themes of the Qur'an* (Chicago: Kazi Publications, 1989).

8 On the early history of Fatah, see, for instance, Helena Cobban, *The Palestinian Liberation Organisation* (Cambridge: Cambridge University Press, 1984); Y. Sayigh, *Armed Struggle and the Search For State* (New York: Oxford University Press, 1997); and A. Frangi, *The PLO and Palestine* (London: Zed Press, 1983). On Islamic Jihad, see Meir Hatina, *Islam and Salvation in Palestine: the Islamic Jihad Movement* (Tel-Aviv: Institute for Palestinian Studies, 2001). On the early history of Hammas, *Khaled Hroub Hamas* (Washington Institute for Palestinian Studies, DC, 2000); Ziad Abu Amr, *Islamic Fundamentalism in the West Bank and Gaza* (Bloomington: Indiana University Press, 1994); and A. Nusse, *Muslim Palestine* (London: Routledge, 1998). See also Edward Said, *The Politics of Dispossession: the Struggle for Palestinian Self-Determination, 1969–1994* (New York: Pantheon Books, 1994); and *Covering Islam*, revised edn (New York: Vintage Books, 1997).

9 For a useful discussion of discourses around the notion of 'enemy', and the ways this plays out in the relationship between Islam and the West, see, for example, Gil Anidjar, *The Jew, the Arab: a History of the Enemy* (Stanford: Stanford University Press, 2003); Carl Schmitt, *The Concept of The Political*, trans. George Schwab (Chicago: University of Chicago Press, 1996); Norman Daniel, *Islam and the West: the Making of an Image* (Edinburgh: Edinburgh University Press, 1960); Allan Cutler and Helen Cutler, *The Jew as Ally of the Muslim: Medieval Roots of Anti-Semitism* (Notre Dame: University of Notre Dame Press, 1986); Franco Cardini, *Europe and Islam*, trans. Caroline Beamish (Oxford: Blackwell, 2001); Tomaz Mastnak, *Crusading Peace: Christendom, the Muslim World, and Western Political Order* (Berkeley: University of California Press, 2002); and Hent de Vries and Samuel Weber (eds), *Violence, Identity and Self-Determination* (Stanford: Stanford University Press, 1997).

12 Religion, 'race' and multicultures

1 For some helpful discussion around issues of migration into Britain, see, for instance, Robert Miles, *Racism* (New York and London: Routledge, 1989); Marie Louise Pratt, *Imperial Eyes* (New York and London: Routledge, 1992); Patrick Wright, *On Living in an Old Country* (London: Verso, 1985); Paul Gilroy, *There Ain't No Black in the Union Jack: the Cultural Politics of Race and Nation* (London: Hutchinson, 1987); and *Black Atlantic: Modernity and Double Consciousness* (Cambridge, MA: Harvard University Press, 1993); and T. Modood and P. Werner (eds), *The Politics of Multiculturalism in the New Europe: Racism, Identity and Community* (London: Zed Press, 1997).

2 For discussion of the migration of Bangladeshi communities into East London, see, for instance, P. Lewis, *Islamic Britain: Religion, Politics and Identity Among British Muslims* (London: I.B. Taurus, 1994); J. Rex, *Ethnic Minorities in the Modern Nation State* (Basingstoke: Macmillan, 1996); T. Modood (ed.), *Church, State and Religious Minorities* (London: Policy Studies Institute, 1997).

3 Discussions of how particular visions of assimilation were shaped in national settings, and how these have been challenged in different conceptions of multiculturalism, see, for instance, Bhikhu Parekh, *Rethinking Multiculturalism: Cultural Diversity and Political Theory* (Basingstoke: Palgrave, 2000); C. Willet, *Theorizing Multiculturalism: a Guide to the Current Debate* (Oxford:

Basil Blackwell, 1998); L. Back, *New Ethnicities and Urban Cultures: Racisms and Multiculture in Young Lives* (London: UCL Press, 1996): G. Baumann, *Contesting Culture: Discourses of Identity in Multi-Ethnic London* (Cambridge: Cambridge University Press, 1996); H. Afshar and M. Maynard (eds), *Dynamics of Race and Gender* (London: Taylor and Francis, 1994); H. Mirza (ed.), *British Black Feminisms* (London: Unwin Hyman, 1997); P. Werbner and R. Modood (eds), *Debating Cultural Hybridity: Multi-Cultural Identities and the Politics of Anti-Racism* (London: Zed Books, 1997); R. Baubock and J. Randall (eds), *Blurred Boundaries: Mitigation, Ethnicity and Citizenship* (Aldershot: Ashgate, 1998); A. Gutman (ed.), *Multiculturalism* (Princeton: Princeton University Press, 1994); A. Phillips, *The Politics of Presence: Issues in Democracy and Group Representation* (Oxford: Clarendon Press,); J. Kekes, *The Morality of Pluralism* (Princeton: Princeton University Press, 1993); A. Heller and A. Zolberg (eds), *The Challenge of Diversity: Integration and Pluralism in Societies of Immigration* (Aldershot: Avebury, 1996); D. Goldberg and A. Quayson (eds), *Relocating Postcolonialism* (Oxford: Blackwell, 2002); and R. Baubock (ed.), *From Aliens To Citizens: Redefining the Status of Immigrants in Europe* (Aldershot: Avebury, 1994).

4 Discussions that relate to issues of appropriate forms of representations with liberal democratic cultures are offered in R. Bellamy, *Liberalism and Pluralism: Towards a Politics of Compromise* (London: Routledge, 1999); Brian Barry, *Liberty and Justice: Essays in Political Theory* (Oxford: Clarendon Press, 1991); S. Benhabib (ed.), *Democracy and Difference: Contesting the Boundaries of the Political* (Princeton: Princeton University Press, 1996); M. Canovan, *Nationhood and Political Theory* (Cheltenham: Edward Elgar, 1996); A. Guttman and D. Thompson, *Democracy and Disagreement* (London: The Belknap Press, 1997); and A. Grillo, *Pluralism and the Politics of Difference: State, Culture, and Ethnicity and Comparative Perspective* (Oxford: Clarendon Press, 1998); and S. Mulhall and A. Swift (eds), *Liberals and Communitarians* (Oxford: Basil Blackwell, 1996).

5 For a discussion of some of the issues raised by the Rushdie affair, especially in relation to the claims of identity and belief, see, for instance, P. Jones, 'Blasphemy, Offensiveness and Law', *British Journal of Political Science* 10(2) 1980: 129–148; and 'Respecting Beliefs and Rebuking Rushdie', *British Journal of Political Science* 25 1990: 415–437. For the diversity of reaction with the Jewish and other communities, see B. Parekh (ed.), *Free Speech* (London: Commission for Racial Equality, 1990). For a collection of relevant discussions that relate to the Rushdie affair, see L. Appignanesi and D. Maitland (eds), *The Rushdie File* (London: Fourth Estate, 1989); K. Malik, *The Meaning of Race: Race, History and Culture in Western Society* (London: Macmillan, 1996).

6 For some interesting discussions that can help to reflect upon issues of trust and secrecy across different boundaries of personal and social life, see, for instance, V. Ware and L. Back (eds), *Color* (Chicago: University of Chicago Press, 2003); D. Morely and K. Chen (eds), *Stuart Hall: Critical Dialogues in Cultural Studies* (London: Routledge, 1996); F. Anthias and N. Yuval Davis, *Racialised Boundaries: Race, Nation, Gender, Colour and Class and the Anti-Racist Struggle* (London: Routledge, 1993); John Solomos, *Race and Racism in Britain* (London: Macmillan, 1993); Commission on the Future of Multi-Ethnic Britain, *The Future of Multi-Ethnic Britain* (London: Profile Books, 2000); and J. Donald and A. Rattansi (eds), *'Race', Culture and Difference* (London: Sage 1992).

7 For discussions that open up a dialogue between diverse cultural traditions and feminism, see, for instance, S. Moller Okin, with respondents, *Is Multiculturalism Bad For Women?* (Princeton: Princeton University Press, 1999); Susan

Mendus, *Toleration and the Limits of Liberalism* (Atlantic Highlands: Humanities Press, 1989); A. Phillips, *Engendering Democracy* (University Park: Pennsylvania University Press, 1991); and *Democracy and Difference* (Philadelphia: Pennsylvania University Press, 1993); and Iris Marion Young, *Justice and the Politics of Difference* (Princeton: Princeton University Press, 1990).

8 For some illuminating reflections upon the development of feminism in Britain during this period, see, for instance, Sheila Rowbotham, *Women's Consciousness, Man's World* (Harmondsworth: Penguin Books, 1973); and her collected essays, *Dreams and Dilemmas* (London: Virago Press, 1983); H. Mirza, *Young, Female and Black* (London: Routledge, 1993); and H. Mirza (ed.), *Black British Feminism* (London: Unwin Hyman, 1997); R. Frankenberg (ed.), *Displacing Whiteness: Essays in Social and Cultural Criticism* (Durham, NC: Duke University Press, 1997); Caroline Ramazanoglu, *Feminism and the Contradictions of Oppression* (London: Routledge, 1989); and M. Wandor (ed.), *The Body Politic* (London: Stage 1, 1972); and Lynne Segal, *Is The Future Feminine?* (London: Virago, 1994).

9 For discussions about the development of race relations in Britain after the migration of Afro-Caribbeans in the 1950s, see for instance, Les Back and John Solomos (eds), *Racism and Society* (Basingstoke: Macmillan, 1996); and their edited collection, *Theories of Race and Racism: a Reader* (London: Routledge, 2000); Paul Gilroy, *There Ain't No Black in the Union Jack* (London: Hutchinson, 1987); and *Small Acts: Thoughts on the Politics of Black Culture* (London: Serpent's Tail, 1993); J. Rex, *Ethnic Minorities in the Modern Nation State* (London: Macmillan, 1996); J. Pieterse and B. Parekh (eds), *The Decolonization of Imagination: Culture, Knowledge, and Power* (London: Zed Books, 1995).

10 For a more extended discussion of Gilroy's views in relation to multiculturalism and anti-racism in Britain, see his *After Empire: Melancholia or Convivial Culture?* (London: Routledge, 2005).

11 Explorations that share the ways young Muslims from different communities have reflected upon their lives are offered in, for instance, *The Quest For Sanity: Reflections on September 1 and the Aftermath* (London: Muslim Council of Britain, 2002); *Islamic Masculinities* (London: Zed Press, 2006).

12 The significance of exploring a relationship between material and spiritual needs is recognised by Simone Weil, *The Need For Roots* (London: Routledge, 1988) that was written for the regeneration of France after the Second World War. This is a theme that has been further investigated in Lawrence Blum and Victor Jeleniewski Seidler, *A Truer Liberty: Simone Weil and Marxism* (New York and London: Routledge, 1991). For more general discussions about the relationships of religion to spiritualities, and reflections upon a 'spiritual crisis' in the West, see, for instance, Paul Heelas (ed.), *Religion, Modernity and Postmodernity* (Oxford: Blackwell, 1998); and Paul Heelas, *The New Age Movement: the Celebration of the Self and the Sacrilization of Modernity* (Oxford: Blackwell 2004); Susan Griffin, *Made from this Earth* (London: The Women's Press, 1982); Sarah Ruddick, *Maternal Thinking: Towards a New Politics of Peace* (London: The Women's Press, 1990); Victor Jeleniewski Seidler, *Man Enough: Embodying Masculinities* (London: Sage, 1999); and articles collected in such magazines as *Resurgence*.

13 For discussions on Qutb as a leading Islamic thinker, see, for example, Emmanuel Sivan, *Radical Islam* (New Haven: Yale University Press, 1985); John Esposito (ed.), *Voices of Resurgent Islam* (New York: Oxford University Press, 1983); Gilles Kepel, *Muslim Extremism in Egypt* (Berkeley: University of California Press, 2003); Johannes J.G. Jansen, *The Dual Nature of Islamic Fundamentalism* (Ithaca: Cornell University Press, 1997); and his *The Neglected*

Duty: the Creed of Sadat's Assassins and Islamic Resurgence in the Middle East (New York: Macmillan, 1986). To explore the confrontation between older and younger generations among the Brotherhood, see Abdel Aziz Ramadan, 'Fundamentalist Influences in Egypt', in M. Marty and R. Scott Appelby (eds), *Fundamentalism and the State* (Chicago: Chicago University Press, 1994).

13 Civilisations, terrorisms and hospitalities

1 For a discussion of the significance of the Algerian war as a turning point in French history and culture, see, for instance, Franz Fanon, *The Wretched of the Earth* (Harmondsworth: Penguin, 1967). To grasp the intellectual and political context of Fanon's writings, see David Macey, *Franz Fanon* (New York: Picador, 2001).

2 For some other interesting reflections on the moral challenges presented by the war in Algeria, see, for instance, Pierre Bourdieu, *Sociologie De L'algerie*, trans. as *The Algerians* (Boston: Beacon Press, 1962); and 'Algerian Landing', trans. Richard Nice and Louic Wacquant, *Ethnography* 5(4) 2006: 415–443. According to Walter Laquer in *No End To War*:

> Algeria produced an ideology which not only justified violence but declared it absolutely essential. This refers to Franz Fanon and his cult of 'cleansing violence' as a means of self-affirmation. Violence seen by Fanon was a liberating force, binding the rebels together. True, towards the end of his life, Fanon began to realize the corrupting influence of the barbarism that ensued ...
>
> (2003: 199)

3 Giovanna Borradori introduces and brings together discussions on the impact of 9/11 and the terms in which to think of the event in *Philosophy in a Time of Terror: Dialogues with Jurgen Habermas and Jacques Derrida* (Chicago and London: The University of Chicago Press, 2003).

4 For some helpful discussions of Carl Schmitt's work, see, for instance, Carl Schmitt, *The Concept of the Political*, trans. George Schwab (Chicago: University of Chicago Press, 1996); *Political Theology: Four Chapters on the Concept of Sovereignty* (Cambridge, MA: MIT Press, 1985); and *Roman Catholicism and Political Form* (Westport: Greenwood Press, 1996). Derrida remarks that, even for Schmitt, reflecting in prison after Second World War on the question of the enemy:

> the question that resounds in this cell is not the converse of the question in *Lysis* (Who is the friend?), or even the geneal or ontological question (*What is* the enemy? *What is* hostility or the *being* – hostile of the enemy?)
>
> (Derrida, *Politics Of Friendship*: 161)

5 For some illuminating discussions of the context of 9/11, see, for instance, the US government report explored in Seymour M. Hersh, *Chain Of Command: the Road from 9/11 to Abu Ghraib* (New York: HarperCollins, 2004).

6 In his way, Derrida is questioning the kind of thinking that informs ideas of a 'clash of civilisations' and so the influential text of Samuel Huntington, *The Clash Of Civilisations and the Remaking of the World Order* (New York: Simon and Schuster, 1996).

7 For Derrida's relevant discussions of Kant, see 'Faith and Knowledge: the Two Sources of "Religion" at the Limits of Reason Alone' and 'Interpretations at War: Kant, the Jew, the German', which both appear in *Jacques Derrida: Acts*

Of Religion, edited and with an introduction by Gil Anidjar (New York and London: Routledge, 2002), pp. 42–101, pp. 135–188).

8 I explored some of the limits of Kant's identification of morality with law and the difficulties it creates for a more relational understanding of ethics in *Kant, Respect and Injustice: the Limits of Liberal Moral Theory* (London and New York: Routledge, 1986). It was also a theme I developed in *The Moral Limits Of Modernity: Love, Inequality and Oppression* (Basingstoke: Macmillan, 1991).

9 In *Unreasonable Men: Masculinity and Social Theory* (London and New York: Routledge, 1994), I explored the notion that modernity, which is so often framed as a secular project, can sometimes most adequately be grasped as a secularised form of a dominant Christian tradition. This can be a difficult idea for those who want to insist they have been brought up within the secularised cultures of the West and made significant breaks with their religious upbringings. But, as Foucault was also exploring in his later writings, the subjectivities that we take for granted in the West can often be best grasped through exploring the resonances with particular Christian traditions. This can help us to grasp differences between, for instance, diverse cultural masculinities in the Protestant north as contrasted with the Catholic south of Europe, while at the same time being careful not to generalise and be open to the diversity of cultural influences within globalised postmodern cultures where so many images circulate across the boundaries of virtual spaces.

10 For a sense of the development of Jonathan Sacks' thinking, see the shifts between his Reith Lectures, *The Persistence Of Faith: Religion, Morality and Society in a Secular Age* (London: Weidenfeld and Nicholson, 1991) and *The Dignity Of Difference: How to Avoid the Clash of Civilizations* (London and New York: Continuum, 2002).

11 I have explored the experience of growing up in post-war Britain in a refugee Jewish family and the politics of belonging within a dominant culture of assimilation in Victor Jeleniewski Seidler, *Shadows Of The Shoah: Jewish Identity and Belonging* (Oxford: Berg, 2000).

12 For some helpful discussions about the shaping of Black British and British Asian identities in the 1980s and 1990s, see, for instance, Les Back and John Solomos (eds), *Racism and Society* (Macmillan: Basingstoke, 1996); and *Race Politics and Social Change* (London: Routledge, 1995). For Black British identities, see, for example, Paul Gilroy, *There Ain't No Black In the Union Jack* (London: Hutchinson, 1987); and his more recent *After Empire: Multiculture or Postcolonial Melankholia* (London: Routledge, 2005).

13 For some relevant discussion about how new technologies have allowed young people to live across and between different spaces, so unsettling traditional conceptions of migration where the Second Generation would settle and identify with the nation state, see, for instance, Nira Yuval-Davis (ed.), *The Situated Politics Of Belonging* (London: Sage, 2006).

14 Paul Gilroy has drawn attention to the significance of Empire and the need to come to terms with its inheritance if we are to shift the terms of multiculture in Britain in *After Empire: Multiculture or Postcolonial Melankholia?* (London and New York: Routledge, 2005). See also, Michael Keith, *After the Cosmopolitan* (London: Routledge, 2005); and the Parekh Report, *The Future Of Multi-Ethnic Britain* (London: Profile Books, 2001).

14 Multicultures, belongings and ethics

1 For some helpful discussions about the emergence of multiculturalism in Britain, with useful contrasts with other countries, see, for instance, Bhikhu Parekh, *Rethinking Multiculturalism: Cultural Diversity and Political Theory*

(Palgrave Macmillan, 2000); R. Baubock, *Transnational Citizenship: Member-ship and Rights in International Migration* (Aldershot: Edward Elgar, 1994); Homi Bhaba (ed.), *Nation and Narration* (London: Routledge, 1993); J. Carens, *Culture, Citizenship and Community* (Oxford: Oxford University Press, 2000); W. Connolly, *Identity/Difference: Democratic Negotiations of Political Paradox* (Ithaca: Cornell University Press, 1991); R.K. Fullinwider (ed.), *Public Education in a Multicultural Society: Policy, Theory, Critique* (Cambridge: Cambridge University Press); Paul Gilroy, *After Empire: Melan-cholia or Convivial Culture?* (London: Routledge, 2005); D. Morley and K.-H. Chen, *Stuart Hall*: Critical Dialogues in Cultural Studies (London: Routledge, 1996); W. Kymlicka, *Multicultural Citizenship: a Liberal Theory of Minority Rights* (Oxford: Clarendon Press, 1995); J. Spinner, *The Boundaries of Cit-izenship*: *Race, Ethnicity, and Nationality in the Liberal State* (Princeton: Princeton University Press, 1994); and C. Willet, *Theorizing Multiculturalism: a Guide to the Current Debate* (Oxford: Basil Blackwell, 1998).

2 For a discussion of Amatya Sen's critical discussion of certain notions of multi-culturalism, see his *Identity And Violence* (London: Allen Lane, 2006).

3 For some discussion around the findings of the Parekh Report, see, for instance, D. Goldberg and J. Solomos (eds), *A Companion Of Racial and Ethnic Studies* (Oxford: Blackwell, 2002). For a grasp of Parekh's own views on these issues, see Bhiku Parekh, *Rethinking Multiculturalism: Cultural Diver-sity and Political Theory* (Basingstoke: Palgrave, 2000). The events of 9/11 in New York and 7/7 in London shifted the terms of the discussion, particularly around the viability of sustaining multiculturalism in the UK, in ways political cultures are still endeavouring to come to terms with.

4 For a sense of the development of Stuart Hall's views and the intellectual shifts he has made from the earlier influence of Althusser, see the interviews and dis-cussions in D. Morley and K. Chen, *Stuart Hall: Critical Dialogues in Cultural Studies* (London: Routledge, 1996).

5 For illuminating discussion around the relationship of the Holocaust to moder-nity, see, for instance, Zygmund Bauman, *Modernity and the Holocaust* (Cam-bridge: Polity Press, 1990); and the concluding chapter in Victor Jeleniewski Seidler, *The Moral Limits of Modernity: Love, Inequality and Oppression* (Basingstoke: Macmillan, 1991) and *Shadows Of The Shoah: Jewish Identity and Belonging* (Oxford: Berg, 2000).

6 For some helpful introductions to the development of the thinking and writing of W.E.B. Du Bois, see, for instance, Paul Gilroy, *The Black Atlantic: Moder-nity and Double-Consciousness* (Cambridge, M: Harvard University Press, 2003); Cornell West, *The American Evasion Of Philosophy* (Basingstoke: Macmillan, 1989); Francis L. Broderick, *W.E.B. Du Bois: Negro Leader in a Time of Crisis* (Stanford: Stanford University Press, 1959). For a sense of W.E.B. Du Bois' own writings, see, for instance, *Black Reconstruction in America* (New York: Atheneum, 1938); *The Souls of Black Folk* (New York: Bantam, 1989); and *Dusk Of Dawn* (New York: Library of America, 1986).

7 For a sense of the intellectual and political development of Malcolm X, see *Malcolm X: Autobiography* (Harmondsworth: Penguin 1970).

8 Simone Weil showed her awareness of the injustices of colonialism while she was in university, while so many of the left remained silent on the issue. This was a theme she was to develop in *The Need For Roots* (London: Routledge, 1988). For some context to her intellectual and spiritual development, see Lawrence Blum and Victor Seidler, *A Truer Liberty: Simone Weil and Marxism* (New York and London: Routledge, 1991). See also the intellectual biography by David McLellan, *Simone Weil: a Utopian Pessimist* (London: Macmillan, 1992).

9 Walter Benjamin developed these notions in his 'Theses on the Philosophy of History', in *Illuminations* (London: Fontana Press, 1978). For helpful discussions of Benjamin's intellectual and political development, see, for instance, Howard Caygill, *The Colour Of Experience* (London: Routledge, 2000); Andrew Benjamin and Peter Osborne, *Walter Benjamin's Philosophy: Destruction and Experience* (London and New York: Routledge, 1994); and Gershom Scholem (ed.), *The Correspondence of Walter Benjamin and Gershom Scholem 1932–1940*, trans. G. Smith and A. Lefevre (New York: Schocken Books, 1989).

10 The disavowal of history and culture, and the way it echoes for Kant the disavowal of emotions, feelings and desires gathered as 'inclinations', was a central theme in Victor Jeleniewski Seidler, *Kant, Respect and Injustice: the Limits of Liberal Moral Theory* (London and New York: Routledge, 1986). This worked to frame rationalist forms of social theory that feminism and gay liberation began to question in their realisation that 'the personal is political', which enabled social theories to appreciate not only the significance of historical and cultural specificities, but also of embodiment and emotional life. In a different way, this was something Stanley Cavell, in *The Claims Of Reason* (Oxford: Oxford University Press, 1979), appreciated in different terms in his recognition of how the sceptical moment within modernity was being redeemed through a recognition of the significance of everyday life.

11 Susan Moller Okin, *Is Multiculturalism Bad For Women?*, provoked a number of responses, some of which were collected and published alongside her original text (Princeton: Princeton University Press, 1999).

12 Some interesting reflections upon the tensions between feminisms, discourses of human rights and concerns with cultural values are explored by Carol Gould, *Globalizing Democracy and Human Rights* (Cambridge: Cambridge University Press, 2004). See also illuminating discussions in M. Nussbaum and J. Glover (eds), *Women, Culture and Development* (Oxford and New York: Oxford University Press, 1995); J. Peters and A. Wolper (eds), *Women's Rights, Human Rights* (London: Routledge, 1995); Robin Cook (ed.), *The Human Rights of Women* (Philadelphia: University of Pennsylvania Press, 1994); and Alison Jaggar, 'Global Responsibility and Western Feminism', in *Feminist Interventions in Ethics and Politics* (Lanham: Rowman and Littlefield, 2005).

13 For an exploration of Michael Walzer's work that followed in the spirit of his *Spheres Of Justice: a Defence of Pluralism and Equality* (New York: Basic Books, 1983), see, for instance, *Thick and Thin: Moral Arguments at Home and Abroad* (Cambridge, MA: Harvard University Press, 1994) and *On Toleration* (New Haven: Yale University Press, 1997).

14 Benjamin Barber's essay 'Jihad vs McWorld' first appeared in *Atlantic Monthly* (March 1992), and eventually became part of the book *Jihad vs McWorld* (New York: Ballantine, 2001).

15 For a sense of the development of Isaiah Berlin's intellectual development, see Michael Ignatieff, *Isaiah Berlin: a Life* (London: Chatto and Windus, 1998). Some of his work on the themes of freedom and diversity have been collected in Isaiah Berlin, *Four Essays On Liberty* (Oxford: Oxford University Press, 1969), *Against The Current: Essays in the History of Ideas*, Henry Hardy (ed.) (Oxford: Oxford University Press, 1979) and *The Crooked Timber Of Humanity: Chapters in the History of Ideas*, Henry Hardy (ed.) (London: Pimlico, 1990).

15 Conclusions: citizenship, multiculturalisms and complex belongings

1 Victor Turner's work was concerned with social transitions while, at the same time, implicitly acknowledging the profound psychological transformations for

individuals during a liminal period. Turner came to see theatre as an inheritor of archaic ritual that functions like a mirror to form a reflective 'metacommentary' on the dramas enacted in their social context. Turner shows how the realms of social and stage drama feed into each other in a spiralling, iterative process which is responsive both to changes in society and the inventions of its individual members. See Victor Turner, *On the Edge of the Bush: Anthropology as Experience*, edited by Edith Turner (Tucson: The University of Arizona Press, 1985).

2 Freud develops his critique of a rationalist modernity, and its vision of progress that works to encourage people to repress their personal and collective histories so they can focus upon the demands of the present, in *Civilisation and its Discontents* (London: Penguin Freud Library). For some helpful discussion on the historical and cultural background to Freud and psychoanalysis, see Peter Gay, *Freud: a Life for Our Time* (Basingstoke: Macmillan, 1989). According to Gay:

> The principles governing Freud's sorties into the domain of culture were few in number, easy to state, but hard to apply: all is lawful, all is disguised, and all is connected. Psychoanalysis, as he puts it, establishes intimate links between 'the psychological achievements of individuals and of society by postulating the same dynamic source for both.'
>
> (1989: 312)

3 Turner frames these discussions of liminality in his paper, 'Betwixt and Between: the Liminal Period in Rites de Passage', in *The Forest Of Symbols: Aspects of Ndembu Ritual* (Ithaca and London: Cornell University Press, 1967). For Turner's work in relation to the theatre and drama as cultural rituals, see *Drama, Fields and Metaphors* (Ithaca and London: Cornell University Press, 1974).

4 For some helpful discussions that have helped to reframe the terms of a Eurocentric tradition within social theory, see, for instance, Paul Gilroy, *The Black Atlantic: Modernity and Double Consciousness* (Cambridge, MA: Harvard University Press, 1993); Alison Jagger, 'Global Responsibility and Western Feminism', in *Feminist Interventions in Ethics and Politics* (Lanham: Roman and Littlefield, 2005), pp. 185–200. Linda Nicholson (ed.), *Feminism/Postmodernism* (New York: Routledge, 1990); Victor Jeleniewski Seidler, *Unreasonable Men: Masculinity and Social Theory* (London and New York: Routledge, 1994); and Nira Yuval-Davis (ed.), *Women, Citizenship and Difference* (London: Zed Books, 1999); and *The Situated Politics of Belonging* (London: Sage, 2006).

5 For some writings of Tariq Ramadan that provide a sense of how he has developed intellectually and spiritually, see for instance, instead *Muslims and the Future of Islam* (New York: Oxford University Press, 2005). *Islam, the West and Challenges of Modernity* (London: Islam Foundation, 2000).

6 For some discussions around the predicaments of identity and belonging within Britain as a multicultural society, see, for instance, P. Gilroy, *After Empire: Multiculture or Postcolonial Melankholia?* (London: Routledge, 2005); M. Keith, *After the Cosmopolitan* (London: Routledge, 2005); B. Alleyne, *Radicals Against Race: Black Activism and Cultural Politics* (Oxford: Berg, 2002); S. Sharma, J. Hutnyk and A. Sharma (eds), *Disorienting Rhythms: the Politics of New Asian Dance Music* (London: Zed Books, 1996); T. Modood and P. Werbner (eds), *The Politics Of Multiculturalism in the New Europe: Racism, Identity and Community* (London: Zed Press, 1997); Zymunt Bauman, *Liquid Love* (Cambridge: Polity Press, 2004); and Nira Yuval David (ed.), *The Situated Politics Of Belonging* (London: Sage, 2006).

7 For some of the writings that show the development of Trevor Phillips' think-ing on British multiculturalism, see, for instance, Chris Smith, Trevor Phillips, Bridget McConnell and Jude Kelly, *Creative Futures: Culture, Identity and National Renewal* (London: Fabian Pamphlets, 1997). Trevor Phillips and Mick Phillips, *Windrush. The Irresistible Rise of Multi-racial Britain* (London: HarperCollins, 1998).

8 For some illuminating discussions of the different ways in which feminisms have questioned traditional patriarchal religious traditions within different Abrahamic traditions, see, for instance, in relation to Judaism, Judith Plaskow, *Standing Again at Zion: Judaism from the Feminist Perspective* (San Francisco: HarperCollins, 1990); Susannah Heschel, *On Being a Jewish Feminist: a Reader* (New York: Schocken, 1995). Christianity, Mary Daly, *Beyond God the Father* (Boston: Beacon Press, 1971). For Islam, Leila Ahmed, *Women and Gender in Islam* (New Haven: Yale University Press, 1992), Karen Armstrong, Yvonne Yazbeck and John L. Esposito, *Daughters of Abraham: Feminist Thought in Judaism, Christianity and Islam* (Florida: University of Florida Press, 2002).

9 For discussion of the secular tradition with France, and the decision to ban 'conspicuous' signs of religion, see, for instance, discussion in D. Goldberg and J. Solomos (eds) *A Companion of Racial and Ethnic Studies* (Oxford: Black-well, 2002); and H. Moghissi, *Feminism and Islamic Fundamentalism* (London: Zed, 1999); and T. Modood and P. Werbner (eds) *The Politics of Multiculturalism in the New Europe*: Racism, Identity and Community (London: Zed, 1997).

10 David Edgar's play *Playing With Fire* was performed at the National Theatre in London in 2005.

11 For some helpful discussions about the history of race relations in France, and the relationship to migrant communities, see, for instance, M. Wieviorka, 'The Development of Racism in Europe', in D. Goldberg and J. Solomos (eds) *A Companion of Race and Ethnic Studies* (Oxford: Blackwell 2002); W. Wilford and R.L. Miller (eds), *Women, Ethnicity and Nationalism* (London: Routledge, 1998); T. Modood and P. Werbner (eds) *The Politics of Multiculturalism in the New Europe: Racism, Identity and Community* (London: Zed, 1997).

12 For an understanding of the growing influence of neo-conservative ideas in the United States, and for a sense of how it became critical within the Republican Party, see, for instance, T. Ali, *The Clash Of Fundamentalisms: Crusades, Jihads and Modernity* (London: Verso 2002); G. Achar, *The Clash of Bar-barism*s: September 11 and the Making of the New World Disorder (New York: Monthly Review Press, 2002); B. Barber, *Fear's Empire: War, Terrorism and Democracy* (New York: W.W. Norton and Co., 2003); N. Chomsky, *The New Military Humanism: Lessons from Kosovo* (London: Pluto, 1999); and B. Latour, *War Of The Worlds: What About Peace?* (Chicago: Prickly Paradigm Press, 2002).

Bibliography

Adam, B. (1990) *Time and Social Theory*, Cambridge: Polity Press.

Adorno, T.H. (1974) *Aspects of Sociology*, London: Heinemann.

Adorno, T.H. and Horkheimer, M. (1973) *Dialectic of Enlightenment*, trans. J. Cumming, London: Allen Lane.

Agamben, G. (1993) *The Coming Community*, Minneapolis: University of Minnesota Press.

Agamben, G. (1998) *Homo Sacer: Sovereign Power and Bare Life*, Stanford: Stanford University Press.

Althusser, L. (1970) *For Marx*, London: Verso.

Altman, D. (1982) *The Homosexualisation of America*, Boston: Beacon.

An Na'im, A. (ed.) (1992) *Human Rights in Cross-Cultural Perspective: a Quest for Consensus*, Philadelphia: University of Pennsylvania Press.

Anderson, B. (1991) *Imagined Communities*, London: Verso.

Anidjar, G. (2003) *The Jew, the Arab: a History of the Enemy*, Stanford: Stanford University Press.

Appignanesi, L. and Maitland, D. (eds) (1989) *The Rushdie File*, London: Fourth Estate.

Archard, D. (ed.) (1996) *Philosophy and Pluralism*, Cambridge: Cambridge University Press.

Arendt, H. (1958) *The Origins of Totalitarianism*, New York: Meridian Books.

Arendt, H. (1958) *The Human Condition*, Chicago: University of Chicago Press.

Arendt, H. (1982) *Lectures on Kant's Political Philosophy*, ed. Robert Beiner, Chicago: University of Chicago Press.

Askew, S. and Ross, C. (1988) *Boys Don't Cry: Boys and Sexism in Education*, Milton Keynes: Open University Press.

Assiter, A. (1996) *Enlightenment Women: Modernist Feminism in a Postmodern Age*, London: Routledge.

Back, L. *New Ethnicities and Urban Culture*, London: UCL Press.

Barber, B. (1995) *Jihad vs McWorld*, New York: Random House.

Bartov, O. (2000) *Mirrors of Destruction: War, Genocide and Modern Identity*, Oxford: Oxford University Press.

Battersby, C. (1998) *The Phenomenal Woman: Feminist Metaphysics and the Patterns of Identity*, Cambridge: Polity Press.

Baubock, R. (ed.) (1994) *From Aliens To Citizens: Redefining the Status of Citizens in Europe*, Aldershot: Avebury.

Baubock, R. (1994) *Transnational Citizenship: Membership and Rights in International Migration*, Aldershot: Edward Elgar.

Baubock, R., Heller, A. and Zolberg, A. (eds) (1996) *The Challenge of Diversity: Integration and Pluralism in Societies of Immigration*, Aldershot: Avebury.

Bauman, Z. (1990) *Modernity and the Holocaust*, Cambridge: Polity Press.

Bauman, Z. (1997) *Postmodernity and its Discontents*, Cambridge: Polity Press.

Bauman, Z. (2000) *Liquid Modernity*, Cambridge: Polity Press.

Bauman, Z. (2001) *The Individualized Society*, Cambridge: Polity Press.

Bauman, Z. (2003) *Liquid Love*, Cambridge: Polity Press.

Beauvoir, S. de (1973) *The Second Sex*, New York: Vintage.

Beck, U. (1992) *The Risk Society: Towards a New Modernity*, London: Sage.

Beck, U. (2000) *The Brave New World of Work*, Cambridge: Polity Press.

Beck, U. and Beck-Gernsheim, E. (1995) *The Normal Chaos of Love*, Cambridge: Polity Press.

Beck, U., Giddens, A. and Lash, S. (1995) *Reflexive Modernization*, Cambridge: Polity Press.

Beetham, D. (1991) *The Legitimation of Power*, London: Macmillan.

Beiner, R. (1992) *What's the Matter With Liberalism*, Oxford: University of California Press.

Bell, V. (ed.) (1999) *Performativity and Belonging*, London: Sage.

Bellamy, R. (1999) *Liberalism and Pluralism: Towards a Politics of Compromise*, London: Routledge.

Benhabib, S. (1997) *Situating the Self*, Cambridge: Polity Press.

Benjamin, J. (1990) *Bonds of Love*, London: Virago.

Benjamin, J. (1998) *Shadow of the Other: Intersubjectivity and Gender in Psychoanalysis*, New York: Routledge.

Benjamin, W. (1973) *Illuminations: Essays and Reflections*, trans. H. Zohn, London: Collins/Fontana.

Berger, M., Wallis, B. and Watson, S. (eds) (1995) *Constructing Masculinity*, New York: Routledge.

Berlin, I. (1969) *Four Essays On Liberty*, Oxford: Oxford University Press.

Berlin, I. (1981) *Against the Current*, Oxford: Oxford University Press.

Bettleheim, B. (1991) *Freud and Man's Soul*, London: Fontana Books.

Bhabha, H.K. (ed.) (1993) *Nation and Narration*, London: Routledge.

Blum, L. (2002) *I'm Not a Racist But ...*, Ithaca: Cornell University Press.

Blum, L. and Seidler, V.J.J. (1991) *A Truer Liberty: Simone Weil and Marxism*, New York: Routledge.

Bly, R. (1990) *Iron John*, New York: Addison-Wesley.

Bock, G. and James, S. (eds) (1986) *Beyond Equality and Difference: Citizenship, Feminist Politics and Female Subjectivity*, London: Routledge.

Bologh, R.W. (1990) *Love or Greatness: Max Weber and Masculine Thinking*, London: Unwin Hyman.

Bordo, S. (1993) *Unbearable Weight: Feminism, Western Culture, and the Body*, Berkeley: University of California Press.

Bordo, S. (1999) *The Male Body: a New Look at Men in Public and in Private*, New York: Farrar, Straus and Giroux.

Borradori, G. (2003) *Philosophy in a Time of Terror: Dialogues with Jurgen Habermas and Jacques Derrida*, Chicago: University of Chicago Press.

Bourdieu, P. (2001) *Masculine Domination*, Cambridge: Polity Press.

Boyarin, D. (1993) *Carnal Israel: Reading Sex in Talmudic Judaism*, Berkeley: University of California Press.

Boyarin, D. (1994) *A Radical Jew: Paul and the Politics of Identity*, Berkeley: University of California Press.

Boyarin, D. (1997) *Unheroic Conduct: the Rise of Heterosexuality and the Invention of the Jewish Man*, Berkeley: University of California Press.

Braidotti, R. (1991) *Patterns of Dissonance*, Cambridge: Polity Press.

Brennan, T. (ed.) (1989) *Between Feminism and Psychoanalysis*, London: Routledge.

Brittan, A. (1989) *Masculinity and Power*, Oxford: Basil Blackwell.

Brod, H. (ed.) (1987) *The Making of Masculinities*, Boston: Allen and Unwin.

Brod, H. and Kaufman, M. (eds) (1996) *Theorizing Masculinities*, Thousand Oaks: Sage.

Buck-Morss, S. (2000) *Dreamworld and Catastrophe: the Passing of Mass Utopia in East and West*, Cambridge, MA: MIT Press.

Buhle, M.J. (1998) *Feminism and its Discontents*, Cambridge, MA: Harvard University Press.

Butler, J. (1990) *Gender Trouble: Feminism and the Subversion of Identity*, New York: Routledge.

Butler, J. (1993) *Bodies That Matter: the Discursive Limits of 'Sex'*, New York: Routledge.

Butler, J. and Scott, J.W. (eds) (1992) *Feminists Theorize the Political*, New York: Routledge.

Canovan, M. (1996) *Nationhood and Political Theory*, Cheltenham: Edward Elgar.

Carby, H.V. (1998) *Race Men*, Cambridge, MA: Harvard University Press.

Cardini, F. (2001) *Europe and Islam*, Oxford: Blackwell.

Casanova, J. (1994) *Public Religions in the Modern World*, Chicago: University of Chicago Press.

Cavell, S. (1979) *The Claims of Reason*, Oxford: Oxford University Press.

Cavell, S. (2005) *City of Words*, Cambridge, MA: Harvard University Press.

Chodorow, N. (1978) *The Reproduction of Mothering: Psychoanalysis and the Sociology of Gender*, London: University of California Press.

Chodorow, N. (1994) *Femininities, Masculinities, Sexualities: Freud and Beyond*, London: Free Associations Books.

Clark, R.T. (1969) *Herder: His Life and Thought*, Berkeley: University of California Press.

Clatterbaugh, K. (1990) *Contemporary Perspectives On Masculinity: Men, Women and Politics in Modern Society*, Boulder: Westview Press.

Cockburn, C. (1983) *Brothers: Male Dominance and Technological Change*, London: Pluto Press.

Cohen, P. (1997) *Rethinking the Youth Question*, Basingstoke: Palgrave.

Collins, P. Hill (1991) *Black Feminist Thought: Knowledge, Consciousness and the Politics of Empowerment*, New York: Routledge.

Connell, R.W. (1987) *Gender and Power: Society, the Person and Sexual Politics*, Cambridge: Polity Press.

Connell, R.W. (1995) *Masculinities*, Cambridge: Polity Press.

Connell, R.W. (2000) *The Men and the Boys*, Cambridge: Polity Press.

Connolly, P. (1998) *Racism, Gender Identities and Young Children*, London: Routledge.

Connolly, W. (1991) *Identity/Difference: Democratic Negotiations of Political Paradox*, Ithaca: Cornell University Press.

Cornwall, A. and Lindisfarne, N. (eds) (????) *Dislocating Masculinity: Comparative Ethnographies*, London: Routledge.

Craib, I. (1989) *Psychoanalysis and Social Theory: the Limits of Sociology*, London: Harvester Wheatsheaf.

Craib, I. (1994) *The Importance of Disappointment*, London: Routledge.

Dallmayr, F. (1998) *Alternative Visions: Paths in the Global Village*, Lanham: Rowman and Littlefield.

Davidhoff, L. (1995) *Worlds Between: Historical Perspectives on Gender and Class*, Cambridge: Polity Press.

Davidhoff, L. and Hall, C. (1987) *Family Fortunes: Women and Men of the English Middle Class 1780–1850*, London: Routledge.

Dawson, G. (1986) *Soldier Heroes: British Adventure, Empire and the Imagining of Masculinities*, London: Routledge.

D'Costa, G. (1986) *Theology and Religious Pluralism: the Challenge of Other Religions*, Oxford: Blackwell.

Deleuze, G. (1990) *Expressionism in Philosophy: Spinoza*, trans. M. Joughin, New York: Zone.

Deleuze, G. (1993) *Nietzsche and Philosophy*, trans. H. Tomlinson, Minneapolis: University of Minnesota Press.

Deleuze, G. and Guattari, F. (1997) *Anti-Oedipus*, Minneapolis: University of Minnesota Press.

Derrida, J. (1978) *Writing and Difference*, Chicago: University of Chicago Press.

Derrida, J. (1998) *Monolingualism of the Other*, Stanford: Stanford University Press.

Derrida, J. (1999) *Adieu: to Emmanuel Levinas*, Stanford: Stanford University Press.

Derrida, J. (2002) *Acts of Religion*, New York: Routledge.

Dinnerstein, D. (1987) *The Mermaid and the Minotaur: the Rocking of the Cradle and the Ruling of the World*, London: The Women's Press.

Dobash, R.E., Dobash, R.P., Cavanagh, K. and Lewis, R. (2000) *Changing Violent Men*, London: Sage.

Dollimore, J. (1998) *Death, Desire and Loss in Western Culture*, London: Penguin.

Donzelot, J. (1979) *The Policing of Families*, London: Hutchinson.

Dreyfus, H. and Rabinow, P. (1983) *Michel Foucault: Beyond Structuralism and Hermeneutics*, Chicago: University of Chicago Press.

Dworkin, R. (1985) *A Matter of Principle*, Cambridge, MA: Harvard University Press.

Easlea, B. (1981) *Science and Sexual Oppression: Patriarchy's Confrontation with Women and Nature*, London: Weidenfeld and Nicholson.

Edwards, T. (1994) *Erotics and Politics: Gay Male Sexuality, Masculinity and Feminism*, London: Routledge.

Eisenstein, H. (1985) *Contemporary Feminist Thought*, London: Unwin.

Elam, D. (1994) *Feminism and Deconstruction*, London: Routledge.

Elias, N. (1982) *The Civilizing Process: State Formation and Civilisation*, trans. E. Jephcott, Oxford: Oxford University Press.

Elliot, A. and Frosh, S. (eds) (1994) *Psychoanalysis in Contexts: Paths Between Theory and Modern Culture*, London and New York: Routledge.

Elshtain, J.B. (1981) *Public Man, Private Woman*, Princeton: Princeton University Press.

Fanon, F. (1986) *Black Skin, White Mask*, London: Pluto Press.

Featherstone, M., Hepworth, M. and Turner, B.S. (eds) *The Body: Social Process and Cultural Theory*, London: Sage.

Flax, J. (1990) *Thinking Fragments: Psychoanalysis, Feminism and Postmodern in the Contemporary West*, Berkeley: University of California Press.

Flax, J. (1993) *Disputed Subjects: Essays on Psychoanalysis, Politics and Philosophy*, New York and London: Routledge.

Foucault, M. (1975) *Discipline and Punish: the Birth of the Prison*, Harmondsworth: Penguin.

Foucault, M. (1976) *The History of Sexuality*, vol. 1, London: Penguin.

Foucault, M. (1980) *Power/Knowledge: Selected Interviews and Other Writings, 1972–1977*, New York: Pantheon.

Freud, S. (1960) *Totem and Taboo*, London: Ark Paperbacks.

Freud, S. (1963) *Civilisation and its Discontents*, New York: Dover.

Freud, S. (1977) *On Sexuality*, Penguin Freud Library vol. 7, London: Penguin.

Frosh, S. (1994) *Sexual Difference: Masculinity and Psychoanalysis*, London and New York: Routledge.

Frosh, S., Phoenix, A. and Pattman, R. (2002) *Young Masculinities*, Basingstoke: Palgrave.

Fullinwider, R.K. (ed.) (1996) *Public Education in a Multicultural Society: Policy, Theory, Critique*, Cambridge: Cambridge University Press.

Gallager, C. and Laqueur, T. (eds) (1987) *The Making of the Modern Body: Sexuality and Society in the Nineteenth Century*, Berkeley: University of California Press.

Galston, W.A. (1991) *Liberal Purposes: Goods, Virtues and Diversity in the Liberal State*, Cambridge: Cambridge University Press.

Gay, P. (1988) *Freud: a Life of our Time*, London: Macmillan.

Geertz, C. (1973) *The Interpretation of Culture*, New York: Basic Books.

Giddens, A. (1991) *Modernity and Self-Identity: Self and Society in the Late Modern Age*, Cambridge: Pluto Press.

Giddens, A. (1993) *The Transformation of Intimacy: Sexuality, Love and Eroticism in Modern Societies*, Cambridge: Polity Press.

Gilligan, C. (1982) *In a Different Voice: Psychological Theory and Women's Development*, Cambridge, MA: Harvard University Press.

Gilmore, D.G. (1990) *Manhood in the Making: Cultural Concepts of Masculinity*, New Haven: Yale University Press.

Gilroy, P. (1987) *There Ain't No Black in the Union Jack*, London: Unwin Hyman.

Gilroy, P. (1993) *The Black Atlantic: Modernity and Double Consciousness*, Cambridge, MA: Harvard University Press.

Gilroy, P. (2000) *Between Camps: Nations, Cultures and the Allure of Race*, London: Allen Lane.

Gilroy, P. (2005) *After Empire: Multicultures or Postcolonial Melancholia*, London: Routledge.

Glazer, N. (1997) *We are All Multiculturalists Now*, Cambridge, MA: Harvard University Press.

Goldberg, D.T. (1993) *Racist Culture: Philosophy and the Politics of Meaning*, Oxford: Basil Blackwell.

Gorz, A. (1985) *Paths To Paradise*, London: Pluto.

Gramsci, A. (1971) *Selections From the Prison Notebooks*, London: Lawrence and Wishart.

Gray, J. (1995) *Elightenment's Wake: Politics and Culture at the Close of the Modern Age*, London: Routledge.

Griffin, S. (1980) *Pornography and Silence*, London: The Women's Press.

Griffin, S. (1982) *Women and Nature*, London: The Women's Press.

Grillo, A. (1998) *Pluralism and the Politics of Difference: State, Culture and Ethnicity in Comparative Perspective*, Oxford: Clarendon Press.

Grosz, E. (1994) *Volatile Bodies: Towards a Corporeal Feminism*, Bloomington: Indiana University Press.

Gutmann, A. (ed.) (1994) *Multiculturalism*, Princeton: Princeton University Press.

Gutmann, A. and Thompson, G (1997) *Democracy and Disagreement*, London: The Belknap Press.

Hall, C. (2002) *Civilising Subjects: Metropole and Colony in the English Imagination 1830–1867*, Oxford: Polity.

Hall, L.A. (1991) *Hidden Anxieties: Male Sexuality 1900–1950*, Cambridge: Polity Press.

Hall, S. (ed.) (1984) *Representation: Cultural Representation and Signifying Practices*, London: Sage.

Hall, S. and Jefferson, T. (eds) (1976) *Resistance Through Rituals*, London: Hutchinson.

Hampshire, S. (1983) *Morality and Conflict*, Oxford: Basil Blackwell.

Hearn, J. (1998) *The Violences of Men*, London: Sage.

Hearn, J. and Morgan, D. (eds) (1990) *Men, Masculinities and Social Theory*, London: Unwin Hyman.

Heckman, S.J. (1990) *Gender and Knowledge: Elements of a Postmodern Feminism*. Cambridge: Polity Press.

Held, D. (1986) *Models of Democracy*, Cambridge: Polity Press.

Held, V. (1993) *Feminist Morality: Transforming Culture, Society and Politics*, Chicago: University of Chicago Press.

Hewitt, R. (1986) *White Talk Black Talk: Inter-Racial Friendships and Communication Amongst Adolescents*, Cambridge: Cambridge University Press.

Hochschild, A.R. (1989) *The Second Shift*, New York: Avon Books.

Hochschild, A.R. (1997) *The Time Bind*, New York: Metropolitan Books.

Honig, B. (1993) *Political Theory and the Displacement of Politics*, Ithaca: Cornell University Press.

hooks, b. (1991) *Yearning: Race, Gender and Cultural Politics*, London: Turnabout.

hooks, b. (2000) *All About Love*, New York: HarperCollins.

hooks, b. (2001) *Salvation: Black People and Love*, New York: HarperCollins.

Ignatieff, M. (1993) *Blood and Belonging: Journey into the New Nationalism*, New York: Farrar, Strauss & Giroux.

Irigaray, L. (1985) *The Sex Which Is Not One*, Ithaca: Cornell University Press.

Irigaray, L. (1985) *Speculum of the Other Woman*, Ithaca: Cornell University Press.

Jackson, S. (1999) *Heterosexuality in Question*, London: Sage.

Jagger, G. and Wright, C. (eds) (1999) *Changing Family Values*, London: Routledge.

Jameson, F. (1972) *The Prison-House of Language: a Critical Account of Structuralism and Russian Formalism*, Princeton: Princeton University Press.
Jardine, A. and Smith, P. (eds) (1987) *Men in Feminism*, London: Methuen.
Johnson, S. and Meinhof, U.H. (eds) *Language and Masculinity*, Oxford: Blackwell.
Kaufman, M. (1987) *Beyond Patriarchy*, Toronto: Oxford University Press.
Kekes, J. (1993) *The Morality of Pluralism*, Princeton: Princeton University Press.
Kimmel, M.S. (ed.) (1987) *Changing Men: New Directions in Research on Men and Masculinity*, Newbury Park: Sage.
Kimmel, M.S. (ed.) (1995) *The Politics of Manhood*, Philadelphia: Temple University Press.
Kimmel, M.S. (1996) *Manhood in America: a Cultural History*, New York: Free Press.
Kymlicka, W. (1989) *Liberalism, Community and Culture*, Oxford: Clarendon Press.
Kymlicka, W. (1995) *Multicultural Citizenship: a Liberal Theory of Minority Rights*, Oxford: Clarendon Press.
Lang, Berel (1990) *Act and Idea in the Nazi Genocide*, Chicago: University of Chicago Press.
Laqueur, T. (1990) *Making Sex: Body and Gender from the Greeks to Freud*, Cambridge, MA: Harvard University Press.
Lasch, C. (1977) *Haven in a Heartless World: the Family Besieged*, New York: Basic Books.
Lasch, C. (1991) *The Culture of Narcissism: American Life in an Age of Diminishing Expectations*, New York: Norton and Co.
Lash, S. and Urry, J. (1987) *The End of Organised Capitalism*, Cambridge: Polity Press.
Lennon, K. and Whitford, M. (eds) *Knowing the Difference: Feminist Perspectives on Epistemology*, London: Routledge.
Levi, Primo (1989) *The Drowned and the Saved*, New York: Vintage International.
Lloyd, G. (1984) *Man of Reason: 'Male' and 'Female' in Western Philosophy*, London: Methuen.
Lyotard, J.-F. (1994) *The Postmodern Condition: a Report on Knowledge*, Manchester: Manchester University Press.
Mac An Ghail, M. (1994) *The Making of Men: Masculinities, Sexualities and Schooling*, Buckingham: Open University Press.
MacInnes, J. (1998) *The End of Masculinity*, Buckingham: Open University Press.
MacIntyre, A. (1985) *After Virtue: a Study in Moral Theory*, London: Duckworth.
McNay, L. (1992) *Foucault and Feminism*, Cambridge: Polity Press.
McNay, L. (1994) *Gender and Agency*, Cambridge: Polity Press.
McRobbie, A. and Nava, M. (eds) (1984) *Gender and Generation*, London: Palgrave.
Maguire, M. (1995) *Men, Women, Passion and Power*, London: Routledge.
Mamdani, M. (2001) *When Victims Become Killers: Colonialism, Nativism and the Genocide in Rwanda*, Princeton: Princeton University Press.
Mangan, J.A. and Walvin, J. (1987) *Manliness and Morality: Middle Class Masculinity in Britain and America*, Manchester: Manchester University Press.
Mastnak, Tomaz (2002) *Crusading Peace: Christendom, the Muslim World and Western Political Order*, Berkeley: University of California Press.
Mattar, Philip (1998) *Islam in Britain, 1558–1685*, Cambridge: Cambridge University Press.

May, L. (1998) *Masculinity and Morality*, New York: Cornell University Press.

Mayer, Hans (1982) *Outsiders: a Study in Life and Letters*, Cambridge, MA: MIT Press.

Mendus, S. (1989) *Toleration and the Limits of Liberalism*, Atlantic Highlands: Humanities Press.

Mercer, K. (ed.) (1994) *Welcome To the Jungle*, London: Routledge.

Merchant, C. (1982) *The Death of Nature: Women, Ecology and the Scientific Revolution*, London: Wildwood House.

Messner, M.A. (1997) *Politics of Masculinities: Men in Movements*, Thousand Oaks: Sage.

Miller, D. (1995) *On Nationality*, Oxford: Oxford University Press.

Miller, S. (1983) *Men and Friendship*, London: Gateway Books.

Minsky, R. (1998) *Psychoanalysis and Culture: Contemporary States of Mind*, New Brunswick: Rutgers University Press.

Mitscherlich, A. (1993) *Society Without Father: a Contribution to Social Psychology*, New York: HarperCollins.

Modood, T. (1992) *Not Easy Being British: Colour, Culture, and Citizenship*, Stoke-on-Trent: Trentham Books.

Modood, T. (ed.) (1997) *Church, State and Religious Minorities*, London: Policy Studies Institute.

Modood, T. and Werbner, P. (eds) (1997) *The Politics of Multiculturalism in the New Europe: Racism, Identity and Community*, London: Zed Books.

Moore, R.I. (1990) *The Formation of a Persecuting Society: Power and Deviance in Western Europe, 950–1250*, Oxford: Blackwell.

Morgan, D. (1992) *Discovering Men*, London: Routledge.

Mort, F. (1996) *Cultures of Consumption: Masculinities and Social Space in Late Twentieth Century Britain*, London: Routledge.

Mosse, G.L. (1996) *The Image of Man: the Creation of Modern Masculinity*, New York: Oxford University Press.

Nancy, Jean-Luc (1993) *The Experience of Freedom*, Stanford: Stanford University Press.

Nardi, P.M. (ed.) (1992) *Men's Friendships*, Thousand Oaks: Sage.

Nardi, P.M. (ed.) (2000) *Gay Masculinities*, Thousand Oaks: Sage.

Nicholson, L. and Seidman, S. (eds) (1996) *Social Postmodernism: Beyond Identity Politics*, Cambridge: Cambridge University Press.

Nicholson, L.J. (ed.) (1990) *Feminism/Postmodernism*, New York: Routledge.

Nietzsche, F. (1967) *On the Genealogy of Morals*, New York: Vintage.

Nietzsche, F. (1968) *The Will to Power*, New York: Vintage.

Nietzsche, F. (1974) *The Gay Science*, New York: Vintage.

Nietzsche, F. (1997) *Daybreak*, Cambridge: Cambridge University Press.

Nirenberg, David (1996) *Communities of Violence: Persecution of Minorities in the Middle Ages*, Princeton: Princeton University Press.

Nixon, S. (1996) *Hard Looks: Masculinities, Spectatorship and Contemporary Consumption*, London: UCL Press.

Oliver, K. (1997) *Family Values: Subjects Between Nature and Culture*, New York: Routledge.

Parekh, B. (ed.) (1990) *Law, Blasphemy and the Multi-Faith Society*, London: Commission for Racial Equality.

Parekh, B. (2000) *Rethinking Multiculturalism: Cultural Diversity and Political Theory*, Basingstoke: Palgrave.

Pateman, C. (1988) *The Sexual Contract*, Stanford: Stanford University Press.

Phillips, A. (1991) *Engendering Democracy*, Philadelphia: University of Pennsylvania Press.

Phillips, A. (1993) *Democracy and Difference*, Cambridge: Polity Press.

Phillips, A. (1995) *The Politics of Presence: Issues in Democracy and Group Representation*, Oxford and New York: Oxford University Press.

Pieterse, J. (1990) *Empire and Emancipation: Power and Liberation on a World Scale*, London: Pluto Press.

Pieterse, J. and Parekh, B. (eds) (1995) *The Decolonisation of Imagination: Culture, Knowledge and Power*, London: Zed Press.

Plummer, K. (1995) *Telling Sexual Stories: Power, Change and Social Worlds*, London: Routledge.

Poster, M. (1998) *Critical Theory of the Family*, London: Pluto Press.

Rajchman, J. (ed.) (1995) *The Identity in Question*, London: Routledge.

Ramazanoglu, C. (1989) *Feminism and the Contradictions of Oppression*, London: Routledge.

Ramazanoglu, C. (ed.) (1992) *Up Against Foucault*, London: Routledge.

Rawls, J. (1971) *A Theory of Justice*, Cambridge, MA: Harvard University Press.

Rawls, J. (1993) *Political Liberalism*, New York: Columbia University Press.

Raz, J. (1986) *The Morality of Freedom*, Oxford: Oxford University Press.

Raz, J. (1994) *Ethics in the Public Domain: Essays in the Morality of Law and Politics*, Oxford: Clarendon Press.

Rex, J. (1996) *Ethnic Minorities in the Modern Nation State*, London: Macmillan.

Ricoeur, P. (1992) *Oneself as Another*, Chicago: Chicago University Press.

Rifkin, J. (1996) *The End of Work*, New York: Putnam.

Robinson, S. (2000) *Marked Men: White Masculinity in Crisis*, New York: Columbia University Press.

Roper, M. and Tosh, J. (1991) *Manful Assertions: Masculinities in Britain since 1800*, London: Routledge.

Rose, N. (1989) *Governing the Soul: the Shaping of the Private Self*, London: Routledge.

Rowbotham, S. (1972) *Woman's Consciousness, Man's World*, Harmondsworth: Penguin.

Rowbotham, S. (1973) *Hidden From History*, London: Pluto Press.

Sacks, J. (1991) *The Persistence of Faith: Religion, Morality and Society in a Secular Age*, London: Weidenfeld and Nicholson.

Sacks, J. (2002) *The Dignity of Difference: How to Avoid the Clash of Civilisations*, London: Continuum.

Said, E. (1979) *Orientalism*, New York: Vintage.

Said, E. (1993) *Culture and Imperialism*, London: Chatto and Windus.

Samuels, A. (1993) *The Political Psyche*, London: Routledge.

Sandel, M. (1982) *Liberalism and the Limits of Justice*, Cambridge: Cambridge University Press.

Sawicki, J. (1991) *Disciplining Foucault: Feminism, Power and the Body*, New York: Routledge.

Schmitt, Carl (1984) *Roman Catholicism and Political Form*, Westport: Greenwood Press.

Schmitt, Carl (1985) *Political Theology: Four Chapters on the Concept of Sovereignty*, Cambridge: The MIT Press.

Schmitt, Carl (1996) *The Concept of the Political*, Chicago: University of Chicago Press.

Scholem, Gershon (1971) *The Messianic Idea in Judaism*, New York: Schocken.

Scott, S. and Morgan, D. (eds) (1993) *Body Matters*, London: Falmer Press.

Segal, L. (1990) *Slow Motion: Changing Masculinities, Changing Men*, London: Virago.

Seidler, V.J.J. (1986) *Kant, Respect and Injustice: the Limits of Liberal Moral Theory*, London: Routledge.

Seidler, V.J.J. (1989) *Rediscovering Masculinity: Reason, Language and Sexuality*, London and New York: Routledge.

Seidler, V.J.J. (1991) *The Moral Limits of Modernity: Love, Inequality and Oppression*, Basingstoke: Macmillan.

Seidler, V.J.J. (1991) *Recreating Sexual Politics: Men, Feminism and Politics*, London and New York: Routledge.

Seidler, V.J.J. (1993) *Unreasonable Men: Masculinity and Social Theory*, London and New York: Routledge.

Seidler, V.J.J. (1994) *Recovering the Self: Morality and Social Theory*, London and New York: Routledge.

Seidler, V.J.J. (2000) *Man Enough: Embodying Masculinities*, London: Sage.

Seidler, V.J.J. (2001) *Shadows of the Shoah: Jewish Identity and Belonging*, Oxford: Berg.

Seidler, V.J.J. (2005) *Transforming Masculinities: Men, Cultures, Bodies, Power, Sex and Love*, London and New York: Routledge.

Seidler, V.J.J. (2006) *Young Men and Masculinities: Global Cultures and Intimate Lives*, London: Zed Press.

Seidman, S. (1996) *Contested Knowledge: Social Theory in the Postmodern Era*, Cambridge, MA: Blackwell Press.

Sennett, R. (1998) *The Corrosion of Character: the Personal Consequences of Work in the New Capitalism*, New York: W.W. Norton.

Sennett, R. (2004) *Respect: the Formation of Character in an Age of Inequality*, London: Penguin Books.

Sennett, R. and Cobb, J. (1971) *The Hidden Injuries of Class*, New York: Vintage.

Shilling, C. (1983) *The Body and Social Theory*, London: Sage.

Smith, A. (1991) *National Identity*, Harmondsworth: Penguin.

Southern, Richard (1962) *Western Views of Islam in the Middle Ages*, Cambridge, MA: Harvard University Press.

Spinner, J. (1994) *The Boundaries of Citizenship: Race, Ethnicity and Nationality in the Liberal State*, Baltimore: John Hopkins University Press.

Spivak, G.C. (1999) *A Critique of Postcolonial Reason: Towards a History of the Vanishing Present*, Cambridge, MA: Harvard University Press.

Squires, J. (1999) *Gender in Political Theory*, Cambridge: Polity Press.

Stanley, L. and Wise, S. (1993) *Breaking Out Again: Feminist Ontology and Epistemology*, London: Routledge.

Staples, R. (1982) *Black Masculinity: the Black Man's Role in American Society*, San Francisco: Black Scholar Press.

Stecopoulos, H. and Uebel, M. (eds) (1997) *Race and the Subject of Masculinities*, Durham, NC: Duke University Press.

Steinberg, L., Epstein, D. and Johnson, R. (eds) (1997) *Border Patrols: Policing the Boundaries of Heterosexuality*, London: Cassell.

Steiner, George (1967) *Language and Silence*, London: Faber and Faber.

Stone, A. (1985) *Radical Conflict in Contemporary Society*, Cambridge, MA: Harvard University Press.

Sydie, R.A. (1987) *Natural Woman, Cultured Men: a Feminist Perspective on Sociological Theory*, Milton Keynes: Open University Press.

Tamir, Y. (1993) *Liberal Nationalism*, Princeton: Princeton University Press.

Taylor, C. (1989) *Sources of the Self*, Cambridge: Cambridge University Press.

Thomas, L.M. (1993) *Vessels of Evil: American Slavery and the Holocaust*, Philadelphia: Temple University Press.

Todorov, T. (1993) *On Human Diversity: Nationalism, Racism and Exoticism in French Thought*, Cambridge, MA: Harvard University Press.

Turner, B. (1984) *The Body and Society: Explorations in Social Theory*, Oxford: Basil Blackwell.

Turner, B. (1992) *Regulating Bodies: Essays in Medical Sociology*, London: Routledge.

Turner, V. (1967) 'Betwixt and Between: The Liminal Period in "Rites de Passage" in *The Forest of Symbols: Aspects of Natombu Ritual*, Ithica: Cornell University Press.

Turner, V. (1985) *On the Edge of the Bush: Anthropology as Experience*, Tucson: University of Arizona Press.

Vries, Hent de (1999) *Philosophy and the Turn To Religion*, Baltimore: Johns Hopkins Press.

Vries, Hent de (2002) *Religion and Violence: Philosophical Perspectives from Kant to Derrida*, Baltimore: Johns Hopkins Press.

Vries, Hent de and Weber, S. (eds) (1997) *Violence, Identity and Self-Determination*, Stanford: Stanford University Press.

Wallace, M. (1979) *Black Macho*, London: Calder.

Walzer, M. (1983) *Spheres of Justice: a Defence of Pluralism and Equality*, New York: Basic Books.

Walzer, M. (1994) *Thick and Thin: Moral Arguments at Home and Abroad*, Cambridge, MA: Harvard University Press.

Walzer, M. (1997) *On Toleration*, New Haven: Yale University Press.

Wasserstrom, Steven (1995) *Between Muslim and Jew: the Problem of Symbiosis Under Early Islam*, Princeton: Princeton University Press.

Weber, M. (1970) *The Protestant Ethic and the Spirit of Capitalism*, London: Allen and Unwin.

Weeks, J. (1989) *Sex, Politics and Society*, Harlow: Longman.

Weeks, J. (1991) *Sexuality and its Discontents: Meanings, Myths and Modern Sexualities*, London: Routledge.

Weeks, J. (1995) *Inventing Moralities: Sexual Values in an Age of Uncertainty*, Cambridge: Polity Press.

West, C. (1993) *Race Matters*, Boston: Beacon Press.

Williams, B. (1985) *Ethics and the Limits of Philosophy*, London: Fontana.

Williams, R. (1980) *Problems in Materialism and Culture*, London: Verso.

Willis, P. (1977) *Learning To Labour*, Aldershot: Gower.

Winch, P. (1989) *A Just Balance: Reflections on the Philosophy of Simone Weil*, Cambridge: Cambridge University Press.

Winnicott, D.W. (1974) *Playing and Reality*, Harmondsworth: Penguin.

Wittgenstein, L. (1958) *Philosophical Investigations*, Oxford: Blackwell.

Wittgenstein, L. (1980) *Culture and Value*, Oxford: Blackwell.

Woodward, K. (ed.) (1997) *Identity and Difference*, London: Sage.

Yerushalmi, Y.H. (1982) *Zakhor: Jewish History and Jewish Memory*, Seattle: University of Washington Press.

Young, I.M. (1990) *Justice and the Politics of Difference*, Princeton: Princeton University Press.

Young, I.M. (1990) *Throwing Like a Girl and Other Essays in Feminist Philosophy and Social Theory*, Bloomington: Indiana University Press.

Young, R. (1990) *White Mythologies*, London: Routledge.

Zizek, Slavoj (1989) *The Sublime Object of Ideology*, London: Verso.

Index